William T
Politics of A

MW00979074

William Terry Couch and the Politics of Academic Publishing

*An Editor's Career as
Lightning Rod for Controversy*

ORVIN LEE SHIFLETT

McFarland & Company, Inc., Publishers
Jefferson, North Carolina

Frontispiece: WIlliam Terry Couch at the University of Chicago Press, ca. 1945 (courtesy Special Collections Research Center, University of Chicago Library).

LIBRARY OF CONGRESS CATALOGUING-IN-PUBLICATION DATA

Shiflett, Orvin Lee, author.
  William Terry Couch and the politics of academic publishing : an editor's career as lightning rod for controversy / Orvin Lee Shiflett.
    p.   cm.
  Includes bibliographical references and index.

  ISBN 978-0-7864-9981-6 (softcover : acid free paper) ∞
  ISBN 978-1-4766-2241-5 (ebook)

  1. Couch, William T. (William Terry), 1901–1988.   2. Couch, William T. (William Terry), 1901–1988—Political and social views. 3. Publishers and publishing—United States—Biography. 4. Editors—United States—20th century—Biography.   5. University of North Carolina Press—History—20th century.   6. Scholarly publishing—United States—History—20th century.   7. University presses—United States—History—20th century.   8. United States—Intellectual life—20th century.   I. Title.

Z473.C767S48 2015
070.5092—dc23   2015022624

BRITISH LIBRARY CATALOGUING DATA ARE AVAILABLE

On the cover: William Terry Couch, ca. 1940
© University of North Carolina at Chapel Hill,
North Carolina Collection Photographic Archives

Printed in the United States of America

McFarland & Company, Inc., Publishers
  Box 611, Jefferson, North Carolina 28640
    www.mcfarlandpub.com

For Benjamin Weintraub, who taught us
that reference works are made by people

Acknowledgments

I thank Louisiana State University for granting me a sabbatical in fall 1996 to begin this work and the University of North Carolina at Greensboro for relieving me of administrative duties to enable me to complete it. I also thank my Louisiana State University former students William Coscarelli and Rebecca Woolbert Hines for their research assistance and my students at the University of North Carolina at Greensboro, Hallie Fields and Megan Bennett, for their close reading of the work.

I am grateful to Andrew Wetheimer for pointing me toward some significant resources and Daniel Singal for his excellent editorial suggestions. I am especially grateful to my colleague, James V. Carmichael, Jr., in the Department of Library and Information Studies at the University of North Carolina at Greensboro for his close reading of the text and excellent suggestions for improvement and to my wife, Mary Ellen, for her constructive criticisms and for her constant support through the writing.

I am particularly grateful for the unfailing help and assistance of the archivists and librarians at the Southern Historical Collections at the University of North Carolina at Chapel Hill, the University of Chicago, the University of Illinois, the American Library Association, the University of Oregon, Duke University, and the School of Information at Florida State University.

Table of Contents

Introduction

Virtually every general history of the South that deals with the intellectual development of the region or with the history of race relations in the twentieth century mentions William Terry Couch. As the first functional director of the University of North Carolina Press, Couch created a new beast in the world of American publishing, a university press that was involved in a form of scholarly publication that ventured beyond the specialized academic monograph to reach out to the general reading public. He attempted to bring the results of academic scholarship to the people who could effectively institute social, political, and economic change in the South. His approach to academic publishing made the University of North Carolina Press a southern trade publisher.

William Terry Couch joined the liberal crusade against southern traditions and values when he was appointed assistant director of the University of North Carolina Press in 1925, while still an undergraduate student at the university. Though his title was assistant director, he quickly became the functional head of the press and was spectacularly successful at developing a publication program that challenged the traditions keeping the South from achieving parity with other regions of the United States. His talents as a publisher and editor served him well at the university. In a scant decade, he made the University of North Carolina Press a major regional publishing house, but it was only regional and the major flaws of the South were the low fruit of American culture and society. Couch was successful enough at this endeavor that he was promoted to director of the press in 1932 when the titular director, Louis Round Wilson, left North Carolina for the University of Chicago.

There has been little published about Bill Couch beyond the brief mentions in the general histories. Elizabeth Villeponteaux wrote an excellent master's paper on Couch at the library school at the University of North Carolina in 1989, "William Terry Couch and the University of North Carolina Press, 1925–1945," under the direction of Edward G. Holley. Daniel Joseph Singal's

1

Bill Couch at U.S. Army Boot Camp, ca. 1921 (courtesy Southern Historical Collections, Louis Round Wilson Special Collections Library, University of North Carolina at Chapel Hill).

chapter on Couch in *The War Within: From Victorian to Modernist Thought in the South, 1919–1945*, published by the University of North Carolina Press in 1982, presents the most comprehensive picture of Couch thus far, reinforcing the view of Couch as a social, racial, and political liberal. While Singal's chapter on Couch, like Villeponteaux's paper, was limited to his time at the University of North Carolina, this period marked only the beginning of Couch's long career in publishing. His work at the University of North Carolina did establish his reputation as a liberal champion of progressive change, but his experiences there also began his active involvement in conservative and even reactionary causes.

His subsequent career has been largely ignored. It was in those later years that, as a publisher and editor, he actively used his editorial positions to promote conservatism in America through seeking and publishing manuscripts, through encouraging conservative authors, and through joining the emerging conservative community in America as an active and vocal participant.

Couch left Chapel Hill to become director of the University of Chicago Press in 1945. The aggressive approach to publishing that had proved so effective at North Carolina failed him at Chicago, and he was fired in 1950 by Chicago's chancellor, Robert Maynard Hutchins. Couch left Chicago under a well-publicized cloud, but the national reputation as a publisher of vision and uncompromising integrity he had earned at North Carolina and embellished at Chicago was well established.

For Couch, the press was the only unit of a university that could address the real issues confronting American society and he used it at both the University of North Carolina and the University of Chicago to present topics and issues that could not or would not be integrated into the curriculum. His vision of the role of university presses was to stir the social, cultural, and intellectual torpor of the United States, to incite controversy, and to actively promote social and political change. The classrooms and curricula of the universities, focused as they were on increasing minutia of academic specialization and dependent on the financial support and political influence of state legislatures, donors, and foundations, were incapable of making a difference. University presses were the only academic agencies that could change America. Though his career as head of a university press ended with Chicago, Bill Couch found other avenues through which he could assail the liberal forces subverting American society.

In 1952, he became editor-in-chief of *Collier's Encyclopedia*. Couch's career at *Collier's Encyclopedia*, however, raised different issues from those he had encountered at university presses. As a general interest encyclopedia, *Collier's* depended on acceptance by American libraries for financial success and on librarians for eventual acceptance by the general public. While home sales were the primary market for such works, the publishers had to impress librarians to whom their potential buyers would turn for recommendations. Without the enthusiastic acceptance of American librarians, the new encyclopedia had no chance of success against the much older and more established compilations available.

Couch came into direct conflict at *Collier's* with the American Library Association and its commitment to freedom of information, to objectivity, and to balance in presenting all sides of controversial issues. The aggressive editorial positions he had pursued at North Carolina and at Chicago came to full flower at *Collier's* in an editorial policy that went far beyond the standards of objectivity nominally expected from general encyclopedias. His work on the yearbooks, in particular, brought him into conflict with the liberal leadership of the American Library Association and of other organizations that he was convinced were leading the nation into collectivism and ultimately, into Communism. Couch's growing commitment to conservative causes led him to editorial decisions at *Collier's* that were anathema to his liberal superiors in the company and led to an inevitable clash that resulted in his firing in 1959.

After an abortive attempt from 1959 to 1963 to revise the *Oxford Junior Encyclopedia* for an American market for publisher Little & Ives, Couch accepted an appointment as director of publications at the William Volker Fund's Center for American Studies in California. It was a position that held for him the greatest potential for furthering his basic and essential beliefs and his commitment to promoting right-wing political, economic, and social causes. This experience proved that there were borders to conservatism that he could not cross. He was personally committed to the conservative values promoted by the center, but it had been pushed too far to the right even for him.

Bill Couch's conservatism had always been strongly based on European and American traditions. He was intensely aware that the fringes of a conservatism based on dogmatic adherence to any ideology would be dismissed by the majority of intellectually active Americans almost automatically. Couch was concerned that he be taken seriously and was careful that he knew where the boundaries between acceptable political discourse and the lunatic fringe lay. For him, liberals held the field and he did not want his own positions to be summarily dismissed as part of the nether world of right-wing polemic. Even so, he continually pushed the boundaries as far as he could. The eventual public association of the Center for American Studies with Nazis and with a radical form of fundamentalist evangelical Christianity led to an implosion that destroyed the endeavor and led Couch to retire to North Carolina in 1964.

William Terry Couch was a publisher who fully understood the power of books and ideas to change the world. To Bill Couch, publishing was a crusade to change American society. Through his career as an editor and publisher, he continually sought to probe the limits of what he could do to challenge the serious reader. At North Carolina, it was through books that addressed the major social and economic problems of the South, including race. At Chicago, it was through books with broader national import. At *Collier's*, it was through designing and implementing a new conception of an encyclopedia—one that embodied his own definitions of objectivity and significance by engaging the major figures in the conservative intellectual movement to contribute to their cause through the encyclopedia and its annual yearbook supplement. In all cases, Couch came under heavy criticism from his superiors, from liberals, and from the institutional powers that controlled research and publication—the major foundations and the American Library Association. But, he kept faith with his commitments to truth and to his vision of publishing. He had a deep understanding that the university presses and the encyclopedia offered the greatest potential to reach the public he wanted to influence to counter the propaganda of the liberal mass media.

William Terry Couch was a central figure in the renaissance of American conservatism, though his role has been largely unrecognized. As an editor and publisher, William Terry Couch was an impresario. Conservative icons such as Russell Kirk, Donald Davidson, Albert Hoyt Hobbs, Willmoore Kendall, and Richard Weaver bowed on center stage, but William Terry Couch managed the theater. As director of the University of North Carolina Press and the University of Chicago Press, and particularly as editor-in-chief of *Collier's Encyclopedia*, Couch pursued a career during which he had editorial and intellectual control over nationally influential publishing venues. His increasingly conservative political and economic convictions and his active promotion of conservative policies in his editorial and publishing decisions forced him into direct conflicts with superiors who held the liberal ideas against which Couch crusaded after leaving the University of North Carolina Press in 1945.

I interviewed Bill Couch in 1986 while working on a biographical study of Louis Shores. In the 1950s, Shores had served as a consulting editor for *Collier's Encyclopedia* while Couch was editor-in-chief. Shores took Couch's job when Couch was fired from *Collier's* in 1959. My interest in Shores had grown out of my own earlier work on the history of academic librarianship in the nineteenth and early twentieth centuries. Shores's promotion of the Library-College Movement in the 1960s was the major development in academic libraries after the 1920s. I was interested in what Couch might be able to tell me about Shores.

A few hours before I was to meet Couch at his home in Chapel Hill on December 17, 1986, I talked with the dean of the library school at the University of North Carolina at Chapel Hill, Dr. Edward Holley. Holley had been a member of the University of North Carolina Press's Board of Governors when Couch had presented his complaints about his mistreatment in Daniel Singal's book. When I told Dr. Holley that I would be interviewing Couch that evening about Shores, he was not encouraging. He told me that I would get nothing out of the meeting: "Couch's brain is fried."

Holley was only partially right. I did not get much useful insight from Bill Couch about Louis Shores, but his brain was certainly not fried. He was, however, quite deaf and no matter how much I tried to keep him on the course of Louis Shores and *Collier's Encyclopedia*, he was off on a wide-ranging monologue. Our interview lasted almost three hours, during which Couch, in a rich

Tidewater Virginia accent, talked of everything from Aristotle to Ronald Reagan. All of this was within the frame of a logical and coherent narrative that, unfortunately, did not get to his experience at *Collier's* or, in any significant way, to Louis Shores. That evening, Mr. Couch was eloquent, coherent, and deaf.

Bill Couch was intensely aware that he was in danger at each point in his career and that his insistence on his own editorial decisions and policies would be challenged by others with more authority in the institutions he served. He did not own the press, but as long as he exercised editorial control, he was committed to his cause and to his vision of publishing as an anodyne to the corrosive effect of liberalism on American society and politics.

At each stage of his career, his neck was in the noose and he knew that the noose could be tightened. This did not deter him from following his own sense of editorial integrity and his commitment to publishing as an intellectual cause. Couch suffered from akrasia, frequently and knowingly acting against his own best interests in pursuing his causes to the point of handing the end of the rope to those who joyfully tightened the noose. He was in constant conflict with his superiors in every organization that employed him.

The liberal causes espoused by the people who controlled publishing affronted Couch's own clear and unwavering vision of the truth. It was a truth that found its way in the post–New Deal rise of neoliberalism and defined itself in anti–Communism. It was a truth that rejected the relativism of social sciences and demanded that the disinterested objectivity that characterized academic discourse incorporate values. The question to which he wanted answers was not how people lived, the dry statistics that were basic to American social science, but how people should live. Above all, he sought to change the thinking of Americans through the books and articles that he published to bring about a better society in America.

1

A University Press
in the South

William Terry Couch was appointed to the job as acting director of the University of North Carolina (UNC) Press by the press's director, university librarian Louis Round Wilson, almost by accident. Wilson spent most of the 104 years of his life in precarious health and in 1925, at the age of forty-nine, had been advised by his physicians to take yet another leave to restore himself. He turned to Couch, then an undergraduate student worker in the library, to accept the management of the press during Wilson's absence for $50 a month. Couch had been the editor of *Carolina Magazine*, a student publication of UNC, which he had used as a lectern from which to attack religious fundamentalism and the foibles and hypocrisies of the South. Wilson recognized Couch's ability but was also aware of his tendency to editorial recklessness. In making the temporary appointment, Wilson warned Couch that the press had to avoid controversial topics. Couch proved reluctant to accept this advice.

Wilson had handled all the work of the press himself since it had been established in 1922 and simply pointed Couch to the drawer in the filing cabinet in which the working documents of the press were kept and left Chapel Hill to recuperate. Couch's first job was to find out what a university press should be doing and, more importantly, what an acting director of a university press should do.[1]

His first challenge came immediately. When Couch took over, the press had just published *Can a Man Be a Christian Today* by William Louis Poteat, president of Wake Forest College, a Baptist institution. The book had emerged from a series of lectures given by Poteat under the sponsorship of the John Calvin McNair Fund in the spring of 1925 at UNC. The fund had been established to support an annual lecture series on the relationship between science and religion. Poteat had had difficulties with Baptist fundamentalists who objected to the teaching of evolution at Wake Forest and was in real danger of losing his job over the issue. Poteat and Wilson had some hopes of calming the opposition of Baptist fundamentalists through the book's publication. Wilson had rushed the manuscript to press, rushed the review copies out, and rushed out the door leaving Couch with the job of selling the book.

While Couch had no idea of what the acting head of a university press should be doing, he did know that the job involved selling books. He began building on the demand that Wilson created by distributing review copies to North Carolina newspapers. He loaded a Ford he had borrowed from Howard Odum's Institute for Research in Social Science at UNC with copies of the book, which he placed in every store in North Carolina willing to display them.[2]

Couch's plan to plant articles about the book and about the author in North Carolina newspapers as a means of generating popular demand was firmly vetoed by Wilson who feared repercussions to the university from the state legislature. Poteat was already a controversial figure in North Carolina and Wilson was apprehensive about publicly having his name associated with the UNC Press. When Wilson told Couch that it was "a subject that was too dangerous for us to touch," Couch expressed his disgust for an administration that would allow itself to be browbeaten by a state legislature to Nell Battle Lewis, a reporter and editorial columnist for the *Raleigh* (NC) *News and Observer*. Lewis had already taken the university to task in a national forum, the *Nation*, for caving to the threats of the North Carolina Cotton Manufacturers' Association to cut the university's funding from the state legislature. The association objected to Howard Odum's Institute for Research in Social Science pursuing its investigations into labor conditions in the North Carolina textile mills under a grant Odum had received from the Rockefeller Foundation. In his letter to Lewis, Couch attributed the timidity of the university's administrators to the university's aspiration to be Harvard or Yale. Couch told her, "If the University Press, like Harvard or Yale, is to devote itself to bringing out nice inoffensive books—perfect examples of modern scholarship—it seems to me that the legislative gentlemen who protest at our expenditures have a real reason for their protests."[3]

His promotion of Poteat's book was successful enough that Couch quickly realized a second printing would be needed and went to the university's business office to arrange for it to be completed in time to enable him to deliver the books to the stores before public interest waned. The business office, however, held the request and failed to forward it to the printer until it was too late for the books to be produced and distributed before demand faltered. This was the first of a long series of clashes between Couch and business offices and accountants that plagued his career as a publisher.[4]

It was not an encouraging start for Couch, but he recovered and persevered. Early on he decided that the UNC Press had a mission that was beyond mere scholarship. It could change the South from a cultural, intellectual, and economic backwater into a dynamic force in America. To accomplish this, Couch knew he had to challenge the culture and traditions that kept the South from realizing its potential.

Daniel Singal appropriately opened the chapter on William Terry Couch at the UNC Press in his book, *The War Within*, with the story of the controversial publication of Edward Clarkson Leverett Adams's *Congaree Sketches*. Couch himself considered it the major event in his tenure at the press and it was, undoubtedly, the incident that established him as a major force in the intellectual life of the University of North Carolina.[5]

As assistant director of the press, Couch sat at the meeting of its Board of Governors in May 1927, against a backdrop of political apprehension while the issue of *Congaree Sketches*, a collection of African American tales collected by Adams, a South Carolina medical doctor, was considered. It was a book that stepped into the muck of southern race relations and could expose the university to public condemnation. Technically, there was no relationship between the University of North Carolina and the UNC Press. When the press was founded, it was placed under a Board of Governors and operated independently from the university. This was, though, a legal fiction structured to keep the press from imposing financial obligations on the university. If the University of North Carolina could not be held accountable for the press legally, it would be accountable in public opinion. The members of the Board of Governors facing Couch that morning were all drawn from the UNC faculty. The president of the university was the final authority on all of its decisions, even though this was not specified in the charter.[6]

Couch probably displayed no open sign of unease as he faced the members of the press's Board of Governors who had been called to this emergency session. He was twenty-five years old and had only recently completed the requirements for his bachelor's degree at the university when he was called to this meeting by the university's president, Harry Woodburn Chase. The members of the board, all men much older than Couch who held appointments as full professors in various departments of the university, could have intimidated a lesser man than Couch, but they had little effect on him. Though young, he was an eloquent speaker with the intellectual agility necessary to hold his own in any situation. He had the poise needed to face the members of the board and the university president as equals.

The issue at hand was the publication of *Congaree Sketches*. The tales themselves were innocuous enough for southern white sensibilities, but the introduction to the book, contributed by social activist and UNC playwright

Paul Green, was potentially dangerous.[7] Paul Green won a Pulitzer Prize in 1927 for his play, *In Abraham's Bosom*. By the time he was asked to contribute the introduction to Adams's book, Green had achieved an international reputation for his plays and a local reputation for his involvement with radical causes, particularly his commitment to racial justice and the civil rights of African Americans.

Many years later, Couch recalled that Adams had asked him to arrange for Paul Green to write the introduction to the book. That may have been possible, but it would have also been natural for Couch himself to have turned to Green for the task. Paul Green had been an active reader and editor for the press and he and Couch had become close friends when Couch was an undergraduate student at Chapel Hill. Couch had been a regular visitor to Green's home in Chapel Hill since at least 1924. There, Couch met Green's sister, Caro Mae Green, a woman to whom Couch was briefly married (1967–1970) much later in both of their lives. Couch took care of the Green's home in Chapel Hill from the summer of 1928 to the summer of 1929 while the Greens were in Europe on a Guggenheim fellowship.[8]

In his introduction to Adams's book, Green pled for racial justice and equality. He began by quoting W. E. B. Dubois and Booker T. Washington, asserting that Dubois was right. Washington's careful approach to economic equality and gradualism in race relations paled in comparison to DuBois's lyric defense of African American humanity and dignity. Racial equality and the integration of black and white in America were, in Green's vision, vitally necessary for the full realization of the country's destiny. He used a metaphor of the African American digging a ditch with the white man directing the work to conclude:

> The negro is crawling out of his ditch to stand on the bank with the white man. And the white man is reaching a hand to pull him up: but let it be a stronger hand and one that reaches further than before. It may be that they will stand in their separate place apart, but I doubt it. They have too much in common not to pass a word with one another after the gesture of brotherhood has been made. And in the light of such benefits to hand I see no sense in the talk of segregation, back to Africa, and the like, which many of our politicians and faddistic souls enjoy.[9]

This was a sentiment with which some members of the board present may have agreed in principle. They were, however, unwilling to commit the University of North Carolina to racial integration or even comity through the university's imprint.

The vote was taken. The men around the table, all major figures in the university community—university librarian and titular head of the press Louis Round Wilson, graduate school dean James French Royster, sociologist Howard

W. Odum, historian J. G. de Roulhac Hamilton, biologist William Chambers Coker, and Robert H. Wettach of the law school—voted to suppress the introduction as inflammatory. Couch, however, informed them that it was too late. Review copies had already been sent out and to re-release the book without the introduction would only draw attention to the original objectionable piece. The board members reconsidered and took no action.[10]

The members of the Board of Governors and President Chase should have known that Couch was capable of causing trouble and would be eager to do so if given the opportunity. A month before the meeting over Adams's book, he had written a blistering letter to the editor of the *Durham* (NC) *Morning Herald* to set its readers straight on the nonsense the paper's editors had written about the Sacco and Vanzetti case. The editors responded, feigning respect for Couch's erudition, but insisting that he was wrong in his interpretation of the issues and wrong for maligning the South. As titular head of the press, Wilson received some adverse criticism of Couch for this letter, notably from UNC President Harry Woodburn Chase, who called both Couch's letter and the editorial response "equally unbalanced and intolerant." Eugene Cunningham Branson of the university's Department of Rural Social Economics told Wilson, "Couch is 'bodaciously' pugnacious and hopelessly superficial. It would seem that anyone would realize the unwisdom of rushing into public print with a controversial subject of this sort. The University will probably hear more from this." Wilson sent these comments to Couch expressing "no special opinion" except that "the trouble with us when we go to right wrongs is that we usually have to exaggerate and if our antagonists are reasonably clever, they usually have the satisfaction of seeing us bested." Wilson's mild rebuke failed to deter Couch, who sent copies of his letter and the Durham newspaper editorial to the *Nation* and the *Christian Century* hoping to further fan the flames of indignation nationally.[11]

The UNC Press's Board of Governors' meeting over *Congaree Sketches* was not the culmination of an unfortunate series of events. Couch knew that the book's introduction would be controversial and was fully prepared to champion it. Years after the event, he claimed that he simply wanted to know how far the press could go in exercising intellectual freedom and had he brought the issue of the introduction to the board before sending out the review copies it "would have led to endless discussion and would have been fatal to the chances for a reasonable measure of freedom of opinion in our publications." Couch knew his actions were risky, but they had no repercussions for him or for the press. The only adverse reaction seems to have come from the author of the book who had not approved the introduction prior to publication and who turned the book over to Scribner for subsequent printings without the introduction.[12]

Through the 1930s, Couch was a southern liberal—a man thoroughly committed to a New South that could recover from its fall in 1865 and the ignominy imposed by Reconstruction to emerge as an economic and intellectual power in America. Couch was less sanguine in his appraisal of the South's potential as an economic power than the early boosters of the New South such as Henry W. Grady or William D. Kelley.[13] He did, however, see that there was potential in economic and industrial development, in equality of economic opportunities between African American and white workers in the South, and in the improvement of Southern institutions to enable the changes necessary to raise the social and economic conditions of the South to the level of other regions of the United States.

Couch was not alone in this crusade against the political and social conservatism of the South, but his views created a potentially inflammatory situation when he took over the press. Howard W. Odum, the head of the university's sociology department, the School of Public Welfare, and the newly founded Institute for Research in Social Science, had already challenged conservative sensibilities in North Carolina. The university, ever dependent on public support, was in a politically dangerous position even without Couch. The January 1925 issue of Odum's journal, *Social Forces*, had published articles by Luther Lee Bernard and Harry Elmer Barnes which many religious fundamentalists in the state considered affronts to Christianity.[14] The university and Odum himself had been roundly attacked in the state newspapers and in the pulpits. Occurring in the midst of a related controversy over the teaching of evolution in the schools, the incident helped to convince the legislators of the state that UNC was a center of anti–Christian activism. The issues of the Adams book and its potential to harm the university and Odum's Institute came only a year after Odum had been forced to retreat from his research into textile mill labor conditions by the North Carolina Cotton Manufacturers Association.[15]

In facing down the press's Board of Governors over the publication of *Congaree Sketches*, Couch established himself as the functioning head of the press. When Couch was appointed assistant director of the press by Wilson in 1925, book publishing was only a minor function of the press. Couch soon changed that situation. For Couch, publishing was intellectual activism. He knew that the disinterested objectivity promoted by academic disciplines, particularly in the social sciences, had reduced academic scholarship to a sterile and meaningless compilation of facts and data. The objective of a university press was to publish books that gave meaning to the data accumulated by academic researchers. Unfortunately, academic researchers were the people least able to write the kinds of books that had meaning, though Couch did find some few who could.

Couch saw that the major problem with university scholarship lay in the fragmentation of disciplines. Academic scholarship had become focused on small problems and issues, on methodology and technique, and on detail at the expense of synthesis and meaningful understanding. He directly blamed the structure of American higher education for this:

> It has split into numerous departments, and it has exhausted its energies in developing techniques. When a new problem arises today, a new department has to be created. And, mainly because our thinking is fractional, the solution we give to any problem is fractional; and that solution, because of its fractional nature, necessarily gives rise to numerous additional problems. We then have to organize more departments and more courses.

Couch saw the press as the one unit within a university capable of rectifying the situation by publishing books that could "cover the whole range of thought and knowledge, as well to explore the unknown." Its work could not be limited to the artificial confines of the academic structure. Couch felt that the models provided by established university presses like Harvard's and Yale's did little or nothing to promote this unified vision. If he had any model in mind for the UNC Press, it was that of Oxford University Press which he praised for following, for four and a half centuries, a policy of using its commercial publishing venture to pay for its scholarly publishing with outstanding quality in both areas. He touted the Oxford model to Frank Graham, Harry Woodburn Chase's successor as the UNC president, as an example of what the University of North Carolina Press could become with adequate university support.[16]

Couch had little patience with the kinds of books that represented the norms of academic scholarship. The general interest trade books, the kinds of books published by Harper, Scribner, or Macmillan, most attracted Couch. Under his direction, the press moved increasingly toward books that filled that niche in the southern publishing landscape rather than to those adding to what he considered the mulch of traditional academic scholarship. Certainly, many of the books that were published as products of academic scholarship were essential to understanding the South. These were not, however, the books that could influence or be sold to the general reading public in the South. As an editor, he insisted on excellent research from his authors, but he insisted equally that they eschew the academic jargon that obscured the meaning for the intelligent reader who had no special knowledge of the arcane conventions of scholarly discourse in sociology, anthropology, or even literature.

Couch made every effort to operate the press as if it were a trade publisher rather than a typical university press, attempting to reach beyond the academic community to influence the general public. A survey of university presses conducted by Association of American University Presses (AAUP) in the 1940s singled out the UNC Press for special mention for the aggressive marketing approaches adopted by Couch, approaches that reflected those of the major trade houses. Couch sent out review copies to and advertised in major newspapers and magazines. He sent flyers to general book stores. The press even sponsored a banquet in honor of one author in Charlotte, North Carolina.[17]

Couch, of course, did not feel that all books published by any university press—or even by the UNC Press—should receive such treatment. He had a solid sense of the market for books and recognized that promoting most of the books he published to a general audience was wasteful. For scholarly books, sending review copies to appropriate specialized journals and flyers to selected scholars in the field was sufficient. Trying to sell scholarly books to bookstores was, he knew, "a serious mistake." Good general interest books could be promoted through bookstores, but trying to interest booksellers in the more scholarly books could only lead to their balking at the truly saleable books on a publisher's list. He maintained, "The only legitimate market, the only market worth cultivating for highly specialized books, is the scholarly group already working in the field."[18]

This view became a source of contention between Couch and the foundations supporting the work of Odum's institute. The press suffered from underfunding by the university to the extent that Couch found it difficult to maintain the ambitious publishing program he envisioned. The grant supplied by the Laura Spelman Rockefeller Memorial Fund to Howard Odum and his Institute for Research in Social Science had been crucial to the continued financial health of the press from the beginning of Couch's appointment. When he took over from Wilson in 1925, the press had a scant $250 a year to support speculative books and only $5,000 a year for its established monographic series. Odum's grants were essential if the press was to continue operating. The Rockefeller Foundation was anxious that the press actively and aggressively promote the books written by the institute's authors. Couch maintained that extensive national advertising of those books could never generate enough additional sales to offset the costs and would be a waste of money. To Couch, the foundation sought to promote the Institute for Research in Social Science and Howard W. Odum, but what was needed instead was support to strengthen the UNC Press.[19]

As Couch gained control of the press's operations, he began to assume an aggressive role in the acquisitions process. The press had to acquire good manuscripts to produce good books and without good books, the operation was doomed. For the first several years, he complained that "it was not considered appropriate for the staff to participate in criticizing and judging manuscripts, particularly if the author happened to be a member of the faculty of the Uni-

versity." The function of the press's staff then was simply to look after the physical production and distribution of the books. The financial strictures placed
on the press by the Great Depression, though, called for the press's staff to
ensure that manuscripts submitted for publication were both intellectually competent and marketable. There was no money to produce badly written books
with no potential for sales. Couch began to work as an editor and critic with
authors who presented potentially good books and began to reject books that
failed to meet his standards of acceptability. He also began to actively solicit
manuscripts and recruit authors who could write books that he envisioned
rather than passively waiting for submissions from academic authors. Rather
than simply accepting a manuscript as it was submitted, his editorial work
included extensively rewriting texts at times.[20]

In 1932, the press published Virginius Dabney's *Liberalism in the South*.
Dabney was the liberal editor of the *Richmond* (VA) *Times-Dispatch* who won
a Pulitzer Prize in 1948 for his editorials against segregated public transportation and the poll tax. During the book's writing, Couch and Dabney engaged
in a long series of correspondence about the book in which Couch instructed
Dabney with pages of criticism and suggestions. Daniel Singal asserted that
"most of the more outspoken passages in *Liberalism in the South* can be attributed directly to Couch's influence" and that the final concluding chapter was
more the work of Couch than Dabney: "It might be more accurate to say, in
fact, that Couch drafted the chapter and Dabney edited it—surely an unusual
role for a publisher."[21]

The specific letter that Singal cited in this exchange certainly is a masterful
piece that gave Dabney an outline and direction for his concluding chapter.
Couch called for a definition of liberalism and gave Dabney one definition:
"the notion of the dignity and worth of the individual." He told Dabney that
he needed to summarize the effects of liberal thought and action and told him
the results to be included. He told Dabney this section must address the failures
of liberalism and what those failures were. Couch's letter to Dabney was an
essay on liberalism disguised as editorial advice and Dabney took it to heart.
Dabney's summation chapter of the book followed Couch's recommendations
item for item to reach the same conclusions Couch had specified.[22] Dabney's
revisions were not slavish, but he did closely follow Couch's suggestions for
revision. Couch may not have put his own words on an author's page, but he
was an active and aggressive editor and was not reluctant to tell authors what
he wanted them to write about and what their conclusions and evidence should
say.

Couch's work on Dabney's book was more extensive than the efforts he
made on behalf of most press authors. Because of objections by Howard Odum

to publishing the book, the manuscript went to eight outside readers rather than the usual three, probably in an effort to convince Odum of its scholarly reputability. During Couch's tenure at the press, he could and did publish books over the objections raised by Odum who was a member of the governing board of the press. As the professional sociologist of the South, Odum maintained definite and fixed ideas of reputable research that differed significantly from what Couch wanted in books the press published.

Couch left routine proof-reading to members of his staff, but was painstaking in reviewing content himself. While most books did not require the intensity of effort he put into *Liberalism in the South*, he did insist that press authors express themselves with clarity and precision and, when their arguments and rhetoric became muddled, he did not hesitate to point to the specific problems and suggest alternative possibilities. When he was working on John B. Holt's manuscript *Under the Swastika* in 1935, he sent the author a list of questions and suggestions ranging from the mundane, such as admonitions to spell the names of people consistently, to the more crucial issue of Holt's use of the word *collectivism* to describe both Germany under Hitler and the Soviet Union under Stalin. Holt accepted Couch's criticism gracefully and revised the text accordingly.[23]

He was harder on Rupert Vance's manuscript for *Human Geography of the South* which the press published for the Institute for Research in Social Science in 1932. When Couch received Vance's first chapter, he took him to task for his failure to give "any definite statement indicating precisely what the regional concept is," complaining that Vance only indicated a "relative position" that completely failed to differentiate the South from any other region of the country except that it was east of west and below north on the map. Vance had entirely failed to convey the cultural distinctions that would differentiate the South from any other region. He asked Vance, "Within this area to what extent do the physical and cultural sub-regions coincide, to what extent do they overlap; and in what ways are these physical and cultural sub-regions different from or similar to sub-regions of other regions?"[24]

Couch was quoted by Chester Kerr in his survey of university presses published by the AAUP as having observed: "In order to be a good editor, one must be a sort of suspicious unabridged human dictionary, an intelligent, self-operating ready-reference library, a compendium of good and bad English usage, and an expert at discovering what is meant when something else, or nothing, is said."[25] Couch was a sedulous editor by this definition.

In most cases, Couch's editorial advice to his authors was no more than a gentle prod, but there were occasions when a gentle prod or even an aggressive thump was insufficient to move a book in the right direction. Couch conceived the *Culture in the South* project in 1928 when he proposed a book on southern life modeled on Harold Stearn's *Civilization in the United States* that would be published under the title "Civilization below the Potomac" in collaboration with the trade house W. W. Norton. He contracted with Howard Mumford Jones, then in the English department at UNC, to undertake the work, assuring Jones that he would have complete editorial control. When Jones delivered the first chapters in 1930, Couch was appalled. Except for Donald Davidson's chapter on literature, the work was incompetent, and Couch lost no time in telling that to Jones.

On December 15, 1930, Couch wrote Jones with a detailed critique of the chapters he had received. Couch's reaction ranged from mild approval of the piece on southern politics by historian and journalist George Fort Milton with the tepid comment that "the article could be printed without disgracing anyone" to his condemnation of the religion chapter written by Baptist minister Archer B. Bass that "this chapter might be printed as an exhibit to show why the power of the churches is declining in the South; but as an intelligent discussion of religion in the South, I think it is next to nothing." Couch concluded thrashing Jones with the admonition that Jones had "to do some hard work and consistent labor in the way of organizing the writing of the various chapters, and in eliminating incompetent writing as soon as it appears."[26]

Jones bristled at the criticism and immediately replied to Couch that he was certain that the letter was "more tactless than you had intended it." He pointed out that the contributors had been chosen for their expertise and not for "their literary skill" and "no notion was entertained of securing skillful journalists." Jones protested that what he had sent to Couch were first drafts and Couch's editorial indignation was inappropriate. Jones told Couch that the job assigned to him as editor of the work was simply to ensure that the people writing the sections "avoid egregious blunders in style and to prevent duplication of material." With contributors selected for their special knowledge rather than their ability as writers, a compilation with variegations in literary polish would be expected. If some sort of literary merit was expected, "one could have put together something as smooth and vapid as *I'll Take My Stand*," the manifesto of the Vanderbilt Agrarians. Rather, Jones had attempted a significant work of scholarship.

Jones concluded that while he was willing to accept criticism from "proper persons," he would not accept Couch's demands for such major changes. He totally rejected Couch's critique, telling him, "you will get no better work from other people by and large; and ... I can not admit that either my work or the work of the authors concerned is as dull or as incompetent as your letter makes it out to be."[27]

On January 29, 1931, Jones resigned from the project. The immediate reason Jones gave was that Couch, without Jones's knowledge, had approached potential contributors to the book. Couch tried to apologize with a letter that claimed it was a misunderstanding, but Jones was not appeased and his resignation was final.[28] Howard Mumford Jones was adamant. He wanted nothing to do with the project or with Couch, and Couch had to find a replacement. Couch contacted virtually every scholar in the South who he thought might be appropriate, but none would agree to serve. Finally, in desperation, Couch took over himself and kept tight control over the authors to keep the book from becoming yet another academic sociological tome. Couch wanted a book that would capture the emotional complexity of the South with an emphasis on the values of southern culture, primarily those of the common people of the South. It was a focus intended to vivify the region with all of its flaws and imperfections.[29]

When Couch took control of the project, he abandoned most of the chapters procured by Jones and began anew with the conception of the work. Among the potential contributors he considered was Andrew Lytle, one of the Nashville Agrarians and a contributor to *I'll Take My Stand*, for an article on workers in the forest and lumber industries of the South. When Couch contacted Lytle, he gave him the option of doing this topic or one on the southern backwoods. Couch was frank to Lytle that he preferred him to do the one on the lumber workers because he had no idea of who else might do it, but he was open to the other topic and clear on what he wanted for that. He demanded that Lytle describe the lives of people in the isolated communities of the South. He wanted particular attention on the transformation occasioned by modernization, "the changes occurring through improvements in transportation and communication." This was, Couch charged, to be accomplished in thirty to forty typed pages.[30]

Lytle accepted the assignment for the chapter on the backwoods. He sent Couch a draft of the chapter in September 1932, which Couch complained took too much of an historical approach to the assignment. Couch wanted a description of life in the remote rural South as it existed in the present—the life of people in area where there were no good roads, no schools or churches, and no "modern conveniences." In particular, Couch specified that he wanted Lytle to write about

> What kind of life do these people live? What do they talk about, what do they think, what do they read? What are their homes like? What furniture, what books, pictures, carpets, curtains do they have, and what sort of taste do they have in their selection? Finally, in what ways are their experiences better or worse than those of their kinsmen in towns, in cotton mills and factories?

He allowed Lytle a month to revise the article for the book and urged him to do so.[31]

Lytle flatly refused, telling Couch that his conception of the hinterlands of the South did not exist. There was no difference between those who lived five or even twenty miles from the main road and those who lived on it. A few days prior to writing to Couch with this refusal, Lytle had written to Allen Tate, a fellow Agrarian at Vanderbilt University, complaining that Couch had rejected the piece:

> The North Carolina people [i.e. Couch] turned down my essay on "The South as Backwoods"; they wanted me to write a purely descriptive something about something that no longer exists; and I scared them, I think, when I said a state could no more be founded on private property than a marriage on a bed. I took the thesis that the South was in the eyes of the rest of the country a backwoods, and I tried to define what that meant. They wanted, so they said, to know what kind of window curtains the folks hang up in their cabins five miles from the arterial highway. They ought to have sense enough to know that folks have quit hanging up curtains; they are wearing them.

Of course, Couch had not rejected Lytle's contribution to the book. He had only asked Lytle to make the changes he felt necessary to suit the piece for the compilation. After Lytle repeatedly refused to continue on the project, Couch wrote Donald Davidson, another Agrarian, asking him to intervene with Lytle to no avail.[32]

Couch should have known better. Andrew Lytle was a poet. He was not a social scientist. While he did dabble in history, he was a creative artist, not a compiler of statistics. This, of course, was primarily why Couch wanted him for the project. Couch wanted someone who could breathe life into the data and Lytle, he thought, was capable of that. Unfortunately, a man who could made good poetry did not necessarily make good sociology. He already knew from his experience with Odum and his institute that people who make academic sociology rarely made good literature.

Couch's antipathy to the kind of research and publication in the social sciences that had become the norm in American universities had been intensified by the books produced by Howard Odum and the faculty members and graduate students in his Institute for Research in Social Science. To Couch, their work was only marginally competent with its reliance on statistics without a narrative to make its significance real to anyone but another academic sociologist. Couch's insistence on editing the books submitted to the press by Odum's institute was a persistent point of friction between the two men.

Over the years, Couch compiled a litany of offenses that Odum had committed against him and the press. In 1938, he wrote to Frank Graham enumerating his conflicts with Howard Odum. Odum's attempts to control the policy of the press by using his position on the press's board to reject books Couch wanted and to publish books Couch thought unworthy headed his list of complaints. Odum tried to keep the press from publishing books that might compete with the publications of Odum's institute, even when those books had not been submitted to the UNC Press, but to other publishers. When the institute did submit manuscripts to Couch, Odum's demand that they be published immediately rather than subjecting them to any editorial intervention resulted in significant costs for in-press corrections. When Couch returned Odum's manuscript for *Southern Regions of the United States* because it was so poorly written, Odum demanded its immediate publication as it was delivered because it was subsidized by Odum's foundation grant.

Couch maintained that he had made every effort to accommodate Odum and the institute by paying the publication costs when the institute could not fund its own publications. This extended even to Odum's journal, *Social Forces*, when it encountered financial difficulties in 1937 and the UNC Press covered the deficit the journal had incurred. Couch professed to UNC president Frank Porter Graham that he had tried his best to placate Odum's outrageous demands and to support the publishing activities of the institute, but had been thwarted at every juncture by Odum. Odum's command that Couch refrain from approaching foundations for funding of the press was another block. Odum insisted that foundation funding was his domain and that Couch was not to tread on that ground.[33]

Couch provided Odum with an example of what he wanted in academic publishing with his own chapter, "The Negro," in *Culture in the South*. The statistics were there—average annual income of tenant farmers, rates of venereal disease, and birth and death rates—but Couch used them, in the midst of his parade of facts, to construct a tableau of a typical black sharecropper family. The parents, Jim and Maggie, had been married twenty years and had seven living children. The oldest of these, Doreen, was nineteen years old and had worked as a housekeeper for a white family in town until she became pregnant. The next oldest, Tom, worked away from home at the sawmill occasionally and also on the farm. Three of the younger children labored the fields with their parents. The "mere hovel" in which the family lived was furnished with broken and crudely mended cast-offs "from kindly white families." The schooling their children received was meager. Jim's Saturday night excursions into town were events where, "so long as he is sober he is careful how he mixes up with town slickers, but once he has a little liquor in him, he feels like anybody's equal." Sunday, of course, was the day of repentance from the sins of Saturday night and the church held the promise of a heaven where "everyone is white and has a harp, a shining white robe, and wings."

Couch depicted a family with little and small hope for anything more, one in which "white men have cut the pattern, the Negro just follows it." The forms of living were established by whites and what was available to the African American was a crude reflection of that: "The Negro's liquor is meaner, his women are blacker (the mulatto women who are loose usually have white men), his craps a little more likely to end in carving."

Couch's vision of the plight of the African American sharecropper in the South was vivid and had, certainly, elements of a reality based on the data available, but it also shared in the prejudice common to most white southerners. It was a prejudice so deeply held that it was simply a fact: African Americans were a separate people who should remain separate. Couch did, though, condemn the results of that prejudice. He deplored the inadequate schools for African Americans and the lack of access to public libraries. Couch censured the South for the political disenfranchisement of the African American. He condemned lynching, but regarded it unlikely to stop even if the officials in southern states enforced the law "rigidly and unsparingly to those who committed crimes against Negros." The cause of the dilemma of African Americans in the South derived from the economic situation: "an economic system that is running in the wrong direction, that thrives on struggle between the poor and the less poor, that forces on the white laborer the fear that he will lose his job to a Negro" willing to work for lower wages. For Couch, the central issue was not race, but poverty, which could and should be addressed.[34]

Like most southerners, Couch had been raised to understand and to adhere to the customs that formed the basis of racial interaction in the South. Couch was philosophically and emotionally committed to segregation, but could still be counted as a liberal in race relations in a South where Jim Crow set the rules under which whites and African Americans coexisted fitfully. He certainly recognized the evil of segregation as it was practiced in the South, but continued his argument that the issue was not one of race, but economics. Simple prejudice had no justification, but the racial issues of the South were not that simple and could not improve until the economic positions of both black and white workers had been ameliorated. Couch blamed the essential problem on the "cheapness and servility of labor" in the South and that could only be improved when all workers of both races achieved a modicum of economic security. As it was, though, Couch affirmed the necessity for continued segregation and that raising even exceptional black individuals to the level of the white majority would be doing a disservice to the African American population by removing them from their people and "the closest possible community of interest with the class from which they come." Integration was a false issue raised by people who failed to see that separation of the races was both necessary and desirable. The points that aroused the most ardor were symptoms of a deeper and undiagnosed malaise that derived from an economic system that pitted the poor white laborer against the poor black laborer.[35]

In his preface to *Culture in the South*, Couch took pointed issue with the recent manifesto of the Agrarian movement, *I'll Take My Stand*. This collection of essays written, according to the title page "by twelve southerners," was the work of men almost all of whom were members of the faculty or students at Vanderbilt University. All were strongly committed to the resurrection of an idyllic agrarian South from the ashes of the Civil War. In the book, Frank Owsley of the Vanderbilt history department rejected the notion that the war had been over the issue of slavery, but was rather an act of aggression by the industrialized North to maintain the captive southern market for its goods. Herman Clarence Nixon, also of Vanderbilt's history department, celebrated the agrarian economy of the South, viewing the industrialism of the region with alarm: "It is deplorable that the South's agricultural philosophy is imperiled by a non-philosophical pattern of society in which the highest aim of life is success in industry." Andrew Lytle warned that industrialization would inevitably lead to socialism, then to Communism, and ultimately to Sovietism and the South "should dread industrialism like a pizen snake." Donald Davidson raised his voice in the chorus to deny the ability of any industrialized economy to produce art.[36]

I'll Take My Stand was essentially a white poetic response to the problems of the South. The writers had little in the way of a unified theme, but all affirmed the value of the white yeoman farmer who, living close to the land and raising his family in a harmonious society, was an ideal that rising industrialism in the South was threatening. The book began with an unsigned introduction subtitled, "A Statement of Principles," written by John Crowe Ransom who attempted to find common threads among the essays. Ransom maintained the essays took aim at proponents of the New South who could only offer "an undistinguished replica of the usual industrial community" which presented a deplorable future for the South. For Ransom, the basic issue was "a Southern way of life against what may be called the American or prevailing way." The American way was industrialism which, the authors agreed, could offer nothing to the South and must be abandoned if the South was to prosper on its own as an agrarian society.[37]

Couch may have been quite right when he simplified the sometimes convoluted essays of the authors into a straightforward conflict between industrial and agrarian forces, condemning Agrarianism as a "serious error" in his preface to *Culture in the South*. Allen Tate, a major participant in the Agrarian movement, took up this challenge when he reviewed *Culture in the South* for the literary journal, the *American Review*, accusing Couch of completely misreading

I'll Take My Stand. While Tate did praise a few of the authors of chapters of Couch's book, notably Donald Davidson, he generally condemned the book as nothing more than the work of liberals with his observation, "that liberalism has no programme and that, however brave and pious its criticism may be, it is ultimately futile." Tate pointedly took Couch to task because he "betrays the general paralysis of the political sense." Tate's objection to *Culture in the South* was that the book represented a typically liberal response to the problems of the South: "Although Professor Couch weeps for the poor-white, he proposes, so far as I can see, to do nothing but study him."[38]

Couch could not fail to respond directly to Tate's criticism and enthusiastically dove into the fray. Couch began by asserting that he had thought it inappropriate to recommend ameliorative measures in a work that was intended to be purely descriptive. But, he did hint at his own solution to the problems in the preface to *Culture in the South* when he wrote of the distinctions between individualism and collectivism in which the gamble of speculation by the farmer could be replaced by the economic security of collective farming.[39]

Couch published an elaborate response to Tate in the summer, 1934, issue of the *American Review* in which he described a vision of a utopian agricultural society designed to cure the malaise of the South. The piece was explicitly framed as a response to Tate's criticism of *Culture in the South*, and published in a journal that was designed by its founding editor, Seward Collins, to be a forum for conservatives, traditionalists, and, specifically, for the Agrarians.[40] Couch blamed cotton, the major cash crop for the South, for the essential problems throughout the history of the South. Cotton was responsible for the institution of chattel slavery and for the continuation of virtual slavery through the sharecropping system that had become established after the Civil War. Cotton was to blame for the depletion of southern soil, for the poverty of the lower classes, white and black, and for the continued economic subjugation of the farmer in the South. New Deal legislation passed to aid agriculture had proven a failure. It "brought assistance mainly to the commercialized agricultural interests rather than to the farm-owning family or the tenants or labourers."

The utopian community Couch proposed had its prototype in a New Deal project under the Subsistence Homestead Program that, beginning in 1932, established a number of communities throughout the country from Minnesota to Mississippi and Georgia to Washington. The project at Arthurdale, West Virginia, was a particular interest of Eleanor Roosevelt. In North Carolina, there was a specific project near Burgaw with which Couch was most familiar, the Penderlea Homestead Farms. It had been developed by real estate promoter Hugh MacRea and sold to the federal government in 1934. Penderlea was only one of several farm villages that MacRae had founded since 1905. By the 1930s, his design for these contained many of the elements incorporated into Couch's answer to Allen Tate.

Couch proposed a five-year program to build four to five thousand villages throughout the South for one to three hundred farm families each with modern housing, community centers with libraries, playgrounds, swimming pools, and commercial and professional buildings. Couch's plan called for the commercial buildings to be collectively owned by the residents and rented to shopkeepers based on a sort of civil service examination for "high standards of service." Doctors and lawyers would be salaried by the village rather than paid for individual services. Capitalism would be eliminated within the farm village: "No opportunity would be given for the financial interest of any one individual or group of individuals to dominate the life of the village." Investments by residents would be limited to government bonds and individual riches would be kept in check through income and inheritance taxes. Of course, African Americans would have separate-but-equal villages. This was a pointed jab at Tate and the Agrarians who, Couch maintained, were enthusiastic for owners of small farms "until the Negro is mentioned as a candidate for farms—then small ownership becomes positively pernicious."[41]

Couch's solution to the problems of funding such a project to redevelop the basis of southern society is a parody of New Deal idealism and double-talk that should have been noticed by anyone who read, "The wealth of this country is internally owned. Every debt that is owed by anyone is also owned by someone. The payment of the cost of building the villages would be a simple bookkeeping transaction: a mere matter of taxing those who owned the debt incurred for building and paying them with the money collected from them."[42] This was certainly a creative approach to financing.

Michael O'Brien, in his perceptive book, *The Idea of the American South, 1920–1941*, called Couch's proposal "collectivist."[43] It was. But, O'Brien took Couch's article as a legitimate proposal and what Couch had offered Tate was actually a parody of a plan. Couch's imitation of Tate's affected use of the British spelling of *programme* in the article is one indication of his intent. The spelling had been used consistently by Tate and Donald Davidson in reference to the Agrarian ideas while *I'll Take My Stand* was in its planning stages, a convention of which Couch would have been aware.[44] It is almost as if Couch had been muttering under his breath while writing, "If Tate wants a programme, I'll give him a programme."

Allen Tate had been a confirmed anti–Communist for several decades by this time. He had insistently urged that the volume that was eventually published as *I'll Take My Stand*, be titled, *Tracts against Communism*. Tate could see only two alternatives for the future of the South, Agrarianism or Communism. He and Couch had an altercation over this at the May 1936 meeting of the Southern Policy Committee in Chattanooga when Couch hotly contested Tate's options and was shouted down by the Agrarians as expressing his own personal opinion. Couch, of course, thought he was expressing the opinion of the majority of the attendees who could easily see other possible futures for the South.[45]

Within a year after the *American Review* piece, Couch published a more thoughtful critique of economic planning in which he took his UNC colleagues, Howard Odum and Rupert Vance, as well as the Agrarians to task for their own failures to offer a workable solution for the South. He easily dismissed the Agrarians who would never get far in promoting small subsistence farming until they recognized that small farmers had already fled to other occupations, regarding farming "as a hopelessly empty and dreary contest with soil, climate, and market." What the small farmer wanted in life did not match the poetic imagination of the Agrarians.

On the other hand, planning by the followers of the social sciences, particularly Odum and Vance, failed because the problems "are not susceptible to any objective, scientific solutions." The answers were political, not scientific. Odum and Vance and others like them had to establish what their objectives in planning were to be and, in doing so, what kind of social and economic order was good. Rather, Couch maintained, the planning services of social scientists were up for sale to anyone who would pay to hire them and those employers were the owners of businesses who controlled the foundations that provided financial support for the research.

Couch did see some possibilities for Communism in southern economic planning at least in its efficiency, but he deplored that prospect. He was probably looking at the growing political presence of Huey Long and his program for economic reform when he predicted that "with the southern public, a fascist, or communist government as bad as fascism, is inevitable and in process of being born."

While he credited Roosevelt as "a far better and more intelligent president than the country has any right to expect," he acknowledged that Roosevelt had failed to turn the country back from the devastation of the Great Depression. The ultimate outcome of FDR's program, Couch predicted, "will be the corruption of the voters of this country, and the training of a great body of people, as well as the organized agriculture and industrial interests, to expect the federal government to give them permanent support."[46]

Agrarian Frank Owsley immediately wrote Couch when the article appeared. The tone of his letter was cordial, but he strongly objected to what he thought was Couch's assertion that the Communists provided the best solution to the racial issues facing the South. Owsley argued that the Communist Party was actively engaged in a program that could only lead to severe racial conflict and violence. Owsley cautioned, "I should hate to see a man of your intellectual stamina and moral integrity go haywire on doctrinaire principles which will cause race conflict and the spilling of blood."

Couch responded to him confessing that he knew little about Communism having read little Lenin and less Marx. He told Owsley that he had simply said that the Communists were the only group attempting to deal directly with the race problems of the South. He was right. In its attempt to organize labor in the South, the Communists had taken a strong stand for integrated labor unions that included black and white workers under one banner fighting for the economic advantage of all. Couch did seem to share one basic belief with the Communists. He agreed that the racial conventions of the South derived from economic causes and not simple prejudice: "If the problem of economic existence is solved for the Negro and the poor white man many of our racial problems will disappear."[47]

Although there should have been many philosophical similarities between Couch and the Agrarians, and there were some, there was also an antagonism that kept them at a distance. The introduction to *Culture in the South* was one point of contention. Couch used it to directly attack the Agrarians to the point that it appeared that *Culture in the South* was a direct response to the Agrarians. Donald Davidson wrote to Allen Tate on January 12, 1934, commending Tate on his excellent review of Couch's book, calling Couch's introduction "an inept and vain attempt to make the book appear like an answer to I'll Take My Stand."[48]

Couch continued his attacks on the Agrarians whenever the opportunity was available. In November 1936, Couch followed Donald Davidson on the program of the Southern Historical Association meeting. After Davidson argued the values of the Agrarians, Couch began his contribution to the discussion by saying that Agrarianism, if it were a serious movement, should have a consistent central body of thought and doctrine, or it was nothing more than "a hodgepodge of medieval dialectic and romantic moonshine." Couch proceeded to enumerate the points of inconsistency, contradiction, and nonsense expressed by the Agrarians to arrive at the conclusion that the Agrarians "have been touched with the distemper of the renowned knight of la Mancha, and if they have no Sancho, they do have a Rosinante and an inexhaustible supply of metaphysical windmills." Couch's audience contained many of the Agrarians. When he took on the Agrarian argument that the soil was the salvation of the South, he told them that by this they were arguing against white supremacy. The African American sharecropper was much closer to the land than the white overseer on his horse. John Crowe Ransom rose in fury to defend himself and his writings. The Agrarians in the audience, including Donald Davidson, were enraged by Couch's attack.[49]

When Couch wanted to publish Davidson's *Attack on Leviathan*, for the UNC Press, Davidson talked with other Agrarians before accepting. He wrote to Allen Tate on March 31, 1937, to explain that he could not see withholding "the book simply because he [Couch] has irritated me." While Davidson "would prefer a true Confederate to do the job," he knew that the UNC Press is "the nearest thing to a Southern publishing house that we have."[50] Tate agreed with Davidson's assessment of the UNC Press and went beyond Davidson to denigrate Bill Couch. When he was considering submitting his novel, *The Fathers*, to the UNC Press, he wrote to literary critic Cleanth Brooks, "Couch has to be handled carefully as so all stupid and ignorant persons whose vanity is on their sleeves."[51]

Couch did publish *Attack on Leviathan* in 1938. Much of the book contained essays Davidson had already published and revised for this book, but he included several new pieces all tied together in thematic clumps and all eloquent expressions of the values of the Agrarians. Davidson's literary talents were considerable, and Couch accepted the copy Davidson provided with only minor proofreading corrections. Twenty-five years later, Couch said it was one of the two most important books he had ever published.[52]

Though a southerner, Couch could never be considered a "true Confederate" by Davidson. Couch was firmly convinced that the central issue in the South was not race but economics. He referred to the bottom of the social and economic levels in the South as "American peasants," people white and black who shared many cultural characteristics arising from poverty rather than race.[53] In a letter to a friend in 1933, he explained his view:

> In my opinion much of the conflict between the races will disappear once the whites find a way to live without keeping the Negro in practical slavery. I don't believe there is very much "natural" antipathy between the races—most of it is induced by economic relationships. The Negro can't be freed until the white man is freed—both are in bondage in the same chaotic system. Perhaps the Negro can never have equal freedom alongside the white man. I'm not willing to be fanatical on the subject, that is, to the extent of demanding "rights" to intermarry and mix freely. I don't think this part of the racial controversy is of any importance in comparison with the desirability of educational facilities, schools and libraries, recreational opportunities, parks and playgrounds, and sanitation and hospitals and other modern needs for Negroes.

Couch maintained that the essential needs and public services could be provided on a separate basis and saw no reason to go beyond segregation of the races.[54]

His quarrel with the Agrarians, though, did go beyond economics to strike through the romantic mist through which Allen Tate and his group attempted to mask the South. The Agrarians demanded that the folkways, the values, and the customs of the South be respected. Couch granted that they sounded eloquently reasonable in this demand, but anyone deluded by the "earmarks of perfect amiability and reasonableness" of the Agrarian argument for respect failed to "realize that lynching, the excessive homicide rates, and numerous other customs and habits equally as reprehensible constitute a part of those things which the Agrarians wish to have respected." The Agrarians, in their crusade to preserve the ideals of the Old South, directly opposed people like him who seriously studied the problems of the South and sought ways to make southern life better. To Couch, the basic difference between him and the Agrarians was "that between the reactionary and the liberal."[55] While Howard Odum engaged the reactionaries of the South behind a safe barricade of statistics, Couch engaged the reactionaries, the Agrarians, in public forums and Couch's principle armament was the University of North Carolina Press. The Agrarians offered poetry. Odum and his institute offered statistics. Couch was trying to offer a vision, essentially, a vision for a New South.

These Are Our Lives, published by the press in 1939, demonstrated Couch's vision for a new social science. The book had its origins in a 1938 letter from Henry G. Alsberg, director of the Federal Writers' Project (FWP), requesting Couch's help in resuscitating the program in the South. Couch proposed using FWP staff members to create a collection of narratives from typical representatives of southern life. The staff members were to be sent out with instructions from Couch on collecting the stories and a detailed outline of the kinds of questions that should be answered. Couch told the interviewers, "The purpose of this work is to secure material which will give an accurate, honest, interesting, and fairly comprehensive view of the kind of life that is lived by the majority of the people in the South."

Couch gave the writers a detailed outline, but he also encouraged them to avoid rigidity in their narratives: "Insofar as possible, the stories should be told in the words of the persons who are consulted." Couch wanted specifics, details, and "literary excellence." He also wanted accuracy, but recognized that the writers could not completely verify the truth of what was said by the respondents. *Accuracy*, Couch elaborated, "meant simply write what you smell, see, hear."

In his introduction to *These Are Our Lives*, Couch expanded on his vision when he wrote about the story of Irma and Morrison, a white sharecropping couple, in "Get Out and Hoe," one of the narratives collected for the volume. Couch said, "I feel as if I know Irma better than I possibly could from mere statistical facts concerning tenant farmers ... this, which tells what kind of person Irma is, cannot be contained in any tabulation or subjected to any statistics." Irma's monologue revealed a woman stolidly surviving her life—children dying, a philandering husband, abuse as a child, and grinding poverty—with hope revived by the New Deal when she said, "It seems like that man in Washington has got a real love for the poor people in his heart, and I believe it's due to him and his helpers that the poor renters are goin' to get a chance."[56]

Couch used only a few of the narratives collected for the project in *These Are Our Lives*. He selected those with the greatest literary value leaving the rest for a projected series of books, hoping that this preliminary volume would demonstrate the value of his approach to research sufficiently to enable him to secure foundation funding for the series. However, the book was not accepted by social scientists as legitimate research. Couch complained that the editor of the *American Journal of Sociology* compared it to *Tobacco Road*.

From this modest beginning, Couch became increasingly involved in the FWP. In April 1938, he proposed an ambitious series of twenty books he thought appropriate for the FWP to support. The topics he offered ranged from studies of recreational facilities in the South to biographies of condemned criminals and included book proposals on such subjects as rural slums and lease agreements between tenant farmers and land owners. It was a broad assortment of ideas. He had ideas for possible authors for most of these and had approached Howard Odum's institute and the Southeastern Folk-Lore Society, both of which expressed interest in cooperating with him on projects. In May 1936, he was asked by Henry Alsberg, director of the FWP, to serve as associate director for the North Carolina state guide project with a salary of $15 a day plus expenses for the duration of the project. That summer, he was offered the position as a regional director of the FWP.

Couch's appointment as regional director was held up in Washington because Couch was not a sociologist. Couch objected, saying that the work he proposed had nothing to do with sociology, but was broadly interdisciplinary. Couch had carefully consulted with all members of the UNC community about the appointment before committing himself to the job, but Howard Odum objected. Odum told Couch that members of the Institute for Research in Social Science would assist on Couch's projects, but the institute could not do so officially since whatever Couch would produce would not be scientific. He told Couch, that the FWP in the South should concentrate on collecting "descriptions of old homes." Couch was unaware that Odum had communicated this opinion to the Works Progress Administration (WPA) officials in Washington who were to make the appointment.

Couch's appointment finally came through, but Couch had already become involved in constant bickering with the bureaucrats of the WPA over credit for authorship on the books sponsored by the FWP and the dispersal of royalty payments. The WPA insisted that *Works Progress Administration* be on the title pages as the author and it had no mechanism for handling royalties. When Couch was instructed to transfer the money received from sales of the book to the United States Treasury, he was livid. He had already received at least two conflicting instructions for the dispersal of the money and the WPA officials, he claimed, refused to respond to him when he asked for clarification, Couch was convinced that the situation had devolved to this because the WPA officials did not think that he was the person at the university who was authorized to handle the money, and he feared that the UNC administrators would consider him "unreasonable" in his complaints against the WPA since they knew nothing about the issues.[57]

At a meeting of the press's board on May 14, 1940, Couch detailed his objections to the pettiness to which he had been subjected by the WPA officials. The minutes report:

> The Director stated that WPA officials had made such a nuisance of requesting copies of agreements that had been furnished previously and of having conferences about matters that had been discussed in the greatest detail and then of failing to read the agreements and of not keeping notes and of making errors on matters that were supposed to have been settled a number of times that he had finally found it necessary to write a letter which he sent to a number of WPA officials to the effect that he could not waste any more time on this matter.[58]

Couch's patience with Washington bureaucrats was as limited as his patience with the bureaucracy of the UNC business office. Finally, Couch resigned from the Federal Writers' Project in disgust.

These Are Our Lives was not sociological research in the constricted methodology of Odum's institute, but was rather a literary endeavor intended to vitalize the data into a personal encounter with the participants in the true South. Couch thought his fictionalized approach presented a new model for reporting social science research, but Howard Odum was as reluctant as other professional sociologists to accept it. At Chapel Hill, Howard Odum had defined the social sciences, and Couch desperately wanted to influence Odum with his conception of research and publication in the social sciences. Odum's intensely academic approach to research was only intelligible to other sociologists and Couch wanted to reach a wider general reading public. Odum's grants had been essential to the finances of the press and Couch appreciated that, but Couch's relationship with Howard Odum was always a tortured one.

In Odum's eyes, Couch was unfit to head a university press. When Wilson left the University of North Carolina to become dean at the University of Chicago's Graduate Library School in 1932, Couch was the logical person to assume the office of director of the press. He had successfully held the job if not the title since 1925. He was appointed director of the press by Frank Graham with the support of most of the press's Board of Governors, but over the strong objections of one board member, Howard Odum.[59]

Odum's working relationship with Couch had been troubled from the beginning and he had frequently complained to the titular head of the press, Louis Round Wilson, about Couch's treatment of manuscripts submitted by Odum and the members of his institute. Wilson replied to one such complaint in January 1929, when Odum was incensed at Couch's condemnation of the quality of manuscripts the press was receiving from the institute that "the youngster [Couch] has an unfortunate way of seeming to give his opinion when frequently it is not his opinion at all but one that he has gathered elsewhere." Louis Round Wilson, the peacemaker, was saying this more to mollify Odum than from his own certainly. He knew that Couch had strong opinions and that they were his own convictions. Wilson assured Odum that Couch "will sin less in that respect in the future than he has in the past" even while he knew it was a promise that could not be kept. Couch was responsible for handling manuscripts submitted to the press and for the contracts under which they were to be published. His insistence on policies and procedures to which Howard Odum objected was a matter of Couch simply performing his job.[60] Wilson's words failed to reassure Odum.

Odum was cautious, even timid, after being attacked for challenging religious fundamentalism in *Social Forces*. He refrained from anything that could be considered overt criticism of southern customs or traditions. Bill Couch was committed to an aggressive form of scholarship that, he maintained, "must deal with controversial subjects directly and honestly and fearlessly." Couch added that the UNC Press had an emphasis on the social sciences because of the great need for scholarly work in sociology, economics, and government in the South, though any area of study "in which sound intellectual work can be performed" was acceptable. But, he preferred work that addressed instrumental problems, the solutions of which would make a difference. He cautioned, "The farmer or business man who ultimately pays for scholarship has the right to ask of what importance is astronomy when the economic structure of a society is cracking to pieces."[61] Odum found it sufficient to map the cracks—Couch wanted to fill them.

From 1924 until 1945, the press published about fifty books for the institute. The contractual arrangement for these publications varied during the early years, but generally the institute paid the costs of production and, if sales were sufficient, the profit was used to support books that did not sell as well. Couch's reluctance to publish books that did not meet his standards of scholarly and literary excellence and his insistence on putting the institute's manuscripts through a full editorial process galled Odum, who was paying the production costs through his grants and viewed the UNC Press as a printing shop for the institute. Odum was incensed when he tried to get a manuscript by North Carolina folk singer Isaac Garfield Greer through the press in 1929 and was blocked by Couch's insistence that the dialect written by Greer needed to be worked over by a linguist to ensure its accuracy and consistency.[62] Odum wanted the manuscript printed and distributed as it had been submitted to the press. Ultimately, the book was not published by the press.

It was not just in editorial matters that Odum objected to Couch's control of the press and his treatment of manuscripts from Odum's institute. When Harriet L. Herring's 1929 book, *Welfare Work in Mill Villages*, was in press, Odum asked Couch for a book design "of some sort of attractive lightness." When Couch delayed the publication for several weeks for the printer to acquire the type font he wanted for it without clearing either the font or the delay with Odum, Odum was furious. Odum knew that Couch would tell him "how the angels themselves approved or would approve this particular type," but Couch's arrogance in "not letting the institute have anything to do with its own work" only confirmed Odum's low opinion of Couch's ability and good sense.[63] Howard Odum and his institute were paying for the publication through his grants and Couch had no business throwing barriers to block what he wanted published in the form he wanted when he wanted it.

When Couch had earlier protested the procedure of tacitly accepting whatever copy was sent by the institute as ready for publication to UNC President Harry Woodburn Chase, Chase reproached him: "Dr. Odum is a competent authority in the field of sociology, and you are not." The Rockefeller Foundation, Chase told Couch, was upset with the press and with the university over the way Odum and the institute's publications had been treated. The subsidy that supported the press was endangered by the belief of the foundation that Couch was "deliberately trying to throw obstacles in Dr. Odum's way."[64]

In 1929, an arrangement with the press was negotiated under which institute staff members would have manuscripts read by three readers, edit the copy, and deliver the manuscripts to the press ready for printing. Books published under this agreement would carry an imprint statement saying that the book was published for the Institute for Research in Social Science by the University of North Carolina Press, thus removing the press from intellectual responsibility.[65] To some extent, this eased one point of contention between Couch and Odum, but the animosity continued.

Couch and Odum did have a common ground for coexistence in their fundamental need to have a thriving press. In public, their relationship remained civil. In 1946, Couch acknowledged the debt owed to Odum and the institute for sustaining the press through the late 1920s. For his part, Odum supported Couch's plans for certain publishing ventures. Privately, though, the two had encounters that strained the bonds of civility. At one point in 1933, Couch wrote to Odum about a confrontation in Couch's office, saying, "I do not object to criticism if offered courteously, but I do object and will not submit to the continuance of spluttered charges and hasty departure. I write this letter to request you not to allow this sort of thing to happen again."[66]

Every university campus has some local institutions that function as an extra-curricular center of intellectual activity. It might be a coffee house, a tavern, or a book shop. At the University of North Carolina in the 1930s, it was The Intimate Bookshop, usually simply referred to as *Ab's*, after its proprietor Milton Abernathy, located on Franklin Street directly across from the campus. Milton Abernathy, a self-proclaimed Communist, published the literary magazine, *Contempo*, from his shop in addition to numerous leftist and labor tracts. Abernathy's shop specialized in an assortment of leftist political pamphlets and *avant-garde* literature, attracting a following of faculty members and graduate students who appreciated the exotic intellectual climate it offered. Paul Green and William Terry Couch were frequent visitors to the shop as was C. Vann Woodward, a young graduate student in history. Howard Odum had obtained a fellowship for Woodward and was upset to find that Woodward had associated himself with the disreputable group at Ab's, instructing him to find more appropriate company.[67]

Couch and Odum each viewed the South as his own intellectual territory. At its heart, their mutual hostility and distrust derived from radically different concepts of the social sciences and the role of a university press. Odum masked the radical notions he and the institute were addressing under technical jargon and obscure rhetoric. Couch wanted books on the same subjects that would "be as far as possible written so people of good intelligence, but no special training, would have a chance to understand them." Dabney's *Liberalism in the South* and Couch's own *Culture in the South* were two such books that he could point to as examples of this effort to make the issues accessible.[68]

In *Culture in the South*, Couch delineated his objections to academic social sciences as practiced by Odum and the members of the Institute for Research in Social Science:

> In order to have any conception of what society ought to be, it is necessary to have a scale of values. It is necessary to have points of view, and the excellence of a scale of values depends on the way in which it hangs together, the interdependence of its parts, and the lack of fundamental contradictions ignorantly held. Among one class of writers today the delusion prevails that the professional fact-finder can

gather raw data in such a manner that out of them will come inevitable and unambiguous conclusions. The social scientist of the 1850s, laboring under this delusion as do many of his successors of today, in all probability would have reached the same conclusion as that of the Supreme Court if the Dred Scott case had been placed before him. The Court rested its decision on a large body of historical data interpreted in the light of the dominant opinions of the time. Here and there, to be sure, were little meager facts, of no comparative numerical importance, indication that some few Negroes might be able to live and thrive as free men and citizens. But the fact-finding statistician in averaging up his findings could have given them no more than a few remarks—they would have been eliminated as freaks from his calculations. The social planner who was not a seer at that time would have charted no course of freedom for the four million slaves.[69]

For Couch, the significance of sociology lay in its explication of societal values. Any sociology that failed to incorporate values or that drew back from conclusions about the worth of a phenomenon was irrelevant. Odum had abrogated the central purpose of the social sciences, to contribute to the betterment of society, by retreating from the central issues of society into a safe timidity, abandoning the notion of values—and particularly a scale of values—by which the worth of social phenomena could be measured.

Couch's insistence that the press publish books that could appeal to and benefit the literate southerner was only one focus of his publishing program. Couch also wanted the press to publish textbooks for the public schools and the press did make significant progress in this effort with such titles as Alex Mathews Arnett and Walter Clinton Jackson's *The Story of North Carolina* (1934), Robert E. Coker's *This Great and Wide Sea* (1947), *North Carolina Today* by Samuel Huntington Hobbs, Jr., and Marjorie N. Bond (1947), and Nellie M. Rowe's *Discovering North Carolina* (1933), among many others. Some were specifically for North Carolina schools and some for a broader range of southern states. In his vision of what the press should be accomplishing, Couch viewed textbook publishing as one activity in which the press could have a major impact, but he had difficulties convincing the press's Board of Governors of that need. One of the most important press contributions was the *Natural Progress* series edited by Carrie S. Smith from Appalachian State University in Boone, North Carolina. This series was designed for elementary school children who were not able to read at the level expected for their grade in school. It was a marginal financial success, but the Board of Governors denied funding its continuation in 1940.[70]

In 1942, Couch singled out the state of Georgia for special emphasis by another audience, America's librarians. He wrote in the pages of the major research journal in librarianship, *Library Quarterly*, that the state desperately needed a good documentary history suitable for school and public libraries that would be inexpensive enough for individual purchase. Almost every state prescribed particular textbooks by state law and he objected to the limited and narrow approach to education this fostered saying, "The history neither of Georgia nor of any other state can be contained within the covers of any one single book, and to give the impression to the young mind that this can be done is an educational error of large magnitude."[71] Couch argued that the functions of a university press should go far beyond publishing scholarly books to publishing books that fostered the education of everyone at all levels. Universities had people with the expertise and knowledge who should be writing and publishing for the public, not simply for a small group of specialists. Couch strenuously objected to the standard history textbooks used in the schools to inculcate "State Pride, State Patriotism" (he insisted on the capitalization) at the expense of learning. History textbooks used in the public schools were "written by people who have little knowledge of the past, little judgment, no imagination and less skill in writing—by people whose chief qualification is that they have friends in influential positions." Such books "victimize the children and make state pride and patriotism shabby affairs." Regional publishing, the kind of publishing to which he had committed the press, could promote pride and patriotism with a level of historical accuracy that was not available from the shoddy texts adopted by the states.[72]

The educational possibilities extended beyond schoolbooks. While Couch had no wish to involve the press or the university in any systematic program of adult education, he did see virtue and purpose in university presses making sound, inexpensive editions of important works in the western intellectual tradition available to the public—a tradition stretching back to fifteenth century Venetian printer Aldus Manutius who printed inexpensive small-format editions, though Couch apparently was unaware of his contribution to publishing. The failure of university presses to produce good affordable basic texts derived not from the lack of potential sales of such books but from "faulty ideals of scholarship." Editing and publishing good editions of important works was not valued in the academy. The inconsequential accumulation of data was. The intelligent reading public was as much in need of good editions of standard works as the classrooms and the university presses were in a unique position to supply them.

While other university presses did publish school textbooks, Couch was clearly moving beyond the commonly accepted functions of university presses—the staid boundaries of academe—into what he referred to as *experimental publishing*. Couch actively developed publishing projects and sought authors to complete them. One such project was for interlineal translations. In 1934, he recounted his own difficulty in learning to read German when he felt the need to study the history of printing and publishing and found the essential texts were in German. He had taken several courses in German as an undergraduate student which failed to prepare him to actually read the language. Couch reported that he thought it would be worthwhile for him to read an English translation and then read the same text in German, but he could not find a literal translation of anything that suited his needs.

An interlinear method that gave the reader the original text with a literal word-by-word translation into English in alternate lines of text had the potential to help students of languages, but found that no attention had been given to the method in educational research. Further, there seemed to be an antipathy toward any technique that facilitated learning languages as being too easy. Research in such areas as "studies of eye movements and other equally important problems" to the neglect of what he had found to be a functionally useful approach was considered more important in the academic environment. He asked the rhetorical question, "Why?" but already knew the answer. Even in such a practical field as pedagogy, research had become fragmented into smaller and smaller insignificant pieces. He felt that the publication of interlinear translations to aid foreign language learning would be a major contribution to education that could be made by university presses. This, of course, would assume that the technique had research to demonstrate its value over other methods of instruction. Couch called it "an opportunity for experimentation."[73]

Couch was revisiting an idea he had expressed in print several years before in the pages of the *Modern Language Journal* when he proposed a thorough study of foreign language instruction including the use of interlineal translations. At that time, he saw little hope for improvement because instruction in foreign languages was not highly regarded by universities and instructors in elementary language courses knew that they had to "become philologists or literary specialists" and publish in those fields in order to become successful academics. Any real research into the best methods for teaching would not be highly valued in university foreign language departments.[74]

Couch formally introduced a proposal to the press's governing board in January 1937 to publish a series of interlineal translations of German writings to be done by Milo Spann of the UNC faculty. The proposal was referred to outside readers and, in 1937, the press published the *First Interlinear German Reader*, a paperbound pamphlet of eighty-four pages, designed to "enable teachers to test the effectiveness of the interlinear method." This was followed the next year with a more substantial offering, the *Second Interlinear German Reader*, at one hundred twenty-eight pages that was, like the first, "designed to test the usefulness of interlinear texts in learning foreign languages." Couch may well have been influenced in this idea by Howard Russell Huse of the UNC faculty, who published a book, *The Psychology of Foreign Language Study*, with the press in 1931. Huse advocated additional experimental study of the use of interlineal translations in foreign language acquisition among other techniques that needed further research. The press did publish another book by Huse in 1945 on foreign language teaching, but it only made glancing reference to the idea of utilizing interlinear translation to teach foreign languages. It did, however, include a chapter on textbooks that echoed Couch's own feelings that foreign language textbooks "are not those that appeal to responsible experts, but rather those that fit in with the passing notions, principles, and dogmas of an academic mediocrity."[75] The books were not intended to enable the reader to actually do anything. Their function was only to enhance the academic credentials of their authors.

He was in a position to implement some of his ideas through the press, but not all. Doctoral dissertations had been a traditional source of manuscripts for university presses, particularly in a period when the research work for the degree was expected to be published. In his 1934 address to the Association of American Universities, Couch made a proposal that was not too far ahead of its time, but somewhat outside of the normal territory of a university press. He called for abolishing the publication requirement for doctoral dissertations and establishing a centralized clearing house at a university press that would collect information on all completed and in-progress dissertations to publish an ongoing comprehensive bibliography. Multiple copies of the dissertation would be deposited in the library of the university at which the dissertation was completed and made available through inter-library loan to those interested in the research. As part of this system, he proposed that the central bibliographic agency collect the reactions of people using the dissertation as to the quality of the research and their recommendations for publication. He specifically wanted to know if the reader would buy a copy if the work was published.

Couch seems to have been unaware that requiring publication of the dissertation was a practice inherited by American universities from earlier German models when he blamed the requirement on the dissertation director who was seeking "to shift critical responsibility from himself and his department to the book reviewers" of the published dissertations. Faculty members who directed dissertations were, Couch argued, simply too lazy to maintain high standards of scholarship and his proposal would hold their work up to public scrutiny.[76] Of course, University Microfilms undertook this project at the end of the decade and the requirement for publication was fulfilled through microfilm.

Through his first decade with the UNC Press, Bill Couch pushed the boundaries of academic publishing with an aggressive agenda that rejected the notion that the university press existed to serve the needs of the university and the local academic community. His insistence on literary quality as well as scholarly merit brought him into direct conflict with important members of the UNC faculty, but he persisted. He was a man of strong liberal convictions who refused to allow his own views intrude on his commitment to publishing important books of whatever political persuasion. At the same time, he was never hesitant to express his own convictions in a public forum. He refused to shrink from direct conflict with either Howard Odum or the Agrarians. He originated ideas for ventures that expanded the established role of the university press and established himself as a major figure in the university, in the South, and in the world of academic publishing.

2

Culture in the South

The Great Depression severely affected the University of North Carolina (UNC). The economic situation in the United States after 1929 proved a major obstacle to Couch's aspirations for the university and for his press. Frank Porter Graham had barely assumed the presidency of the university when the North Carolina legislature slashed the university's state appropriations by twenty-five percent in 1929/1930 and another twenty percent in 1931. Graham managed to fight back and received some small increases, but the direction of support for the university from the North Carolina legislature continued downward through the 1930s as did the economic situation of the state and the nation.[1]

The federal election of 1932 gave the Democratic Party an impervious majority in the U.S. House and Senate and placed Franklin Delano Roosevelt in the White House. Roosevelt's plan to bring the country back to economic stability, the New Deal, was a bold instance of planning that called for major restructuring of the American economy and, in many instances, American society itself.

Will Rogers notoriously quipped, "I am not a member of any organized political party. I am a Democrat." He was stating a truism. Franklin Roosevelt's Democratic Party was an uneasy alliance of factions with major regional differences united under a single banner, but divided by issues of substance. It effectively functioned only in opposition to the Republican Party in America. Prior to the 1932 election, the southern states had provided the majority of Democrats in Congress. After that election, southern Democrats were a minority in Congress but, Roosevelt needed them to pass the legislative agenda of the New Deal. The South had been solidly Democratic since reconstruction, but southern Democrats were not the same as the newly elected Democrats from the North. More importantly, southern Democrats, having been longtime members of Congress, controlled most Congressional committees because of their seniority.[2] While southern Democrats supported major parts of Roosevelt's program, there were pieces of the New Deal that were anathema.

Southerners had supported Roosevelt at the beginning. He offered the South hope to escape the combined effects of the depression and the legacy of Reconstruction that had, for many southerners, an aura of colonialism in which the means of production and the capital to foster economic development had been controlled by the North. Southern members of Congress could support Roosevelt's plan only as long as it did not violate the conventions and traditions that ensured the subjugation of African Americans under Jim Crow laws and customs. For southerners, the racial policies of the South, both legal and extra-legal, were essential to the culture of the South and white southerners had a long investment in maintaining them. Those policies were not matters for discussion. They were a matter of the rights of the individual states which were not subject to federal intervention.

Roosevelt was careful to assure the South that he had no plans that would include the intrusion of the federal government into the racial equilibrium of the South and that white supremacy would be maintained. Roosevelt was forced to mollify the South by allowing elements of his legislation to be amended to exclude African Americans from many New Deal programs that could put them on an equal basis with whites. Roosevelt and members of Congress from the North were willing to politely ignore the racial situation in the South preferring to focus attention and energy on the economy and to treat the South as simply another region of the United States that was more impoverished than the rest. As long as the South controlled the mechanisms through which the New Deal programs operated thereby putting its instrumentalities in the hands of local politicians, southern members of Congress could support those programs.[3]

After Roosevelt's failed move to restructure the Supreme Court in 1937, southern Democrats made a serious attempt to join with Republicans to directly challenge the New Deal with a *manifesto* written in part by North Carolina Senator Josiah Bailey. It called for removing regulations constraining business, balancing the federal budget, lowering taxes (particularly those on capital gains), ending the power of labor unions, and maintaining state rights. To its authors, private enterprise and faith in "the heart of the American people" would suffice to bring the country out of the economic depression. While the authors admitted that the federal government had performed a necessary service for the country, it had to unleash private investment and businesses to truly restore America to greatness. With this, southern Democrats had begun to form a bi-partisan effort to join forces with the Republicans in Congress to directly oppose Roosevelt and the northern Democrats in a conservative coalition.[4]

For southern Democrats, the major point of contention was racial segregation and the preservation of the Jim Crow system under which this was maintained. Roosevelt knew that he could remove the conservative southern Democrats from the political equation and, perhaps, form a viable coalition with moderate northern Republicans by taking a strong stand on civil rights for African Americans. He also knew that this could be a dangerous strategy for his legislative program. He could lose the support of progressive Democrats in the South since no politician in the South could stand for reelection on a platform that threatened the system of custom and law that maintained white supremacy.

Southern opposition to the Fair Labor Standards Act, the wages and hours bill, led by Senator "Cotton Ed" Smith of South Carolina, infuriated Roosevelt who considered the legislation an essential element of the New Deal. Southern Democrats rose in opposition wanting to keep labor costs low and fearing that a guaranteed minimum wage would raise African American laborers to the same level as white workers. They joined with the northern Republicans who opposed any legislation favorable to labor to stall the bill in the House of Representatives.[5]

In June 1938, Roosevelt, specifically citing the wages and hours bill, directed the National Emergency Council to prepare a report on economic conditions in the South that would enumerate region's problems. One month later, the report was delivered to the president.

Clark Foreman was responsible for planting the idea for the report with Roosevelt. Shortly after his election, Roosevelt had been approached by Edwin R. Embree, president of the Julius Rosenwald Fund, about appointing someone in the federal government charged with ensuring that African Americans would be treated equitably by the New Deal programs. Foreman, then with the Rosenwald Fund, was appointed as an advisor to Interior Secretary, Harold Ickes, on the economic status of African Americans with his salary paid by the Rosenwald Fund. Foreman was called to the White House in spring, 1938, by Roosevelt who asked him to recommend liberal Democrats who might run against the southern conservatives plaguing him in Congress. Foreman had no specific suggestions, but took the opportunity to push the idea of a survey of southern conditions. Roosevelt asked Foreman to undertake the project and Foreman produced the first draft.[6]

The report was little more than a pamphlet, a scant sixty-four pages that covered southern issues from natural resources to education, labor, housing, and health, to the condition of women and children. It documented deplorable conditions across the entire spectrum of southern life. Extreme poverty, illiteracy, and abysmal labor conditions were normal throughout the South. Almost pointedly, the report did not touch on racial issues in the region.[7]

Joseph Gelders, a somewhat covert member of the Communist Party, had been active in the labor movement in the South. He had been introduced to Eleanor Roosevelt by a mutual friend, Lucy Randolph Mason of the Congress of Industrial Organizations, and, through Mrs. Roosevelt, had met the president. Gelders had sought to mount a southern-wide conference on labor and civil rights issues and Roosevelt encouraged him to proceed with this plan suggesting that it be based on the report on economic conditions in the South.[8] This meeting became the Southern Conference for Human Welfare (SCHW). From June through October 1938, Gelders, as the only paid staff member for the conference, worked to organize the gathering envisioned by Roosevelt. Gelders drafted William Mitch, Alabama director of the Congress of Industrial Organizations and president of an Alabama local of the United Mine Workers, to assist in organizing the conference. When the conference was held in November, Gelders kept a low profile, accepting the leadership of the Civil Rights Committee charged with abolishing the poll tax, but appearing in none of the major leadership positions.[9]

UNC President Frank Porter Graham, had chaired the advisory committee charged with editing Foreman's draft of the *Report on Economic Conditions of the South*. He had not been at an organizational meeting for the SCHW held in Birmingham, Alabama, in July 1938, but was pleased to accept the invitation of the conference organizers to deliver the keynote address for the meeting to be held in November 1938.

The first SCHW convened on November 20–23, 1938, in Birmingham, Alabama. Frank Porter Graham delivered his keynote address to a group of some 1,200 delegates and about as many guests. While there seem to have been no registration lists kept, one estimate has approximately twenty-five to thirty percent of the delegates as African American. Other historians of the event put the attendance at different levels. But, all confirmed a large attendance with substantial African American representation.[10]

The conference attracted a wide diversity of attendees and participants. Judge Louise Charlton, a United States Commissioner, presided. Congressman Luther Patrick of Birmingham and Brook Hayes, a Democratic national committeeman from Arkansas, headed the Sponsorship and Participation Committee. Senators John Hollis Bankhead, III of Alabama, and Claude Pepper from Florida spoke as did, of course, Eleanor Roosevelt. Hugo Black was there to receive the Thomas Jefferson award for "equal and exact justice to all men" in his first public appearance after being appointed to the U.S. Supreme Court. Swedish economist and sociologist Gunnar Myrdal was there and the University of North Carolina was represented by Paul Green, William Terry Couch, and Frank Porter Graham among others.[11] Educators, sharecroppers, politicians, and reporters—all of liberal persuasion—and their supporters joined together in fellowship to celebrate a new South.

Graham's opening address on "equal and exact justice for all," calling for equality of opportunity, for federal aid to schools, for fair treatment for everyone, and "for building a new South rather than tearing down an old one" through the combined efforts of religion and education, was inspirational.[12] Graham set the tone for the four day meeting which was devoted as much to uplift, sanctification, and communion as it was to an instrumental attempt to grapple with the social and economic problems of the South.

In an almost self-immolating gesture, the African American and white delegates and guests sat intermingled in the Birmingham Auditorium. The size of the group, its mission, and its nation-wide representation should have made the organizers aware that segregation, particularly at a public facility such as the Birmingham Auditorium, would have been mandatory. At noon on the second day, November 21st, the police ordered the separation of the races in the auditorium in accordance with Birmingham city ordinances. Couch attributed this action to a complaint filed by someone who was not a delegate to the conference who "wanted to make trouble, and that someone or more than one, had influence with the police." There is evidence that this, indeed, was the case. A publicist for the Republican Party in Alabama sought and was rejected for a publicity job with the conference. It was he, J. D. Brown, who went to the Birmingham Commissioner of Public Safety, Theophilus Eugene "Bull" Connor, who ordered the imposition of segregation on the audience, purportedly proclaiming, "I ain't gonna let no darkies and white folk segregate together in this town."[13] The order came when most of the delegates were in afternoon meetings and at 4:30 p.m., fifteen police officers entered the auditorium threatening arrests if the conference was not immediately segregated. Eleanor Roosevelt defiantly took a seat in the black section, but according to tradition and lore, when she was told by the police that she could not sit there, she and her group moved to a place between the two segregated sections.

This story of Eleanor Roosevelt may have become embellished over the years. The reaction of the delegates was not. A resolution against segregating the conference meetings was passed. It was a resolution that Couch opposed, fearing that any hint of integrationist sentiment would lay the SCHW open to harsh criticism in the South. He was right. This simple resolution, one that deplored the actions of the Birmingham police and urged the conference officers to schedule future meetings in places that would not require that the ignominy of segregation be imposed, was reported in southern newspapers as a general condemnation of segregation. It was not. It specifically referred to segregation as it affected the conference sessions and requested the conference officers "to avoid a similar situation, if at all possible" by finding meeting places at which segregation would not become an issue. The organizers, leaders, and speakers were careful to bow to southern conventions. The object was to raise the Negro from the ditch, not to place him on the same side of the ditch as the white man. The ditch itself would still divide them. One commentator said: "The conference wished, in a phrase, to refurbish Jim Crow's cage until it resembled the white dove's aviary. Here was true separation with equality."[14]

In his report on the conference in the pages of the *New Republic*, Couch publicly reproached Eleanor Roosevelt for her failure to adequately address the situation. She had, Couch maintained, the ability to quell the radicals. When she addressed an audience of some seven thousand crowded into the auditorium, she should have, according to Couch, argued that this was not a "social gathering" but something different that was not covered by the Birmingham ordinance. In chastising Mrs. Roosevelt, Couch noted: "It was, therefore, of the greatest importance that someone who had the attention of a large audience explain the difference between a conference and a social gathering; that it be made clear there are many kinds and degrees of segregation, some good, some bad, some indifferent."[15] Eleanor Roosevelt, of course, could only see the bad in segregation, not the good, and was constitutionally incapable of being indifferent to it. Couch knew this. Eleanor Roosevelt was a crusader for human rights with a pointed interest in the plight of African Americans. While she was forced by the conservative climate in Washington to separate whites from African Americans at White House functions, she would not be forced to acknowledge segregation's morality.[16] Couch was mocking Mrs. Roosevelt when he derided her for not making the fine distinction between a business meeting and a social event.

Couch had a major role in the 1938 conference. He had been impressed into service by Graham to chair the Program Committee. He chaired the meeting of the Labor Relations and Unemployment Section. He was appointed chair of the Committee on Permanent Organization and charged with developing a plan for continuing the effort. The plan developed by Couch's committee was adopted by the conference on November 23, the final day of the meeting.[17] It called for the SCHW to hold annual meetings, but since the organization was ever in a precarious financial state, there was no 1939 meeting and the next event was in Chattanooga in April 1940.

Charges of Communist influence and Communist control were leveled against the SCHW from the beginning. The line between liberal and conservative has always moved in relation to whatever current issue might be at the front. In the 1930s, the issue of segregation was so central to the core of the South that the position of the liberal was pushed far to the right. The segregation of races—black from white—was the norm. The moderate position, if the separate-but-equal position can be said to represent a moderate position, was one from which the utilization of lynch-law to maintain social conventions could be regarded as a slightly right-wing perspective, and anything approaching acceptance of African Americans into the mainstream of American life would be far to the left. If the moderate mainstream position on race relations was the preservation of white supremacy, the maintenance of an economic and social system under which African Americans were subject to the indignities and domination of the white ruling class, anything that promoted the humanity of the African American, could readily be condemned as radically left.

In the South, the Communist Party had become closely associated with the issues of racial equality. In the 1930s, it made concerted efforts to organize workers in textile mills, the coal and steel industries, and tenant farmers and sharecroppers into racially integrated units dedicated to improving working conditions. The Communist Party was the only organized force in the South committed to resisting the Jim Crow laws and customs regulating southern labor. Any attempt to deal seriously with the issues of race in the South would almost automatically be branded by the white majority as part of a Communist conspiracy if it demanded anything approaching equality of white and black.[18] The Southern Conference for Human Welfare was no exception.

Frank Graham knew from the start that there were Communists present at the conference, but welcomed them as a part of the southern landscape. As long as their activities were not covert or disruptive, their contribution to the SCHW would be welcome.[19] However, Graham also recognized that any charge of Communist control of the conference was a serious one that could destroy the credibility of the conference, especially among white liberals who were crucial to its success. He was so concerned that he reversed his own refusal to accept the chairmanship of the conference for the 1940 meeting to assure others that the organization was led by legitimate liberals and not by Communists. In accepting the leadership of the group, Graham said, "I refuse to run in the face of Communist intrigue on one side or smearing by powerful and privileged groups on the other."[20] Even with Graham providing a stabilizing rudder to the conference, the Dies Committee, the House Un-American Activities Committee chaired by Martin Dies, concluded that the conference had been conceived and controlled by the Communist Party as a "most deviously camouflaged Communist-front organization" and that the conference's "professed aims in southern welfare is simply an expedient for larger aims serving the Soviet Union and its subservient Communist Party in the United States."

The charge of the Dies Committee that the SCHW was under the direct control of the Communists was strained and has been largely disproven. Couch, however, believed that Communism was a major force in the conference, telling

Graham on April 15, 1940, "I cannot escape the view that the real issue is whether the Conference is dominated by Communist influence." Couch had become convinced of the Communist influence at the 1938 Birmingham meeting when a resolution was passed condemning "the persecution of religious groups by Nazi Germany and other European countries." It was a modest resolution in the midst of many others dealing with equality of education, job opportunities, child labor, public health, prison reform, social security, freedom of speech, the poll tax, and many other pressing southern issues. Couch spoke against this resolution on the grounds that it violated the avowed purpose of the conference to address specifically southern problems. Couch was the only one present who spoke against the resolution and it passed with only his dissenting vote. Couch, "not wanting to be obstructive, and believing the membership was sincere in its vote," withdrew his objections to make the vote unanimous.[21]

Couch brought his own revision of this resolution to the 1940 Chattanooga meeting. The non-aggression pact of August 23, 1939, between Germany and the Soviet Union had radically changed the situation under which the earlier 1939 resolution against the Nazis had passed. He had, prior to the meeting, become concerned, as he told Frank Graham on April 12, 1940, "over the way liberals forget or minimize the crimes of Hitlerism." He also was troubled that "the majority of the Conference will insist that the Conference should limit itself to dealing with Southern problems and assert that affairs in Europe are no concern of ours." Couch went on to tell Graham that he did not see any purpose in attending the Chattanooga conference if the resolution he was bringing that condemned the Soviet Union for its treaty with Germany would not result in the same approval as the earlier resolution condemning Germany.

The resolution Couch presented read:

Whereas, the Southern Conference for Human Welfare at its first meeting in November 1938, went on record as follows: ...

"Resolved: that this Conference express its vigorous condemnation of the persecution of religions groups by Nazi Germany and other European Countries, and that we commend President Roosevelt's action in expressing the indignation of the American people, and Be it further Resolved: that we endorse an American peace policy such as proposed by President Roosevelt and Secretary of State Hull, to promote the national security of our country, to curb aggression and assist the democratic peoples of the world to preserve peace, liberty and freedom."

Whereas, the only essential changes in the European situation since this Conference passed this Resolution are that Communist Russia has formed a pact with Nazi Germany, and Communist Russia has become an aggressor with Germany as her virtual ally:

Therefore, be it Resolved that this Conference reaffirm its position previously taken with the proviso that that portion of the previous Resolution relating to measures to "curb aggression and assist the democratic peoples of the world" be interpreted as any measures that can be taken within legal neutrality such as those now being effected by the Congress and the President.

Couch had prepared the way by mailing copies of his resolution to members of the conference executive committee with a memorandum laying out his reasons for the resolution. This essentially said that if the SCHW took a stand against Germany in 1938, it had to take the same stand against the Soviet Union in 1940:

> It will now be fatal to the Conference to fail to extend this explicitly to include the Communists. To fail to do this will lay the Conference open to the charge that it is Communist-dominated and condemns aggression only when it suits the purposes of the Communists to do so. Far worse than this, it will lay under grave suspicion the intelligence, honesty, and good faith of the Conference.[22]

Couch, of course, already had reservations about the intelligence, honesty, and good faith of the SCHW. He fully expected that his resolution would be summarily rejected.

At the conference's first business session on April 14, 1940, Couch, at the urging of Graham, introduced the resolution. There are differing accounts as to what happened, but it was evident that the more left-leaning members of the assembly were prepared to do battle. Couch was forcibly removed from the microphone. Graham, attempting to restore order in the ensuing melee, pounded on the podium with his glasses, breaking them. When order was restored, Graham overruled those seeking to kill Couch's resolution for not being within the scope of the conference and forwarded it to the Resolutions Committee. There were Communists on the Resolutions Committee who vigorously attempted to derail the resolution. The committee sessions were long and arduous, lasting late into the night. At one point, there was a call to remove all adjectives from the resolution with the argument that this would make a more forceful statement. It would also have removed all references to Communism. Graham stopped this effort.

Ultimately, a diluted form of the resolution was passed by the membership of the conference. It read:

> We deplore the rise of dictators anywhere, the suppression of civil liberties, the persecution of minorities, aggression against small and weak nations, the violation of the neutral rights and the democratic liberties of the peoples by all fascist, nazi, communist and imperial powers alike which resort to force and aggression instead of to the processes of law, freedom, democracy and international cooperation.

By this time, Couch had left Chattanooga and his involvement in the Southern Conference for Human Welfare ended. Couch left convinced that his prediction made to Graham on April 15, 1940, that if the resolution failed, it would be because the conference was under Communist control, was the case. On May 6, 1940, Couch wrote to Howard Lee, executive secretary of the SCHW, requesting that his name be removed from the list of members.[23]

The SCHW struggled on for a number of years, but the taint of Communist control caused members of the leadership, the white liberals necessary for the success of the endeavor, to fall away and membership declined. Assessments of how deep Communist involvement in the conference went differ radically from a few people who were representing organizations and groups with Communist ties to complete domination by the Communist Party. The exact extent is not relevant. Couch's firm belief that the Communists were in control and, more importantly, that Frank Porter Graham's attitudes had enabled the Communists to gain control is important.

In 1971, Kenneth Douty wrote a study of the Communist influence on the conference under a grant from the Fund for the Republic through Cornell University. Couch was asked to respond to the accuracy of Douty's assertions. He wrote a detailed response adding that Frank Graham could not by any stretch be considered a Communist himself: "Frank Graham is distinguished, as few people in this world are, by his wide, deep, and genuine sympathies for people—all people, even those with whom he disagrees on basic matters." Graham was also a man who was ignorant of the dangers of Communism. Couch particularly mentioned the meeting of the executive board that preceded the first business meeting at which Couch introduced his resolution when Graham "did not stand up as I thought he should."[24] The incident did not destroy Couch's respect for Graham, but it undoubtedly placed strains on their relationship.

Couch's estimation of Graham was written over thirty years after the event, but it reflects a basic ethical assumption he held throughout his career. Couch expected—even demanded—complete loyalty from his subordinates in any organization that employed him and he offered his complete loyalty to his superiors in the organization. In turn, he expected support from his own superiors in the organization. He respected and valued Graham for his willingness to listen to those with whom he disagreed, but could not accept Graham's enthusiasm to listen and even cooperate with those who threatened the foundations of civil discourse. Couch went to Chattanooga fully anticipating that his resolution against the Soviet Union would be rejected. He did not foresee that Frank Porter Graham would allow the Communists and closet Reds to exert such a decisive influence on the proceedings.

For Couch, any society had values and customs governing interactions which formed the basis of its existence. Dialogue among opposing factions and ideas was important to any functioning group, but the Communists had ignored the line between dialogue and intimidation in Chattanooga. He had been simply disappointed in Graham's behavior at the conference, but the Communists had made an enemy of Couch by forcibly insisting on their view. Indeed, any group that threatened the essential values of western civilization through intimidation and threats would make an enemy of Bill Couch.

There were, though, issues such as racial segregation in which the attacks on white southern values did not have to be raised to the level of intimidation. In 1944, the UNC Press published *What the Negro Wants* under the editorship of Howard University history professor Rayford W. Logan. Logan was among the foremost of his generation of African American scholars and held a PhD from Harvard. He was an established and respected historian who, in 1941, had submitted a manuscript to the press dealing with international perspectives on race. Couch declined to publish this, but, on the recommendation of UNC sociologist Guy B. Johnson, suggested to Logan that the press would be interested in an edited anthology by African Americans writing their own visions of blacks in American society. In March 1943, Logan agreed to this and was guaranteed by Couch that he would have a free hand in developing the project. Couch's only direction to Logan was to tell him that a broad representation of opinion including both liberal and conservative authors would be desirable.

Logan set to work and assembled a list of authors who represented the full spectrum of African American political persuasions and social outlooks. When the completed manuscript was delivered to the press in early September 1943, Couch was horrified. He had assumed that the array of opinions of African American intellectuals would parallel those of white intellectuals— that liberal and left-leaning African Americans would hold essentially the same opinions and values as liberal whites and that conservative and right-wing African Americans would assert the same opinions and values as conservative and right-wing whites. He was prepared that leftist African Americans would condemn segregation. This was in keeping with his commitment to publish controversial books. He was not prepared for the complete unanimity of the African American authors that an end to racial segregation was essential.

Couch submitted the manuscript to reviewers for the press who were equally appalled by the demands of the contributors. One of these was Howard Odum who may well have been acting as a gadfly to Couch when he argued for publication on the grounds that it would expose to the world the harm that African American leaders were capable of doing. Couch forwarded these reviews to Logan demanding extensive revisions including the excision of insistent calls from several authors for an end to laws against inter-racial marriage that Couch and other reviewers thought too radical for any press to publish.

Logan agreed to some revisions, but could not reach agreement among his contributors for the extensive changes Couch wanted. When Couch told Logan to find another publisher for the book, Logan threatened to sue. Couch agreed to publish the book under the University of North Carolina imprint only if he could add an introduction.[25]

Couch's introduction to the book was a masterpiece of intellectual obfuscation in which he rejected the notion of cultural relativism, the assumption that all cultures had equal value and that the essence of sociological and anthropological study was in their differences, in favor of a set of essential values and standards by which cultures can and should be evaluated. According to Couch, there were universal standards that characterize a civilization and any group can be measured by its values in relation to those universal ideals. He argued that an end to segregation would be a disservice to African Americans: "If the Negro tries, every decent white man will help him—but if the white man thinks that he alone, that he, the white man, can raise the Negro, if he acts on this notion, imagining that he can relieve the Negro of what the Negro himself needs to do, he only fixes the inferiority of the Negro more certainly, more firmly."[26] Racism in the South was not a problem for white southerners. It was a problem for African Americans.

Couch had argued similarly a decade earlier in his chapter, "The Negro in the South," in *Culture in the South* when he asserted that African Americans preferred to live in segregated communities. Because of the difficulties they had in finding decent housing in the sections of towns set aside for citizens of their race, families occasionally lived in white sections and neighboring whites assumed it was because the black families were demanding social equality. This, Couch asserted, was not the case: "There may be such Negroes, but there is no question that the great majority, the illiterate and the educated, the untutored and the cultivated, would prefer to live among people of their own color." The issue, Couch maintained, was the quality of housing available to African Americans, not the location. This held for education and schools, also: "With things as they are, no worse punishment for Negro children in the South could be imagined than to send them to schools with white children." Couch deplored the low condition of African Americans in the South, but asserted the necessity for racial segregation. He refrained from an attempt to deal with prejudice considering it to be unimportant and blamed much of the South's racial problems on the approach of the social sciences that could only collect data without recognizing that the true measure of what a society should be had to be based on its scale of values.[27] In the South, the scale of value placed whatever culture African Americans might have attained at a lower level than the value of the white Anglo-American culture.

In his "Publisher's Introduction" to the Logan book, Couch paid special attention to attacking the recently published study by Swedish sociologist Gunnar Myrdal, *An American Dilemma: The Negro Problem and Modern Democracy.*[28] The work had been funded by the Carnegie Corporation of New York, and Gunnar Myrdal was chosen to direct the project precisely because he was not an American and, presumably, could thus view the racial situation in America as an objective outsider. Couch acknowledged that Myrdal's conclusions agreed with those of the authors of the chapters in Logan's book, but maintained that agreement did not validate the conclusions of either work. Rather, it reflected a common error. Logan's group of authors and Myrdal had fallen into the erroneous assumption that the dilemma of African Americans was due to simple prejudice and "the consequent disabilities inflicted on the Negro by the white man." This, Couch maintained, was complete nonsense, but it was "the dominant view of the day, is subscribed to by most sociologists and anthropologists, and is taught in many of the schools and colleges and universities of the country." Its acceptance, Couch reasoned, rested on at least one major fallacy: the values expressed by a culture are irrelevant to any meaningful understanding of the culture. He again asserted that there is a set of universal standards by which a culture can be measured and that Myrdal and other sociologists had failed to recognize this as "a valid basis for comparing and evaluating cultures." Social scientists "assumed that one standard or set of standards cannot be shown to be superior to another—therefore no set of customs and habits, no culture can be regarded as superior to another."

To Couch, this view was dangerous. He was as incensed by Myrdal's conclusions as he was by Myrdal's fallacious reasoning and incompetent methods. Couch complained that even if the perspective from which the research was conducted was one of scientific objectivity, Myrdal, like other social scientists, failed completely to recognize his own assumptions in arriving at his conclusion that racial segregation was an evil instrument under which African Americans were victimized by the white majority. The fallacy in this lay in the underlying assumption that the races are equal when it was impossible to compare cultures and races in a meaningful way without recourse to external standards of value. If social scientists refuse to acknowledge the existence of cultural standards by which the value of a culture can be measured, they cannot make any valid assertion on the relative value of cultures:

> Relativistic anthropological and sociological arguments concerning race prejudice in western society cannot be effective in the way intended by those making the arguments. The treatment of certain classes of persons in Germany or in the South, in India or in Africa—all have to be looked at merely as phenomena of particular times and places, neither good nor bad. But nothing could be more abhorrent than this view. Those who promote it have to go along with other civilized

people and refuse to accept it when they see its consequences. But in doing so they
destroy their assumptions of equality and the non-existence of universal values.

Couch's central charge against Myrdal and other sociologists, including Howard
Odum, was that their research was shallow. They failed to deal meaningfully
with the human condition. He charged, "social scientists generally are content
to work at such superficial levels and seem unaware that there are any deeper
levels at which work has to be done."[29]
      Couch's introduction to Logan's book did not go unnoticed. He received
letters from southerners who privately applauded his attack on Myrdal, but
were reluctant to do so publicly. Myrdal's study was widely praised in the northern press, but largely ignored in the South where it was reviewed with skepticism
if at all. Couch's assault on Myrdal was one of the few southern voices raised
in public protest over the book.[30]
      Couch's introduction to *What the Negro Wants* was written for a white
audience, but Couch was willing and even eager to present similar arguments
to an African American audience. In 1945, he published an article in the *Negro
Digest* presenting a convoluted argument that the social sciences, in an attempt
to be scientific and objective, had abandoned one basic element of responsibility—value. It was obvious to Couch that there were significant differences
between African Americans and Americans of European descent. The simple
fact of difference meant that there were differences in the value of each. While
all men were created equal, their abilities made them different and those differences, both physical and mental, made them unequal: "Anyone not utterly
blind has to admit the existence of glaring inequalities among men."
      Couch tortured logic by moving from the obvious differences between indi-
vidual people to extrapolate to races, concluding that "a number of people with
a lot of talents and goodness in them are superior to a comparable number with
less of these qualities or with their opposites in them." Scientism had obscured
this simple fact to the detriment of the social sciences. Couch concluded,

> The great problem of the modern world is to get people to be decent to each other
> in spite of differences. Nothing could be more as if calculated to cause endless
> hate and misery than the argument for decency on the basis of an equality that
> doesn't exist. Nor can any better basis be found for the development of civilized
> life than equality which does exist.[31]

The issue was neither race nor equality, but a common human decency that
recognized the differences and, more importantly, that there were differences
of value to society itself. As a group, African Americans were simply of less
value to American society that whites.
      At a meeting of the Board of Governors of the press on Saturday, June

26, 1943, Couch proposed publishing a companion volume to *What the Negro Wants* collecting essays by prominent white southerners on the issue of the African American in the South. North Carolina Governor Joseph Melville Broughton, he reported, had already agreed to contribute to the book.[32] Fortunately, nothing came from this plan. The damage to the university's reputation caused by Couch's introduction to *What the Negro Wants* was already sufficient. W. E. B. DuBois, among others, deplored the fact that none of the contributors to the book nor its editor saw the preface prior to publication. DuBois concluded, "The University of North Carolina may gradually be receding from its leadership of liberalism in the white South."[33]

What the Negro Wants went to three printings for a total of 10,000 copies before its November 4, 1944, publication date and received strongly positive reviews in the northern press.[34] Couch did not expend great effort or incur great expenses in producing or designing the book. A cursory comparison of the physical book with others produced by the press in 1944 reveals that the paper was cheaper, the binding shoddier, and the general presswork more slapdash than other press productions even under the war-time standards for conserving paper and materials for book production that affected all publishers. It was not a book that Couch wanted for his back list at the press.

While the intellectual issues of editing manuscripts and finding suitable authors for the books he wanted to publish were his essential concerns, there were other problems with the press that troubled Couch. In addition to being Couch's intellectual crusade, the press was also a business. Through the years, much of Couch's dissatisfaction with the press at North Carolina had derived from the administrative relationship of the press to the university. In his annual report for 1940–1941, he professed dismay at finding that the university's position was that the press was a legally separate entity from the University of North Carolina. The situation came to a head in 1941 when Dunn and Bradstreet sent a letter to the university administration inquiring into UNC's level of responsibility to its press's creditors, many of whom were using outstanding press bills as assets when applying for their own loans. Couch had known that this was coming months before and had written to the university administration and the UNC business office to alert everyone to the impending problem. His warnings went unheeded.

With the university controller, Couch wrote a letter to Dunn and Bradstreet explaining that the press was an autonomous unit with no legal connection to the university and, thus, the university had no legal responsibility for the press's debts. However, the letter added, with the approval of Frank Graham, "The University administration, at all times, will do everything in its power to assist the Press in securing funds to meet its obligations."

While Couch did assist in drafting this letter, he expressed serious doubts that the press could continue operating without the university taking ultimate financial responsibility. Further, in his 1940–1941 annual report, Couch expressed bemusement over the assertion that the press and the university were legally separate entities since he had assumed from the beginning that the press was a unit of the university and had pursued credit to keep the press in operation based on that assumption. It was an understanding for which he had earlier received support from the UNC administration. He quoted a letter from Graham written in the early 1930s and approved by the North Carolina Attorney-General that simply stated, "The University controls the Press and is responsible for its obligations." Couch had specifically requested this letter to use in applying for credit for the press.

Couch was deeply concerned about the reluctance of the university to back the press, calling it a "breach of faith." He was more concerned, though, that the university business office had sent Dunn and Bradstreet a copy of a deeply flawed audit report on the press without telling Couch and, apparently, with no explanation of the defects in the audit about which Couch had previously told the business office.

The issue of the press's status in the university extended far beyond credit and responsibility for paying the bills. In his 1940–1941 annual report, Couch observed that he had been operating under the assumption that the press was a unit of the university and had told the North Carolina Department of Revenue that the press was exempt from taxes because the university was. Since it now had been pointedly brought home to him that this was not the case, he would have to find out what the tax status actually was and how much the press might owe the state in current and back taxes. He also noted that he had only recently become aware that the press should have been charging state sales tax on books sold in North Carolina.

The problematic status of the press in the university was paralleled by the ambiguity of Couch's status as director of the press. He had assumed when he was appointed director that he would be considered either a member of the administration or of the faculty, but his status at the university had never been made clear to him or anyone else at the university. The situation of the press having no legal relationship to UNC and its director's role undefined by the university was intolerable for Couch.

The ambiguous relationship between the press and its director to the university was part of the administrative and procedural incompetence that was the source of his major issues with the university. He pointedly addressed his dissatisfactions in his 1940–1941 annual report:

Almost uniformly in his relations with the University, the Director has first had to discuss policies, reach agreements, then after he has gone ahead on the basis of agreements he has found they have not been put into writing by the University officials, and he then not only has to do his job but has to be constantly struggling to get the University to do things to which it freely committed itself.

Couch desperately wanted a university press that was committed to the educational programs of the university, but his vision of the possibilities of such a press had been thwarted by the inability of faculty members, university administrators, and others, to understand the potential benefits of the press.

The ambiguity of the administrative structure complicated that understanding, but Couch did his best to hammer home his theme:

> The inter-relation of the University and faculty and the press is so clear it would seem unnecessary to discuss this problem. However, the University for years has had resources which it has used apparently without considering this interdependence. It would seem that any agency connected with the University doing anything in the way of making plans for books would want the Director of the Press to be aware of what is [*sic.*] was doing and might consider asking him to take part in its plan-making.

Though Couch did not explicitly make the accusation here, he was referring to the publication program of Odum's institute. Couch asserted that until the press and its director were "taken into full partnership" in all publishing activity of the university, the press could not be functional. While UNC may want to have a university press, "its desire is vague, undefined, unformed."

Couch was vitally concerned that resolving these issues was crucial to the survival of the press and essential if the press was to achieve the purposes he envisioned. Couch knew that the only way to save the press would be to secure adequate funding that was independent of the university or the state of North Carolina. In defiance of Howard Odum's injunction against contacting foundations, Couch drafted a letter to the Rockefeller Foundation on October 6, 1941, with an appeal that it reconsider its policy against funding university presses. Couch acknowledged that most presses had been established by universities "to secure favorable publicity," but the UNC Press had, under him and President Frank Graham, early abandoned that simple purpose. The UNC Press was not concerned with any favorable public opinion but with "serving the ideals of scholarship." This was "the only basis on which the existence of either the University or the Press could be justified."

He wanted the foundation to consider funding university presses directly rather than individual researchers or groups of researchers such as Odum's Institute for Research in Social Science. He pointed out that the Rockefeller Foundation and the Laura Spelman Rockefeller Memorial Fund had given $92,500 from 1926 to 1932 to support the publications of Odum's institute and much of that had been wasted because of "violation of the most basic elementary publishing standards." By funding publication costs through authors rather than through the presses, the foundations had created a situation under which publication proceeded without regard for the merit of the work.

Couch's argument was that the practice of the foundations, particularly the Rockefeller Foundation, encouraged the publication of mediocre books that had bypassed the mechanisms of scholarly review that ensured manuscripts would meet minimum standards of scholarly reputability. The process of sending manuscripts to qualified readers who could assess the quality of the work and the careful double-blind review process under which the reviewers were kept ignorant of the identity of the author and the author ignorant of the identity of the reviewers was essential to the intellectual integrity of the publishing process. None of this was possible if the author controlled the funding for publication.

He argued that the process of submission, evaluation, and the careful editing of the manuscript was vital to the progress of scholarship. He urged the publication subsidies given by the foundation be awarded not to the author, but to the publisher only when the press certified that the manuscript had been thoroughly evaluated and found worthy of publication. Of course, not all university presses could be included in such a program. There were only a few in the country that maintained the standards of the UNC Press, but establishing the approach to funding would raise the standards of scholarly publishing across the country.

When he drafted this letter, Couch knew he was blindly seeking a solution to the problem he faced at UNC. The letter was never sent, but it did express his central belief that with some degree of financial independence, a university press could become a major force in the intellectual and cultural future of America and that the foundations could be a decisive factor if only they would redirect their efforts from supporting individual researchers to directly supporting the presses themselves. Directing the grants for publication to the researcher only gave them the keys to the gates of scholarly reputability when the entry should be in the hands of the publishers.

This abortive attempt to approach the foundations came from Couch's desperate attempt to find some way out of the deplorable financial condition of the UNC Press. It was a situation that put him, as director of the press, in a subservient position at UNC when he should have had much more power and prestige in the academic community.

The major issue that Couch addressed in the 1940–1941 annual report was, of course, financial. Couch complained, "The Director of the Press is ashamed of the piddling requests for funds that he has had to make through the years." He blamed himself for his own inability to plead the case for the press in a way that would "catch the imagination of people who have spent millions on other work of negligible importance" compared to what the press could do for the university. He reported that for the period 1937–1941, the press was generating losses of an average of $10,000 a year with no hope of catching up and suggested that in addition to the capital funds of $100,000 needed and additional subsidies for specific books, the press needed $200,000 to $300,000 to be raised in the next ten to fifteen years as an endowment to subsidize book publishing, an endowment to be controlled by the press and not by other units of the university such as the Institute for Research in Social Science or the business office.

In essence, Couch attributed the press's problems to the failure of procedures, the lack of documentation, and the inattention to detail on the part of the university. The university had followed a non-policy of benign neglect toward the press for too many years. These problems were not the result of malice or ill-will and could be addressed to create a strong university press that was integrated into the educational and research efforts of the university.[35] At this point, Couch still had hope for the future of the press.

Couch's prospects for change, however, relied on the continued active interest of President Graham and the eventual fulfillment of his promises to Couch of adequate support for the press. Unfortunately, Graham would not be able to fulfill his commitments to Couch. On March 30, 1941, Franklin Roosevelt appointed Frank Porter Graham to the eleven-member National Defense Mediation Board charged with calming labor unrest that threatened to hinder the effort to supply war materials to the allied powers.

Graham's work on the board was time consuming, but when Roosevelt asked him to serve on the War Labor Board, created on January 12, 1942, after the United States entered World War II, he could not refuse. From then until the end of the war, Frank Porter Graham spent most of this time in Washington working on the issues of labor and the war industries, neglecting his duties at Chapel Hill. His absence from the campus created deep distress among faculty members and administrators of the university to the extent that in the spring of 1944, a faculty resolution unanimously passed condemning his lack of leadership. On October 2, 1944, the Board of Trustees added its voice to that of the faculty, requesting Graham to return to Chapel Hill as a full-time administrator. Roosevelt prevailed. While Graham made attempts to get back to Chapel Hill on weekends, he had entered a phase of his life of public service that went far beyond the university.[36]

Graham's absence from the university campus put Couch in a quandary. Graham had, for the most part, only given promises and assurances, but promises were better than no promises and Couch, trusting Graham, accepted his assurances. Without Graham's presence, though, Couch was left with little hope for the future of the press. Couch reported to the press's Board of Governors at a meeting on December 14, 1941, that he had met with William Chambers Coker, professor of biology and chairman of the Board of Governors of the press. Coker had pointedly asked Couch what the press needed to cover its current deficit and, if it could not be covered, what the consequences might be.

Couch had no answer for Coker. The status of the press as an independent agency had drastically modified the terms under which Couch had sought credit in the past, and Couch had informed the press's creditors about the situation. He told the board that the entire $60,000 currently owed by the press could be called immediately, and he had no idea of what might happen should that occur.

Couch reported to the board that university controller, William Donald Carmichael, Jr., affirmed that the university would continue to support the press, but would demand more control over the press and, in fact, wanted "a continual check on the financial operations" of the press. Carmichael wanted the university's business office to take over the bookkeeping and accounting for the press. Couch objected. During the early days of the press, the account books had been kept in the business office and total confusion had resulted. The press did not have immediate access to its own records and purchase orders were delayed to a point where the demand for a title had frequently evaporated before additional printings could be approved. Couch had managed to have the working files of the press moved to the press offices in the early 1930s when the financial contributions of the university to the press were negligible, and he was not about to return to a system he found intolerable for an ongoing business. He told the Board of Governors that such a move would be unacceptable. He had worked under that situation and "most of his time and energy were taken with trivial detail." He continued, "if the University wanted to wreck the Press one way to do it was to remove the bookkeeping of this organization from the offices of the Press and keep the books in the office of the University."[37] The business office never regained control over the press's records and books during Couch's tenure, but the threat was sufficient to keep Couch in a perpetual state of anxious agitation.

By this time, it had become evident to Couch that Graham's commitment to the press and the university had eroded in favor of other considerations that offered his talents greater scope on a national scene. Graham's promises to Couch would not be kept and the press would continue only under the parsimonious scrutiny of Carmichael and the university business office. Couch's aspirations for a university press that would be a vital force in the university had no hope for success in the future.

While Graham's career was expanding beyond the confines of Chapel Hill,

Couch was, by the early 1940s, also earning national attention and recognition. Couch had been active in the Association of American University Presses (AAUP) from its founding in 1936. Donald Bean, head of the University of Chicago Press until he went to the Stanford University Press in 1944, had been primarily responsible for the formal organization of the AAUP. Bean credited a new generation of university press men for creating the organization in 1936. These were Datus Smith of Princeton University Press, Joseph Brandt who succeeded Bean as head of the University of Chicago Press, Rollin Hemens of the University of Chicago Press, Savoie Lottinville who became head of the University of Oklahoma Press in 1944 when Brandt left there to assume the job at Chicago, and William Terry Couch.[38]

In 1941, Couch became president of the AAUP and organized a symposium on regional publishing for the annual conference.[39] This position may have been one of the reasons that he was approached with an offer to become head of the Princeton University Press in March 1941. Graham countered by doubling Couch's salary to $6,000 a year that was to be paid out of the university's and not the press's accounts. Graham also offered Couch an appointment at the rank of professor in the university with the retirement benefits that came with that position.

More important for Couch was Graham's promise of an endowment sufficient to enable him to do what he needed to do with the press. Couch wanted $100,000 and Graham promised him he would do what he could. Couch had no real expectation that this amount would be achieved, but at the time was willing to follow Graham and trusted him to do his best. While the Princeton offer was tempting if only because of the solid financial basis Princeton University had compared with UNC, Couch turned it down. Unfortunately for Couch, Graham put neither the offer of a professorship at $6,000 a year nor the commitment to raise $100,000 as an endowment in writing to him or to the university's business office and Graham's promises came to nothing.[40] Couch did not expect Graham to actually raise the entire endowment, but he did expect Graham to make some attempt. Graham failed even to make the effort.

Couch clearly was becoming a man of consequence beyond the confines of Chapel Hill and even beyond the South. His work with the AAUP brought him national exposure and other opportunities. In 1942, Everett Fontaine, head of the publishing unit of the American Library Association (ALA), and Carl Milam, executive secretary of the ALA, had decided that ALA publishing needed to be placed on a firmer business basis than it had been in the past. Milam and Fontaine did not have far to go for help. ALA headquarters were in Chicago and the University of Chicago was home to the Graduate Library School, the only program in the United States engaged in training librarians at the graduate level. Milam and Fontaine contacted Donald Bean of the University of Chicago Press who directed them to Couch as a man capable of and willing to act as an outside consultant.[41]

Couch's report on ALA publishing was a masterpiece. ALA publishing was a small operation, but the income from publishing represented a significant resource for the organization. Further, the production and distribution of its highly specialized list of books and periodicals on librarianship were important in fulfilling the ALA's educational mission. Couch's report, submitted on June 18, 1942, affirmed, in essence, that the operation was financially sound. Whatever problems there were, were not with the unit itself, but with the leadership of the American Library Association. Couch concluded, "From its beginnings in 1886 until the present, A.L.A. Publishing has flourished or faltered according to the interest and vitality of the leadership in the field. This basic dependence is not likely to change."

Couch effusively praised Fontaine for his work as head of the operation. Fontaine served as chief editor and as the book designer for virtually every project. Fontaine's ability and his close attention to the details of publishing were exceptional. While Couch did recommend tightening the accounting system used by the ALA, he cautioned that this in itself could do no good if there were no good books to publish and he laid this responsibility directly in the leadership of the ALA. He flatly rejected as impractical Carl Milam's idea that the ALA could increase sales through trade channels for the specialized books it published. Fontaine had already rejected this possibility when Milam had earlier proposed it, and, indeed, Couch had rejected it when the foundation funding Odum's institute had insisted on it for the books published through the UNC Press. No matter how you sold them or what booksellers carried them in stock, you could not make best-sellers of such books.

Couch gave ALA publishing and Fontaine high marks in a report that considered all of the possible avenues that might be taken in order to improve the division's financial situation. It was a report that was, quite properly, favorable to both Fontaine and to the operation. Everett Fontaine must have felt gratified by the positive report produced by Couch.[42]

On February 6, 1945, Couch was invited by the University of Texas to consult on establishing a university press. He visited Austin in March 1945 for several days and delivered a report to the University Press Advisory Board that drew on his long experience at the UNC Press. He recommended establishing a press at Texas and gave a detailed business plan that, depending on the level of funding, would either start the press in a small way or, with sufficient funding and support, establish a press that could quickly become one of the leading university presses in the country. It was this last approach that he recommended.

In addition to a dedicated building, a full-time director, a printer-designer, and other staff members, he called for a subsidy from the university of at least $50,000 a year in addition to the $8,900 already appropriated, and an endowment of at least $100,000.[43] It is no surprise that this level of funding approximated what Couch had been seeking from Graham.

By the mid–1940s, Couch had established the UNC Press as a major force in American academic publishing and had, himself, attained a national reputation as a publisher. In a survey of university presses conducted in 1947–1948 by the American Council of Learned Societies, the University of North Carolina ranked seventh in the number of books published in the previous decade among the thirty-five members presses surveyed. The report of this survey singled out North Carolina as a press notable for its regional publishing program and clearly placed the press in a group of peers above those of UNC itself. Couch had responded to the request for information from the survey about the focus of the press from the AAUP, saying that regional manuscripts were favored and that the press had published a wide variety of books "from a natural science primer for the region to fiction with a southern regional background." While the list remained strongly regional, he mentioned his interest in publishing "more general interest trade items."[44] The regional emphasis of the press was, of course, at least partially a matter of the kinds of manuscripts submitted to the press, but it did reflect Couch's vision of the press as a general southern publishing house rather than a purveyor of academic scholarship characteristic of other established American university presses. While other university presses published academically reputable books, Couch committed his press to books that would affect people. The general literate public, not the academic community, was Couch's primary audience.

Couch's emerging national reputation and recognition as a publisher and his growing dissatisfaction with what he considered an intolerable situation at UNC made him increasingly susceptible to other possibilities. On August 10, 1945, Couch resigned from his job as head of the UNC Press, telling Frank Porter Graham that he had accepted a job as director of the University of Chicago Press beginning October 1, 1945. He expressed deep appreciation for Graham's support for the press and for him personally through the years, but pointedly cited the finances of the press as the major reason for his resignation.[45]

The relationship between Couch and Graham continued to be cordial and each man retained a strong respect for the other. When Henry Regnery published Russell Kirk's book, *Academic Freedom: An Essay on Definition* in 1955, Graham was sent a copy and was dismayed to read Kirk's account of the conflicts he had had with Couch on issues of academic freedom. Kirk reported that Graham had told Couch when he began with the press "that the press there would destroy itself if anything was published which dealt seriously with race, religion, or economics." Graham expressed his objection to this interpretation to William F. Strube, vice-president of the Henry Regnery Company, saying that he had not been president of the university when Couch became acting director in 1925 and thus had no knowledge of what Couch might have been told about the publishing of controversial books. Graham, however, was president when Couch was promoted to direct the press in 1932 and told Strube, "I was most happy with the selection of Mr. Couch for the very reason that he favored dealing seriously and courageously with matters of economic, social, cultural and general concern to the Southern people." Graham went on to aver that he and Couch had never had arguments over issues of academic freedom.

Graham sent a copy of this letter to Couch who wrote back confirming what Graham had said, but adding, in an odd interpretation, that he had taken the passage Kirk wrote "as a warm expression by Kirk of his admiration for your genuine exemplification of the principle of freedom of discussion." Couch went on to thank Graham for not firing him when he held the series of books commemorating the sesquicentennial of the university until adequate financing had been found because no funding had been specifically appropriated to support the publication of the series. Graham could have legitimately penalized him for the events at the meeting of the Southern Conference for Human Welfare—an issue that had nothing to do with the press, but everything to do with Couch's relationship with Graham—or even for the introduction to *What the Negro Wants*. Couch assured Graham that Russell Kirk did not mean this passage to be a condemnation of Graham, as Graham interpreted it, and expressed his own gratitude to Graham: "The important point is that you gave constant support to genuine freedom of discussion. Such freedom, in my opinion, is more important than anything else in this world today; and I am sorry to say I know very few people, left or right, who are standing up for it."[46] For Couch, the problem with Frank Graham at the UNC Press had not been one of intellectual freedom, but one of money.

3

Books That
Ought to Be Written

William Terry Couch found the prospect of an established, well-funded operation compelling after twenty years of penury in North Carolina. He had struggled for two decades to create a press in North Carolina that could make a difference, but had been hindered at almost every turn in constant battles over money, control, and intellectual freedom. Chicago offered a salary that was much more than Chapel Hill could ever offer, but there were further inducements for Couch to accept the job. The University of Chicago was a glowing land of intellectual freedom and scholarly activity where, under the chancellorship of Robert Maynard Hutchins, Couch expected that the entire range of ideas could be explored and where he would not have to consider the effect of the press's publications on the prejudices of a state's voters or the whims of a state legislature that controlled the budget. As a private university, Chicago enjoyed much greater freedom than any state supported institution could. Couch had been grateful for the full support of President Frank Graham at the University of North Carolina (UNC), but the continuous battles with members of the faculty, particularly Howard Odum, and the pressures that could be exerted on a state university by legislators, religious fundamentalists, and the southern public, made the relative insulation of a private university in the liberal North an alluring prospect.

Hutchins's widely publicized position on intellectual freedom was also attractive to Couch. In the early 1940s, Hutchins had established a national reputation as a defender of academic freedom. By the end of the decade, he had become the nation's authority. Hutchins's testimony before the Subversive Activities Commission of the Illinois State Legislature in April 1949, defending the University of Chicago against the charge that it was promoting Communism, would be anthologized in Howard Mumford Jones's *Primer of Intellectual*

Freedom where Jones placed Hutchins in the company of John Milton, Oliver Wendell Holmes, Jr., and Francis Bacon.[1]

Hutchins's views on the purpose of higher education must have also influenced Couch's decision. Hutchins's fear that "the pursuit of knowledge for its own sake is being rapidly obscured in universities and may soon be extinguished" by the rise of vocationalism certainly fit well with Couch's sentiments.[2] Couch's education at Chapel Hill had been in the liberal arts and his broad range of personal reading had thoroughly convinced him that the university was not a place to train people to do jobs, but to educate them. His vision of a press as an organic unit of a university that could fill the educational holes left by academic specialists fit well with Hutchins's view of a holistic university education. In all, Couch expected Chicago to be a place in which he could grow and expand his vision of what a university press could be, a place from which American society could be positively influenced by the important books he published. At a later date, Couch reflected on his view of Hutchins when he took the job:

> I saw Mr. Hutchins before I went to Chicago, and until the end of my stay there, as the best hope of education in America, brilliant and fearless in the pursuit of truth, large-minded, generous and just, capable of descending from the clouds on which university presidents too often seem to dwell and entering the battle to maintain the conditions that are necessary to decent life among human beings on this earth. Hutchins ... did not just talk. He took risks and did things.[3]

The problem with Chicago, as Couch was to find, was the very things that Robert Maynard Hutchins did.

Couch anticipated joining a university press at Chicago that would offer him the organizational autonomy necessary to publish important books. His predecessor at the press, Joseph A. Brandt, had certainly tried to guarantee the independence of the press and the authority of its director. Brandt had come to the press in 1944 and immediately engaged in a campaign to change the policies under which the press operated. He had been particularly concerned about the composition of the Board of University Publications, which he found too large to be of any functional use, the status of the director of the press, and the reporting structure of the organization. Brandt particularly urged that the director of the press report directly to the university's president rather than to the business manager and that the director be recognized as a member of the university community through appointment as a full professor.[4] These issues had all been areas of contention for Couch at Chapel Hill.

Brandt only stayed at Chicago for eighteen months, leaving for a job with trade publisher Henry Holt in New York. When Couch negotiated with Hutchins, though, he pursued the issues Brandt had raised. His major concerns about the job were related to the mechanics of the press's operations. Couch insisted on proper accounting procedures, on placing control of the printing plant under the university press, and on stabilizing the operation's financing. He averred that he and Hutchins were in substantial agreement about the most important issue of "how to recognize and promote excellence," even though this question was one that Couch said he and Hutchins had only vaguely raised before he went to Chicago.[5] It did, however, prove a consideration that Couch and Hutchins should have discussed in more detail before Couch took the job.

Hutchins was anxious enough to secure Couch's services that he acceded to his demand for the rank of professor, a concession Couch had been unable to obtain from UNC. Joseph Brandt had recommended the press director be appointed with faculty rank, but Couch insisted on it. Bill Couch knew about the experience of Louis Round Wilson, his mentor at UNC. When Wilson was offered the job as dean of the Graduate Library School at the University of Chicago in 1932, he found that the appointment was only as a dean which was an entirely administrative position. He invested seventy-two cents in a telegram to Chicago saying that he would only accept the job if he was given the rank of a professor of library science with tenure. Later, Wilson said it was the best investment he had ever made. When he arrived, he found that the university had cut administrative salaries, but not professorial pay. Since his appointment was ⅚ professorial and only ⅙ administrative, his portion of the cut only affected ⅙th of his salary. He calculated that his telegram gained him almost $17,500 over the decade he was there. Wilson told Couch to insist on faculty rank with tenure before he accepted Hutchins's offer.[6] Couch wisely followed Wilson's advice and demanded similar terms.

Increased academic freedom and greater autonomy were important to Couch, but a major consideration in his decision had to have been the salary. Hutchins offered Couch $12,000 a year beginning on July 18, 1945.[7] It was an offer that Couch could not refuse. Frank Graham attempted to counter the offer, but failed. The best he could manage to offer was a Kenan Professorship, the highest academic rank available at the University of North Carolina, with a salary of $7,000 a year. But, Graham could only offer to take that prospect to the trustees of the University of North Carolina if Couch would agree to stay beforehand. He gave no guarantee of success.[8] This vague prospect was insufficient and Bill Couch was off to Chicago.

Unfortunately, this new life at the University of Chicago was not all that Couch hoped. Even before his arrival, Couch was contacted by the university president, Ernest Cadman Colwell, who wanted him to fire Rollin Hemens from his job at the press. Hemens had been with the press for some twenty years, serving as interim director between the departure of Donald Bean in 1940 and the hiring of Joseph Brandt in 1943, and again in the same capacity between the directorships of Brandt and Couch in 1945. Couch had worked with Hemens on the Association of American University Presses (AAUP), but he was unenthusiastic about Hemens's ability and unimpressed with his accomplishments. He was, though, reluctant to fire anyone with Hemens length of service and Colwell left the issue at that. Couch's resistance had nothing to do with Hemens himself. Couch was a sentimentalist who valued the loyalty and longevity of his employees.

In 1947, Couch reviewed Roger Burlingame's book on the history of Scribner for *Library Quarterly*. He felt compelled to recount the story told by Burlingame about Charles Scribner's inability to remove incompetent employees including a cashier whom Scribner fired after employing him for twenty years. The man refused to be fired and continued to appear for work each day for another decade until he died, still on the Scribner payroll. Couch delighted in the anecdote, concluding, "In a House where business was so personal and loyalties so intertwined with all its detail, a man's very heartstrings, if there were such things, are twisted, after twenty years, around his chair."[9] Bill Couch's experience at the University of Chicago began badly. Prior to Couch's arrival, the press had become involved in a venture that probably no university press should have undertaken. In 1944, the directors of the Foundation for the Advancement of the Social Sciences at the University of Denver had approached Brandt about publishing a biography of James H. Causey, a western financier and promoter of world peace, who had endowed the foundation in the 1920s. Causey had been widely known for his international philanthropic activities and widely applauded for his selfless devotion to humanitarian causes.

The representatives of the foundation asked Brandt to recommend a scholar to undertake the writing and agreed to pay for the publication of the book. Though the foundation undoubtedly had someone from the University of Chicago faculty in mind, Brandt had other ideas. Brandt had headed the presses of the University of Oklahoma and Syracuse University and had served as president of the University of Oklahoma, but he was a journalist at heart. He was not a supporter of the kind of writing he found in most scholarly work and, like Couch, felt that better writing would result in a larger audience for academic books. He ignored the collection of faculty members at Chicago and found a professional writer for the job. George Milburn, a fiction writer, did not hold the academic credentials of most university press authors, but he had published *The Hobo's Hornbook*, a compendium of folksongs, which Brandt thought represented the quality of research worthy of a doctoral dissertation. Brandt hoped that by bringing Milburn into the project, he could eventually persuade him to write a biography of Will Rogers for the University of Chicago Press. Unfortunately, Milburn's scholarship was too thorough. He uncovered details about Causey's financial dealings that did not reflect favorably on his memory.

When the manuscript was delivered to the press six months after Couch assumed control, it was obvious to Couch that the family and the officials of the foundation would be offended. Couch was prepared to reject the book, but his assistant at the press, Fred Wieck, convinced him it was an important piece of scholarship. Couch was appalled when the lawyers for the University of Chicago business office advised him not to publish the book because of the possibility of a lawsuit from the Causey family. He began negotiations with the family and the foundation to allow publication of the book, but was stopped when Milburn accepted a settlement from the family for his work and agreed to drop his contract with the foundation. The incident gave clear evidence to Couch that the power of foundations to suppress the truth and to control research was ubiquitous and that Chicago could offer no more insulation against their power than he had at North Carolina.[10] The University of Chicago's reaction to even the mere possibility of a lawsuit and Milburn's acceptance of a pay-off were both egregious violations of scholarly integrity.

Couch went on to develop an impressive list of books for the press. Though he had strong personal opinions bordering at times on prejudices, he recognized that his opinions, except for judgments of quality, were irrelevant in considering the manuscripts submitted to the press. He was aware of the difficulties in following this principle, but maintained, as his general editorial policy, "I am as much interested in publishing a good statement with which I thoroughly disagree as I am in publishing one that I endorse."[11]

Of the more than two hundred books published by the University of Chicago Press while he was director, Couch was most pleased with Richard Weaver's *Ideas Have Consequences,* a book that Couch claimed won him the antagonism of the university's trustees. Weaver was a member of the English department at the University of Chicago. He had earned his bachelor's degree at the University of Kentucky in 1932 where he was active in socialist political causes. Failing to find a job after graduation, he went to Vanderbilt University to work on a master's degree in English and fell under the influence of the Agrarians, particularly John Crowe Ransom. When he completed that degree, he took a teaching job at Texas A&M University and spent three miserable years in College Station.

In 1940, Weaver entered a PhD program at Louisiana State University. His work was completed under the direction of Cleanth Brooks in 1943, with a dissertation titled, "The Confederate South, 1865–1910: A Study in the Survival of a Mind and Culture." Brooks was enthusiastic about Weaver's abilities and assisted him in finding a permanent teaching job which was probably the reason that a University of Chicago faculty recruiter sought Weaver out in Weaverville, North Carolina, where he was offered a job at Chicago in the Great Books Program. As a southern Agrarian in Chicago, Weaver was out of place. While he was less unhappy with Chicago than College Station, it was not a joyous life for him. The University of Chicago, however, was among the great universities in the United States and Weaver knew he could not do better. Weaver needed a book for promotion and tenure and offered Couch his doctoral dissertation, a customary first publication for a newly appointed instructor. Couch rejected the dissertation because it was too southern for the University of Chicago Press. The idea for Weaver's book, *Ideas Have Consequences*, apparently came from Couch himself after he declined to publish Weaver's dissertation, and Bill Couch seems to have worked on Weaver's book to much the same extent as he worked on Virginius Dabney's *Liberalism in the South*.[12]

In *Ideas Have Consequences*, Weaver argued that the only metaphysical right remaining in American society was that of private property. The secular state in which religion enjoyed no official sanction had destroyed the communal foundations of society and the modern compulsion to accept cultural diversity as a hallmark of a civilized state ignored the essential differences among cultures that derived from the notion of value. The traditions, customs, and culture of one society were either better or worse than those of another. The demand that "we must not define, subsume, or judge; we must rather rest on the periphery and display 'sensibility toward the cultural expression of all lands and peoples,'" was an attitude that Weaver contemptuously dismissed as "a process of emasculation."

Weaver identified music as one of the major symptoms of the decay of the Western world. The music of the eighteenth century, especially that of Mozart, was the last that truly expressed the ideals and values of a civilized society, demonstrating "what is possible with freedom and law." Music of the nineteenth century, particularly that of the Romantic period, represented the degeneracy of all that was good and pure and beautiful when composers such as Beethoven "sought effects, designed contrasts and imitations, strove for climaxes, as, like their literary contemporaries, they turned to the expression of bizarre or perverse feeling."

His harshest condemnation was reserved for jazz, which he found to be "the clearest of all signs of our age's deep-seated predilection for barbarism." Originating in the "dives of New Orleans," jazz had infected the world. Its popularity was inevitable: "something in the Negro's spontaneous manifestation of feeling linked up with Western man's declining faith in the value of culture" to destroy the delicate balance between structure and feeling that formed the foundation of Anglo-American civilization. Jazz "often sounds as if in a rage to divest itself of anything that suggests structure or confinement." It was a degenerate music suited to a degenerate society.

If the last great music was that of the eighteenth century, the last great society was that of the fourteenth in which people knew their place in the social order and class distinctions based on each person's worth to society were universally recognized. The source of the evil that destroyed this societal synthesis was, of course, egalitarianism and democracy. The idea that everyone was equal in a legal sense was not one to which Weaver objected. The belief that everyone was equal in a social sense, though, was one that was anathema: "equality is a disorganizing concept in so far as human relations mean order." To Weaver it was obvious that people individually were different and that these differences could be measured by an objective scale. The modern idea of liberal democracy, of egalitarianism, could only lead to chaos. The individual, who assumed equality with everyone else could only envy people who had accumulated more of the ultimate right, private property. The hierarchy of merit made the unequal distribution of wealth a natural phenomenon. Superior people deserved more than their inferiors. This was not an occasion for envy but for rejoicing in the perfection of the proper order in a society.[13]

Weaver's book brought mixed reviews and some negative reaction on the Chicago campus. In the final analysis, though, the judgment of Henry Regnery is undoubtedly accurate: Weaver's book, Friedrich August von Hayek's *The Road to Serfdom*, and Russell Kirk's *The Conservative Mind* formed "the intellectual basis for the modern conservative movement."[14]

Couch was convinced from the beginning that Weaver's book was important and committed the press to promoting it. He took out a full-page advertisement in the major magazine of the publishing world, *Publishers Weekly*, as well as national literary magazines such as the *Saturday Review*, the *New Republic*, the *Atlantic Monthly*, and the *Nation*. He sent letters to all potential book reviewers comparing Weaver's book to Frederick Hayek's *The Road to Serfdom*, which the University of Chicago Press had published in 1944. He clad the book in a dust jacket plastered with what appear to be alarmist headlines ripped out of newspapers and sent out promotional displays that were described as "surrealist" to book and department stores. The advertising campaign disturbed Weaver who disapproved of the dust jacket and the displays complaining that someone had said, "It reminded one of advertisements for prophylactics."[15]

Weaver was equally displeased with the title Couch forced on him for the book. Weaver's original title was *The Fearful Descent*, but Couch insisted on *Ideas Have Consequences*. Weaver submitted reluctantly.[16]

The books that Couch published at Chicago differed from those he had published at North Carolina. Of course, the preponderance was still scholarly works in literature, history, and the sciences, the kind of books that formed an essential backlist for any academic publisher. But, the books he championed, books that had the potential to change people's thinking, differed. At North Carolina, he had built a regional press and a publishing program consciously designed to awaken the South from its traditionalist torpor. While UNC was, by most estimations in 1945, the best public university in the South, it was still a regional and not a national institution, and Couch wanted and acquired manuscripts that dealt with particularly southern problems there. The University of Chicago was national and even international in its scope. Accordingly, Couch sought and published books that seriously attacked national and international problems. Bill Couch was prepared to attack and, if he could not find an author to join him, was fully capable of jumping in himself.

He had become increasingly infuriated over the collusion between American book-trade associations and the United States Department of State that resulted in the incorporation of the United States International Book Association (USIBA) as a non-profit corporation in 1945. It was a cooperative effort that was, at the start, enthusiastically supported by American publishers. The USIBA was a consortium of 145 publishers at its peak membership led by Chester Kerr, head of the Book Division of the United States Office of War Information. For American publishers, the major object of the USIBA was to promote the sale of American books abroad. For the Department of State, the object was to promote American ideals and the spread of American democracy throughout the world. By late 1946, the two objectives were at odds. The State Department put its efforts into elaborate and expensive book shows abroad to bring favored books to the attention of foreign booksellers and an international reading public to the detriment of American publishers interested in opening foreign markets to all the books they produced. American publishers and their trade associations were more interested in expanding international markets for all American books than advertising America by singling out books that promoted American values and United States policies to a world devastated by war. This dissention was fatal and the USIBA was terminated at the end of 1946.[17]

Couch was upset with the USIBA and its tactics, but equally upset with the American Book Publishers Council for lobbying Congress for special treatment. He refused to "have any part whatsoever in any effort to secure support from the Department of State or any other agency of the Federal Government in the effort to get foreign markets for books or anything else."[18] He wrote the editors of *Publishers Weekly* on more than one occasion in 1947 to express his opposition to policies dealing with the international book trade that were being promoted by the American Book Publishers Council and the American Textbook Publishers Institute. His particular target was the intimate relationship that he found "thoroughly pernicious between the publishers associations and the U.S. Department of State to develop foreign markets." The lobbying activities carried on by the publishers associations to influence federal legislation particularly concerned Couch. He was enraged about a proposal from the State Department that would require countries accepting loans from the United States to rebuild after the war to commit part of the money to purchasing books from American publishers through the Marshall Plan.[19] He was furious over a proposed requirement that publishers submit books to UNESCO to evaluate their "treatment of other nations." This was pure censorship. The other provisions were simple cultural imperialism. If other countries really wanted American books, they could use the loans to purchase them without being required to do so as a condition for the loans. The efforts of the publishing associations abetted by the State Department were a move toward centralization and statism that were anathema to Couch.

Couch's letters to the editors of *Publishers Weekly* condemning these proposals were never published. Couch reported that the editor, presumably Frederick Melcher, had told him, "I had not the faintest idea of what you were talking about." In desperation, Couch, through conservative publisher Henry Regnery, published his objections in a pamphlet in which he elaborated on his theme, accusing the publishing associations of being cartels that used government support to force their goods on foreign countries. He drew parallels between the American publishers and the Nazis and even the Soviets. The proposals were "a caricature of everything democracy is supposed to stand for" and could only lead to contempt for the United States abroad. The argument that the publishers' program would spread American ideals and democracy through books was dismissed as preposterous. Europe had a longer tradition of democracy than America and its own body of literature that surpassed anything American social scientists had produced.[20] With its myriad of social problems, the United States had little to offer the rest of the world.

Couch's pamphlet, *It Costs Us Nothing*, was a surprising success. While the editors of *Publishers Weekly* were perplexed by his arguments, others fully understood Couch's objections. The pamphlet received positive notices in the *Washington Post* and the *New York Times*, prompting interest and wide distribution.[21]

Couch was so frustrated by the failure of the *Publishers Weekly* editors to understand what he was saying that he finally admitted,

> In attempting to explain, I run into the problem of communication, into the practical impossibility of saying anything of importance that anyone today can understand.... And when I make an argument and it is not understood, and I repeat with

variations, and it still does not register, I hope that I will not then prove myself another one of those who know it all and were going to save the world and end up by wanting to use force to make people understand.[22]

Couch never resorted to force, but never stopped trying with multiple variations on his themes. His variations, however, failed to convince the editor of *Publishers Weekly* that the proposed program represented nothing more than cultural imperialism.

He was particularly opposed to the publishing associations' attempts to lobby Congress to promote the trade in American books to foreign countries. In 1948, the American Textbook Publishers Institute, the American Book Publishers Council, and the AAUP, banded together to sponsor a pamphlet, *Books in World Rehabilitation*, to be distributed to members of the U.S. Congress and the executive departments of the federal government to prompt federal legislation promoting the exporting of books. Couch opposed this move. The issue to him was that American publishers were attempting to "prey on the destitution of the world" when Europe and Asia were in "dire need and starvation" by forcing countries to buy American books as "a condition of loans and gifts." When the AAUP proposed establishing a central office to promote American university press books internationally, Couch expanded his objections telling David Stevens, director of the Division of Humanities for the Rockefeller Foundation, that the proposal of the AAUP should not be funded: "I think there would be serious danger, if we had an office engaged in operations of this kind, that we would find ourselves under obligations to the Federal Government and under the virtual necessity of supporting whatever foreign policies might be followed."[23] Couch insisted on the right to criticize the federal government and certainly felt that a major purpose of university presses was to criticize the government.

By then, though, Couch had already completed his break with the AAUP. He refused to support any of the efforts made to further international book sales and, particularly, to contribute to the efforts of the publishers associations to lobby the government. When the associations published *Books in World Rehabilitation* in 1948, they included a list of the members of the American Textbook Publishers Institute, the American Book Publishers Council, and the AAUP from which the University of Chicago Press was absent. It was pointedly conspicuous because the section in the pamphlet listing the AAUP members that supported the effort carried the gloss, "The University of Chicago Press dissents from the foregoing recommendations."[24]

Couch's clash with the leaders of the American book trade seems to have invigorated him, and Weaver's book had generated some refreshing controversy. Neither event, though, prepared Couch for the tumult that developed when he accepted a manuscript by Morton Grodzins on the internment of Japanese Americans during World War II for publication. Grodzins had been recently appointed an assistant professor in the political science department of the University of Chicago when he submitted the revision of his doctoral dissertation completed at the University of California to the University of Chicago Press in the summer of 1948.

The decision Couch faced should have been a simple one. The manuscript either represented a competently executed piece of research on a topic of some significance or it did not. If it did, the work should be subjected to further evaluation. If not, then Couch's duty would be to reject it politely, with a form letter informing the author that the work did not fit the publishing program of the University of Chicago Press. It was a ritual Couch had performed numerous times during his career. If Couch thought it had merit, a manuscript was sent to readers or referees, favorably reviewed and, as is the course for such matters, accepted for publication by the press. If the review was unfavorable, it would not be accepted. The procedures through which university presses handled submissions of manuscripts were well established.

Morton Grodzins complicated the process at the beginning when he told Couch that the manuscript had already been rejected by the University of California Press and, further, that officials at the University of California would oppose any effort of any other press to publish the book. Couch dismissed this, assuming it to be "the fanciful creation of a young author," and proceeded with plans to publish Grodzins's book.[25]

Grodzins was right, though. When officials at the University of California found out that Couch would publish the book, they immediately objected. Dorothy Swaine Thomas, the director of the Evacuation and Resettlement Study, a unit established in 1942 in the University of California College of Agriculture, wrote detailing her objections to the publication. She informed Fred Wieck, the assistant director of the press who had confirmed to her the plans to publish the book, that Morton Grodzins had been hired as a research assistant in her unit and had worked on the project for approximately three years, during which time he had collected the data he used in his doctoral dissertation.

Thomas assured him that Grodzins's data was the property of the University of California which had placed severe restrictions on its use. She said that Grodzins had been allowed to use the information in his doctoral dissertation, but pointed out that he had acknowledged this permission in the introduction to his dissertation. Further, the strictures on the information were such that even copies of his dissertation held by the university were kept "in locked files rather than in the General Library." She asserted that Grodzins himself had been repeatedly warned that the data he used was still controlled by the university and he had been denied permission to publish or even to allow anyone else to view it. She told Fred Wieck, "Publication by you would be an appropriation of materials belonging to the University of California and a breach of trust by Morton Grodzins."

As if this were not enough, Thomas went on to state that the directors of the study had encouraged Grodzins to write about the project and would have been pleased to have used the subsidy provided by the Rockefeller Foundation to publish his work if Grodzins had produced an acceptable manuscript. What he had written was unacceptable because of its scholarly deficiencies and the directors of the study had already committed to other members of the University of California faculty to publish a monograph based on material collected by Grodzins. She cautioned Wieck that "the prior and unauthorized publication of Grodzins's manuscript would, of course, constitute an infringement of these commitments."[26]

Thomas's position left Couch in a quandary. The subsidy by the Rockefeller Foundation was a problem, encountered before at Chapel Hill, to which he had earlier objected when it was used by Howard Odum to control publications by the University of North Carolina Press. He had, however, never encountered a rejection of a manuscript from someone controlling the subsidy when the money would not have gone to the press publishing the book. It was bad enough for the Rockefeller Foundation to award money for publication subsidies to authors rather than the publisher, but giving it to a third party who felt that they controlled all publication rights was a bizarre perversion of academic publishing. Further, he wanted to publish Grodzins's book and the statement that she considered it shoddy work undoubtedly rankled. It was the kind of book he wanted for the University of Chicago Press: it had the potential to incite controversy. Nevertheless, if there were a problem with the ownership of the material Grodzins used, Couch knew that he was ethically and perhaps legally bound to decline the book.

In September, Couch wrote to Jacobus tenBroek, Thomas's successor as head of the project, attempting to clarify the situation. What concerned Couch most were the conditions that might have been attached to Grodzins's use of the material he had collected as a research assistant on the project. He told tenBroek that, as he saw it, he had to believe one or the other of the parties in the dispute. Either Grodzins had, as he claimed, the right to publish the material in his dissertation or he did not. TenBroek countered that the assertions of the two sides were not, as Couch seemed to imply, equal in their claim to the truth. There was only a right side and a wrong side and the side of the University of California was the right side. Grodzins was only a research assistant and had been hired only to collect data on the project. It was, he said, a "common understanding" in American universities that this position implied no right to use that data in any way not authorized by the directors of the project.

TenBroek went too far with Couch when he claimed that even if there was no formal contract between Grodzins and the university explicitly stating the limitations placed on his use of the material, Grodzins was obliged to respect the constraint and had, indeed, recognized the necessity for permission when he acknowledged the help of Dorothy Thomas in his introduction with the phrase, "due to the generosity of Dr. Dorothy S. Thomas and others." This, tenBroek claimed, was proof that Grodzins felt the necessity to secure permission to use the material.[27]

Couch was amazed that the polite convention quoted to him could be construed as proof that Grodzins accepted the prohibition placed on his use of the data. He wrote tenBroek asking for a copy of the entire introduction telling him, "If it contains acknowledgment of the restrictions that you and Mrs. Thomas say existed, I see no course but for us to tell Mr. Grodzins we cannot publish for him." TenBroek failed to send Couch the introduction. With no specific agreement, Couch concluded that the University of California's objections to Grodzins's use of the data were invalid. If the University of California Press did not want to publish the book it should reject it, but it had no right to deny Grodzins the opportunity to publish it with another press.[28]

The day after Couch sent this letter to tenBroek, he wrote to his friend Samuel T. Farquhar, director of the University of California Press, to tell him that his understanding of the issue was whether California would let Grodzins publish at all or, more importantly, "whether he is to be permitted to interpret the materials as he thinks they should be interpreted." Couch was already convinced that the central issue was not a question of intellectual property as the California officials insisted, but intellectual freedom. For Couch, the answer was clear and one which he had resolved before at the University of North Carolina Press:

> If Mr. Grodzins' study had been made under the auspices of a research committee in the Southern United States, if his subject had been the Negro, and if he had then the same experience that he has had with the research committee in California, I think if I were running my own publishing concern I would go ahead and publish his book, and I don't believe anybody anywhere could stop me. There are certain kinds of materials that by their nature belong to the public, and if public or philanthropic funds are spent in the collection of this material, it cannot honestly be kept indefinitely from the public. I would not respect any customs or agreements of any kind whatsoever, existing in any southern states, designed to keep information concerning southern white treatment of the Negro from the

public at large. If this is a sound position to take with reference to the South it is a sound one to take with reference to the West.[29]

Couch was unable to see beyond the basic principles. Essentials were essentials and the fine nuances argued by the University of California were simply not relevant to the case.

Jacobus tenBroek, however, had been trained as a lawyer and had a reply. The case he had earlier presented against publication had rested, he said, on "considerations of ethics, customary and current practice, and inter-university comity," but there were legal arguments upon which he had not touched. He went on to quote sections from *Corpus Juris* and *Corpus Juris Secundum* he felt relevant to the argument that the publications of anyone employed to produce intellectual work were the property of the employer and not the employee contracted to produce the work. This, he asserted, was the crux of the case. Grodzins was an employee hired by the University of California to collect data. Inasmuch as that data formed the basis of the book, the rights of publication were owned by the university and not by the employee.[30] This was an argument that Couch was more than prepared to reject. The legal basis cited by tenBroek was clearly written for private industry, not universities. The environment of employment and the expectations of employees were radically different from private companies or even governmental agencies.

On October 25, 1948, Couch prepared a summary of the case in which he refuted each of the arguments put forth by Thomas and tenBroek for suppressing the book. He dismissed any implied contract with the University of California and the notion that Grodzins was employed merely to collect data: "One of the purposes of research assistantships is training for the assistant. A part of this training often is the collection of material—frequently to be used by someone else, but, unless there is definite agreement to the contrary, custom also prescribes that it may be used by the original collector. It is difficult to see how any other custom can be justified in tax-free institutions using educational and philanthropic funds." Further, the fact that Thomas had expressed the hope that Grodzins would write about the Japanese internment was evidence that he would be expected to do so. This was evidence that permission to publish had already been granted and it could not be rescinded.

With oblique reference to his experience with Odum at North Carolina, Couch wrote: "I have run into a good many cases of abuse of power by scholars controlling research funds, but I have never run into a more flagrant case than this." For Couch, Thomas and tenBroek were, by abusing their power, in a completely immoral position. If the University of Chicago refuses to publish the book, it "helps California sanctify and universalize its yellow dog contracts. If it refuses to be frightened by threats that California will sue or gossip, and goes ahead and publishes Grodzins['s] book as it planned to do before California made its claims, it helps make custom and law conform to decent standards of morality." Couch asked the rhetorical questions, "Is the University of Chicago willing to accept the view that universities have the right to suppress manuscripts they do not want to publish? Is the University of Chicago willing to accept the view that property claims can legitimately be used to control the expression of opinion? Is a practice that is wrong when committed by private property interests, right when engaged in by universities?"[31] The answer to all of these was, of course, understood to be *no*. At that point, Couch was clearly committed to publishing the book not only as a legitimate work of scholarship, but as a cause.

Robert Maynard Hutchins and other administrators of the University of Chicago disagreed with Couch on the matter. Ernest Cadman Colwell, president of the University of Chicago, was a man who seems to have had much in common with Couch, at least in his view of what a university press should be. Colwell had read a paper at a meeting of the AAUP in 1946 that roundly condemned the practice of university presses publishing the dissertations produced by their university's students. Most were simply not worth publishing either on literary merit or as substantial contributions to knowledge. Publishing the work of faculty members simply because they were members of a university's faculty was equally deplorable. It was more a way for members of the faculty to advance their careers than to contribute to learning. He knew that "professional progress is directly related to the length of the bibliography." Faculty researchers chose the simple problems, the ones that were not really important either to society or to the researcher, and ignored the complex and important ones to enable them to publish more. Colwell went on record when he asserted that one of the major purposes of a university press was to reach the general public and the people on university faculties were frequently not the best authors for books that could accomplish that end.[32] These were ideas with which he and Couch were in total agreement.

Colwell should have been more in sympathy with Couch, but he was not. Colwell fell in line with Hutchins, telling Couch and the Board of University Publications that Grodzins's book should not be published "because of inter-university comity." Couch exploded to him, "If we adopt as our great principle not offending anybody, you will reduce this University to an intellectual bawdy-house."[33]

Colwell's position, which infuriated Couch, was that Chicago's Central Administration only wanted to ensure that the rights of all parties in the dispute were protected. Bill Couch knew that the Central Administration had only intervened after it found that the issue would not go away because he would not let it go. When the lawyers at the university's business office affirmed that the university press did not have the right to publish the book and Couch insisted on bringing in an outside lawyer with experience in literary property, Colwell flatly refused. He ordered Couch to reach a resolution with Thomas and tenBroek himself on the issue. Thomas and tenBroek, however, only had one acceptable solution—the book would not be published.

Hutchins stayed above the fray, refusing to meet with Couch. Couch did corner him at a dean's luncheon in early November 1948, where Hutchins told him that that the University of California's protest against the book's publication was legitimate and the final decision would be made in the chancellor's office. Bill Couch refused to accept any *ex cathedra* decision from Hutchins. He wanted a reason, at least. He reported that Hutchins "seemed to imply that in a controversy between two parties, one little and one big, the wishes of the big party had to be granted."

Hutchins did authorize Malcolm P. Sharp of the University of Chicago law school and a member of the Board of University Publications to try to resolve the matter with tenBroek. Sharp was not chosen simply because he was a lawyer and a member of the board. Sharp had become friends with tenBroek when tenBroek was employed on a temporary appointment at the law school in 1940–1942. Sharp also knew Couch beyond his contact on the publishing board. Sharp's son, Jonathan, had recently married Couch's daughter, Betsy. Sharp reported back to the board that everything he had found supported Couch's and Grodzins's claims and the University of Chicago Press should proceed with plans to publish the book.

While Couch pounded on Hutchins and his henchmen with the bludgeon of moral rectitude and scholarly independence, Morton Grodzins was waging his own campaign to have his book published. For Couch, it was an ethical and moral issue. For Grodzins, it was an academic career. Grodzins needed the book published for tenure at the University of Chicago.

Grodzins had enjoyed a close relationship with Dorothy Thomas while he was writing his dissertation. She was a member of his doctoral committee and Grodzins and his wife had been close friends with Thomas and her husband. When Grodzins applied for the job at the University of Chicago, Thomas wrote a strong letter of recommendation for him. She praised his "unusually alert intelligence" and his "capacity for productive research." She went on to say that his dissertation could be reworked into "two extensive monographs" with the judgment, "the basic data has been very well organized, the analytical framework is superior, and the manuscript is well written." Unfortunately, the high opinion she expressed did not last.

On August 9, 1945, long before he offered the manuscript to Couch in the summer of 1948, Grodzins wrote to her in an attempt to clear up her opposition to publishing the book about which he had warned Couch at the beginning. This letter and Thomas's reply undoubtedly formed the grounds for Grodzins's original warning to Couch that the University of California would not look favorably on anyone publishing the book.

He began by telling her that while he subscribed to the original intent of the secrecy covenant on which Thomas had insisted for the duration of the study, the agreement was made when everyone thought the war would last much longer than it did. By August 9, 1945, the end of the Pacific war was apparent. The need for secrecy for the project was over and he urged her to proceed with plans to publish the results of the study and, particularly, to publish his dissertation.

Thomas's reply to Grodzins was devastating. She began by asserting that he had no claim to publish anything. He had been hired to collect data and, as an employee of the University of California, he had been paid. Any publication was to be entirely at the discretion of her and Charles Aikin who had chaired Grodzins's doctoral committee and was a close personal friend of tenBroek. She reaffirmed what she had evidently told him before. She would allow him to use the dissertation and the report he had prepared for the study only after she and Aikin had determined a publication schedule for the whole of the study and that she would write to him with her permission to publish his dissertation at that time. In this letter, Thomas expressed her belief that the dissertation was unpublishable without significant revision. It was, she said, "verbose" and "includes a number of intemperate and immature judgments about the behavior and misbehavior of government officials."[34]

This last charge was the central issue to Couch. At the time of the internment, Earl Warren was the attorney general of California and the major political player in the decision to evacuate Americans of Japanese ancestry from the Pacific coast. He fared badly at Grodzins's hands in the account. As governor of California and a close personal friend and political ally of the University of California President Robert Gordon Sproul, there would seem to be an almost natural inclination on the part of the University of California to suppress the book.

Earl Warren and Sproul had known each other since they were undergraduates at Berkeley and clarinetist Earl Warren had marched directly behind drum-major Robert Sproul in the University of California band. Sproul delivered the speech nominating Warren for president at the Republican national convention in 1948 as a California favorite son. While Warren failed to achieve the nomination for president, he was selected as Thomas Dewey's running mate for vice-president on the 1948 Republican presidential ticket. In one of the few modern analyses of the Grodzins incident, Peter T. Suzuki made a compelling case that the essential reason for the attempt to suppress Grodzins's book was his treat-ment of Earl Warren. While the participants from California denied any polit-ical motives and those from Chicago almost pointedly avoided the imputation of them, it is evident that Thomas's charge of scholarly intemperance against Grodzins was, indeed, the crux of the matter.[35] Morton Grodzins had taken too many politically powerful groups and individuals to task for their actions in the internment of Japanese Americans.

In September 1948, Grodzins put Thomas's claim that the entire group of graduate assistants had been sworn to secrecy and that she alone controlled the publication of the material to the only test he could devise. With the lack of any corroborative written evidence, it amounted to the word of one graduate assistant in the project against that of a senior professor. Grodzins contacted the other assistants he could locate and all confirmed his own memory that whatever secrecy they had subscribed to was to last only for the duration of the war. Rosalie Hankey, one of the assistants, added that she had been surprised later when Thomas wrote to her to say that all the material she had collected belonged to the study and not only could she not publish it, she could not even use it in her lectures. Further, she told Grodzins, Thomas's letter "contained an order that I was not even to testify in court—were I asked to do so—on the suit instituted by the Japanese who had renounced their citizenship." She told Grodzins that she was outraged by this demand.[36]

Ultimately, it was Grodzins who broke the impasse. The November 1948 election killed Earl Warren's immediate political aspirations and there was no further need to protect his name. On December 30, 1948, Fred Wieck told Couch that Grodzins had said that Robert Sproul had telephoned him to authorize Hutchins to allow the press to publish the manuscript. Grodzins had been told to expect the call and had Malcolm Sharp at his side to talk to Sproul as well. After Sproul obtained concessions from Grodzins dealing with the omission of certain names and materials used in the dissertation, he granted him unofficial permission to continue with the publication plan. Sharp and Grodzins prepared a memo to Hutchins detailing this agreement, but Hutchins was obviously already prepared for this and in a terse, inelegant communication to Couch sent the same day, granted the press permission to publish the book.[37]

Couch's enthusiastic support of Grodzins through this derived, at least partly, from his appreciation of Grodzins's approach to the subject. It resonated with Couch's own views of research in the social sciences. One recurring charge made by Grodzins against Thomas was that their views of social science research differed radically. While Grodzins viewed his conclusions about the political aspects of the internment essential to understanding the phenomenon, Thomas held the belief that there was a standard of objectivity that precluded the kind of analysis that Grodzins pursued in his manuscript. She felt "social science can be a value-free discipline and that the social scientist should not, as a scientist, be concerned with problems of social policy." While Grodzins early on was amenable to any changes or revisions that would not compromise his scholarly integrity and, indeed, on numerous occasions professed his willingness to revise his work for Thomas's approval, he could not, as he told Couch, alter "the sense of what I believe to be true and important" or modify his conclusions to fit Thomas's concept of scientific research. This was an attitude with which Couch was in complete sympathy.

At least part of Thomas's and tenBroek's opposition to the publication of Grodzins's book is attributable to this view of reputable research. Another perhaps equally significant factor was the desire of senior members of the study to publish the final reports under their own names. To a great extent, Grodzins's exasperation with the situation came from his assumption that Thomas's early plan for publishing a series of books on the project was, indeed, a plan. At the time he was working on the project as an assistant, he understood that the final reports of the study were to be published in a series "of eight to ten or more monographs" dispersed over the various areas and phases of the project. These were to be written by the various principal investigators on the project and by the assistants who would, it was assumed, receive appropriate authorial credit for their work. By the fall of 1948, it was obvious this would not happen.

In a letter to Couch on October 7, 1948, Grodzins expressed bemusement over the dramatic change in Dorothy Thomas's thinking from their early relationship during which she had frequently complained about what she termed *academic feudalism*, the practice of people with established reputations in the academic community using the work of their graduate students and assistants without acknowledgment. Grodzins reported being encouraged when Thomas referred to the number of monographs published by students working under her direction when she was at Yale. Yet, it was apparent to Grodzins and to the other assistants who had worked on the project that, by 1948, she and tenBroek intended to retain all rights to the material and reserve publication credit for themselves. In the case of Grodzins's material, this is precisely what happened.[38]

Thomas had already published one volume of the study, *The Spoilage*, in 1946, which was written before the war was technically over. In this book, she was listed as the author and gave credit to Grodzins and other research assistants on the title page for their contributions. Only one other volume in the originally planned sequence, as understood by Grodzins, followed. In 1952, *The Salvage* was published with Dorothy Swaine Thomas listed as sole author with a notation acknowledging the research assistance of Charles Kikuchi and James Sakoda on the title page. In 1954, the University of California Press published tenBroek's reworking of the Grodzins material on the political process behind the internment under the title, *Prejudice, War and the Constitution*, with tenBroek, Edward N. Barnhart, and Floyd W. Matson listed on the title page as joint authors.[39] It is evident that Thomas and Aiken intended to block Grodzins's ability to publish his dissertation almost from the beginning. In the summer of 1946, Thomas and Aikin had already formalized publication plans to the extent that Thomas wrote Grodzins in July telling him that because of "the propagandistic nature of your writing, and your tendency to over-dramatize," she and Aikin had contacted Milton Chernin of the University of California faculty asking him to completely rewrite Grodzins's dissertation for publication. Chernin was to share joint authorship with Grodzins and the book was to be published as part of a projected series. This plan was indignantly rejected by Grodzins. Chernin, though, was not the only person Thomas and Aikin contacted. When he declined the task, Thomas asked at least three other candidates to undertake the revision before Jacobus tenBroek finally completed the job.[40]

Jacobus tenBroek's contribution to the literature was finally published specifically to counter Grodzins. In his preface, tenBroek only mentioned Grodzins's book, noting that its conclusions differed from tenBroek's official report and were, at times, contradictory. The issue of Grodzins's book was raised later in the text by tenBroek when he attempted to demolish Grodzins's argument that the California civic groups, local public officials, grower's organizations, and chambers of commerce that forced the establishment of the internment camps were motivated by greed for the lands, businesses, and resources owned by Japanese Americans living in California. TenBroek and his collaborators claimed that Grodzins's evidence for this conclusion was at best slight and could not be accepted as proof that each segment of California's population was in favor of the resettlement program.[41]

One disingenuous method tenBroek and his collaborators used in this effort to discredit Grodzins's work was surveying the various groups Grodzins cited as supporting the removal and internment program. Almost overwhelmingly, the respondents denied that they or the groups and organizations with which they were associated had supported the program. This denial was not surprising since after the war and particularly after Grodzins's book was published, the whole incident was viewed by most people as a deplorable event in American history.[42] In the end, Couch had won. The Grodzins book was published by the University of Chicago Press in 1949 and, Couch hoped, the incident would be forgotten or at least fade into the background. By this point in his editorial career, Couch was used to fighting battles. As a publisher, he knew that such victories and losses were irrelevant to the long-term objective of maintaining the supply of good books from the press. For him, the Grodzins affair was simply one in a series of events in a career committed to the larger goal of publishing, and he was ready to move on to the next book for the press. While he had been battling for the publication of Grodzins's book, he had also been deeply involved in another project, publishing A. Frank Reel's *The Case of General Yamashita.*

Reel was a member of the team of military lawyers assigned to represent Lt. Gen. Tomoyuki Yamashita, commander of the Imperial Japanese Army in Malaya, Singapore, and the Philippines. Yamashita was tried for war crimes by an American military tribunal in Manila from October 29 to December 7, 1945, and sentenced to death for atrocities committed by the troops under his command in the Philippines and Singapore against civilians and prisoners of war. The book raised serious questions about the nature of Yamashita's guilt in the crimes of which he was accused and about the legality of the military tribunal that condemned him.

Couch accepted the book after it had been rejected by several New York trade publishers. He knew the book was important and that it could only be published by a university press. The subject, a defense of a Japanese commander, would arouse too much public opposition to be undertaken by any American trade house so soon after the war. Couch compared Yamashita's "judicial lynching" to the illegal execution of African Americans in the South, about which he had published books at North Carolina. He felt compelled to publish Reel's book. Couch had no real illusions that it would be a financial success, but this did not stop him from aggressively promoting the book more than any other publication at either the Chicago or the North Carolina press.

He sent review copies to every newspaper, magazine, and other potential reviewing medium in the country. He focused his efforts on law journals, pounding the editors for reviews and even enlisted the author in a letter-writing effort to newspapers and journals promoting the book. He sent copies to Japanese publications and made every attempt he could to interest a Japanese publisher in sponsoring a Japanese translation of the book.

His attempts to have the book noticed were successful. Couch secured reviews of the book in all of the major law reviews and many major newspapers. It was reviewed in the *Chicago Sun*, the *Christian Science Monitor*, the *New York Herald Tribune*, the *New York Times*, and even the *London Times Literary Supplement*. The *Saturday Review of Literature*, the *New Republic*, the *Nation*, and even the *New Yorker* gave it space. And library book selection periodicals *Booklist*, *Library Journal*, and *Kirkus* noticed it. The reviewers were laudatory, even if they sometimes caviled over Reel's passionate advocacy for Yamashita. It was recognized as an important book and Reel's passion was what Couch wanted in an author.

Couch's efforts led him into some odd territory. He made a nuisance of himself with the Book-of-the-Month Club pushing Reel's book. As was his custom, Couch always approached the person at the top. In this case, it was Harry Scherman, the founder, to whom Couch wrote on several occasions, making a case for Reel's book. Scherman finally responded, complaining about his "advance pressure tactics, which very few publishers have engaged in." He told Couch, obviously not for the first time, that he had nothing to do with choosing books for the Book-of-the-Month. The selection committee had considered the book, but had already rejected it for inclusion.[43]

Couch put his every effort into getting the book noticed to the point of demanding that General Douglas MacArthur, commander of the U.S. Occupation Forces in Japan, respond to the charges in hopes his reaction might arouse interest in the book. Couch sent out flyers promoting the book with the heading, "Whose Iron Curtain Is This" with the prominent conclusion, "One thing is certain, this iron curtain does not belong entirely to General MacArthur. President Truman has a big share in it." Couch's flyers with their oddly mismatched typography and strangely spaced and justified phrases looked more like a promotion for a cut-rate drug store or a crude ransom note than a product of a major university press. After trying all else, he wrote Reel on January 31, 1950, "I am convinced that our policy of getting MacArthur to talk is a necessary one if we are to have any chance to continue getting attention to *The Case of General Yamashita*." Couch was right. A statement from MacArthur would undoubtedly draw attention to the book. MacArthur was one of the principal targets in Reel's sights and had, in Reel's account, viewed the entire trial as only an unfortunate delay in Yamashita's execution. The reviewers, particularly the authors of the longer ones, recognized this and joined in the condemnation of MacArthur. One went as far as to question the fitness of MacArthur should he follow the expected route of running for public office after leaving the military.[44]

Couch's enthusiasm for publishing Reel's book is an instance of his commitment to publishing important books even when he was in disagreement with their authors. He did respect Douglas MacArthur and, even though he had severely criticized the general, he thought enough of MacArthur that he encouraged Henry Regnery to make the attempt to get a book out of him.[45] This tepid approval, though, was insufficient to keep him from hammering at MacArthur for a response to Reel's book.

MacArthur remained silent through this, leaving an assistant, Brigadier General Courtney Whitney, to answer Couch. Whitney came close to accusing Couch of treason when he expressed shock "to see Americans join in the campaign of vilification, adding their weight to existing pressures directed at undermining Japanese faith in American justice and morality" against the American Occupation Forces that were already "constantly facing formidable subversive propaganda from the Asiatic mainland."[46]

When the October 7, 1949, issue of the *Chicago Tribune* published a note that the Occupation Forces had asked the Japanese newspapers to refrain from mentioning Reel's book, Couch found a new approach for his campaign. It became an issue of freedom of the press since a request from the Occupation Forces was tantamount to a direct order to the newspaper publishers. Couch immediately telegrammed every major newspaper and newsmagazine in the United States with the same message. The suppression of the press in Japan by the U.S. government was equivalent to the suppression of a free press by the Communist government of the Soviet Union, telling the editors, "I have hope you will feel this subject is important enough to see that real attention is given to it."[47]

To Couch, the issue of MacArthur's control of the Japanese press was one that came to have more significance than the miscarriage of justice in the execution of General Yamashita. He sent copies of Reel's book to members of the U.S. Congress in an attempt to generate a reaction to MacArthur's censorship efforts, accusing liberals in government of either ignorance or cynical apathy. Couch even attempted to enlist the aid of the American Civil Liberties Union (ACLU) in the case. The ACLU did not get far and its attempts to inquire into the situation were deftly parried by Whitney who assured it that the requirement that publishers receive permission from the Occupation Forces was only a mechanism to allow the authorities "to assist Japanese publishers toward a well balanced program." Whitney calmly informed the ACLU that even though "obviously inflammatory matter" would not be allowed, it could not be considered censorship. It was, rather, part of MacArthur's plan to develop and nurture democracy in post-war Japan.[48]

In an eighty-two page memorandum dated November 22, 1949, Whitney gave the only full public response from the U.S. Army that described the prosecution's case against General Yamashita. The prefatory material to the piece made it clear that it was a direct answer to Couch's attempt to interest a Japanese publisher in issuing a translation of the book. Whitney noted that "an unusual number of free copies of this book were distributed in Japan" but only one publisher, Hosei University Press, had inquired about translation rights and, after talking with a U.S. Army representative, had been dissuaded. Indeed, Whitney averred that if any Japanese publisher asked to publish the book, the request "would be disapproved both because of the textural nature of the book and the inflammatory advertising material publicly circulated by the publishers to stimulate sales." To the American Occupation Forces, Couch and the University of Chicago Press shared responsibility for this almost treasonable action with the book's author. Whitney went on to condemn the book as "an attack on our American system" and its author as engaged in "an almost hysterical endeavor" to retry a case that had been legitimately and legally lost.[49] It was not until after the occupation of Japan had ended that a Japanese language version of Reel's book could appear, translated by Muraji Shimojima and published by Nihon Kyōbunsha in 1952.

4

A Case History
in Book Publishing

On Monday, November 20, 1950, William Terry Couch was called into the office of the University of Chicago's vice-president for business affairs, James A. Cunningham, and fired from his job as director of the University of Chicago Press. Couch flailed around trying to find an explanation. He wrote one close friend, Lucille Crain, blaming it directly on the antagonism of the Chicago trustees for having published Richard Weaver's book, *Ideas Have Consequences*. To another correspondent, he blamed Robert Maynard Hutchins's disappointment that Couch was not a liberal, and was not aware that Couch had become a committed opponent of Communism when he hired him.[1] Couch, though, was convinced even at the time that the underlying reason was his insistence on publishing Morton Grodzins's *Americans Betrayed* over Hutchins's objections. The administration of the University of Chicago certainly considered Couch precipitous in his evaluation of the evidence given by the University of California.

A perhaps a more balanced assessment of the reasons has been given by Stephen Murray in his analysis of the incident when he ascribed the firing to Couch's "intemperance rather than the content of a controversial manuscript." Couch certainly had been intemperate. His battle for the Grodzins book and his unorthodox promotion of Reel's book on General Yamashita must have engendered serious concern from Hutchins and other administrators at the university about Couch's competency to head a major university press. Both books were more anti-government polemics than the exempla of dispassionate scholarship that had characterized the books of the University of Chicago Press in the past.

The official cause for his dismissal, though, was not a matter of intellectual freedom, but rather his inability to manage the internal operations of the press.

Neither freedom of the press nor issues of academic freedom were considered relevant by the Chicago administration. Management issues proved the major problem for Couch, at least according to the Chicago administrators.

In the midst of Bill Couch's battle with the university's administration over the Grodzins book, James A. Cunningham was appointed vice-president for business affairs at the university. The first assignment he was given by members of the Central Administration was to rid the University of Chicago of Bill Couch. Cunningham demurred. Just as Couch had done when he arrived at Chicago and had been ordered to fire Roland Hemens, Cunningham refused to fire someone as his first act in office without having a full understanding of the situation and circumstances involved.[2]

Days before Cunningham arrived at Chicago in November 1948, Couch sent Ernest C. Colwell, president of the university, a memorandum that was unrelated to Grodzins's book. Here, he addressed the management of the press. Couch was concerned about the dearth of good manuscripts being submitted for publication. He was also deeply troubled that the press's sales force had been decimated by resignations and there was no one left to even process book orders should someone want to buy a book. Income from sales funded the ongoing operation of the press to a significant extent and, if sales fell, the press had to immediately cut its expenses to absorb losses.[3] The easiest and quickest way to reduce expenses was, of course, to reduce number of employees. The alternative strategy, reducing expenses by delaying publications, would only create more significant problems in the future.

Colwell's response was not helpful. He expressed astonishment that Couch would even want more good manuscripts since he had, not long before, complained to him that there was not enough money to publish the ones already accepted by the press. Couch's other management issues would have to be referred to the new vice-president for business affairs, James A. Cunningham. Colwell promised to forward Couch's request for a meeting to Cunningham and to bring those particular items to his attention.[4]

Apparently, Colwell failed to send this on to Cunningham, but he did forward a letter from an angry customer of the press. In November 1948, Professor Frederick C. Grant of the Union Theological Seminary wrote directly to Colwell complaining about the time it took the press to fill orders for the textbooks he needed for classes. He wrote to Colwell because Colwell was the author of the book, *The Study of the Bible*, which Grant used in his classes. Grant had been ordering the book in the early summer for use in the fall semester for several years and the books had never been received until the part of the course using the text was almost over. Colwell forwarded this letter on to Cunningham, who in turn sent it on to Couch with the demand, "Will you please explain the reason for such delays and I will reply to Mr. Grant."[5] Couch replied to Cunningham with the record of the orders for the book that had been received and filled for the Union Theological Seminary bookstore, expressing surprise that the time between the receipt of the orders and the shipment of the books was as prompt as it had been, since "we do not keep our people long enough to get them trained to do anything properly." The time lapse was anywhere from one to two weeks and the delay about which Grant complained probably came from the Union Theological Seminary's bookstore which held requests from faculty members for several months to accumulate orders from individual publishers to obtain larger discounts. This was a common practice in college book stores.

Couch reminded Cunningham that he had already spoken with him about the one hundred percent turnover in staff each year for the past several years. In a sarcastic aside, he asserted that the press's personnel situation might appear to be a problem, but it was obviously not. He had been unable to interest anyone within the Central Administration with the power to do anything about it to take the situation seriously. He told Cunningham that if the press had anyone on the staff to sell textbooks, Grant's problem would not exist.[6] Orders could go directly from the salesman to the press without going through a campus book store. The press could be a profitable business if anyone in the Central Administration wanted to support Bill Couch. No one, evidently, did at this point.

The absence of an advertising and sales staff for the press may well have been the reason for Couch's own exuberant campaign for A. Frank Reel's book. A competent sales staff with people who understood book sales and the book trade and who could be more realistic than Couch about the possibilities for Reel's book might well have kept Couch from overextending his efforts. By the end of 1949, it was evident to all, including Couch, that his elaborate promotion of Reel's book had been a blunder. Couch reported that the press had "disposed of somewhere between 4500 and 5000 copies at an advertising and publicity cost of close to $2 per copy." This was an extravagant amount for a book that retailed at $4. Couch maintained, though, that it was a rational expenditure if it generated a large enough public response to eventually pay off.[7] He may have thought this, but his enthusiasm for the book definitely outran that of the reading public.

Despairing of relief from the business office or the Central Administration, Couch brought his problems to the Board of University Publications meeting on April 8, 1949, and laid them before the members. He told the members that it was impossible to get any vitally needed decisions from the administration on the questions to which the press needed answers. Couch said that he would accept any decision, "right or wrong." He preferred right answers, but had been unable to obtain anything.

The members of the board debated whether it had the authority to address the problems raised by Couch at the meeting. The members knew that the board's jurisdiction was limited to the vague arena of educational policy, but what Couch argued seemed certainly to impinge on that. They agreed with Couch's central argument that the editorial functions of the board were inextricably intertwined with the financial problems from which the press suffered. Couch made a strong case that most scholarly books and journals published by the press could not support the costs of their publication through sales, but some could produce enough income to support others that were less successful. This balance, however, depended on a healthy publishing program. Couch told the board, "Our great problem, besides that of getting good books, is to keep the costs of scholarly publishing down. This can only be done by having a going concern, supported with money earned on good and profitable textbooks and trade books that require salesmen to sell them."

Couch's vision of the press was holistic. Resolution of the financial concerns were central to the editorial issues that were the official concerns of the Board of University Publications. Ultimately, the board members present appointed a committee to study the question of the relationship of the press to the university and help the board members decide what action might be appropriate.[8]

Malcolm Sharp was appointed chairman of this three member committee and, almost immediately, carried the story about Couch's complaints against the administration to Robert Maynard Hutchins. Hutchins preferred not to directly confront Couch, and he referred the problem to Cunningham who called Couch into his office on April 18, 1949, to give him an official reprimand for his actions. Couch reported that Cunningham "wanted to know what I meant by getting my Board worked up and having people bother the Chancellor about matters over which the Board had no authority." To Couch's surprise, Cunningham said Couch should have come to him with the problems and that Couch could have hired replacement personnel for the press himself. Couch knew that Cunningham and the business office had to approve hiring and he had been completely unable to force any decision from anyone from the business office about the issue. Cunningham professed to agree with Couch on many of the issues facing the press, but bringing them to the board's attention was "discourteous and ungentlemanly." More seriously, Cunningham directly accused him of "trying to play politics with the faculty."

Couch claimed to have been conciliatory with Cunningham at this meeting, but Cunningham told him if he "did not call off the Committee that the Board had appointed, he would drop his efforts to help him get the Press on a sound basis." Couch had seen no evidence that Cunningham was willing to help him or the press and refused. Cunningham's implied threat merely confirmed Couch's belief that there was no hope for help from the business office. He told Cunningham that he would inform the board about his objections to the committee's appointment, but refused to direct the board or its committee to drop the matter. Cunningham answered, whatever the board did could not help him.[9]

Hutchins knew he could not ignore the board's committee and directed Cunningham to informally work with it, even though Cunningham made the members aware from the start that he questioned the validity of the committee's charge. On May 18, 1949, the committee delivered its report to the board. The three members addressed all of Couch's pressing problems; the need for financial reserves to protect the press from fluctuating sales income, the need for a budgetary process that would protect the press from losses derived from administrative meddling in the production schedules and the subsidies available to the press, and the necessity for personnel policies and procedures that would enable the press to attract and retain competent people. It was a report that Couch himself could have written. Indeed, he had written the same account of the problems and solutions using the same examples and wording in a barrage of memos to everyone concerned with the press over the preceding year.[10] Cunningham seemed ready to let the issue go with that.

While the press and Couch suffered from neglect by Chicago's Central Administration in financial and personnel matters, the ambiguous relationship of the printing plant to the press caused greater problems. Couch had been concerned about the high cost of printing and book production the press incurred by using the university's own printing facility since he had accepted the job at Chicago.[11] The need of the university press for editorial responsibility and integrity and the need of its printing department for a constant flow of copy to keep the presses running placed Couch in an ambiguous position as titular head of both operations. He had to ensure the integrity of the editorial process and to maintain a constant and sufficient level of work in the print shop. The flow of copy from the editors was not a constant stream, though. There were times of overwhelming work for the printers and times of idleness.

By the end of November 1949, Couch was dismayed to find that the Central Administration had begun to question the need for a printing plant at all. Couch knew that it would cost the press twenty-five to thirty-five percent more to have all printing done by outside presses than by an in-house operation and encouraged the administration to commission a study of the printing operation by someone who understood printing and scholarly publishing. He told Howard B. Matthews, associate business manager for the university, "I would prefer not to have my time taken by people who are ignorant of the subject."

By this time, Couch had begun to despair of obtaining a commitment from the university administration for a coherent approach to the needs of the press. He told Matthews that the constant battles with the administration over the press and its printing operation were damaging to the press and, ultimately, to the university itself:

> In continually asking questions of this kind [i.e. the need for a printing facility] the University is doing to me somewhat the sort of thing they would do, say, to the director of one of its institutions if when he said he needed a cyclotron and he needed one that met certain specifications, he was then asked by someone in the Central Administration whether he didn't really need a baby carriage, whether this wouldn't serve his purpose just as well or better. This sort of procedure is anything but intelligent.[12]

Any respect Bill Couch may have had for members of the university's administration had severely eroded.

Even though Couch was fully aware that he was making a powerful enemy of Robert Maynard Hutchins, he almost felt compelled to challenge him on multiple fronts. Couch took Hutchins to task in February 1950 over Hutchins's failure to provide the leadership that would encourage the faculty of the University of Chicago to seriously examine the use of force in international relations. The University of Chicago had made major contributions to the war effort with the Manhattan Project, but it had completely failed, under Hutchins, "to make any contribution to the understanding of the moral issues involved." It was, Couch charged, "one of the most scandalous intellectual and moral failures of all time."[13] It was, also, hardly a diplomatic juncture for Couch to personally attack Hutchins's integrity.

In May 1950, Couch received a report on the management of the press from the consulting firm of Booz, Allen and Hamilton. The report, commissioned by James Cunningham, may have been in response to the recommendation of the committee of the Board of University Publications from a year earlier. It may have been prompted by Cunningham's own conviction that he needed more information on the press's operations than he had. Or, it may have been ordered by members of Chicago's Central Administration looking for weak points to attack Couch. It was probably not occasioned by Couch's desire to have someone who knew something about scholarly publishing examine the operations of the press.

It was certainly not a report produced by someone familiar with publishing. And, it was not a report to be used by the Board of University Publications. Indeed, Cunningham and Colwell seemed to have wanted to keep the report a secret from everyone. They took Couch to task for even mentioning its existence to the members of the board and were furious that he allowed the heads of the departments of the press to see it.[14]

Couch submitted a brief reaction to the consultant's report to Howard B. Matthews shortly after receiving it. He acknowledged to Matthews that a number of the points made by Tom Wood, the consultant sent by Booz, Allen and Hamilton, were valid and worth implementing. He had serious reservations about others, though. Couch particularly objected to the praise Wood gave to the Printing Department. He maintained to Matthews that the problems with the printing operation were much more severe than those of other units and the issues between the editorial staff and the printing plant were of utmost importance to the successful operation of the University of Chicago Press.[15]

He was much more detailed in his response to Tom Wood after he had time to study the report. On July 7, 1950, he addressed his concerns in a detailed, fifty-five page letter to Wood. He opened by expressing disappointment that Wood had failed to send him the report in a preliminary draft before sending a final version to Cunningham. He told Wood that there was much in the report that was reasonable, but also that Wood should have met with him before the final version was released because "at present there is much in the Analysis that seems to me wrong, and much omitted that should have been given attention." The range of his comments, both substantial and caviling, made evident his displeasure at spending his time with someone with no understanding of scholarly publishing. Couch picked apart every error, real or imagined, that Wood had made in describing the work of the University of Chicago Press. He found many.

Most of Couch's quibbles with Wood's report dealt with accounting procedures and printing terminology. All of this was interspersed with a narrative explaining his differences with the business office and the Central Administration and his own vision of academic publishing. Much of Couch's problem with the report derived from Wood's failure to address issues that Couch considered critical. Where Wood found the printing operation to be efficient and effective, Couch found inefficiencies and waste. He pointed out to Wood that for every hour a Chicago press composer worked at the Linotype keyboard, it took someone else twenty-four minutes to correct his errors. Composition cost the press some $300,000 a year and forty percent of that was lost in correcting mistakes. This waste, Couch maintained, was something that should have been addressed in any competent consultant's report.

Couch dismissed as nonsense Wood's assertion that the low cost of production in the printing facility was the result of the low non-union wage scale. If he were allowed by the business office to increase the pay-rate of the printers in the department, he would and could hire more competent pressmen who would decrease the total costs of the operation. As he told Wood, "Good management has known for a long time that it is not always true that low wages mean lower operating costs." Higher wages bought better workers who were more productive.

The editorial unit came under severe criticism from Wood who found, "The leisurely pace of the employees in the Publications Department offices indicates that the supervisors do not require enough attention to work from the employees reporting to them." Couch was incensed, pointing out to Wood that the appearance of a leisurely pace was deceptive. It was not the result of lax supervision, but from "a deficiency in knowledge and skill in the staff from top to bottom." Forcing a faster pace would only increase the errors and decrease the quality of the work. He was aware of the problem, but assured Wood, "these deficiencies have been corrected as far as certain University policies permit." Until he was be authorized to hire people better trained and prepared for their jobs, the editorial work would have to remain deliberate. Couch attributed the problem of low salaries in the Publications Department—the unit charged with editing and sales—to a matter of university policy that was beyond his control. This point, he maintained, needed to be part of Wood's analysis. At many major points in his critique of the report, Couch noted that Wood failed to ask the right question or to provide useful answers. Wood did agree, however, with one major point Couch had been trying to make to the administration since he arrived at Chicago.

Wood observed that the head of the university press must be part of the administration of the university and his responsibilities should not be divided. Couch had been arguing for this on essentially the same terms since he arrived. He had accepted the job with the understanding that he would be reporting directly to Hutchins.[16] Hutchins, however, had delegated the editorial oversight that he should have been exercising to Ernest Colwell and the financial oversight to James A. Cunningham. The trifurcation of responsibility was, as Couch had been persistently asserting, the source of the major problems of the press.

Couch concluded his extended memorandum to Wood with his own set of recommendations. These were essentially what he had been consistently urging on the members of the Central Administration and the business office in the past. His central concern was that the press must be an autonomous operation. A university press was a speculative enterprise that needed budgetary flexibility and accurate accounting, and its director needed to hold and to exercise complete control over the operation if he was to be held responsible for the success of the press. The practice of members of the business office and the Central Administration directly interacting with members of the press staff in an official capacity and making instrumental decisions about costs, employee salaries, hiring, and prices without consulting the director could only be detrimental to the success of the press. He told Wood, "The criteria used by the business management of the University ought to be more of the nature of those of a banker considering the lending of money to a corporation than of a higher officer in a staff giving orders to subordinates."[17]

At the Board of University Publications meeting on April 28, 1950, the Committee on Finances, the committee that Cunningham had ordered Couch to abolish a year earlier, reported. After a year, the committee was still trying to determine the dimensions of its responsibilities and authority and readily acknowledged that what it could do was limited. It did conclude, though, that any committee charged with examining the finances of the press would inexorably be drawn into considering the ways in which costs were allocated among the publishing ventures in which the press engaged. The three members of the committee knew that by examining the costs of the press, they would intrude on larger issues that affected the financial affairs of the university, but felt that they could give some assistance to Couch in arriving at decisions about the publishing program. They defined a measured charge that purposefully limited their activities to a purely advisory role in the press's operations.[18]

Cunningham called Couch into his office for a meeting with him, Colwell, and Matthews, on May 26, 1950, and told him to bring the minutes of the latest meeting of the publications board. This was the minutes for the April 28th meeting at which the finance committee reported. Couch brought the minutes of the March 29, 1950, meeting, which were the latest that had been distributed. Cunningham objected that were not the minutes he had demanded. Couch assured him that those were the last minutes that were distributed and Cunningham replied that that Colwell had the minutes from the April 28th meeting. Cunningham then went to Colwell's office and retrieved the April minutes, triumphantly laying them before Couch. Cunningham told Couch that he should have known that the minutes were available, accusing Couch of lying about not having them. The minutes Colwell had were the original typewritten ones. Couch replied that the distributed minutes were always mimeographed and that he had no idea of how Colwell had gotten the set that Cunningham produced.

Cunningham turned to the last pages of the April 28th minutes containing the report of the board's finance committee, demanding an explanation from Couch for having this report in the document. Cunningham reiterated his position from a year earlier, telling Couch that a committee of the board had no authority to deal with financial matters and that Couch should not have allowed the committee to continue its work or to allow the report in the minutes since in doing so it established a university policy that could not be countenanced by the administration. Couch knew that this statement was complete nonsense, but held his tongue. When Colwell jointed the meeting to harangue Couch over the matter, Couch asked him to specify precisely which questions the publications board was forbidden to consider. Colwell told him that any financial issue was completely outside the limits. Couch objected to this, again, telling Colwell and Cunningham that the board needed to understand the financial situation in order to make reasonable decisions about editorial policies. To this, Colwell reiterated his position that the board was only concerned with judgments on particular manuscripts submitted to the press for publication. Cost was not and could not be part of its purview.[19]

After the adversity cooled somewhat, Colwell and Couch met again to discuss the role of the board and its committee and Colwell finally acknowledged some value in having the board establish a committee to advise Couch on allocating university funds used to subsidize books and journals that were expected to incur losses because of limited sales potential. Couch pointed out to Colwell that these were issues that board members had to fully understand. Colwell's dictum that the board refrain from considering costs prohibited Couch from fully informing the board of pertinent information. The board needed to know the costs and an order from Couch to curtail in-press changes and other production costs would be insufficient. Couch bluntly told Colwell, "I do not see how I can administer a decision of this kind by issuing a ukase."[20] This argument proved persuasive to Colwell and he relented.

One direct result of the Booz, Allen and Hamilton report was effected with the beginning of the new fiscal year on July 1, 1950. Couch was given permission by Cunningham to allow the press to do outside production work in an attempt to maintain the staffing level of the Printing Department and avoid laying off personnel. At the same time, Couch began contracting with European printers for specific books that could be produced abroad at a significantly lower cost than at the Chicago facility. Charles Trout, head of the Printing Department, objected to the policy of sending projects abroad while the local facility was scrambling to find work. When Couch suggested the possibility that the Printing Department might reduce its rates, Trout was outraged.

On November 6, 1950, Couch brought the acting business manager of the university, Weston Krogman, into the discussions of printing costs. Krogman supported Trout, immediately objecting to Couch's practice of sending books abroad, saying that they should have been held to create a backlog for the Printing Department. There was no sense in sending books abroad to be printed when the facilities of the university were idle and the differences in cost could be made up by charging higher prices for the books. Couch countered that the result of this policy would be to price University of Chicago Press books out of the market and the result would be even greater losses. Couch knew well that publishing and bookselling were price sensitive and any single title costing significantly more than a comparable title would suffer in sales. Couch offered to follow Krogman's advice only if Krogman would commit the university to absorb any losses incurred. Krogman was unwilling to underwrite the effort.

At this meeting, it became apparent to Couch that Charles Trout was taking orders directly from James A. Cunningham, who had earlier directed Trout to increase the income of the printing operation by ten percent. Couch reminded Trout that Cunningham was not his boss and any problems they had should be worked out together. According to Couch's account of the meeting, Trout "repeated several times that he was taking orders from Cunningham." The next morning, Couch called Trout into his office for a browbeating over Trout's failure to fall into line and support the policies Couch had established. When Couch told him that he was the boss and that Trout's role was to follow his orders, Couch reported that Trout seemed to agree.

While Trout may have seemed to agree then, it became evident to Couch at subsequent meetings on the problem of the Printing Department that Trout was not supporting him. Krogman berated Couch for formulating and implementing policies without discussing them with the staff. Even though Charles Trout had been an active participant in the managerial decisions, he remained silent. But, there was little reason for Trout to support Bill Couch. Couch's authority at the press was severely limited and did not extend to Charles Trout.

In August, Cunningham had, without Couch's knowledge, gone before the trustees' Committee on the Budget and gained a salary increase for Trout. When Krogman notified Couch about Trout's raise, he told him, "We should appreciate your conveying to him our appreciation of the high caliber of management he is exercising over the printing plant," Couch objected. He refused to approve the raise because Trout had been given five salary increases in as many years and was already being paid a third more than any other department head at the press. Further, other people would be more difficult to replace than Trout. If any department needed to be strengthened, it was the Publishing Department. It, not the Printing Department, brought sales. Couch was particularly incensed that the increase was to be paid out of the sales income of the press. Had the trustees appropriated the money to pay Trout, it might be a different matter and he would, he asserted, be delighted at Trout's good fortune. Since this was not the case, he would not approve an increase for Charles Trout.[21]

Trout's raise was, to Couch, only another instance of administrative interference in the operation of his press. The crux of the issue, though, was the failure to assimilate the Printing Department into the structure of the press itself. The interference in the operation from Krogman, Colwell, and Cunningham, abetted by Trout, derived directly from the imperfect assimilation of the Printing Department into the university press operation.

Krogman claimed that he had assumed that he could and should go directly to Trout about issues that concerned the Printing Department, especially when Couch complained directly to him about Trout's operation. When Couch objected to Krogman "that all questions involving the operations of the Press ought to be taken up with me before they are taken up with any members of the staff of the Press," he elaborated: "In order for me to be responsible for the Press, I believe it is necessary that no decisions of any kind whatever be given to any of my subordinates in the Press except through me, and, of course, I cannot be responsible for decisions I do not make or do not agree to." Krogman was conciliatory and said that he had no intentions of by-passing Couch: "If we have in any way been remiss you will understand, I am sure, that our sins are ones of innocent omission and not deliberate commission." He promised to go directly to Couch in such matters in the future.[22] This was at the beginning of August 1950. Krogman promised to do better, but continued to go behind Couch in matters concerning the press and its operations.

Couch said later he only became fully aware of the whole situation at the meeting on November 10, 1950, when he realized it was impossible for him to deal with Krogman. Every suggestion Couch made to solve the printing issues was rejected, and Krogman's only contribution was to tell Couch that it was his problem and he had to solve it. Couch stormed out of the meeting telling Krogman that, "further discussion with him was a waste of time."[23]

Couch stewed over this and reacted on November 13, 1950, with a series of memos. He sent three separate ones to Krogman, each with the heading, "Financial and Managerial Policies," that detailed his rational and business-like approaches to the printing problems and Krogman's irrational reactions to them. These issues were ones Couch evidently had intended to discuss with Krogman on November 10, but Krogman's intransigence precluded any rational approach.

Couch's first memo in the series was a summary of the November 10th meeting. Krogman had affirmed that he wanted the books that Couch was contracting out to European printers given to the Printing Department of the press. When Couch asked him about the increased costs of printing using the Chicago facility, Krogman refused to authorize any increase in the university subsidy to the press. When Couch showed him the sales accounts of the press and pointed out that they were not accurate because the press had no one on the staff qualified to handle the complexities of publishing accounts, Krogman had attacked him for being unfair. He told Couch that Couch's job was to defend his staff, not to denigrate it. Krogman had also refused to authorize a higher salary to hire a qualified accountant. Couch concluded his first memo observing, "You were more interested in finding fault than in helping me solve the problems of the Press." By then, finding fault with Bill Couch may have become part of Weston Krogman's informal job description.

The second memo of the day focused further on the issues that were raised by the Printing Department. Couch had been forced to use the Printing Department's own Purchasing Department to locate and contact foreign printers to bid on jobs. This unit, under the direction of Charles Trout, proved ineffective at either finding foreign printers or in securing bids from them. Trout's people had no meaningful inducement to enable competition, so Couch turned the task over to Fred Wieck who was successful. Krogman, however, had undercut Couch by telling him in the presence of members of the Printing Department's staff that there was no reason to send printing jobs abroad. But, Krogman refused to authorize the additional funds that would be needed to meet the higher costs of Trout's work and Trout refused to lower the rates he charged the press. Couch told Krogman that he had gotten no help or direction in determining what books would be suitable to hold back or how to tell authors that their books had been demoted to a back-log.

Couch's third memo of November 13th, opened by cancelling a meeting scheduled for November 22, 1950, at which the substance of the memos he was sending was to be discussed in an open forum. He told Krogman, "Further discussion in the presence of my staff, particularly members below the top level, until we are in agreement, will only damage the authority of the management of the Press." Here, Couch laid out his issues with Krogman and, by extension, with the business office and the administration of the University of Chicago.

By this time, Bill Couch was on the attack. Couch had less respect for Krogman than he did for the other members of the Central Administration. He almost directly accused Krogman of either duplicity or stupidity when Krogman ordered Couch to use the Printing Department for all printing jobs while prohibiting him from requiring Trout to meet the prices of the competing printers and refusing to give the press subsidies to make up the difference in costs. Krogman had offered the suggestion that the funds available to the press were fungible. Couch could use all of the subsidies available to fund all of the books he needed to produce. It was a simple equation, but Krogman included books that had subsidies from outside sources including foundations and other universities. Even author contributions were to be used.

Couch had dealt enough with similar issues at the UNC Press to know that Krogman's solution could only work for a short time. The subsidies Krogman wanted to use were dedicated to specific projects and could not legitimately or legally be used for others. Eventually, such action would be found out and the responsibility for the practice would be on William Terry Couch. In this last memo of the day, Couch bluntly told Krogman, "The scholarly publishing

program of the University does not exist to support a Printing Department."
His fear was that the printing issues would overwhelm those of the press itself
and become "an obstacle to scholarly publishing."

At the end of this third memo, Couch distilled his complaint for Krogman:

> If the policies I am trying to establish for the Press are wrong it is very important
> that I be shown that they are wrong and that I be given other policies and con-
> vinced that they are sound. This would be a great improvement, but this alone
> would not be enough. The work of the Press cannot be conducted successfully as
> long as the same set of sound policies is not accepted and understood—or at least
> followed—by everybody who has any authority in the operations of the Press.

Here, Couch expressed his complete frustration with the system that had been
imposed on him by the University of Chicago. He had attended the November
10th meeting with the hope of resolving his problems with the business office
and the Central Administration, but had become involved in a shouting match
with Weston Krogman, a relatively minor person in the administrative hierarchy. Couch had been used to having open access to the upper administrators at
UNC. Frank Porter Graham had relied on Couch's judgment in university press
matters and Couch had relied on and trusted Graham to do what was right.
Robert Maynard Hutchins, though, was not Frank Porter Graham.

These three memoranda represent Couch's frustration with the University
of Chicago administration in mid–November 1950. He had no hesitation in
sending them to the man who exercised direct supervision over him, Weston
Krogman. He also sent copies of the three memos to Charles Trout, probably
as a matter of record, and to University of Chicago President Ernest C.
Colwell.[24]

Couch's three memos to Krogman may or may not have been written
before his memo to Charles Trout sent the same day, November 13, 1950. He
wrote to Trout demanding an explanation for his duplicity at the meeting with
Krogman on November 10th. Couch commanded Trout to commit himself to
supporting Couch's policies, requiring Trout to give him a written statement
affirming that Trout had never been opposed to any means through which the
university could reduce its publishing costs. This statement was to include an
affirmation that Trout was in in full support of any cost cutting measure even
if it meant reductions in the Printing Department's staffing and equipment.
Couch required that Trout declare complete fealty to him.

Trout failed to satisfy Couch. He did write a response that barely gave the
statements of contrition Couch demanded, but also mounted a detailed defense
of his actions and his positions on the issues confronting the press. He protested
that all he had done was within the reporting structure of the university and

that it was the ambiguity created by Couch himself that had caused the difficulty. He professed his loyalty to the university, to the press, and to Couch concluding, "I regret that this one serious difference in opinion makes you question my loyalty. After twenty-six years of conscientious service (five with you) it hurts deeply to have my loyalty and performance questioned for the first time."[25]

The one serious difference Trout referred to was that Couch sent manuscripts to foreign printers for bids and refused to allow the Printing Department to examine the bids received. It was a difference that Couch found to be major. Couch read Trout's reply and called Trout into his office on November 16, 1950. He also called in his secretary to record his response to Charles Trout. He opened, "You are not facing the issues, Charlie." He made it clear that he considered the bidding process closed to the Printing Department from the outset. Couch was not going to permit Trout to examine the bids and then produce his own bid that would be, he assumed, lower than those received by foreign printers. He was willing to allow the Printing Department to submit its own bids, but only on the same basis as those of outside printers. In this competition, Charlie Trout's operation was equal to any other outside printing business. He further made it clear to Trout that he did not consider him capable of underbidding the foreign printers the press had been using for the jobs. That question was closed as far as Couch was concerned.

For Couch, printing was no longer the central problem. The issue had become Charles Trout himself and his failure to stand with Couch in the corner into which the administration of the university had backed him. Trout's failure to make it clear to Krogman and other members of the administration that Couch had indeed discussed the problems of the press with important members of the staff was a sin that could not be absolved and Trout's written defense of his position was inadequate. Couch concluded, "There is much in this memorandum that you have written that is correct. There is some that is incorrect, much of it is irrelevant and missed the issue completely. The issue is Charlie Trout's character. And I am shocked beyond words over that."

Couch may have been shocked, but he was never beyond words. He was stunned almost to the point of incoherence, though, in his verbal response to Trout when he told him that the source of his anger was Trout's relationship to members of the Central Administration and the business office and Trout's perfidy in going behind his back to Cunningham and Krogman. Couch said, "I can give you some pretty good evidence that I don't think you would care to refute. I think you would regret my giving that evidence to anybody. I think you would regret it very much. I would regret it. You want me to state what that evidence is? I take it your silence means that you want me to state it." Couch went on to denounce Trout's habit of telling him one thing and Krogman another. Couch ended by giving Trout no evidence at all: "There are some things I can't tell you. There are some things that if you knew about you wouldn't like. My duty requires that I not tell you these things and I am not telling you these things."

Buried within his response was Couch's admission, "If the time ever comes when the Administration feels my judgement [sic] is so far wrong that they cannot support me as Director, it is up to the Administration to tell me so."[26] Ultimately, the administration did.

Charles Trout was furious over Couch's abuse. When he left the meeting, he immediately went to Roland Hemens who had his own reasons for hating Couch. Three days before, Couch had demoted him at the press and promoted Fred Wieck to his place in charge of the editorial functions and to share Couch's authority over all units of the press including printing.[27] The two immediately went to Cunningham and Krogman to complain about Couch's actions. Cunningham made the decision to fire Couch that Thursday afternoon. On the morning of Friday, November 17, 1950, Cunningham met with Ernest Colwell to confirm the decision and notified two members of the publications board. Neither Cunningham nor Colwell consulted with the board members. They were simply notified that Bill Couch was being fired. Cunningham tried to call Couch that afternoon, but could not reach him until the following Monday.[28]

Shortly after 10:00 a.m. on Monday, November 20, 1950, James A. Cunningham called Couch into his office and demanded his resignation. Couch refused to give it and Cunningham told him his services were no longer wanted by the University of Chicago. Rollin Hemens gloated to Donald Bean, Couch's predecessor at the Chicago press who had moved on to the Stanford University Press, that Couch had blustered about suing the University of Chicago. Because of this threat, Colwell did not want Couch around collecting evidence that could be used in a civil suit and ordered him out of the building by 5:00 p.m. Cunningham then put the firing into writing and sent Couch a check for $6,263.64 to pay off his contract.[29] Couch refused the check, returning it on December 9, 1950, telling Cunningham that he considered the termination of employment invalid. He had been hired with the rank of full professor and could only be discharged under the policies of the university for misconduct or inadequate performance, neither of which had been charged by Cunningham. Couch told Cunningham, he expected his salary to continue to be paid as usual.[30] Couch had already begun his assertion of this right to full faculty status on the day Cunningham fired him when he contacted Paul C. Hodges, chair of the Faculty Senate Committee on the University Press, calling for a full investigation of the firing and of the operations of the press.[31]

The members of the Board of University Publications were aghast at the news of Couch's dismissal and met immediately to consider what action to take. They drafted a letter to Colwell defending Couch's ability and integrity, expressing their dismay over the celerity of the firing and the complete absence of any consultation with the publications board. They dismissed any suggestion that Couch's managerial ability was the cause for the administrative action. Rather, the letter expressed the conviction that "Mr. Couch has been the victim of organizational complications." The origin of this was, the letter's authors maintained, the battle over the publication of Morton Grodzins's book. The management problems were merely an excuse for the firing: "They were an occasion rather than the cause for dismissal."[32]

Couch knew that it would be impossible to keep his job under the circumstances. He demanded, however, that the university administration issue a public apology to him—one that he would have the opportunity to approve before it was announced—and a public statement explicitly stating that his work at the press was excellent. The statement was also to include the reasons for the dismissal. If this statement was provided, Couch said, he would be willing to take a leave of absence until the end of his current contract and would resign then.[33]

While the ostensible reason for the firing given by administrators of the University of Chicago was Couch's inability to work peacefully with either those under him or with his superiors, Couch attributed it directly to his insistence on publishing the Grodzins's manuscript over the objection of Robert Maynard Hutchins. The administration had, according to Couch, merely waited until the Grodzins affair had died down before seeking the ultimate solution.[34]

Couch may have been right, but his enthusiastically unorthodox promotion of A. Frank Reel's book most certainly offended the dignity of the members of Chicago's Central Administration and contributed to their dissatisfaction with Bill Couch. His continual pounding on members of the administration and the business office for answers to questions for which answers were not forthcoming and his string of memoranda to Hutchins proposing publishing projects that were clearly beyond possibility were also major factors in the decision.[35]

The firing became somewhat of a *cause célèbre* nationally. Articles appeared in the stridently anti–Hutchins *Chicago Tribune* and even in the *New York Times* on the incident, and the Association of American University Presses sent an open letter to Hutchins expressing its official dismay and its support for Couch's integrity in the matter. There was neither a response from Hutchins nor an official defense from the University of Chicago administration.

Robert Penn Warren took up the cause and did some work publicizing Couch's cause as did others including educational philosopher and recovering

Communist Sidney Hook. *Publishers Weekly* immediately published a report on the incident that drew heavily on Couch's version of the events since Cunningham refused to respond to the editor's inquiries.[36] Frank Hughes, a reporter for the *Chicago Tribune*, who even then was writing an exposé of the Communist influences in Robert Maynard Hutchins's Committee on Freedom of the Press and its report, *A Free and Responsible Press*, published a piece on the incident in the journal, the *Freeman*, a Libertarian monthly published by the Foundation for Economic Education. Hughes made a strong case for Couch, but his piece was probably written, at least in part, by Couch himself. This was rejoined by a surprising Hutchins supporter, Alex L. Hillman, treasurer of the *Freeman* and president of Hillman Periodicals which published *Pageant Magazine*. Hillman, a University of Chicago graduate, maintained that the issue with the Grodzins book and Couch's dismissal had nothing to do with academic freedom or freedom of the press, but was about the ownership of intellectual property. He sided with Hutchins and affirmed that Grodzins's book had been based on materials owned by the University of California and should not have been published.[37] Through all of this, the Hutchins camp remained silent.

In June 1951, the University Council Subcommittee on the Couch Dismissal made its report on the affair. Couch claimed that this report provided total vindication, particularly since the members of the sub-committee had been appointed by Hutchins himself. The report cited the cooperation the subcommittee had received from the administration in the conduct of its investigation at the outset, but noted that when the members of the subcommittee had become convinced that Couch had been wronged, the administration's cooperation ended. The subcommittee confirmed Couch's conviction that the immediate business problems of the press were not the cause of the dismissal: while "friction between Mr. Couch and officers of the business administration had been developing for some time," specifically beginning with his confrontation with Hutchins over the Grodzins book, and "during this time Mr. Couch became openly and tactlessly critical of the business administration who regarded themselves as his superior officers," the reporting structure of the university press was ambiguous and it was unclear to whom Couch should report. Since his original agreement called for him to report only to Chancellor Hutchins, Couch's position was justified. He certainly could not be dismissed by a business manager or even the president of the university.

Further, Couch's status as a full professor was an odd arrangement, but one which the administration had accepted from the beginning of his employment. Even though the wording of Couch's contract did not call for indefinite tenure as it did for all other professorial contracts, the administration had accepted his status as a faculty member in retirement benefits, membership in the University Senate, "and various other courtesies implying recognition of his academic status." His firing was, in effect, "a violation of tenure."

The subcommittee recommended that the University Senate go on record to express its dismay that the firing could have taken place without the prior knowledge of the Board of University Publications or the Faculty Council. It called for the university administration to come to a more satisfactory settlement with Couch than it had offered. And, it recommended the council request "the Board of University Publications to study and report to the Faculty Council on the extent to which business interests may have affected the basic scholarly functions of the Press and to provide safeguards in the future."[38]

Couch may have been vindicated, but it brought him no peace. Hutchins remained aloof from the proceedings and Couch blamed him personally for the whole affair. Couch eventually cashed Chicago's check, but protested that it was only a monetary settlement and continued to demand an apology, preferably from Hutchins himself.[39]

He never received one. On December 9, 1950, Hutchins resigned from the University of Chicago to become associate director of the Ford Foundation in Pasadena, California, and, eventually, to head The Fund for the Republic. Hutchins left Chicago with more than the Couch affair to trouble him. There was widespread faculty dissatisfaction with his autocratic administration. Hutchins had frequently overruled faculty recommendations in hiring, promotion, and tenure decisions. These essential academic decisions were often based on his own perception of the value of a faculty member's or potential faculty member's research. His persistent attempts to expand his power over the faculty and to control the educational policies of the university had led a significant portion of the Chicago faculty to actively distrust Hutchins. This dissatisfaction, added to the financial problems faced by the university after World War II, had made Hutchins's position at the university difficult. For Robert Maynard Hutchins, Couch's firing was just one more troublesome incident added to a long list.[40]

While Couch and his supporters cried for Hutchins's response, their voices were lost in the chorus of protest over many other faculty grievances that Hutchins chose to ignore, refusing to respond to what he called "even the most absurd reports."[41] While Hutchins would have preferred to ignore the clamor of outsiders, he was unable to do so completely. The AAUP's letter writing campaign on Couch's behalf in the fall of 1950 forced him to respond. Almost every head of every university press in the country wrote Hutchins to protest the firing and to demand reasons. Hutchins's letters to almost all of them were short, terse, and formalistic. Even Louis Round Wilson wrote Hutchins to express his dismay over Couch's firing. It was, for Wilson, an uncharacteristically impassioned letter in which he assured Hutchins that whatever offense Couch had given was the result of "excessive zeal" rather than "improper motives." He told Hutchins, "The combination of imagination and zeal in some way resulted in the achievement of a distinctive record as publisher which his sudden dismissal brings to an abrupt end." Hutchins's entire response to Wilson on November 30, 1950, was typical: "I think Mr. Couch is a good editor, and that he could operate a small enterprise. I think that the University of Chicago Press is too large and complicated for Mr. Couch."[42] Hutchins felt compelled to expand on this when he wrote Howard Mumford Jones, by then a more influential man in America's academic hierarchy than Wilson, in response to his demands for an explanation. Hutchins told Jones that Couch was a good editor, but a poor administrator, adding that intellectual freedom was not relevant to Couch's situation when he told Jones, "Academic freedom is, I suppose, designed to protect independence of thought. Mr. Couch's thoughts are not involved in this matter. We simply feel that it is impossible to operate the Press as long as he is its chief administrative officer."[43]

The administration attempted to further defuse the situation through the appointment, to Couch's surprise, of Rollin Hemens as acting director of the press. For Couch, though, the ultimate insult was the subsequent appointment of Morton Grodzins as the permanent director of the press. Couch reported that he had been assured by the chairman of the Board of University Publications that Grodzins's appointment had no relationship to his charge that the Grodzins book was the real reason for his termination, but he refused to believe it and added Grodzins to his own list of enemies at the University of Chicago. Couch complained that Grodzins had written him about the appointment calling it a "vindication," but Grodzins said in the same letter that the charge that the book was the primary reason for the dismissal was not true. Couch wondered how Grodzins could hold two contradictory versions of the truth.

Bill Couch was appalled that Grodzins could be so perfidious after what Couch had done for him. Couch began a letter to Grodzins in November with: "I am sure you don't realize you are being purchased, but that is the cold truth." Couch concluded, "After I saved you from a lynching, you, in the public eye, are willing to consider joining my lynchers."[44]

Following Couch's dismissal, there were several changes at the press. Fred Wieck, who fully supported Couch, resigned in protest to take a short-term job with the Newberry Library and eventually landed an editorial job with publisher Henry Regnery. Several other staff members at the press followed Wieck and Couch in leaving Chicago. The Printing Department with Charles Trout in charge was moved out of the university press and placed directly under the business office. The income from printing was to go into the university's general fund, and the losses of the press were to be paid by annual subsidies from the university.[45]

Couch's experience with the University of Chicago had soured him on university presses and academe in a profound way. He felt that the Chicago firing had made his chances of finding another job in academic publishing impossible. As long as the cloud hung over him and the issue failed to get the thorough public hearing he wanted, no university press would hire him. Even the natural defender of intellectual freedom, the academic community, could not help. He wrote to his friend, Virginius Dabney, editor of the *Richmond* (VA) *Times-Dispatch*, that he had been told by friends on the Chicago faculty not to expect help from that sector "because I was not a Communist, was not suspected of being a Communist—was not even a Communist sympathizer." Couch knew that the only offenders who could hope for a fair trial in academe, especially when Hutchins sat as judge, were Communists.[46]

Couch blamed Robert Maynard Hutchins directly for the firing and took every opportunity he had to make his case. In May 1954, he submitted an article on Hutchins to *Collier's Magazine*. The piece, entitled "Hutchins and Full, Frank, Free Discussion," was rejected for publication.[47] The thrust of Couch's argument was that Hutchins, while pretending to be a champion of intellectual and academic freedom, had had the temerity to take Senator Joseph McCarthy to task in the pages of *Look Magazine* for what Hutchins condemned as McCarthy's chilling effect on the substance of academic discourse. Couch countered that anyone who could be "cowed" by a mere accusation was unworthy of respect and that McCarthy, unlike Hutchins, had never been responsible for getting anyone fired without giving them a hearing. His own experience at Chicago proved Hutchins a worse offender of intellectual freedom than McCarthy.

Couch proceeded to compare his treatment under Hutchins to what Hutchins himself had written condemning Joseph McCarthy. In all particulars, Couch attempted to demonstrate that the actions of Hutchins were more detrimental to the concept of academic freedom that those of McCarthy. Prior to the rejection of the piece by *Collier's Magazine*, Couch had tried to sell it to the *American Mercury*. He wrote to William F. Buckley, Jr., a staunch supporter of Senator McCarthy, that he was not enthusiastic about publishing it, but many friends who were concerned about Hutchins's attacks on McCarthy had urged him on.[48] The *American Mercury* declined the article, but Couch continued to revise the piece for years afterward hoping to find a publisher.[49]

In the articles Couch prepared for general publication, he accused Hutchins of many errors in judgment, fallacies in logic, and, frequently, failures to live up to his own high ethical standards. Couch drew back, though, from what he came to perceive as the essential problem between him and Hutchins: he was a conservative, Hutchins was a Communist.

Couch was not the only one who thought Hutchins a Communist. Most conservatives through the 1950s and later viewed him as a clear danger to America. Perhaps the basis for this charge began as early as January 12, 1944, when Hutchins, addressing the annual dinner sponsored by the University of Chicago Trustees at Chicago's South Shore Country Club, said, among other startling pronouncements, that the customary means of determining faculty compensation was wrong in any situation that demanded the sort of close communal activity that characterized American higher education. According to Hutchins, "The only basis of compensation in a true community is need." Hutchins, who was undoubtedly the best known college president in America and probably the best known educator, may or may not have been a "Brooks Brothers Bolshevik" as Milton Mayer once characterized him, but he did become known to Americans as the epitome of liberalism and was continually castigated in the conservative media for his leftist views. Most commentators even on the right would not have gone as far as the editors of the *American Legion Magazine* who professed horror that a man such as Hutchins, when he became head of the Ford Foundation's Fund for the Republic, could control fifteen million dollars to promote Communism when the source of the funds, the Ford Motor Company, did not spend that much to sell Fords. The editors concluded, "For this amount he may not be able to prove that black is white, but he's doing a pretty good job of selling unthinking Americans the idea that red is really red, white and blue."[50]

Though Couch frequently protested that he wanted to forget and have his unfortunate career at Chicago forgotten by everyone, his antipathy to Hutchins was widely known. Late in 1952, he was approached by Edward C. Kennelly, a lawyer for the U.S. House of Representatives Select Committee to Investigate and Study Educational and Philanthropic Foundations and Other Comparable Organizations Which Are Exempt from Federal Income Taxation, a committee created to determine the extent to which Communist influences extended into tax-exempt philanthropic foundations. Kennelly was interested in what Couch knew about Hutchins's leftist leanings. While Couch had much to say on the subject, he was reluctant to involve himself in the investigation. Couch was unimpressed with Kennelly's ability, characterizing him as "dumb," when he complained to Fred Wieck that Kennelly was "looking for something, but doesn't know what it is he's looking for, and not capable of finding out." Couch was apprehensive of facing a congressional committee if people with Kennelly's limited intellectual ability were involved, but concluded that he would "have to take the chance" if called upon to testify.[51] Fortunately, he was not called.

One major reason for the committee's failure to call Couch was, probably, Couch's insistence on rewriting its agenda. The problem, Couch insisted to Kennelly, was not the overt influence of Communists on the foundations, but the subtle drift to the left "by people who honestly think they are defending or developing democracy." He dismissed the notion "that the intellectuals of the country have been consciously working for Communism" as absurd, assuring Kennelly that the more basic problem was caused by an intellectual elite that controlled the foundations and failed to recognize that it was leading the country into Communism.[52]

Couch attempted to interest Kennelly in his version of the situation. Even though he offered what he considered compelling evidence that Hutchins was a Communist, Kennelly remained unmoved. To be sure, Couch's evidence was slender, consisting of hearing Hutchins, on more than one occasion, make the statement at meetings of the deans of the University of Chicago "that a real university would have a convinced Communist on its faculty." Couch said that he would have asked Hutchins why he did not hire Nazis also, except he already knew the reason. Communists were acceptable. Nazis were not.

The House committee, chaired by Representative Edward Eugene "Goober" Cox of Georgia, issued its final report in January 1953. The committee found that, except for a few instances, the foundations were remarkably free from Communist influence. After the report of the Cox Committee became public, Couch wrote about his meeting with Kennelly to George de Huszar, a public enemy of liberals, foundations, Communists, and the University of Chicago, who shared Couch's antipathy toward Hutchins and his respect for Joseph McCarthy. He said that Kennelly was not interested in his testimony before the committee unless Couch had "evidence that Hutchins was a card-carrying Communist." Couch told de Huszar that he had been asked to write an article for the *Chicago Magazine* in which he maintained "that willingness to hear advocacy of Communism along with unwillingness to hear advocacy of Nazism was one of the tests for the presence of pro–Communism." The editors declined to publish his article and Couch had been forced to submit another on a safer subject. Couch concluded, "The academic world has been so tender in its feeling toward Communism that it has been incapable of examining this feeling and being rational about it."[53]

Even after his travail at the University of Chicago was over and Couch had eventually moved on to other endeavors, he continued to brood over his mistreatment by Robert Maynard Hutchins for the rest of his life. In 1955, the Henry Regnery Company published Russell Kirk's book, *Academic Freedom:*

An Essay in Definition. In it, Kirk devoted considerable attention to Couch's firing at Chicago. Kirk, while obviously using information about the event supplied directly by Couch, did not castigate Hutchins as vehemently as Couch himself did. Kirk concluded that Hutchins's opposition to the publication of Grodzins's book probably "was taken in hasty support of his subordinates; and, having once decided, Mr. Hutchins was too proud to turn back."[54] To be sure, Kirk did not exonerate Hutchins, but he did refuse to go as far as Couch in placing the blame entirely on the former chancellor of the University of Chicago.

Couch was concerned over Kirk's publication of his story. He wrote to Fred Wieck expressing his apprehension over the reaction of potential employers to the spread of his reputation as a difficult employee.[55] Yet, Couch himself had done his utmost since leaving Chicago to keep the episode alive in the public forum. He even had Kirk's publisher, Henry Regnery, send out complementary copies of Kirk's book to many of his supporters.[56]

When Daniel Singal interviewed Couch in 1970 for the Columbia University Oral History Office, Couch maintained that the only contact he had had with Kirk about the Chicago affair was when he sent him some documents relating to the problems Couch had had with Hutchins. This may have been true, but Couch's memory at many points in his narrative was faulty, and he more probably offered Kirk as much assistance as he did to E. Merrill Root, the poet laureate of anti–Communism, who included the story in his 1961 book *Collectivism on the Campus: The Battle for the Minds in American Colleges.*

Root approached Couch about his story in 1954 and Couch was pleased to give him every assistance including sending Root proof copies of the Kirk article on academic freedom which was then in press for the 1954 *Collier's Encyclopedia Year Book.* He also sent a piece written by Fred Wieck on the affair which had been rejected by the periodical, *Poetry,* because of, according to Couch, pressure from the University of Chicago. Couch did all he could to help Root and the words in Root's conclusion to his account of Couch at Chicago, "The Couch affair is an instance of a conservative falling among 'liberals,'" reflect Couch's own comment to Root on the incident."[57]

Couch considered several alternatives after Hutchins fired him, some holding more appeal than others. Couch was in no pressing need to find employment. The settlement he had reached with the university left him with some resources. He did receive an immediate job offer from Stanley Pargellis of the Newberry Library in Chicago who had hired Fred Wieck. Couch had served as an evaluator of the applications for the Newberry Library Fellowships for several years. He declined this offer, feeling that he could not successfully pursue his case against Hutchins from a library.[58] He and his wife, Elizabeth, toured the South looking for a place to settle, but found property costs too high, especially in Chapel Hill, where he preferred to live. They finally settled on a run-down farmhouse on nine acres of land in Medfield, Massachusetts. He was accepted at Harvard to begin graduate work in political science in February 1951, but never began classes there. At the age of fifty, he thought himself too old for such a dramatic career change.

By April 1951, he had had enough of professional idleness and earnestly began a job search by contacting trade publishers about potential employment. He wrote Nicholas Wreden of Dutton, Kurt Wolff of Pantheon, and Fred Melcher of Bowker, among others, asking each of them to meet with him about job prospects. At the same time, he considered the possibility of joining Prentice-Hall which was starting a Canadian subsidiary, but this prospect had fallen through by the summer. He was approached by the publisher of *Compton's Pictured Encyclopedia* about a job as managing editor, but declined. He said that even though he knew about editing and something about children's books, he did not consider himself qualified for the kind of work that editing a children's reference work would entail.[59]

The possibility of working for conservative publisher Henry Regnery was one that appealed to him, but Regnery couldn't pay Couch what he needed for the job.[60] When Russell Kirk published *The Conservative Mind* in 1953 with Henry Regnery, Couch regretted his decision. He wrote his friend at Regnery, Fred Wieck, expressing his pleasure: "In twenty-five years of publishing, years during which I was anxiously looking for MSS like Kirk's, I received two, Donald Davidson's *Attack on Leviathan* and Richard Weaver's *Ideas Have Consequences*. If I had done nothing else during my twenty-five years, I feel that I would have justified my existence as publisher by making these volumes available to the public. But they do not do the job that Kirk does."[61]

Couch clearly conceived of publishing as a crusade. The idea or cause did not always have to be one with which he totally agreed, though it is obvious that the causes of Russell Kirk, Donald Davidson, and Richard Weaver were ones that Couch supported. It was, rather, the intellectual combat that was of transcendent importance to Couch. He came to feel that his best possibility was in the arena of trade publishing, though the idea of a career in the commercial sector was foreign to him. He wrote to Carter Harrison, a five-term former mayor of Chicago, in June 1951, when he was contemplating taking the job with Prentice-Hall: "I'd enjoy working for a time on a job on which my sole concern was making money. I'd feel that I was doing something clean and honest, thoroughly admirable. I don't know enough about PH to say that working for them would be like working for an honest bawd, but I can say, without knowing this, that working for an honest bawd is better than working for a dishonest one."

Couch's dishonest bawd was the University of Chicago. He compared his ouster there to a lynching and Hutchins and the Chicago administration were the mob. But, he also acknowledged his own culpability in the matter. He had expected the administration at the University of Chicago to act within the constraints of academic integrity and it had not. Going with a commercial publisher, he recognized, would imply a different basis of action and a different purpose. While he could not expect to be paid as much as he had been at Chicago, that was the price he would have to accept and, he admitted, he would be willing to pay more. But, with a trade publisher, the price buys a different commodity: "It is not honest, in my opinion, to accept a job with such a firm, a job that implies willingness to work to make money, and then not work with everything you've got to serve this purpose."[62] The clear purpose and function of trade publishing was attractive after the years of ambiguity with university presses. Issues of intellectual freedom and ideals of scholarly integrity were not important to publishing for profit.

Bill Couch was also considering other possibilities. He had been corresponding for the past year with Lucille Cardin Crain, a woman who had made a career of anti–Communism and right-wing causes. Crain was the editor of the *Educational Reviewer*, a journal sponsored by the Conference of American Small Business Organizations. The journal had begun with modest funding from William F. Buckley, Sr., as a Catholic answer to the insidious intrusion of collectivist and Communist propaganda into American schools and colleges.[63] A. J. Liebling has suggested that the Conference of American Small Business Organizations was of unknown membership, the sponsor of anti-labor propaganda, and may have had ties to the old America First Committee, which had opposed the entry of the United States into World War II until the attack on Pearl Harbor.[64] He may have been correct on at least two of these charges. In 1950, the U.S. House of Representatives Select Committee on Lobbying Activities published its report on the Conference of American Small Business Organizations which found that even though the organization claimed a dues-paying membership of some 2,875 including businesses and trade organizations as well as individual members, the actual membership and, more importantly, the names of contributors to the organization were hidden. It was evident also that the definition of small business was being stretched as far as it could go. The House committee identified several multi-million dollar corporations giving substantial support to the group. Further, the conference urged its members to limit their contributions to $499 to avoid the necessity of having to report them to Congress and encouraged large corporations to purchase memberships for their executives and employees. The committee found that rather than operating as an organization dedicated to consensual action, the agenda and the activities of the conference were largely controlled by its chairman, Fred A. Virkus, a Republican Party activist who had served in the Illinois legislature, and a few of his close associates.

The House committee addressed one of its harshest criticisms to the *Educational Reviewer*, which the report characterized as an "ingenious contribution to the encyclopedia of pressure tactics." What the report deplored were not the views expressed in the *Educational Reviewer*, but that the conference was attempting to establish those views "as the standard of orthodoxy in the schools of the Nation." As the report explained, "the review of textbooks by self-appointed experts, especially when undertaken under the aegis of an organization having a distinctive legislative ax to grind, smacks too much of the book-burning orgies of Nuremberg to be accepted by thoughtful Americans without foreboding and alarm."[65] It is evident, though, that the large amounts of money raised by the Conference of American Small Business Organizations was used almost exclusively for lobbying activities and little of it went to the journal. The *Educational Reviewer* was financially straitened and finding money to continue publishing was a major activity of Lucille Crain.

The journal itself was a poor, homely affair, more of a newsletter than a quarterly, photo-offset on cheap paper, and rarely numbered as many as ten pages. From the beginning, it proclaimed that it was not a partisan effort, but was "biased in favor of both personal liberty and economic liberty, which are indivisible, and which are the basis of the American system." Lucille Crain announced in the first issue, the *Educational Reviewer* "will rest its case on the premise that the encroachment of centralized political power upon the initiative of the individual and groups of individuals is the greatest threat both to liberty and to material well-being."[66]

Typically, each issue opened with an editorial, some written for the issue by various people and some reprinted from newspapers and other magazines, and contained lengthy reviews of three to five books. High school and college textbooks in the subjects of history, economics, and political science or civics were emphasized and most were roundly condemned for their conscious or unknowing adherence to Soviet propaganda. A review that appeared in the second issue of the *Educational Reviewer* of the high school text, *American Democracy Today and Tomorrow* published by Harcourt, Brace in 1942, typifies the editorial perspective of the journal when it complained, "The authors have done a capable and adroit job of undermining the principles of private enterprise, yet concealed this propaganda among the words so that the text must be completely studied to understand its full implications." While this review is representative of the type of criticism leveled against the textbooks, it was atypical in that it was not signed by an individual author but rather by the Baker County Chamber of Commerce of Baker, Oregon, and concluded with the note that the use of the book in the Oregon public schools had been discontinued.[67]

An occasional book won the approval of the reviewers. But, more often, textbooks were found fatally defective in representing American values to students. One, designed for colleges of education, was roundly condemned by Milo McDonald, executive director of the American Education Association, for promoting membership in the competing National Education Association. McDonald objected that the book "is filled with traps for the unwary so that they may be caught and so become propagandists for the Social Frontier thinkers of 'progressive education' who, by means of our schools would lead American youth along the road that will end in socialism."[68]

Even literature textbooks were subject to criticism if not for their contents, for their representation of leftist authors. Felix Wittmer, identified as a former associate professor of social studies at the New Jersey State Teachers College at Montclair, took one high school textbook, *People in Literature*, severely to task for including "the usual run of Communist fronters and quondam sponsors of Communist causes among the authors." He concluded, "This book follows the line, by now accepted, which has immunized our youth to the collectivist poison which is fast destroying our Constitutional awareness." His condemnation of leftist authors was strong enough that it must have given even Lucille Crain qualms. She appended an editorial comment to the review defending condemning Communists and their sympathizers even though their specific writings were not subverting American values. First, she said, including even their non-political writings in anthologies made all of their work acceptable to the general public. Second, the inclusion of these authors meant excluding others "who have an unblemished intellectual record." And, finally, including subversive authors enhanced their financial resources allowing them to give greater support to the causes of Communism.[69]

At the end of June 1951, Couch wrote Crain to offer her whatever help he could to support the *Educational Reviewer*. He was not offering his editorial expertise. He thoroughly respected her ability in that area. He offered his ability as a fundraiser for the enterprise for the rest of 1951 if she could merely cover his travel expenses. If the job needed his attention beyond the end of the year, he would be willing to negotiate a salary of three or four thousand dollars a year based on the amount of time he devoted to the work. He made it clear to her that his motive was not the salary but his commitment to the ideals expressed by the journal and by Lucille Crain herself. Couch admitted to Crain that he had been a "New Dealer" until the late 1930s when he realized that the

Roosevelt's New Deal was nothing but "a movement toward collectivism." He averred that her work was "of the utmost importance" and told her that if he did not think so, he would not be willing to help in it.[70]

Crain accepted Couch's help and began using him to recruit supporters for the *Educational Reviewer*. Couch wrote letters, lunched with potential donors, and generally made himself available in whatever way she might think most useful. In September, he wrote Crain with his ideas on solving the problems facing the *Educational Reviewer*. He told her that the major difficulty was convincing anyone that the journal needed support. He recommended disassociating the journal from the Conference of American Small Business Organizations. The masthead assured readers and potential financial supporters that the editorial policies were established and the bills paid by the organization, which was not true. Even if that were the case, he continued, he did not think the members of the organization were well enough informed to even care about the problems the journal was addressing. Couch was right on this point and Lucille Crain was aware of it. The American business community was indifferent to her efforts to challenge the inevitable trend toward collectivism. She was dismayed that businessmen would not support her effort to suppress a movement that threatened their own existence and would even support the collectivist propaganda found in American public schools.[71]

Couch's critique of the journal focused on his essential agreement with Crain and her objectives, but told her that what was needed was a larger effort dealing with bigger issues than she had assailed. While the questions raised by the journal had broad implications, Couch asserted that she had not reached out to the next level. He called upon her to envision a more focused purpose than her vague attempt to promote "truth, objectivity, and American ideals." This sort of statement led inevitably to equivocation and was appropriate only for a propaganda sheet. If she was willing to settle for that, Couch admitted, that was fine. He, however, encouraged a more ambitious effort: "If you are trying to start an intellectual movement, one directed toward getting and keeping serious discussion of fundamental problems in our textbooks, you will need a different statement."

Couch avoided formulating such a statement for her. Rather, he wrote of the need for "a larger program, one that is concerned with the development of a sound conservatism." This would necessitate stimulating the interest of universities and foundations—something Couch confessed he had tried and had failed to accomplish. The issues that Couch raised depressed him to the point that he begged off from the task of raising funds for the *Educational Reviewer*, though he continued a vigorous correspondence with Crain and supported her cause whenever he could.[72]

The September 1951, issue of *McCall's* published an article on American education which Couch considered a slander against the *Educational Reviewer*. The article was an exposé of attempts by the radical Right to challenge Communist influences in American schools. It contained interviews with Allen Zoll of the National Council for American Education, retired Major General Amos A. Fries, editor of *Friends of the Public Schools*, and Lucille Crain. The author portrayed Lucille Crain as undereducated, fatuous, and "convinced that any critic of her publication is a Communist."[73]

Couch was furious when he read the article in *McCall's*. The fact that the magazine was read by liberals meant the article was doubly dangerous because those were the types of people who accepted what *McCall's* published uncritically. They were exactly the people the *Educational Reviewer* needed to reach the most. Couch's concern with the disreputability of the lunatic fringe of the Right was real. Above all, he wanted to be taken seriously by people who mattered on the issues he was addressing. Having the support and approval of factions given to irrationality could only hurt the argument and the cause and the article certainly placed Lucille Crain among the irrational elements of the right-wing. Couch urged her to respond to the calumny, telling her, "You can't allow this kind of smear to stand and expect your work to be fruitful of good results. If the smear is not corrected, you will draw the interest and support of the lunatic fringe; and if the smear does not destroy you, this will." He went on to urge her to challenge the attack and promised financial support if she wanted to sue the magazine.[74]

Crain took Couch's advice seriously, but she did not immediately feel that the *McCall's* attack was the disaster Couch feared. In October, she could report to Couch that the lawyers for *McCall's* were taking her threat of a suit seriously and that the article, rather than diminishing trust in the *Educational Reviewer*, had rallied support behind her efforts.[75] Crain may have had hopes at the time. But, she ultimately blamed the *McCall's* article for the eventual end of the *Educational Reviewer* in the fall of 1953. She claimed, in her last editorial statement, that the *McCall's* article "achieved its end by scaring off would-be contributors."[76] Lucille Crain did, eventually, sue *McCall's* and the author of the article, Arthur D. Morse, in 1955. The jury exonerated the defendants.[77]

Couch continued his relationship with the *Educational Reviewer* and with Lucille Crain, but it never became the business relationship he had envisioned. Couch had worked on fund raising and, indeed, seems to have been effective, but on June 16, 1952, he wrote Lucille Crain that he had accepted an offer to become editor-in-chief of *Collier's Encyclopedia*.[78]

5

Objectivity and
Social Science

The twenty volumes of the first edition of *Collier's Encyclopedia* were published in 1950–1951. It was the first new multi-volume general encyclopedia to appear in America in the twentieth century and immediately joined the competition with *Americana* and *Britannica* as basic reference sets for both the home and library markets. The executives of the Crowell-Collier Publishing Company recognized from the beginning that the library market was essential because of its large potential sales, but also because of its impact on the success of any general reference work in the home markets. The availability of the encyclopedia in local libraries and, especially, the recommendations of local librarians were the best advertising an encyclopedia could obtain and were crucial to the commercial success of any general encyclopedia. Without enthusiastic acceptance by librarians, the multi-million dollar investment in a new encyclopedia could be a total loss. Early in planning the set, the company had attempted to enlist the American Library Association (ALA) in its efforts to design the new encyclopedia to ensure its acceptability to librarians.

The publisher contacted Carl Milam, executive secretary of the ALA, about the mechanism for having an encyclopedia approved by the organization. Milam replied that the ALA could only review books as they appeared. It could give no guidance to publishers as to what would constitute an acceptable reference compendium. At the recommendation of Carl Milam and Everett Fontaine, then head of ALA Publishing Services, the company approached Louis Shores, dean of the library school at George Peabody College for Teachers in Nashville, Tennessee, about joining the company as the editor of the new encyclopedia. Shores had a national reputation in the area of reference work, having produced the widely used textbook, *Basic Reference Sources*, and had edited an influential column reviewing new reference works for libraries in the

Wilson Library Bulletin for a number of years before joining the United States Army during World War II. At the end of the war, Shores had reluctantly returned to Peabody but was looking for new challenges and eventually accepted a full-time appointment as the dean of a newly created library school at Florida State University in Tallahassee. He declined the Crowell-Collier offer, but did accept an appointment as a library advisor to the new encyclopedia on a part-time basis.[1]

Late in 1951, Everett Fontaine left the ALA to become director of publications for P. F. Collier & Son, the subscription books division of the publisher, Crowell-Collier. The company's executives felt that *Collier's Encyclopedia* had to have some organic connection to the ALA to give the company's new encyclopedia credibility in the library community. Fontaine certainly could accomplish that. He had been a member of the ALA staff since 1924 and had headed the publishing unit since 1936.[2] Carl Milam and Everett Fontaine were also close personal friends so when Milam left the ALA in 1948 to head the new United Nations Library, Fontaine had few ties to Chicago except for his long tenure at the ALA headquarters and the call to New York and Crowell-Collier was welcome. Among Fontaine's first major responsibilities there was to find a replacement for Frank Price, the man who had accepted the job as editor-in-chief of the encyclopedia after Shores declined. Price had been summarily fired from Crowell-Collier on August 20, 1951, for his inability to meet the production schedule set by the company executives. Fontaine had several possible people in mind for the job, but the one who appealed to him the most was Bill Couch, even though Fontaine was aware that Couch had had difficulties at Chicago, a situation that Fontaine referred to as a "misunderstanding."[3]

Fontaine, of course, already knew Couch from his consulting with the ALA's publishing program in 1942 while Fontaine headed the unit. Couch's command of the issues of publishing impressed Fontaine enough that he recommended hiring him as editor-in-chief of *Collier's Encyclopedia*.

Fontaine hired Couch because of his mastery of the mechanics of publishing. Couch certainly could adhere to publishing schedules, budgets, and the work flow of the operation, skills which the company desperately needed. Fontaine, however, did not know of Couch's turn toward the right after his treatment by the Communists at the Southern Conference for Human Welfare, or of his horror at finding that African American intellectuals were unanimous in their demand for integration through his experience with the Logan book, or of the details of his unfortunate experience at the University of Chicago under the liberal administration of Robert Maynard Hutchins, or of his work with Lucille Crain on the *Educational Reviewer*. Such knowledge would have made little difference to Fontaine at the time. Couch's confirmed anti–Communism, his insistence on racial segregation, and his growing Libertarian sentiments would not have been important. To Fontaine, an encyclopedia was a compendium of facts, and facts are independent of ideology. Fontaine hired Couch for his managerial expertise, not for his political or social convictions.

Fontaine made the offer to Couch in June 1952, at a salary of $8,000 a year. This was substantially less than Couch had been paid at Chicago, but more than conservative publisher Henry Regnery could offer and much more than the income Couch had at the time which was nothing. Couch accepted. Fontaine was anxious to have Couch in New York at the earliest opportunity so that he could attend the 1952 annual American Library Association Conference in New York and meet, as Fontaine phrased it, "some of our library friends."[4]

Couch knew nothing about *Collier's Encyclopedia* when the offer was made. He had used *Britannica*, of course, and had heard of *Americana*, but *Collier's* was new to him. He went to the local public library to look at it and was appalled. The articles were superficial, riddled with factual errors, and the encyclopedia's organization was seemingly arbitrary. He could immediately see room for great improvement.[5] Rather than being discouraged over the poor quality of the set, he saw a challenge to improve it.

Couch accepted the offer with the awareness that he was entering what was, for him, a new world of publishing. At Crowell-Collier, he would be committed to a commercial enterprise, and he held no illusions that the academic and commercial worlds were similar. As he wrote Fred Wieck shortly after arriving in New York to assume his duties, "I haven't yet run into any serious problems on the job. The outfit is obviously toughly commercial and if someone should give me a public smearing I wouldn't have a chance. And, of course, if I'm told not to publish something, it will be absurd for me to argue as I did at Chicago. Of course, anyone who's not an utter fool tries to work with his bosses."[6]

Bill Couch was no fool and he did work. Louis Shores squired Couch around the 1952 ALA Annual Conference and subsequent library gatherings. Shores was a sociable man who believed that the best way to introduce Couch to the library community was to have him meet his own friends in the profession at the multitude of social gatherings accompanying the conference. Shores did have many friends among both the librarians and the publishers of competing reference books. Couch favorably impressed them all.

Shores was one of the most prominent librarians in the South and was president of the Southeastern Library Association (SELA) during its October 1952 meeting in Atlanta. Shores, as an advisor to the encyclopedia, arranged for Couch to attend the conference and for him to have a prominent role. However, Couch had few opportunities to meet the librarians that Shores wanted him to meet in a social setting. The association mandated that all members be given equal access to all meetings that were open to conference registrants. Since the Atlanta hotels refused to serve African Americans and whites together at social functions, these were canceled.[7]

Shores did arrange for Couch to address the fifth general session of the conference on October 31, 1952. His presentation, "Regionalism in Literature," examined the intellectual foundations of the South from an almost Agrarian perspective. At a meeting that was widely known by the attendees to have had problems accommodating its few African American members, Couch rose to the defense of the South in celebrating the vitality of regionalism. Couch asserted that the essence of regionalism lay in the power of customs and habits—the same customs and habits that Atlanta hotels followed as they refused to allow racially integrated social functions. Had any members of the audience been actually listening to the words rather than simply swelling a procession, they must have been amazed when Couch told them that regionalism was the salvation of America. Couch seems to have forgotten that this was precisely what he had condemned the Agrarians for doing at the 1936 conference of the Southern Policy Committee when he objected that the Agrarian insisted on affirming the traditions of the South without realizing that lynching and "other customs and habits equally as reprehensible constitute a part of those things which the Agrarians wish to have respected."[8]

Couch had been well received by the American library community. The recommendation of Louis Shores and Couch's own impressive intellectual presence enabled him to establish himself firmly in the company of librarians. After the 1952 Southeastern Library Association Conference in Atlanta, however, his relations with the library world began to deteriorate.

In November 1953, the University of Georgia and the Georgia Institute of Technology planned ceremonies to dedicate a new joint library building. Porter Kellam, director of the library at the University of Georgia, and Dorothy Crosland, director of the Georgia Institute of Technology library, turned to Robert Downs, library director and head of the library school at the University of Illinois, for advice on speakers for a symposium on the availability of library research materials, which was to be held as a part of the dedication ceremonies. Downs suggested speakers for the proposed topics and submitted the symposium outline to the members of the publications board of *Library Trends*, a quarterly journal published by the library school of the University of Illinois. Each issue of the journal was devoted to a single subject and was edited by different people under the general editorial direction of Downs. The proposed issue was approved and Kellam and Crosland were to be the co-editors of the April 1954 issue which was to consist of the papers presented at the dedication symposium.[9]

On Louis Round Wilson's suggestion, Robert Downs asked Bill Couch to contribute to the event. Downs had known Couch for almost thirty years. Both had worked as student assistants at the University of North Carolina library in the 1920s under Louis Round Wilson and Downs succeeded Wilson as librarian of the university in 1932 when Wilson left Chapel Hill for the University of Chicago and Couch was officially appointed to head the university press.[10]

Couch's paper was politely received by those in attendance, but when he received the proofs of his *Library Trends* article, he was furious. The text he had written had been butchered so badly that he refused to allow its publication under his name. The topic he had been assigned was "problems in publishing results of research from the point of view of the individual scholar." Couch modified that charge and delivered a tirade against the false scholarship of the social sciences based on cultural relativism. He only tangentially mentioned publishing in this screed but the charge that publishing was dependent on the prevailing orthodoxy of scholarship was explicit in his condemnation. American scholarship in the social sciences had accepted the precepts of communalism and even Communism as part of the American landscape and scholarly works that did not adhere to that orthodoxy were unpublishable. It was nothing less than censorship and scholars, publishers, and the ALA were all to blame for the suppression of unpopular views.

Couch protested to Downs, "I'm sorry that someone has seen fit to censor my discussion of censorship and, in view of your public stand on this issue, I am sure that you will disapprove of a procedure of this kind in a publication for which you are responsible."[11] Downs was unsympathetic. He answered Couch that what he had written was simply not on the topic that he had been assigned. What had happened to his article was not an act of censorship, but an exercise in editorial responsibility. Scholarship, Downs asserted, was by its nature, "noncontroversial, at least from the censor's point of view" and discussion of censorship in the context of scholarly publishing was peripheral to the assignment he had been given.[12] Couch's answer to Downs's objections was a forceful insistence that the journal publish all or none of his article:

> I don't see the world as a place neatly divided into parts that are kept separate in differenct [*sic*] compartments. In the world in which I live, economics is mingled with freedom, and freedom with economics. We falsify and destroy when we try to separate one from the other. And I would never consent to talk about one and not talk about the other, particularly when I know, from some experience, that other speakers are going to have opportunities, and are going to use them, to say things that I think are propaganda.[13]

Downs was unmoved by this argument and continued his refusal to publish the unedited article. Couch was forced to seek other channels to vent his anger, which he did through a more sympathetic journal, the *Freeman*, a Libertarian monthly started by Leonard Read, founder of the Foundation for Economic Education.

Under the title, "The Sainted Book Burners," Couch published an account of the *Library Trends* affair that excoriated the ALA for its hypocrisy. Couch's title was inspired by a 1953 article in the *New Republic*, "A Special New Republic Report on Book Burning," which praised the courageous stand the ALA's Intellectual Freedom Committee had taken to oppose censorship. In 1953, the ALA had adopted its *Freedom to Read* statement affirming the right of Americans to be free from censorship and called on publishers and librarians to provide the widest diversity of opinion to the American public, including those that conflicted with the views of the majority of Americans.[14]

In his article for the *Freeman*, Couch took the ALA to task for what he considered its systemic hypocrisy in censoring conservative viewpoints and not liberal ones. The ALA's liberal position on intellectual freedom was a sham: "Americans today, thanks to their intellectual leaders and such agencies as the American Library Association, are forgetting the meaning of censorship and freedom and are progressing toward the condition of the totalitarian, that of freedom to read propaganda."[15]

Couch was pleased with the article. He lost no time in sending a copy to Paul Bixler, librarian of Antioch College and head of the ALA's Intellectual Freedom Committee, who had written the article, "Intellectual Freedom and Censorship," for the 1954 *Collier's Yearbook*, with the sarcastic comment, "In publishing 'The Sainted Book Burners' I am following the current practice of ALA committees of active criticism and opposition to persons and groups engaged in censorial activities. I trust this practice on my part will meet with the approval of these committees even though it leads me to criticize them."[16]

Couch distributed copies of his *Freeman* article as widely as he could, including to Librarian of Congress and ALA President L. Quincy Mumford and ALA Executive Secretary David Clift hoping for their intercession with Downs. He was not successful.

Bill Couch did realize he was in a dangerous situation battling the ALA while working for a commercial press. He wrote Louis Round Wilson in the midst of the clash, "Collier doesn't pretend to provide academic freedom for its employees, and if ALA makes a counter attack and hurts our sales badly enough, out I will have to go.[17] His worries were without substance. There was no real danger of counter attack from the ALA. The Intellectual Freedom Committee was, during the mid–1950s, far too busy with issues that more directly impinged on libraries and library services to pay much attention to Couch.[18]

Couch's article did raise some questions from library trustees, but these were handled adequately by local librarians.[19] Some prominent librarians involved in intellectual freedom issues, though, thought that Couch's argument might find support from American librarians and others and were apprehensive that the incident might become a major issue within the ALA. While the ALA was liberal in its statements on censorship and intellectual freedom, many individual librarians were more conservative and appalled by the liberal positions that ALA adopted. ALA leaders knew that Bill Couch had strong support from influential members of the conservative movement in America, notably Russell Kirk, William F. Buckley, Jr., and Henry Regnery, and Couch had made telling points against the ALA positions on intellectual freedom that even some members of the ALA's Intellectual Freedom Committee found compelling.[20]

Bill Couch, of course, knew there was dissention among librarians over the pronouncements of the Intellectual Freedom Committee when he wrote to Crowell-Collier president Clarence F. Norsworthy linking the ALA and the National Education Association in a program to "scare the hell out of anybody who dares give evidence in public that these leaders are really propagandists fooling the public into believing they are advocates of freedom of speech." Couch cautioned, "If we scare, we will be their tools from now on."

Couch attempted to enlist Norsworthy and other executives of Crowell-Collier in a campaign to promote his cause against the liberals and the ALA. What they could do was simple: insist that the ALA follow its own rules:

> Be polite, attend their meetings, get on their programs, and do what our interests and the country's interests require: Insist that if the ALA is going to defend the freedom of communists and communist sympathizers to speak out in public and delude people with their lies, they must also defend the freedom of non-communists to speak out. We can win on this ground, for ourselves and for the members of the ALA who are being betrayed by their leaders.

It was time, Couch told Norsworthy, for Crowell-Collier to exert strong leadership. To avoid the fight would do damage to the company and to America. Couch assured him, it would be an easy fight. The people who dominate the ALA "are a bunch of sheep, and if we say boo to them, and if we said it strongly, and clearly, and showed we meant it, they'd run."[21] Norsworthy did not take Couch's challenge.

Everett Fontaine felt compelled to intercede at this point. He wrote to Robert Downs on June 9, 1955, in an attempt to distance the company from Couch's crusade against the ALA, telling him that "Couch's remarks about the ALA date back to his troubles at the University of Chicago" when he attempted to bring the case of his firing before the Intellectual Freedom Committee as a case of censorship. The problem, Fontaine explained, was that Couch took the position that a publisher rejecting a book was equivalent to a library refusing to add it to a collection. In both cases, someone is determining what the public can or cannot read. Fontaine admitted that Couch might have a legitimate point, but cautioned that the issue would take careful "study in view of the possible pitfalls and of the crackpots with whom it [ALA] might become involved."

Fontaine assured Downs that neither he nor anyone associated with the company wished to suppress Couch. Crowell-Collier did support free speech, but he also wanted to assure Downs that "Collier's, of course, is not a party to Couch's statements." No one in the company knew of the *Freeman* article until after its publication and, "our officers are disturbed, nevertheless, lest the Couch criticism of ALA be interpreted as a Collier criticism." Fontaine told Downs that he had managed to convince the Crowell-Collier executives that librarians would recognize Couch's diatribe as a personal and not a company attack and, as such, it would not reflect unfavorably on the company in the minds of librarians.[22] Fontaine had contained the potential damage within the company.

This exchange effectively ended the incident, at least as far as Fontaine and the members of the Intellectual Freedom Committee were concerned. Fontaine did not tell Couch about his intervention. As late as September 1955, Couch felt the need to chide Fontaine for his lack of support when he wrote to him: "I am disappointed that you have not yet commended me for writing the article [in the *Freeman*] and given me some reason to believe you were using your strength with ALA to defend my right to write and publish it." Couch pointed out that if Fontaine truly believed in the ALA's statements on intellectual freedom, he would have rushed to Couch's defense, however, Couch apparently had second thoughts about the criticism and never sent this letter to Fontaine.[23]

Acting as a public representative for the encyclopedia was only a minor aspect of Couch's responsibility as editor-in-chief. *Collier's Encyclopedia* was, as were all major encyclopedias, under a program of continuous revision through which approximately ten percent of the articles was revised each year. Since the first publication of the set had been completed in 1951 and Couch began work in 1952, the encyclopedia itself was not an immediate drain on Couch's energy. His work on the yearbook supplements to the encyclopedia, though, demanded his continuous attention for his first years of employment.

Couch's preface to the 1953 yearbook, the first that carried his name on the title page, was not the usual bland statement of some general intent to cover the important events of the year. He proclaimed in his opening paragraph that one of the major problems facing the world was the relationship of a government to the freedoms of its citizens. He pointedly raised the question of "how people can have reasonable opportunities to work and earn enough to feed, clothe, and house themselves decently without a large measure of interference of the kind that came in America with the New Deal." This was the first salvo of his attack on the establishment of institutional liberalism that he used to frame his introduction to the article on statism by Leland Rex Robinson of the business school at New York University in the yearbook. Robinson focused tightly on the threat of government economic control to individual freedom in an affirmation of the intrinsic merit of private enterprise capitalism.[24]

The 1953 yearbook carried several articles that were obviously solicited by Couch himself. It is evident, though, that since Couch had only started in June 1952, many of the pieces used had been commissioned by his predecessor. The 1954 yearbook was the first for which Couch was totally responsible. In the preface to the 1954 yearbook, he set the tone for his issues again when he cited the radical transformation in the liberal perspective in the prior half-century from one that deplored the centralization of power in the federal government to one that supported that tendency through the programs of the Roosevelt administration. He asked, "whether it is possible to develop a conservatism that will be able to gain enough strength to seriously question this new liberalism," which he saw as "one of the crucial questions in America today." For an answer to this question, he called on Russell Kirk for an article on conservatism. Kirk, who had recently published *The Conservative Mind: From Burke to Santayana* with Henry Regnery, reviewed the literature of the past year and came to the unsurprising conclusion that "the American nation, having attained its majority, seems to require a mature conservative philosophy."[25]

Kirk also wrote the 1954 yearbook's article on censorship in which he attacked the recent ALA manifesto, *The Freedom to Read.* The statement represented the official stand of American librarians, condemning censorship in all forms. Kirk took a strong position in favor of suppressing dangerous books and ideas. Additionally, he offered an article, "Academic Freedom and Intellectual Standards," which brought his and Couch's objectivity and *Collier's* validity as a reference work under attack from many directions.

Kirk had left his faculty position at Michigan State College in 1953 in a dispute with the administration of the college over lowering admissions standards. Michigan State, in an attempt to diversify and expand its student body, had moved toward an open admissions policy and a dilution of course and degree requirements. To Russell Kirk, these changes signaled the abandonment of any pretense to academic quality. The decline in the academic rigor and quality of higher education was a direct result of the erosion of standards of performance and achievement that afflicted American society because of collectivism. Excellence had no place in a system that failed to recognize the achievements and merits of the individual.

In the 1954 yearbook, Kirk also took up the case of Frank Richardson, a professor of biology who had been fired from the faculty for challenging the president of the University of Nevada at Reno over attempts to open admission to the university to any Nevada high school graduate. This was the same issue Kirk had had with Michigan State College. Kirk described Richardson's firing and his own case at Michigan State College as instances of overbearing administrators attempting to "reduce the professors to abject obedience."[26]

Jackson Towne, Shores's predecessor at Peabody, who had gone to Michigan State College as librarian in 1932, was incensed by Kirk's article. Towne rose to the defense of Michigan State and Shores felt compelled to mollify him. Shores wrote to Couch about his meeting with Towne at the 1954 Minneapolis Conference of the ALA: "Fulfilling the functions under my contract called not only for editorial work but for library contact. I took it upon myself to ask Jackson Towne to pick up a yearbook and bring it along with him, drink a coke with me in the convention hall, read the article over with me and talk it out. I talked with him before [sic] Jackson Towne went away feeling less unhappy than he felt when he first called the article to my attention." Shores conceded that Towne was still not satisfied after their meeting, but at least was not as determinedly upset as he had been before.[27]

The relationship between Couch and Everett Fontaine appeared doomed from the start. If Fontaine assumed that Couch held views of the world and of politics that were similar to his, he had quickly been disabused of this notion by Couch's editorial positions. Incidents such as the Kirk articles may well have exacerbated the tension between them. Though Couch attempted to view his job as making a profit for Crowell-Collier through the encyclopedia, his natural inclinations made the opportunity to use the encyclopedia as a pulpit inescapable. Fontaine wanted only facts, not opinions, for the encyclopedia. For Couch, the international Communist conspiracy and the destruction of America by the New Deal were not opinions, but facts and it was the duty of the encyclopedia to report the facts. Fontaine, a nominal liberal, objected to what he felt were Couch's obsessions. Couch found Fontaine "dangerously uninformed" about the problem of Communist propaganda in the encyclopedia, but was never successful in his attempt to convince him of his error and complained that Fontaine's "obvious displeasure" over the issues Couch raised made it difficult for Couch to give "proper instruction to the staff on the subject." On May 30, 1953, Couch sent Fontaine his letter of resignation, citing basic differences in editorial policy as the reason.[28] Fontaine refused to accept it, and Couch stayed, hoping their differences could be resolved.

Couch, however, found it impossible to abandon his conservative crusades for *Collier's* commercial interests and continued to use his position to spread his truth. His commitment to his own principles would not allow him to either subvert what he considered basic truths or to submit to the spread of collectivism which he knew would lead to the inevitable destruction of western civilization. The problem, at least as far as Fontaine was concerned, was that Couch used his job at *Collier's* to actively promote his vision of the world. It was a vision which, because of its clarity and vigor, Fontaine found almost a compulsion. What worried Fontaine was not so much the vision, but that Couch insisted on bringing it to the editorial policies of the encyclopedia and that Couch also found numerous other public outlets for his views. As editor-in-chief of *Collier's Encyclopedia*, Couch was publicly associating the encyclopedia with radical causes that Fontaine felt were far beyond the level of moderation appropriate for any commercial endeavor and Couch took every opportunity he was offered to make his positions known.

Couch's outspoken support and enthusiasm for Senator Joseph McCarthy was an area in which he and Fontaine clashed. Couch, never one to allow his opinions to go unexpressed, appeared to Fontaine as a dangerous radical in his esteem for McCarthy during a time when American liberals were defensive. As Couch wrote to Fred Wieck, "I admire McCarthy as I would admire a man who helps me put out a fire that is burning my house down while others do nothing but talk about it. If the talkers shout and say that the fellow who is putting the fire out is a highwayman, and he beats his wife, and his grammar is bad, and he, too, has stolen from the public, and he wants to be a hero and a dictator—well, I just do what I can to see that they don't get in the way of putting the fire out."[29]

Couch saw great value in Joseph McCarthy's approach to the Communist menace to America, but he also recognized that McCarthy was a controversial figure in American politics. Couch had begun his technique of using the *Collier's Encyclopedia* yearbooks to stage debates on controversial topics with the 1954 issue, a practice that he felt necessary to adequately deal with events and issues over which different interpretations could reasonably exist. In the 1954 yearbook, he arranged a series of four essays on Senator Joseph McCarthy under the title, "McCarthyism: A Debate." The two pieces in support of McCarthy were contributed by an early Libertarian and survivalist, Karl Hess, and ardent anti–Communist Victor Lasky. The two were simply identified as free-lance writers in the yearbook. Newspaper columnist Jack Anderson and *New York Post* editor James A. Wechsler wrote against McCarthy. All four participants acknowledged the significance of the Communist menace to America and the free world. Their only differences lay in how to effectively combat it. They, like Couch, saw the fire, but differed as to the credentials of the fireman.[30] Fontaine failed to see the fire. The smoldering embers of collectivism that threatened to burst into a conflagration of Communism were invisible to him.

Couch's continued correspondence with Lucille Crain and his support of the work of the *Educational Reviewer* must also have played a part in Fontaine's growing enmity toward Couch. Couch habitually reported incidents of his association with the *Educational Reviewer* to Fontaine as part of his campaign to convince him that the Communist menace was real and not part of his own overactive imagination. In July 1953, Crain received a letter from Donald Allen Waite, the bookstore manager of the Cedarville Baptist College and Bible Institute in Cedarville, Ohio. Waite asked her to recommend textbooks in the areas covered by the curriculum of the college. The administrators of the college were "well aware of the large number of left-wing textbooks on the market" and needed guidance to choose "only those books that stand for the very highest form of Americanism." He assured her that "we have taken a firm stand in our college division upon the Constitutional free enterprise system of government."[31]

Crain forwarded Waite's letter to Couch asking for his opinion and Couch responded. He gave his approval to any textbook in business administration because, "there is very little danger of slanted material in this field," but found education texts impossible: "The opportunity for slanting for propaganda purposes here is wide open, and most of the writing done during the last twenty years has been slanted." Rather than recommend textbooks, Couch told Crain that students should read Albert Hoyt Hobbs's *Social Problems and Scientism* and Richard Weaver's *Ideas Have Consequences* as well as any of Bernard Iddings Bell's writings on education.

Economics was even worse than education. Couch urged that students be exposed to all points of view, but despaired of finding a good text since he doubted "the competence of textbook writers in this field during the last twenty years." No one teaching economics was competent to give an unbiased presentation of the subject. Geography was no better. The use of the term *republic* by the Communists was deplorable and the worst form of propaganda, but it was universally present in geography textbooks. Political science and sociology were, of course, impossible. There was no body of knowledge that made politics a science and sociology was absurd.[32]

The problem of Communist propaganda in school textbooks was one that bothered Couch as much or perhaps even more than it did Crain, and they worked closely together to counter it. In December 1953, she urged Couch to write to Herbert Stockham, president of Stockham Valves and Fittings in Birmingham, Alabama, who had written her about his own concern over the matter. Couch responded, telling Stockham that the propaganda to fear was not the overt kind, but the kind that was introduced into textbooks by writers who had no idea of what they were doing and who compromised their message with assumptions that were wrong. He recommended Lucille Crain to him as the best person to turn to for help in identifying Communist propaganda, telling Stockham, "She has helped me locate and cut out propaganda about which I would have found it difficult to do anything without her help."[33] Couch relied on Crain's expertise in recognizing Communist propaganda, apparently on a regular basis, to evaluate contributions to the encyclopedia and to the year-books.

Couch was jealous of his own rights as an author. As an editor, though, he allowed authors little deviation from his conception of a piece and, while he rarely put words onto an author's page, he did insist that the writers of articles for the encyclopedia and the yearbook adhere to his vision of the assignments he made. In the fall of 1954, he approached Brand Blanchard of the Yale philosophy department asking him to recommend someone to write an article on objectivity and the scientific method. Couch was specific about what he had in mind. In addition to an overview of the use of scientific methodology in research in the natural and social sciences, Couch wanted "someone willing to give serious attention to the special problems created by the assumption that man is in no respect distinguishable from other parts of nature."

Blanchard recommended William H. Werkmeister of the philosophy department of the University of Southern California, who helped Couch to write four versions of the article. In the course of the revisions, Werkmeister would write, and then Couch would rewrite and return the piece. Couch said he rewrote rather than simply offering criticism "because by doing so, I could make my criticisms clearer than if I simply knocked holes in the author's version." Couch maintained that he did this because he "did not want to put words into the author's mouth or take them out," but he did make clear exactly what it was that he wanted the author to do with the assignment. Ultimately, the article was never published. All the versions written under the co-authorship of Couch and Werkmeister were rejected by Fontaine except the first which Couch thought was nothing more than propaganda.[34] The extensive work by Werkmeister and Couch on the piece had only eliminated the assumptions of cultural relativism that formed the underpinnings of modern social science.

In other instances, Couch published articles about which he had misgivings. For the 1955 yearbook, Kenneth Colgrove had been approached to revise what Couch referred to as the *Republic* article, a piece originally written for the encyclopedia by Franklin Burdette, head of the Department of Government and Politics at the University of Maryland. When Couch received Colgrove's manuscript, he was concerned enough to forward it to Louis Shores for his reaction. While Couch told Shores that there had been few complaints about

Communist propaganda in the encyclopedia, "The company, like everyone else, had to drop a few people who've been found too far to the left in the past." He feared that Colgrove's revision might be overcompensation for the sentiments of Burdette's earlier article in the encyclopedia. Shores responded that "the very tone of the revised article reads more like a crusade than an encyclopedia article." To Shores, Colgrove's revision was much too far to the right and most political scientists would find the piece "unnecessarily biased." Couch finally published the piece in the 1955 yearbook, under both Colgrove's and Burdette's names, with Couch himself adding a signed preface that exceeded the combined contribution of Colgrove and Burdette in length, under the title, "Republic and the Language of War."

Colgrove and Burdette had submitted a short piece that treated the history of the term *republic* and its political overtones from Plato to the present, ending with a sound condemnation of the way the word was used as a propaganda device to deceive the world into believing the totalitarian governments of Eastern Europe and Asia were, in fact, democracies. Their contributions added little to Couch's introduction, though, which was a personalized, almost passionate defense of his decision to include the article and the necessity for guarding against the semantic deceptions of Communism.[35] Shores was right that it was "more a crusade than an encyclopedia article," but it was Couch's crusade.

Couch was troubled by Shores's reaction to the republic article. It was a piece that he thought vitally necessary to present to the encyclopedia's readers who were in constant danger of being deceived by Communist propaganda. In December 1954, he complained to Fontaine that it was "unwise to follow the advice of librarians" when it came to objectivity. He specifically cited Shores's inability to recognize Communist propaganda in the older republic article, written by Burdette, as evidence that librarians "have been propagandized to the point where they cannot see the truth."[36]

Couch failed to recognize that after years of heading the publishing division of the ALA, Fontaine had more sympathy with Shores and the library community than he had with the businessmen who controlled the Crowell-Collier enterprise. The executives of Crowell-Collier had no expectations for the encyclopedia or the yearbooks beyond that sales would profit the company. Couch was simply producing a product for them to sell. Fontaine, however, was charged with ensuring the intellectual acceptability of that product to librarians. Couch continued to use Colgrove extensively as a contributor to the yearbooks, but had to defend him constantly against Fontaine who thought Colgrove's scholarship marginally competent and his rhetoric inflammatory.[37]

In Couch's view, Shores, Fontaine, and American librarians in general suffered from the same myopia toward the threat of Communism as did Robert

Maynard Hutchins. Hutchins's mistreatment of him at Chicago continued to fester in his mind, and he brooded on the injustice he had received at Chicago to the point of obsession. By the mid–1950s, Couch had become convinced that there was a grand design to the activity in which Hutchins had become involved when he left Chicago for the Ford Foundation and became head of the notoriously liberal Fund for the Republic when it was established in 1952. Hutchins's abandonment of the fight over Couch's firing at the University of Chicago was, somehow, a part of this. He continued to work on the diatribe against Hutchins he had begun writing shortly after the firing, reworking it over and over with different emphases and differing presentations. In one version that was probably completed in early 1956, he accused Hutchins of resigning in the middle of the faculty investigation to keep the decision firing Couch from being reversed. At the same time as the Subcommittee on the Couch Dismissal was to make its report to the Council of the University of Chicago's Faculty Senate, Hutchins had appeared before the council to announce his resignation, thus delaying the report to a later meeting. Couch charged that Hutchins did this intentionally to create more difficulties for Couch himself. To Couch, the reason was clear. Hutchins was intensely aware of "the decisive role that scholarly publishing plays in shaping the mind of the country." Couch was a major impediment to his plans to keep the press under his control as "an important channel for his future propaganda." When Hutchins found that "Couch could not be counted on to bend to him on every occasion," he had to go.[38]

Couch's attempts to air his own case in a public forum met with little success. He did profess that he feared the consequences for him at *Collier's* should the issue re-emerge nationally, but his own sense of wrong and his hatred of Hutchins compelled him to keep it a public issue. When Kenneth Colgrove and Willmoore Kendall, who had helped found William F. Buckley, Jr.'s *National Review*, published an article in the July 1956 issue of the *American Legion Magazine* in which they gave Couch's side of the story a full airing, castigating Hutchins for hypocrisy, duplicity, and misuse of power, Couch was pleased. It was, perhaps, not the comprehensive attack on Hutchins and the liberal academic establishment he would have wished, but anything that would discomfort Hutchins was to be applauded.[39]

Couch's enmity toward Hutchins was compounded by the support Hutchins's Fund for the Republic gave to the various causes promoted by the ALA. Couch was convinced that the ALA, represented at Crowell-Collier by Everett Fontaine, with its commitment to spreading Communist propaganda under the guise of freedom of information, had become the source of a major problem in America. The ALA not only controlled what was available to the public in American libraries, it also controlled what was published—particularly by publishers of reference books—and it was abetted in this by Robert Maynard Hutchins. The publication of the ALA Intellectual Freedom Committee's *Intellectual Freedom Newsletter* was only possible with the continuing financial contributions of the Fund for the Republic. This was bad enough, but Hutchins and his fund engaged in more egregious support of subversive activities. In 1955, the Fund for the Republic awarded $5,000 to the William Jeanes Memorial Library, a Quaker institution in Plymouth Meeting, Pennsylvania. Mary Knowles had been fired from her job at the Norwood, Massachusetts, public library in 1953 because she pled the Fifth Amendment before William E. Jenner's Subcommittee to Investigate the Administration of the Internal Security Act and Other Internal Security Laws, a sub-committee of the United States Senate Committee on the Judiciary. She had been hired at the Jeanes Library in 1953. The award was made in 1955 because the library's trustees refused to bend to public pressure to fire her when she refused to sign a loyalty oath. Hutchins took a personal interest in the case, sending a member of his staff there to investigate the circumstances prior to authorizing the award.

Further, Hutchins's Fund for the Republic gave the ALA $30,000 to support the Liberty and Justice Book Awards for 1957 and 1958. These awards, administered by the ALA's Intellectual Freedom Committee under the chairmanship of Robert Downs, recognized outstanding books that were contributions "to the American tradition of liberty and justice."[40] Couch may not have objected to the specific books chosen for the award, but that Hutchins's Fund for the Republic would conspire with the ALA to make the award was in itself cause for outrage. That Robert Downs, a man Couch was convinced had no idea of what censorship and intellectual freedom meant after having clashed with him over those issues, would be in charge of this award was doubly objectionable.

At various times, Couch maintained that his opposition to the universities, the foundations, and to the ALA was prompted not by the liberal leanings of those organizations, but rather by abuse of their power to canonize particular ideas and attitudes. He firmly believed that higher education and the foundations were controlled by liberals who used their power to promote "left-wingism to the exclusion of conservatism." He added, however, that if conservatives were in power and were using that power in the same way that liberals were, he would be opposing them, too and "would do what I could to see that their activities were exposed in public, in the hope that exposure would lead to curbing their power." It was, however, the liberals and not the conservatives who had the power and who exercised it through the universities, the foundations, and such organizations as the ALA "to overwhelm and stifle almost all criticism;

and they have not scrupled to use their power without restraint" in a "determined, continuous, and powerful assault on the standards of civilized life."[41]

Couch's continued attacks on Hutchins in public, his support of various causes, many of which would have been labeled radically reactionary by the company for which he was working, and his persistent search for Communist propaganda in the encyclopedia continued to affect his relationship with Fontaine. While Couch often cited editorial differences for his difficulties with Fontaine, the problems formally addressed by Fontaine frequently had less to do with intellectual matters than with the organization of the company and the logistics of encyclopedia making. Couch's arguments for intellectual freedom in promoting conservative causes were well reasoned and, ultimately, most executives at Crowell-Collier agreed in principle with him. Fontaine could not gain credence with the company's executives by attacking Couch as a right-wing radical, but he could bring Couch's management of the publishing operation into question, just as Robert Maynard Hutchins had done at the University of Chicago.

In December 1953, Couch sent Fontaine a memo in answer to his criticisms of the editorial department. Fontaine had raised two complaints: first, that the editorial department, of which Couch had charge, was submitting unacceptable copy to the printing department and second, that the editorial department was directly responsible for escalating production costs of the encyclopedia. Couch countered that these criticisms were unfair. First, the kind and quality of copy was a matter that was between him and the printers. Fontaine and others in management had neither the right nor the obligation to interfere. Second, he and the other editors under him had no control over the budget of the manufacturing department.[42] The first charge was nobody's business and the second was completely beyond Couch's jurisdiction. The antagonism between Couch and Fontaine clearly had gone beyond the issues of editorial perspective.

Late in 1954, Couch outlined his perception of the organizational dysfunction at Crowell-Collier to Fontaine. Couch accused Fontaine of a management approach that isolated the elements of the organization to such an extent that communication among the various parts was impossible. The immediate issue that prompted Couch's memo was a meeting in which Couch found that the management of the company had planned a new set of illustrations for a projected overhaul of the encyclopedia for 1956. This came as complete news to Couch who had been operating under an earlier directive from Fontaine that instructed him to use about one thousand illustrations from the current set. Couch pointed out that he had objected at the time to reusing the old material but had been overruled because of cost considerations. He had planned the revision assuming that the thousand illustrations would not be replaced. Couch considered this an impossible situation. He protested to Fontaine that the question was never raised about how much time it would take to collect the new illustrations if the old ones were not used.

Couch's memos to Fontaine were almost invariably complex efforts that addressed numerous issues that he had on his mind. This one was no exception. Couch took the opportunity to bring up a number of problems in the procedures and processes at *Collier's*, all of which were involved with planning and coordinating the effort. The major problem Couch saw was the need to provide an organizational structure in which planning could proceed on an orderly and rational basis. He told Fontaine that what he was asking was nothing more than the establishment of procedures that would ensure effective communication of problems at all levels, that would enable regularly scheduled meetings of the editorial staff with the company's management personnel, and that would result in decisions on the problems that arose in the process of producing the encyclopedia. To Couch, this was a reasonable request and one that, he charged, had been rejected by Fontaine. Couch concluded his diatribe to Fontaine by again offering his own head: "I suggest that you either fire me or tear this memorandum up and throw it away."[43]

Though Couch had come to feel that Fontaine was an obstacle to the holistic development and production of the encyclopedia, he continued to give Fontaine reason to keep him in isolation. In the summer of 1954, Couch made the mistake of approaching Sidney Hook asking him to write part of an article on academic freedom for the 1955 yearbook. Couch probably should have known better than to approach Hook. He had attacked Hook only the year before when he had written a letter to the editor of *Saturday Review* taking violent exception to an article it had published by Sidney Hook. Hook's argument was that "the test of freedom is the presence of heresy." But, Hook, writing on American education, failed to point out that American education allowed no heresy. Prior to World War II, teachers in America had allowed no dissent in the classroom and, in 1953, they still allowed none. Education had simply replaced its dogmas. With the New Deal, collectivism had become the prevailing intellectual force and, Couch concluded, "I see little chance that anybody who feels the urge will be allowed to exercise his freedom and commit, in public, the heresy of making a serious attack on this orthodoxy."[44] Hook's sin was that he had not recognized and acknowledged that the conservative intellectual environment of the pre-war schools had been supplanted by a liberal orthodoxy. Couch gleefully pointed that out to Hook and the world.

What Couch now proposed to Hook was simple. He wanted two writers. One to take the position against academic freedom in universities. He suggested approaching William F. Buckley, Jr., for this. The other writer was to support academic freedom and he wanted Hook to argue for this position. He told Hook, "My object is to secure discussion that will help the reader understand the pros and cons of academic freedom."

Had Couch simply made the request, Hook might have simply declined. Couch, however, felt compelled to elaborate on his theme. In his letter to Hook, he attacked the academic community as being against or at least ignorant of the true ideals of academic freedom and assailed the Association of American Universities (AAU) which had gone on record in 1953 against the employment of Communists on university faculties. Couch argued to Hook that in the 1930s and 1940s, membership in the Communist Party was considered by university administrators to be an innocuous hobby. To condemn such membership in 1953 was, in essence, "ex post facto legislation." That the AAU would attempt to cleanse the campuses of Communists not because of a genuine awareness of the threat Communism posed to freedom, but from public pressure was the true abridgement of academic freedom.[45]

Hook's reaction was sharp. He declined Couch's offer, citing the "burden of other writing commitments," but added, "even if I were free I would not accept your invitation." His reasons were several, but he essentially objected to Couch's use of Russell Kirk's article on the Michigan State College affair in the 1954 yearbook as being "blatantly one-sided" and "self-serving." Hook concluded that both Kirk for writing the article and Couch for publishing it were "guilty of the most lamentable disregard of ethical principles." Hook informed Couch that not only would he not write for *Collier's*, he could not "conscientiously recommend others to write."

Characteristically, Couch reacted immediately. He defended having only Kirk's view on the issue in *Collier's* by asserting that he believed that Michigan State would have given him "nothing but a wrangle" had he attempted to obtain an opposing view from anyone there. The administration of Michigan State College had more avenues of public disclosure than were available to Kirk and, Couch concluded, "Michigan State, along with many other educational institutions, doesn't want serious discussion of current educational policies in public by Kirk or anyone else."[46]

Hook answered and Couch replied. The correspondence at each exchange became increasingly heated with detailed charges and counter charges. Hook's final letter to Couch, dated July 20, 1954, was a summation of Hook's opinion of Couch. Hook compared the incident of Russell Kirk at Michigan State to that of Couch at the University of Chicago, asserting that Couch would have been no better a reporter of his own controversy than Kirk was on his. Couch objected strenuously to this comparison saying that he would have been pleased had Hutchins chosen to make his side of the Chicago affair public because all of his efforts to force Hutchins into a public statement had failed.

Hook's response was final and decisive:

> I believe I am the only one, or one of the few, who has spoken up for you in the academic community. I have done this not only in print but even more often in public discussion when the Hutchins-Couch case comes up. I signed a letter of protest in your behalf, I have urged you to lay your case before the public, and even tried to stir up the AAUP [American Association of University Professors]. I don't expect to be thanked for it. But neither do I expect some one whom I have tried to help—what more could I have done within the limits of my energy and other causes I have been fighting?—to spit in my eye?

To this possibility, Hook vowed that he could only "try to keep out of range."[47]

Shortly before this final word from Hook, Couch wrote Russell Kirk informing him of the exchange, sending him copies of the correspondence. Couch acknowledged his own failure in the confrontation when he told Kirk that after consideration, he regretted the forcefulness with which he had pressed the issue: "I wish again, as I have wished many times, that when somebody bangs away at me I could somehow avoid banging back, that we could discuss the problem between us without the use of language and attitudes that evoke anger." However, Couch went on to assert that the banging was necessary if progress was to be made: "I have to bang at Hook in order to bang at the problem."[48] The problem, of course, was liberals who failed to see the extent and depth of the threat of Communism in all its guises to American life.

On July 20, 1954, Couch forwarded the whole series of correspondence to Fontaine saying, "I'm not sure I've done the right thing in showing Hook the courtesy of taking his questions seriously." Fontaine agreed with Couch's assessment, telling him, "I'm sorry this correspondence got as far as it did. The breach widens with each exchange & we antagonize a person who can be useful to us." The next day, Fontaine and Couch agreed to cease all correspondence with Hook.[49]

Couch's concept of objectivity and his opposition to the quantitative methods of the social sciences were central in the exchange between Couch and Hook. His experiences at both the University of North Carolina and the University of Chicago had driven him to the conclusion that social science and its practitioners in American colleges and universities were fraudulent. To Couch, the sort of objectivity demanded by Hook was a dangerous illusion. No one with full knowledge of the facts could be dispassionate, and he wanted people with full knowledge of the facts as writers for the yearbooks. As much as Couch tried to commit himself to the commercial enterprise of Collier's and shroud his own opinion with academic orthodoxy, he could not abandon his commitment to what he knew to be the truth. In 1925, Louis Round Wilson found him brilliant, but contentious. Thirty years had not changed him.

Couch's vision of the social sciences as practiced at both the University of North Carolina and at Chicago had undergone no change during his time at *Collier's*. If anything, he had become more convinced that anyone involved in the academic disciplines of the social sciences was committed to the destruction of western civilization and that any attempt to intrude notions of value, decency, and morality into these academic disciplines was doomed to failure. Couch tried, with varying degrees of success, to convince others of the problem, which was not simply Communism, but the thoughtlessness of liberals who simply accepted the notion that creeping federal control over local issues was necessary and even essential to the public good. At the suggestion of Lucille Crain, he wrote to Holt McPherson, editor of the *High Point* (NC) *Enterprise*, about the problem and his reaction to it in March 1956:

> Since leaving Chapel Hill in 1945, I have learned from hard experience that it is not possible with impunity to criticize or question the current orthodoxy in the social sciences. I put my neck into a noose and jeopardize the interests of the firm for which I work every time I let anything get into print that questions the orthodoxy. It is backed by the great foundations and universities, by all the more powerful opinion-making agencies in the country, and by innumerable organizations from the American Sociological Society to the American Library Association and the National Association for the Advancement of Colored People. In my opinion the interest of the country, not merely the South, requires that the unlimited rule of this orthodoxy be broken.[50]

Though he knew he could be hung for doing so, he was committed to breaking the orthodoxy that was leading America into a fatal error.

Of course, it was not just Communism, socialism, or even statism that Couch found objectionable. He was a southerner and the attitude toward race that had become fixed during his experience at North Carolina still held. As did many white southerners, he opposed the Supreme Court decision that ordered the integration of public schools in the South. He found a sympathetic ear when he wrote to professional southerner and segregationist James Jackson Kilpatrick, editor of the *Richmond* (VA) *News Leader*, in 1956, that the major problem in the South was professors in colleges and universities who taught that segregation was immoral at the same time as they, as cultural relativists, were teaching "that there is no such thing as genuine morality."

He cautioned Kilpatrick that what he had to say on the subject was "not for publication." Indeed, he had found that nothing he truly believed could be for publication. Fontaine and the American Library Association controlled the editorial policy of *Collier's* and liberals controlled the other major outlets. He was impotent to do anything about it. Couch supported segregation, but knew he could no longer do so as publicly as he could at North Carolina. He told Kilpatrick that he had been approached about participating in a radio discussion program on civil rights and had declined. "The South was morally right," he said, but "the desegregationists had the foundations and the universities and the federal government back of them" while "the South had nothing but inertia and feelings, divided feelings it did not understand." Couch refused to serve as a target on the program for those who "had been so completely propagandized."[51]

Couch carried on extensive, sometimes belligerent, correspondence whenever he felt a public figure had fallen into error or whenever he felt the need to support those who were fighting a world of hostile liberals. Even though he could not publicly take a position in the arena of civil rights, Couch often rose in support of what he considered the moderate and rational voice of southern traditions.

On December 8, 1955, Eugene Cook spoke before an audience at the Yale University law school. Cook was the attorney-general of Georgia and had been invited by the Conservative Society of the Law School to explain Georgia's response to the United States Supreme Court decision declaring segregation of the public schools unconstitutional. Georgia's plan was to use public funds to support private schools, cutting off any school or school system that attempted to follow the court's order. It was a lively meeting during which Cook was challenged on his assertion that the National Association for the Advancement of Colored People was committed to interracial marriage rather than integration and Cook dredged up statistics about the comparative rates of venereal disease among the white and black population of the South as evidence of the moral degeneracy of African Americans. The *New York Times* noted that his talk engendered laughter—at him and not with him—and not a few boos and hisses. The *Times* also reported that the audience was, in the main, polite. Cook had excised a large portion of his prepared talk dealing with the African American illegitimacy rate because, the article quoted Cook, "I was afraid of trouble."[52]

After reading the *New York Times* account of the incident, Couch responded with a long letter to Cook marked "Personal and Confidential." He told Cook that the reaction he received could only have been expected: "When you faced the audience at Yale and tried to talk about legitimacy, you were talking to an audience with a set of values shaped by modern social science." It was modern social science that was, Couch again contended, at the heart of America's problem. The social sciences had perverted the western tradition by abandoning the values that shaped the western world. Social science, he wrote, was "taking this country into Communism under the guise of democracy" and was being supported in this subversion by the mass media:

> These teachings are not scientific. They are propagandistic. The social scientists who have been making this propaganda have the backing of the great universities and foundations and other more powerful opinion-making agencies of the country. They, and their backers, have either eliminated or smothered virtually all opposition and criticism. The propagandists of social science are today almost all-powerful everywhere. The New York Times did its best to make your appearance at Yale look absurd. The publications of Henry Luce do the same whenever they pay attention to such affairs. There is no powerful opinion-making medium that reaches into all parts of the country that does otherwise.

The essence of the problem, he continued, was that the social sciences were controlled by the major universities and foundations and southerners interested in the social sciences "are so misguided that they would like to have jobs at Harvard or Yale or Chicago or Columbia, or with Carnegie or Rockefeller or the Ford Foundations, and they have to support the orthodoxy in order to have a chance in this direction."

Couch suggested to Cook that a well-financed research institute at the University of Georgia could be a means to combat the evil. He pointed to his own difficulty at *Collier's Encyclopedia* in making the "articles in the field of social science really objective and honest." The problem was that social scientists and editors had never given serious study to the methodological problems of the social sciences and had "no idea of how dishonest" those methods were. A research institute dedicated to objectivity and to the eradication of propaganda would go far in serving the country by supporting honest work in the social sciences and would give him, as an editor, a place to go for truly objective advice in articles for the encyclopedia.

Couch recommended the work of University of Pennsylvania sociologist Albert Hoyt Hobbs, a vocal proponent of research in the social sciences based on values and morality, as a model for scholarship. He told Cook that "Hobbs is intelligent, honest, courageous—so much so that the propagandists in social science are determined to starve him out and eliminate him from the field." Cook's response to Couch's support was cordial. He wrote back thanking him and agreeing with all he had said about the social sciences, telling him that he was asking the Board of Regents of the University of Georgia to contact Hobbs.[53] The Board of Regents, apparently, did not.

The nature of objectivity in the social sciences was an issue over which Bill Couch had agonized for many years and his attempts to have it specifically addressed in both the encyclopedia and the yearbook were either thwarted by Fontaine or resulted in unsatisfactory solutions. He did publish an article, "Social

Science and Science," by Hobbs in the 1954 yearbook, but this was nothing more than a synopsis of Hobbs's book, *Social Problems and Scientism*.[54] Couch agreed with Hobbs that nothing about the social sciences made them scientific in any meaningful sense and he persisted in his demand that the problem needed further exposition. He was given that opportunity himself when he was invited to contribute to *Scientism and Values*, a collection of essays published in 1960 through Van Nostrand by the conservative William Volker Fund. Couch's principal argument was that social scientists insisted there was an objective reality while they failed to recognize that the value of their research lay in a subjective realm.

In 1934, Howard Odum had given Couch a copy of Ruth Benedict's book, *Patterns of Culture*, when it was first published and he had used the book as something of a touchstone since. In his essay for *Scienticism and Values*, Couch took Benedict to task for her failure to acknowledge that there were universal moral considerations. The differing ways peoples and cultures devised to deal with problems were not equivalent in any moral or ethical sense. There is a continuum to civilization, and specific solutions evolved by one culture to address problems were either better or worse than those created by other societies.

The ultimate problem, according to Couch's analysis, is that people professing to be scientific refuse to acknowledge that their own cultures directly condition what they see. Consequently, "the role of the social scientist is necessarily limited to that of supporting and strengthening the myth of the society to which he belongs." For Couch, even the use of the term *objectivity* by anyone in the social sciences was nothing more than a magical talisman intended to delude the public into following the religion of science when, in fact, it was nothing more than an illusion. The sin of the social sciences and the dishonesty of its practitioners lay in the inability to recognize that the fundamental assumptions underlying their area of study were ones that were liberal, collectivist, and even Communist in sentiment. William Terry Couch had become a firm believer in natural law. For him, the peculiarities that characterized a society were only localized, ephemeral expressions of a deeper reality that was common to all people. It was this deeper reality that should be the proper object of the social sciences and formed the meaningful commonality of human experience that constituted natural law. The specific folkways, mores, and rituals of any specific culture of society were merely transitory reflections of the deeper underpinnings of human existence. He had made this clear when he addressed the general session of the Southeastern Library Association in 1952, saying, "Custom and habit, in spite of their contradictory nature as seen from one people to another, are expressions of natural law, are derived from the nature of things."[55]

Couch's concept of natural law rejected the positivism that controlled the social sciences. Data was less important to Couch than values, and the social sciences had abandoned values in pursuit of a form of scientific objectivity that was anathema to him. Couch rejected the commitment of the social sciences to cultural relativism, the notion that any culture was neither better nor worse than another. They were only different. Collecting data on the differences was important, but explaining the meaning of the data in the underlying natural law of human existence was the essential purpose of the social sciences. For Couch, the social sciences had abandoned their true purpose—to understand the essential human condition through delving down below the superficial layer of cultural differences to the essential nature of human society. In doing this, the social sciences had tacitly accepted a liberal perspective that embraced cultural diversity as a positive value in human society. Without expressly recognizing the fallacy, social scientists were spreading liberal ideas and even Communist propaganda precisely because they failed to examine the assumptions underlying their research.[56]

Couch's idea of natural law was inchoate, but he knew that it was a paradigm preferable to the positivism that prevailed in the social sciences and rejected honest discussion of the central issues of society. He confessed to southern reconstruction historian Howard K. Beale in 1954, "The most difficult question seems to me that of finding a way to distinguish clearly between the honest and dishonest. And I don't know that ability to distinguish is of much value unless we are also committed to refusal to tolerate dishonesty." Couch admitted to Beale that the nuances of this distinction were beyond him. There were too many facts and it was impossible to separate fact from non-fact. Further, the way a fact was announced could "make it the worst kind of lie." He concluded, "I do not see how you can move unless something deeper than fact moves you, something that you may call convictions or values or standards and that somebody else may call bias or prejudice."[57] Ultimately, it was a question of values, not of facts, that moved Couch and created meaning in the world.

Couch tried to realize his vision of objectivity and natural law in his work at *Collier's Encyclopedia*. In November 1955, he recommended a number of editorial policies for the yearbook to Clarence F. Norsworthy, president of the Crowell-Collier Publishing Company, including one on objectivity that stipulated:

> Year Book editorial policy should stand for free society and develop a staff that does not accept the view, supported by the propagandists of the last twenty years, that the truth lies somewhere between communism and free society. To do this is to accept Communist propaganda and open the way for the destruction of free society. The Year Book should serve a genuine objectivity, not one that falls with the purposes of the enemies of free society.[58]

Norsworthy was unimpressed with the necessity to embody Couch's ideas into official company policy.

Implicit within Couch's policy was the notion that the presentation of objective factual knowledge was impossible. The best that could be hoped for was that the highest moral and ethical considerations would form the framework of knowledge around which *Collier's Encyclopedia* could be constructed and this would, of course, be those of the European and Anglo-American tradition. Couch's job as the editor was to find people who could develop their various assignments with some knowledge of the traditions they were to uphold, conservative scholars like Donald Davidson, Richard Weaver, Willmoore Kendall, and Russell Kirk.

Couch's continual use of Russell Kirk as both an advisor and as a writer for the yearbook was the occasion for direct attacks from the library world that infuriated Couch. The opposition of Jackson Towne to the 1954 yearbook article on academic freedom by Kirk did not deter Couch from committing the same error in judgment again. Kirk's article in the 1956 yearbook, "Academic Freedom: A Report," was a straightforward discussion of issues that stuck closely to the major threat to academic freedom of the year, the inquiries into Communist influences in higher education. Interestingly enough, Couch did carry through his original idea of staging a debate on academic freedom in the pages of the yearbook, having Kirk take one position and after Sidney Hook refused to participate in the debate for the 1955 yearbook, Glen Negley of the philosophy department at Duke University defended the practice. Kirk took the opportunity to promote his own new book, *Academic Freedom*, but his contribution was a balanced report, even though Couch's allowed him to write both the introduction and gave him the opportunity to directly rebut Negley's position which did give him an advantage.

However, Kirk also wrote an article that appeared in the same 1956 yearbook entitled "Colleges and Universities" in which he again brought up his firing from the faculty at Michigan State for opposing the loosening of academic standards. This was too much for Eli Oboler, librarian of Idaho State College and an aggressive supporter of intellectual freedom. Even though Couch added a rebuttal to Kirk's contribution from Lyle Blair, head of the Michigan State University Press, who had been delegated the job of replying by the president of the university, Oboler was disturbed. Oboler complained to his friend John Carroll, director of the Library and Education Division of P. F. Collier and one of Couch's superiors in the company, that opinion was easy to find while facts were not and he wanted facts from a reference book, not opinion: "And the Yearbooks of Couch have been loaded—as I can prove, if you wish—with opinion—and most of it on *one* side. Mr. Couch himself stated in a preface to one yearbook that his major purpose in issuing the thing was to combat 'statism'! Some of us think he's seeing things under the bed. I suppose that makes me an anti-anti-anti-anti–Communist!"[59]

Couch sent Oboler's letter and a copy of Hobbs's book, *Social Problems and Scientism*, to Luther Hodges, governor of North Carolina, with his own comment on the insidiously evil nature of the American Library Association, which he said was "manipulated by a clique of which the writer of the enclosed letter is a typical member." The ALA was in a position to abuse the public trust by forcing reference book publishers to follow the liberal line and imposing its own agenda on an unsuspecting public. The letter from Oboler, he asserted, proved his case.[60]

Though he admired Couch's mind and valued his friendship, even Louis Shores could not accept what Couch published in the 1956 yearbook when he allowed Russell Kirk to take up his own cross again, and again, and yet again. Shores mildly rebuked Couch for his breech of ethical editing:

> My admiration for Russell Kirk's style and position is strong. I have, indeed, cited and quoted him most often as evidence of the fact that America does have an intellectual conservative, and that we in the Intellectual Freedom Committee must be equally vigilant on discovering and opposing censorship of the right. But, by placing Kirk in the dual role of moderator ... and advocate for one position ..., our Yearbook, perhaps unintentionally, places itself on his side.[61]

This, to Shores, countered every principle of objectivity he knew. No matter how weak the other side might be, it deserved more than Couch had given it in the editorial process and the presentation, in Shores's view, violated all rules of fair debate.

Many of the debates did, indeed, seem one sided, principally because Couch drew on the authors he knew, people who shared his own conservative views. In all, the yearbooks edited by Couch carried only seven articles which he felt it necessary to structure with multiple authors presenting opposing views. Most of these articles dealt with political subjects, but there were others. For the 1955 yearbook, Couch contacted Howard Whitman, a free-lance writer who had published a series of articles on education in *Collier's* magazine in 1954, and Howard G. Spalding, an engineer who had turned to teaching and was a high school principal in Mount Vernon, New York, for a debate on public education.

Whitman, an educational conservative, argued that the inability of public schools to teach students basic subjects even at an elementary level was principally due to the commitment of progressive education to a collectivist political and social philosophy that ignored the necessary academic rigor that should be the primary focus of the schools. It is evident Couch had hoped that Spalding would confront Whitman's attack on progressive education and the explicit connection he made between that and anti–Americanism. Spalding had the benefit of reading Whitman's contribution before offering his own. When he sent Spalding a copy of Whitman's attack on the public schools, Couch even gave him the cue to his response. Spalding, however, began by pointing to the logistic difficulties of universal public education in response to Whitman's critique of the quality of public education and moved on to a detailed attack on Whitman's qualifications to address the topic. Spalding refused to rise to Whitman's linking progressive education to collectivism, only citing studies indicating that graduates of progressive schools had similar success in higher education to those from traditional high school programs. In his introduction of the participants, Couch tried to blow on the embers of controversy by alluding to the differences in discussion of the topic in Communistic and free societies. Spalding ignored the challenge and the debate faltered.[62] It is probably just as well. Couch did not need any new controversy in his battle with Everett Fontaine.

Certainly Couch had tried Fontaine's patience sufficiently. Fontaine's reaction to Couch's ideas of editorial integrity is best expressed by his summary rejection of a piece on regionalism by Donald Davidson that Couch had planned for the 1956 yearbook. Fontaine called Davidson's contribution "highly contentious" because "All the way through it is striving to prove something rather than explain something, whereas, as I have said often before, an encyclopedia article should be expository and not a one sided debate."[63] This was a directive that Couch found impossible to follow. Bill Couch had complete mastery of the mechanics of publishing. He could plan and direct the operation of the encyclopedia adhering to publishing schedules, maintaining budgets, and producing an acceptable product for the sales department of the operation. These were the skills for which he had been hired by Everett Fontaine. They were not, though, the activities that most interested him. His use of editorial policy to shape public opinion was of overarching interest and, as editor-in-chief, the arena in which he found the greatest rewards and the greatest point of conflict with his immediate superior in the company, Everett Fontaine.

6

The Sainted
Book Burners

Everett Fontaine assumed that with any topic of discussion there was a basic level of truth to be reported to the readers of an encyclopedia. The best person to do this, particularly in the case of topics about which there could be and were differences of opinion, would be an expert on the subject who was capable of objectively and dispassionately explaining the full range of opinions. Bill Couch was intensely aware that any dispassionately objective outsider, someone not engaged in the argument, could not adequately represent all sides of any controversial topic. Someone not committed to a point of view and who was dispassionate about the outcome was incapable of adequately presenting any topic. Couch wanted to publish "the more important competing views as their advocates would present them," but his technique of using multiple authors, each arguing a different perspective on the truth, encountered opposition. In 1956, Couch was ordered by Fontaine to cease using debates between opposing factions as a means of handling controversial topics. Fontaine told Couch that if he wanted to treat a subject in that way he had to submit a rationale for the approach and submit the manuscripts to Fontaine himself for approval.[1]

Fontaine objected to Couch's policy of using advocates, but Couch did have outside support for his approach. The May 18, 1956, issue of the *Catholic Universe Bulletin* contained a review of *Collier's Encyclopedia* contributed by Francis J. McCool, SJ, attacking the entry on Jesus Christ as being too "Protestant." Actually, the single paragraph devoted to *Collier's* in the review took exception to a treatment of Christ that danced around the divinity issue. The *Collier's* articles on Mary and the Roman Catholic Church were acceptable, having been contributed by Catholic scholars. Couch contacted McCool to clarify this sketchy criticism and McCool suggested that three articles, one by a Protestant, one by a Catholic, and one by a Jew, would give a more balanced treatment. This approach was what Couch had been arguing to Fontaine. Couch knew he was already in trouble at *Collier's* with Fontaine and decided to simply follow Fontaine's directive and have the author of the existing article, Otto Piper of the Princeton Theological Seminary, write an introduction to it explaining the development of various views of Christ.[2]

Couch did have a rationale for Fontaine, but having no expectation that Fontaine could understand the reason, Couch had given up on trying to explain it to him. Couch knew that an encyclopedia editor had to be a polymath or at least someone "who had mastered the great books of human experience." It was, essentially, a scholarly and intellectual job and not a mechanical one. His meetings with the editorial board of the encyclopedia exasperated him. The central concerns of these meetings were the costs of paper and presswork, production schedules, and word counts. He wanted to spend the time on matters of editorial substance. As an editor who was well versed in the classics, in literature, and even in the history of the natural sciences, Bill Couch was familiar with Aristotle's works and drew on them in his vision for the encyclopedia. To frame controversial topics, Couch deliberately used what he called Aristotle's "principle of contradictions" in which experts with divergent views would present their contrary arguments to the reader in an attempt to construct a unity of the subject. For Couch, this was particularly necessary in the social sciences where the same set of facts frequently led to radically different conclusions by different authorities.[3]

In an encyclopedia article, representing every side of an issue was impossible if only for space considerations. Couch, typically, tried to find the extremes of the topic and to find people engaged enough to write about it. His interpretation of Aristotle was, "The best argument against any position on any topic must be known before it can be known that there is an adequate or more than adequate defense."[4] While McCool suggested that three religious traditions, Catholic, Protestant, and Jewish, be represented in the article on Jesus Christ in balancing the perspective, Couch preferred the extremes. The truth could not be encompassed by the three approaches McCool suggested, but existed somewhere between the poles of the true believers and the atheists. Had Couch had his way he would have chosen different poles of opinion to represent, perhaps those of the Pope and Madalyn Murray O'Hare. To his credit, Couch attempted to find competent authorities on all sides of the issues. Couch's debates rarely rose to an Aristotelian ideal, but he was making an attempt to formulate an encyclopedia on his own intellectually coherent principles and not to create controversy where none existed, as Fontaine accused him of doing.

By the beginning of 1956, Couch had effectively capitulated to the demands of his liberal bosses at *Collier's*. As he told James J. Kilpatrick on February 25, 1956, he was "practically enslaved by the prevailing orthodoxy. I have no choice, if I am to continue earning my living in editing and publishing, but to print the propaganda that comes from our social scientists."[5] The orthodoxy that Fontaine demanded called for a strict presentation of the facts and Couch knew that facts without interpretation were always colored by the orthodoxy of the social sciences. For him, the critical issue was the assumptions underlying the presentation of factual information.

Couch may have acquiesced, but he was certainly not content. He complained to P. F. Collier President John Ryan that, after the publication of the 1955 yearbook, Fontaine had taken the editorial responsibility for the yearbooks out of his hands. The 1955 yearbook was the last that began with one of Couch's jeremiads on the evils in America and the threats of centralization and statism to a free society. Beginning with the 1956 yearbook, these essays were replaced with a bland "To the Reader" section outlining the major events of the year and telling the purchaser how to use the index. The differences in policy between Fontaine and Couch in the approach that should be taken on controversial issues was so great as to be irreconcilable, and Couch told Ryan that Fontaine's name should appear on the title pages of both the yearbooks and the encyclopedia in place of his own. This was an exaggeration of the difficulty. Fontaine had only forbidden Couch to continue the editorial policies that brought the yearbooks under attack and insisted on a more traditional approach of reporting the events of the past year. Even though Couch considered it a violation of all the ethical principles of editing, Fontaine's approach would protect the encyclopedia from the adverse criticism that it was not objective in its approach to controversy.

Couch did try to acquiesce to Fontaine's demands. In March 1957, he developed a series of policy statements on handling controversy in the encyclopedia that he wrote in preparation for a symposium on encyclopedias to be held at the 1957 annual meeting of the Catholic Library Association. He sent these to Fontaine in yet another attempt to explain his perspective on controversial issues in the encyclopedia. He proclaimed that he would eschew controversy "in the sense of rhetorical arguments" and assured his critics that the reader would only "find all the more important facts of all the great controversies that have raged from ancient times to the present." He went on to say that the position at *Collier's* "has been to state the facts of the beliefs and the facts resulting from the beliefs." That a proponent of a cause believed that something was true was a fact, but the belief itself was not necessarily a fact. This fit with what Fontaine wanted, but Couch could not leave it at that.

The problem was not the facts but their interpretation. To elaborate on this, he chose, of course, the case of the USSR. The rhetoric of Communism expressed ideals that were fine, but "the hooks of fraud and tyranny are baited with melodious words." He allowed that there may be some society in which the lofty ideas of justice and truth were realized in appropriate actions, but countries under Communist control were not among them. The capacity to distinguish between social orders that served the highest ideals of humanity and those that failed were crucial and the purpose of any encyclopedia is to provide the information that would enable people to make that distinction. Of course, putting the facts of anything "cheek to jowl in an encyclopedia article" would do nothing to demonstrate the significance of the facts presented to the reader. But, Couch concluded, such a procedure in explicating any topic with potential for controversy is all that can be done and would, at least, "bring out significance of which most of us have had little or no chance to be aware."[6] This was what Fontaine was demanding.

This position paper was one of several Couch prepared for consideration by the executives of the P. F. Collier Company in preparation for his presentation at the Catholic Library Association Conference in 1957. It was an attempt to find a position he could live with as the editor of *Collier's* and that would satisfy the objections Fontaine and leaders in the ALA had against his practice of presenting controversial topics as debates among proponents of opposing views and his relying on conservative scholars for single-author pieces. This version of the paper at least met Fontaine's demands. In other position papers in this series, he claimed that facts were nothing more than beliefs that were generally accepted and objectivity in presenting them was impossible.[7]

Couch shared the stage at the conference with Walter Yust of *Britannica*, Lavina Dudley of *Americana*, and Carroll Chouinard of the *American Peoples Encyclopedia*, a resurrection of the much older *Nelson's Encyclopedia* that was sold exclusively by Sears, Roebuck and was a poor relation to the three major encyclopedias in America. It was inferior in quality, but still among the majors in sales in the United States. On April 24, 1957, in Louisville, Kentucky, Couch delivered his talk, "Policies, Procedures, and Objectives of Encyclopedia Publishing," which closely followed the statements of policy he had developed for the executives of Crowell-Collier. In the typescript he prepared for his talk, he began by telling his audience of librarians that the two purposes for encyclopedias were to summarize knowledge and to make a profit for the publisher. As a first principle of encyclopedia construction, he cited *interest*. In what is the closest passage to a real conceit Couch ever wrote, he asked the rhetorical question, if there are millions of species of plants and animals, why are only humans singled out for biographical encyclopedia articles? The answer, of course, was that people are interested in people and have no interest, as did Reginald Bunthorne, in "a bashful young potato, or a not-too-French French bean."

With elaborate discursions into Shakespeare's Prince Hal and Falstaff, Couch affirmed that facts are important, but only within "the theoretical schemes in which the facts may be interpreted." For a compilation such as a general encyclopedia, the focus first had to be on interest and creating and maintaining the interest of the reader depended not on individual facts, but on the conceptual context in which the facts are presented: "The important statements on a subject are always efforts to understand the why of the subject and efforts to understand always go beyond the bald statement of facts."[8] If readers wanted only the facts, they could turn to an almanac, or the census, or the publications of the Bureau of Labor Statistics. Encyclopedia readers wanted an interpretation that explained the significance of the facts.

At the Catholic Library Association Symposium, the four encyclopedias representatives were only given ten minutes each to present their statements. Couch was forced to drop his extended discourse on Falstaff and Prince Hal that he used to illustrate the distinction between facts and myths. Couch had been invited to talk about editorial policies and procedures while Walter Yust of *Britannica* was given "The Detection and the Handling of Controversial Topics." Couch was rarely, as a speaker, able to focus on his assigned topic, especially if his conception of the topic differed from that of the organizers of the occasion or if he felt a more important issue demanded the audience's attention. Even without Shakespeare, he went well over his ten-minute allotment. Yust, charged with what to Couch was the essence of the discussion, controversy, took most of his allotted time talking about his own domestic controversies, his wife was a Democrat and he was a Republican. Yust filled out his ten minutes recounting amusing anecdotes about users failing to find articles in *Britannica* because they could not spell the name of the topic.

While Yust had the floor on controversy at the meeting, Couch could not resist the opportunity to bring up the closely related issue of objectivity and authority without, though, relating them to his central topic of editorial policy. He managed to work an allusion to his central theme of the treachery of facts and the failure of authority into his comments on policies and procedures of encyclopedia editing. It was a meek assertion that certainly did not cross Fontaine, but did express his central belief that the simple facts were not what encyclopedia readers wanted or needed.[9]

Couch could mouth the words in a public forum officially representing *Collier's*, but he was dissatisfied with the position on controversy that he had developed to answer Fontaine's objections. Fontaine's insistence that he use only one author for each entry in the encyclopedia distressed him because it was not working. He told Louis Shores, "It could have been known in advance that it would not work, and this would have been known if those of us who have crucial responsibility in the making of policies had any knowledge and skill in dealing with abstract ideas." It was impossible for one author to adequately and persuasively present all of the sides in any controversial subject with any convincing authority. After the Catholic Library Association presentation, he complained to Louis Shores, "To look for such a person is to look for the moral equivalent of God."[10] Unfortunately, He was not available to write for *Collier's Encyclopedia.*

Fontaine's objections to Couch's debates in the encyclopedia were, it seems, limited to topics of political or social import. At the Catholic Library Association meeting in 1957, the discussion of controversial topics appropriately addressed religion which had proven to be a persistent thorny question for all the encyclopedias represented there. *Britannica's* editor, Walter Yust, confessed that his encyclopedia had been using the article on the Virgin Mary which had a decidedly Roman Catholic bias since the ninth edition which was published from 1875 to 1899. He told the audience that he had been trying for twenty years to find a more balanced article, but had failed. At *Collier's,* Couch had his own problems with articles on baptism, on the sacraments, on miracles, and on Jesus Christ.[11] Fontaine seemed not to object to multiple authors as long as Couch used it for topics that were safe. Multiple authors explaining the relation of Mary to the Catholic tradition and the Protestant view would be a safe controversy. Having two authors take adversarial positions on political or social issues was not. Ultimately, Fontaine's objection to Couch's approach had more to do with the use of right-wing contributors than to the format itself. Religion could be safe while economics, politics, and even education were not.

When the 1957 yearbook came out, Eli Oboler still objected, particularly to the consistent use of "the most conservative individuals" for the articles in the social sciences. But, he approved of the general change in editorial policy, telling John Carroll, director of the Library and Education Division of Collier-Crowell, "It looks as though perhaps Mr. Couch or you or somebody is becoming aware of the fact that it is not enough to print articles on two sides of a controversial question, but it is also important to have individual articles on controversial matters written by people who are not fervently prejudiced on one side or the other."[12] Essentially, Oboler framed the American Library Association's definition of *objectivity*, affirming Fontaine's objections to Couch's approach, at least in that overt partisanship was to be avoided.

The arguments over objectivity, over the mechanisms of the debate, and over particular contributors with whom Couch contracted to write the articles were only a part of the editorial controversies. Couch's own notions of what an encyclopedia should be had been highly influenced by his association with Louis Shores. Couch had come to Crowell-Collier with the idea that the responsibility of *Collier's Encyclopedia* was to disclose the truth about whatever subject it addressed and his editorial concern had been focused on finding that truth in the mass of half-fact, propaganda, and opinion that comprised knowledge, particularly in the social sciences. Shores, however, interjected other considerations into the equation when he insisted that ready-reference, the provision of facts, and self-education, the ability of the reader to learn something from the articles, were also primary purposes of encyclopedias.

Shores had engaged in vigorous debate with Couch over the suitability of various authors and the value of various treatments in the social sciences. Shores's objections to Couch's practices led Couch to conclude that Shores was a hopeless liberal who had been completely duped by Communist propaganda. But, Couch eventually did come to accept Shores's idea that encyclopedia purposes were broader than the limited compass he had originally envisioned. Shores argued from the perspective of the general reference librarian and called for an encyclopedia that could be all things to all users. Addressing the students of the library school at Drexel Institute in 1960, he called for an encyclopedia that would be designed not for scholarly use, but for the layman who needed much more diverse knowledge and information than the specialist. He told the audience that the encyclopedia must "augment the subjects every cultured man should know with those the household needs. Bring everyday ephemera into the summary of significance side by side with the eternal verities so that things as well as ideas will have their space allotments." It made sense to Couch when Shores told him that referring an encyclopedia user somewhere else for practical information through bibliographic references was a disservice: "You could refer him to every subject that way an[d] eliminate the need for an encyclopedia."[13]

Shores was effective in his argument for this vision of an encyclopedia. Couch enthusiastically accepted it and promoted it to Fontaine who was firmly opposed. Fontaine maintained that what the encyclopedia said about technique and procedure was simply a part of exposition. Its purpose in an encyclopedia article was to enable readers to recognize the process, not to enable them to reproduce it. If an article on baking was needed, it did not need to delve deeper than describing the process. It should not provide recipes for pound cakes in the detail necessary to enable the reader to make one. While Fontaine confessed that he had had complaints from customers that *Collier's Encyclopedia* failed to give them instruction on arts and crafts or how to build a Conestoga wagon, he believed that this fell outside the purposes of the work. As he told Couch, "This is precisely the kind of information I have always contended does not belong in a general encyclopedia."[14] This, however, was a minor disagreement that was eclipsed by other issues between Couch and Fontaine.

By May 1958, Couch knew that much of his difficulty with Fontaine came from Fontaine's aversion to the causes Couch had supported and began to take steps to protect his position in the company. His retrenchment took the form of disassociating himself from any potential controversy. He had been approached by Chalmers Davidson, librarian of Davidson College in Davidson, North Carolina, who wanted him to suggest names of conservative scholars for the Coe Foundation. The foundation, established by William Robertson Coe, had funded the establishment of academic programs in American studies at several colleges and universities in the United States and endowed professorships at Yale, Stanford, and the University of Wyoming. After Coe's death in 1955, the foundation had turned to promoting Americanism in public schools through educational programs for American history teachers. Davidson was seeking recommendations for a list of possible conservative speakers for high school and college classes. It was an opportunity to further an educational cause that normally would have delighted Couch. But, he was forced to decline saying, "I am still with Collier's Encyclopedia, but of course I can't mix matters of this kind with my job. That, as you must know, isn't possible these days."[15]

Another invitation possibly caused him greater pain. Robert Welch, editor of *American Opinion*, was a man Couch admired and respected. At one point, he had written Welch, "You are one of the few genuine educators in the country today, Bob, and since I'm for education, I'm for you." Couch had planned to attend a meeting called by Robert Welch to be held on April 10–11, 1958, at the Harvard Club in New York. This meeting probably grew out of Welch's role at the time as head of the Educational Advisory Committee of the National Manufacturers Association. This meeting took place only a few months before Welch founded the John Birch Society. Couch wrote Welch that because of the instability of the Crowell-Collier management, he had to decline the opportunity.[16]

The instability to which Couch referred was the appointment of Wilton Donald Cole as chairman of the board of directors of Crowell-Collier and the subsequent changes Cole made in the company. Cole had come to Crowell-Collier in 1956 as a member of the board and had become chairman the next year in a management upheaval precipitated by the company's financial difficulties. Since 1946, Crowell-Collier's primary publications, the mass market magazines *Collier's*, the *American Magazine*, and *Woman's Home Companion*, had been losing money. While subscriptions remained robust, revenues from advertisers had been declining and advertising was the primary source of income for the popular magazines. Cole's first task was to deal with that problem which he did by selling the *American Magazine* and closing down the other two magazines in 1956 and 1957.

Cole had been chief executive officer of the Union Bag and Paper Company prior to moving to Crowell-Collier and he immediately brought in Raymond Hagel as his chief advisor. Hagel was a member of the advertising agency of Smith, Hagel, and Knudsen which had advised Cole at Union Bag and Paper. Hagel's first assignment from Cole was to do a marketing survey for *Collier's Encyclopedia*.[17] Cole and Hagel, however, were too busy straightening out the financial difficulties of the firm's magazines to immediately intrude into the company's major source of income, the encyclopedia. This administrative turmoil must have given Couch concerns, but his immediate problem continued to be Everett Fontaine.

Couch was frustrated. Fontaine had blocked his every attempt to do what he thought right, but seemed incapable of taking any initiative himself to develop and implement editorial policies for the encyclopedia. Rather, Fontaine sent specific directions on handling editorial problems without offering any general policy to guide Couch. In February 1958, Fontaine sent Couch a detailed memorandum on points of editorial policy. Couch picked only one of Fontaine's issues to which to respond. The question of including cities in the encyclopedia was, for Couch, a difficult one and he balked at Fontaine's demand that all cities of over 5,000 population be covered. Fontaine had been pressured by the sales department which felt the policy would be a good selling point to residents of smaller towns. Fontaine had directed Couch to include smaller towns as early as May 1957, but had refused to respond when Couch, on several occasions, asked for guidance on to how this was to be accomplished and still maintain the editorial integrity of the encyclopedia. The question, Couch reiterated, was where to draw the line.

He pointed out that there were some 161 cities and towns with over 10,000 population which did not have separate *Collier's* articles and another 675 places with 5,000 to 10,000 population that were not mentioned at all. The question of whether these could be handled in tables or if a separate article for each town was necessary was one that Couch complained Fontaine had pointedly ignored. He persisted: "It seems to me that somebody or some group of somebodies should have the responsibility of making decisions on the questions we ask. I am willing to take the responsibility for making the decisions. I am willing for you to make the decisions. I am willing to follow a committee procedure. I am willing to provide more information when I can. But I urge that we find some way of getting decisions, and, of course, I do not mean by this that all we need is decisions whether right or wrong."

The situation with Fontaine had made Couch cautious. He gave Shores his home address to use if he had anything to write that might be too candid for his office mail which he suspected Fontaine was reading. He told Shores that he was, for the time, keeping peace with Fontaine. He said, "If I'm not to have a period in the doghouse, I don't write if he says don't write, and if I do write I have to say what he wants me to say." It was a confession to Shores that he had completely capitulated to Fontaine.

Couch unburdened himself of his difficulties with Fontaine to Shores. He confessed that it bothered him so much that he had not "been able to think straight about anything." But, he also recognized that the right in the situation ultimately belonged to Fontaine. He told Shores: "I have hated more than I can say to oppose and distress Mr. Fontaine. If any subordinate of mine opposed me and criticized me so much as I've criticized Mr. Fontaine, I'd get him another job." It had been a bad week for Couch. He told Shores that after he had sent a memo to John Ryan telling him again that he wanted his name removed from the title page and replaced with Fontaine's, Ryan had called him into his office and, according to Couch, "gave me a really rough going over." Couch expected Ryan to fire him, but Ryan did not. Couch asked Shores if he thought he was doing the right thing in removing his name from the title page, and warned him that he would be seeking advice from him in the future.[18]

On February 12, 1958, after his thrashing by Ryan, Couch wrote to Ryan, telling him, "I am deeply puzzled and sorely hurt by the way you have dealt with me in the last few days." He humbly told Ryan that his desire to have his name removed from the title pages "was written in the effort to avoid antagonizing Mr. Fontaine." By that time, virtually anything he did was liable to antagonize Everett Fontaine.

At Ryan's request, Couch had submitted a detailed plan for a substantial revision of the encyclopedia to be completed in 1962. Couch had presented his plan at an August 1957 meeting of the encyclopedia's advisors where Fontaine had made a concerted effort "to shoot holes in details of the plan" and "to get our advisors on record against these details." Couch told Ryan that the advisors were ignorant of the confrontation between Fontaine and Couch that was unfolding at the meeting, but they supported Couch's own plan. Couch was particularly pleased with the support Shores demonstrated for the plan since, he told Ryan, much of the theory behind his idea for the revision came from Shores's ideas.

Couch denounced Shores as a lackey for the ALA to his conservative correspondents, but consistently extolled Shores as the ultimate expert on the construction of encyclopedias to Ryan and other executives at Crowell-Collier. In part, this was because Shores's views of the functions of an encyclopedia fit with many of Couch's own ideas about education and exposition, ideas Couch had begun developing with the German interlineal translations he had promoted at North Carolina. In part, Shore's own conservative views of American society and politics, though never as extreme, were at least compatible with

Couch's. Above all, though, Couch needed Shores and cultivated him as a shield against Fontaine and other executives in the company who viewed Fontaine as the Crowell-Collier link to the ALA and the company's source of legitimacy in the library world.

To his correspondents, Couch sounded as though Fontaine gave no rationale for his opposition and it derived from nothing more than a liberal reaction to a conservative truth. Fontaine, however, frequently did give detailed reasons for rejecting Couch's editorial decisions. Couch had extended some effort to cajole Richard Weaver to write an article on propaganda for the 1956 yearbook, and Fontaine went into extensive detail when he rejected it as "a good example of propaganda" itself. He specifically objected to Weaver's characterization of Lincoln's Emancipation Proclamation, Churchill and Roosevelt's Atlantic Charter, and Woodrow Wilson's Fourteen Points as propaganda. Fontaine pointedly rejected Weaver's assertion that there was such a thing as "good propaganda" in service to a good cause when he had already defined propaganda as inherently bad. His summary rejection was, in essence, a charge against Couch: "I am greatly surprised that the propaganda in this article and the use of propaganda techniques by the author of it have not been recognized."

The antipathy between Fontaine and Couch over the issues of Communist propaganda and the nature of objectivity persisted. When John Ryan was promoted to president of P. F. Collier in January 1958, Fontaine lost no time in complaining to him that Couch had "made a nuisance of the subjects propaganda and objectivity." By this time, Couch had abandoned all hope of leading Fontaine to the light. As he later wrote to one of the encyclopedia advisers, Joseph Gleason, his attempts to get articles on propaganda by Richard Weaver and objectivity in the social sciences by William H. Werkmeister into the encyclopedia and yearbooks had had to be done in the face of Fontaine's evident displeasure and that Fontaine had thwarted his editorial judgment in virtually every possible way. Fontaine's opposition had forced Couch to drop any article to which he felt Fontaine might object and to back away from every policy decision over which he and Fontaine might clash.

Couch asked John Ryan for his support, expressing willingness to subordinate himself to Fontaine as head of editorial policy if Fontaine would actually accept that role and provide leadership. He told Ryan in no uncertain terms: "I can limit myself to taking orders and carrying them out, if that is what is wanted of me." He only asked that Ryan clarify the matter. Ryan did attempt to defuse the situation. On February 19, 1958, John Ryan relieved Fontaine of all responsibility for the encyclopedia and the yearbook. Fontaine was to handle only the routine matters of payroll and bookkeeping.[19]

Fontaine does appear to have made an effort to give Couch a free hand in determining the editorial policy for the encyclopedia. When he was relieved of responsibility, he notified Couch about the items of editorial importance he had on his desk and assured him of his cooperation. On February 21, 1958, he sent Couch a memorandum outlining the decisions made on the cities and towns question in which he pointed out that at the August editorial meeting, Shores had recommended using Lippincott's *Gazetteer* and *Webster's Geographical Dictionary* as points of reference for determining the inclusion of towns, but, he observed, numerous minor issues had yet to be resolved.[20] This was not a satisfactory solution to Couch. The sources recommended by Shores could only tell him which cities to include. They could not tell him how they could be handled in the encyclopedia. He had insisted on guidance and direction from Fontaine for this.

With Fontaine in a reduced role in the company, Couch did begin to feel freer to attack the demons that tormented him—particularly the American Library Association and the American library establishment. He felt free enough to renew his offensive against *Library Trends*.

In the summer of 1958, Couch launched an attack on Raymond Kilgour of the library school at the University of Michigan. Kilgour had contributed an article to the July 1958 issue of *Library Trends*. The issue was entitled *Trends in American Book Publishing* and the issue editor was Frank Schick of the Library Service Branch of the United States Office of Education. The article, "Reference and Subscription Book Publishing," was a modest survey of reference book publishing in America that attempted to cover the entire field in only fourteen pages. Kilgour sinned when he dismissed *Collier's Encyclopedia* in a scant three sentences as a "useful supplement to the major encyclopedias" that "lacks the authority and balance of the older [i.e. *Britannica* and *Americana*] sets."[21]

Couch seized the opportunity to assail Kilgour as a representative of the ALA establishment who gave "evidence that he does not know what he is talking about." Couch fired off a nine page single-spaced memo to Ryan calling for a war against the ALA's *Subscription Books Bulletin* and calling the article "an opportunity" that could be used by the company for *Collier's* "to gain recognition as a major encyclopedia and possibly leadership in the field." He attacked Kilgour's citing the cost of continuous revision of *Britannica* and *Americana* on the grounds that such statistics were meaningless because Kilgour did not go into detail about what, precisely, such costs included. Even if he had gone into detail, it would have been meaningless because much of what was expended on such projects was wasted. Couch objected, "The editors of *Library Trends* [i.e. Robert Downs] should know this even though Mr. Kilgour does not."

Couch had an underlying problem with his attack on Kilgour's article.

Kilgour did not address the issue of objectivity, and Couch was forced to bring it up to scrutiny in order to demolish Kilgour's presumed position. That he did not address it was, to Couch, sufficient evidence that Kilgour and the editors of *Library Trends* had completely and uncritically accepted the Communist propaganda that was promoted in *Britannica* and *Americana*. Once he had constructed the windmill that Kilgour failed to provide, Couch charged.

His attack continued with only passing references to Kilgour's article as Couch considered the problems of the authority of the contributors to encyclopedias, the accuracy and scholarly breadth of the articles, and the format of encyclopedias. He advised Ryan that one course of action would be to approach *Library Trends* about granting equal time for a rebuttal of the article, but concluded that would be unwise. Raymond Kilgour would not back down and the publisher of *Library Trends*, Robert Downs, would undoubtedly defend him. Besides, *Collier's Encyclopedia* should do nothing that could be interpreted as attempting to influence a reviewer's opinion. *Collier's* could ignore this article, but Couch asserted the company must address the issues that were raised if it "is not to continue to be exposed to incompetencies such as Mr. Kilgour."

After suggesting and rejecting several alternatives, Couch finally came to his proposal. He advocated a series of studies to be conducted under the auspices of a library school which "would be designed to find and establish answers to editorial questions that are now being answered in one way one moment and in another the next." The studies would be published as a series of monographs to culminate in a final published work to summarize the results. The purpose of this program would be to standardize encyclopedia practice: "In a year or two after the monographs were available, you would find Britannica and Americana changing some of their current habits and following the recommendations of the monographs. Reviewers would discredit themselves if they failed to follow the recommendations without giving good reasons for doing so."

Financing such a project would have the added benefit of strengthening *Collier's* market position:

> The fact that Collier's Encyclopedia was sponsoring and financing and giving serious continuing attention to a series of studies designed to answer important questions about encyclopedia editing problems would gradually percolate through the library world. The relations that could be established in the conduct of such a program of this kind could guarantee, as far as any guarantee is possible that Collier's Encyclopedia was on the right track and ahead of Britannica and Americana.

Couch further told Ryan that if he thought the program had merit, he must talk to Shores about it as "Louis would be invaluable in a program of this kind." Couch sent a copy of this memorandum to Shores asking him to keep it "strictly confidential" hoping that Ryan would want to consult Shores about the idea.[22]

Couch was undoubtedly intending Shores's library school at Florida State University as the place where such a study should be conducted. Ryan, perhaps wisely, did not follow Couch's advice.

John Ryan supported Couch throughout his difficulties at *Collier's*. Ryan saw and appreciated Couch's talent and, even though Couch proved difficult to work with, Ryan smoothed the way for him in many ways. Couch, though, had ambivalent feelings about John Ryan. While Ryan frequently defended Couch against Fontaine, it was evident to Couch that Ryan did so only because he personally liked Couch and not because of any basic agreement with Couch's ideas or a shared philosophy on what an encyclopedia could be. It was not because Ryan really wanted to improve the encyclopedia or because he understood what Couch was trying to do. Even at that, Couch was grateful for Ryan's continuing support, which gave Couch his single point of security in the organization.

With Ryan on his side of the issues, Couch threw himself into the work on the encyclopedia with particular attention to the projected revision of *Collier's Encyclopedia*. By mid–November 1958, Couch had worked out a plan that called for a thorough evaluation of the articles, a reconsideration of the illustrations and maps, an examination of the indexing, and studies of encyclopedia users. He had even projected a detailed budget of about $55,000 to cover the costs.[23]

On April 2, 1959, Wilton Donald Cole, chairman of the Board of Directors of Crowell-Collier, fired John Ryan from the presidency of the P. F Collier Company and assumed direct control of *Collier's Encyclopedia*. After dropping the financially disastrous magazines the company published, Cole had finally focused his attention on the encyclopedia as part of his attempt to turn the company from general publishing toward specialized educational publishing. Couch's immediate problem, though, was neither Cole nor Raymond Hagel who assumed Ryan's job, but another of Cole's advisors. Cole, naturally looked to his own people for advice about restructuring the enterprise and, to Couch's horror, one of those to whom Cole turned to for advice was Everett Fontaine. Couch firmly believed that it was Fontaine who convinced Cole to fire John Ryan.[24]

The loss of Ryan's support within the company was a major blow to Couch. Couch wrote Russell Kirk in May explaining his position, telling Kirk, "it had taken me years to win Ryan over to my policies." Fontaine, with decades of publishing experience with the ALA, was in a powerful position and his enmity had made the conversion of Ryan to Couch's way of thinking difficult. But, Couch told Kirk, he had accomplished it. The problem, as Couch saw it, was that the groundwork he had laid in the organization with Ryan had been destroyed and now Cole was looking to Fontaine for advice on the encyclopedia. Consequently, Couch was looking for other employment.

A major issue between Ryan and Cole seems to have been the sales practices instituted by Cole for the encyclopedia. Ryan was a salesman who had no real interest in the editorial aspects of the encyclopedia. Couch disparaged him as "a 'bind up the telephone book and we'll sell it' man." But, Couch and Ryan had a mutual respect and Ryan, if he did not support Couch's attempts to produce a better encyclopedia, at least backed Couch himself knowing that the most aggressive salesman could only do so much in moving an inferior product. Cole, however, took Ryan's attitude to a new level. Cole's policy was to increase commissions to the sales staff which would undoubtedly increase the immediate sales of the encyclopedia, but would ultimately have a detrimental effect on profits by shifting the expenses from the editorial and content areas to the door-to-door efforts of the salesmen.[25] While a good sales staff might be able to sell almost anything, Ryan knew that the eventual decay in quality of the encyclopedia caused by neglecting the editorial work would eventually result in a public awareness that it was inferior to other encyclopedias. Cole had no such qualms.

Immediately on assuming control of the company, Cole embarked on a policy that eventually led *Collier's Encyclopedia* before the Federal Trade Commission in the 1960s on charges of deceptive sales practices. The list of offenses charged against the encyclopedia was a long one and represented an inventory of the imaginative devices created by door-to-door salesmen through the years.[26]

As Cole was busily promoting the sales of the encyclopedia to the detriment of editorial work, Couch was apprehensive for his own future with the company and told Russell Kirk that his only real hope there was Louis Shores. According to Couch, Shores's reputation among American librarians was far stronger than Fontaine's and Shores was on his side. Though they had had differences in editorial policy over the years, Shores would support him. Among other reasons, Shores knew that Fontaine was against him, too and Couch had, on occasion, defended Shores when Fontaine attempted to have him removed from the encyclopedia. Couch went on to tell Kirk that the best opportunity he could see if he was discharged from *Collier's* was to sell *Britannica*. Even though it was filled with propaganda, it was still a better encyclopedia than *Collier's* and he could double what *Collier's* was paying him through sales commissions.[27]

Couch was apprehensive for his future, but went forward with the job at hand. It was a job, though, that had been made doubly difficult because of Cole's reliance on Fontaine's judgment in encyclopedia design. Together, the two raised issues that Couch found editorially irresponsible. Cole, prompted by Fontaine, wanted to balance the set by apportioning one volume to each letter of the alphabet, a decision with which Couch might have agreed, but Cole also wanted each volume of the encyclopedia to contain the same number of pages.[28] Knowledge is not equally dispersed alphabetically. Couch had already prevailed over Fontaine when he had brought this idea to editorial meetings, but Couch had had Ryan behind him then.

Cole wanted an encyclopedia that could be as useful to elementary school children as to researchers. He was insistent that this was not merely an advertising ploy, but an attempt to have *Collier's Encyclopedia* directly compete with *World Book, Compton's, Britannica*, and *Americana*. Couch knew that a broad population could be served, but not a population as diverse as that envisioned by Cole. Cole was, however, willing to accept Couch's appeal that more attention be given to a program of revision and to the views of the encyclopedia's advisors, particularly Louis Shores. Couch needed Shores's support against Fontaine and, with it, was almost hopeful for his future at Crowell-Collier.[29]

Indeed, Couch felt sanguine enough that he, hesitatingly, began to reassert his own editorial control over the encyclopedia. Soon after Ryan's dismissal from the company, Couch sent Cole a detailed memorandum outlining his view of the editorial problems of the encyclopedia. At the most basic level, there was a confused idea of who could actually use the set. Couch pointed out that the foreword to the set proclaimed that it was designed to serve everyone, "young and old from the upper grade level through high school and college to the most advanced levels." This universal promise was tempered by the directions the editorial offices gave to authors that the encyclopedia articles are supposed "to meet the needs and interests of the average American family." While the first statement was obviously meant for sales purposes and the second for editorial direction, neither could really function to direct the policy of the encyclopedia.

Couch dusted off his proposal for a series of studies of encyclopedias that he had developed to counter the Kilgore article and that had been rejected by John Ryan and presented it to Cole in somewhat altered form. These studies, approached from a variety of research perspectives, would examine all aspects of encyclopedia design and use. Probably under the influence of Louis Shores, he proposed that library schools be contracted to study the issues of comprehensiveness, space allocation, authority, objectivity, arrangement, redundancy, graphics, and general design. Studies in readability, curricula, and marketing would be conducted by other experts. He urged this on Cole because of the need to move quickly if the projected 1962 revision was to proceed as planned. If Cole's aspiration to establish the company "as a great and genuinely educational publishing house" was to be achieved, such studies, giving the policies "an objective scientific nature," would be vitally necessary.[30] This proposal received similar treatment from Cole as it had from John Ryan. Cole ignored it.

While his major efforts to redirect the encyclopedia did not receive approval, Couch did maintain his own editorial directions. He asked Shores for recommendations for the names of possible curriculum advisors for *Collier's*, insisting that they be people who were not subservient to John Dewey's ideas of progressive education and who could recognize the virtues of teaching basic skills over liberal propaganda. Shores, a professed educational conservative, obliged with the names of men who "opposed the extremes of the Dewey philosophy."[31]

Couch's hopes were not realized. Donald Wilton Cole called Couch into his office on July 20, 1959, and terminated his employment at Crowell-Collier. Couch's reaction to this event was radically different from his firing from the University of Chicago. He had known when he signed the contract at Crowell-Collier that this was a different operation from a university press. Cole was, he was willing to admit, within his rights and, indeed, within his obligations to fire him if that would promote the company's ends.

That was Couch's public presentation. Privately, he bitterly blamed the American Library Association and Everett Fontaine. A few years after the event, he wrote to his friend, James J. Kilpatrick, laying the blame directly on the American Library Association's reaction to his article, "The Sainted Book Burners," and on his persistent attempts to purge *Collier's Encyclopedia* of "a lot of viciously misleading propaganda." He told Kilpatrick that the ALA "tried hard in 1954. They tried again in 1958. They finally got me in July 1959."[32]

One factor that undoubtedly contributed to Couch's firing was the distribution of Ralph E. Ellsworth's bibliography on the American Right. Ellsworth was a well-known academic library building consultant, a former president of the Association of College and Research Libraries, and, since 1958, the director of the library at the University of Colorado. When he was at the University of Iowa library, shortly after World War II, Ellsworth began collecting primary research material on American conservatism. Though it was not published until 1960, the annotated bibliography Ellsworth and his assistant, Sarah Harris, compiled was widely distributed in 1958 and 1959 in a draft that was essentially unchanged in its final published form. It was an idiosyncratic document that lumped politicians like Richard Nixon, Barry Goldwater, and William Jenner together with numerous anti–Semites, segregationists, and isolationists. It also, unfortunately for Couch, linked many of the men whom he had recruited over the years as writers for both the encyclopedia and the yearbook with the demagoguery of the Far Right. Richard Weaver, Kenneth Colgrove, Albert Hoyt

Hobbs, Donald Davidson, and Russell Kirk, all conservative intellectuals, were painted into the same corner with rabble rousers such as Billy Hargis, founder of the Christian Crusade, fundamentalist radio preacher Carl McIntyre, and Gerald L. K. Smith, founder of the America First Party.

It was a controversial document both because of its conclusions and because of its ambiguous relationship to the Fund for the Republic which Robert Maynard Hutchins headed. The subtitle of the essay, "A Report to the Fund for the Republic," led many to assume that the Fund for the Republic was somehow responsible for its production and, by extension, that the fund had some intellectual responsibility for the contents. When Howard Margolis reviewed the pamphlet for *Science*, he called it "simply a long series of samples and summaries of the writings of the fruitiest of the writers on the far fringes of the right" noting that the Fund for the Republic had not given any indication that its name should not be used on the report. Ellsworth responded to this, admitting that the name of the fund was used only to acknowledge the grant to the University of Iowa that enabled him to organize the collection of right-wing material he had amassed for the use of researchers. The Fund for the Republic, he asserted, had no responsibility for the intellectual content or the conclusions of the report.[33]

However, the report did appear under Ellsworth's name. Ellsworth was a major figure in the politics of the ALA as well as being a close friend of the former ALA executive secretary, Carl Milam, who was a close personal friend of Everett Fontaine. It is impossible that Fontaine would not know of the Ellsworth bibliography or that Louis Shores, as a member of the ALA's Intellectual Freedom Committee, would not have a copy of the bibliography. The Ellsworth manuscript linked numerous *Collier's* yearbook and encyclopedia contributors to the most radical right-wing extremists and was produced under what would appeared, to executives of Crowell-Collier, to be the joint approval of both the ALA and the Fund for the Republic. The document itself might not have tipped the scale against Couch. However, accompanied by Fontaine's enmity, Cole's reservations about Couch, and the desire of the newly reformed corporation to legitimately press into the field of educational materials, the decision that Crowell-Collier seek an editor for *Collier's Encyclopedia* who was more closely associated with educational issues than radical causes became imperative. With Bill Couch out of the way, Louis Shores was offered and accepted the job as editor-in-chief of *Collier's Encyclopedia*.

Couch had known that it would be only a matter of time before the ALA and his conflicts with Crowell-Collier caught up with him. He had toyed with the idea of becoming a salesman for *Britannica* because salesmen were paid much more than editorial staff members of any of the major encyclopedias, but that idea was probably engendered more by bitterness than reality. He and John Ryan had made an approach to publisher J. J. Lyons about purchasing the rights to *Chambers' Encyclopedia*, but this was unrealistic and both men undoubtedly knew that.

Cole offered Couch a year's salary and the use of an office for the year. Couch took the money, but declined the office, so there was no immediate need for him to earn a living, but he was incapable of remaining inactive. Couch did have an offer in hand on the day he was fired from *Collier's* by Cole. He began work as editorial vice-president with publisher J. J. Little & Ives on August 31, 1959.[34]

7

Do Intellectuals
Have Minds?

There is a hierarchy in the publishing world. Major university presses hold positions of the highest prestige: those of the University of Chicago, the University of North Carolina, and Oxford University are among the best. Major trade houses such as Knopf, Morrow, and Random House follow at a slightly lower level. They publish many excellent books, but the quality of the research and the scholarship of the author is secondary to the potential sales of a book. At the bottom, the reprint houses, Grosset and Dunlap, A. L. Burt, Blue Ribbon Books, and the myriad of mass-market paperback houses, have held the places of lowest rank in which reprinting popular books in cheap bindings on cheaper paper enabled them to offer popular books at greatly reduced prices to the general public.

Even though the company's owner, Harold Drimmer, had described his publishing venture as "a scavenger operation" to Bill Couch, Little & Ives was more than a bottom-feeder in the publishing pond.[1] Its primary business as a publisher, however, had been in reference sets and specialized books designed to be sold in supermarkets. In an attempt to expand its niche in the ecology of publishing, the company had negotiated an arrangement with the Oxford University Press (OUP) through which it acquired the American rights to the *Oxford Junior Encyclopedia*. While it was loosely associated with the Oxford University Press, an operation Couch had extolled to Frank Graham as a model to be emulated at North Carolina, Little & Ives was not at the same level as the university presses of North Carolina and Chicago, or even that of Crowell-Collier.

The job offer from Harold Drimmer of Little & Ives did not surprise Couch. Drimmer had turned to Couch before to recommend someone to serve as editor-in-chief for the American revision of the *Oxford Junior Encyclopedia*.

When Couch's first nominee, Robert Murphy, failed to satisfy Drimmer, Couch sent him Sarah Martin, one of Couch's editorial assistants at *Colliers Encyclopedia*. Unfortunately, Sarah Martin's performance in the job did not impress Drimmer and when Couch became available, Drimmer acted. He appointed Couch as editorial vice-president of the company. Supervising the Americanization of the *Oxford Junior Encyclopedia* was one of his responsibilities. Even though this was an encyclopedia for young people, the problems in editing and in production were the same as those Couch had encountered at *Collier's*. He had already suffered through similar problems with the sales division, with personnel, with editorial control and, particularly, with the subtle intrusion of Communist propaganda into encyclopedias.

Couch walked into a mess at Little & Ives. Sarah Martin remained editor-in-chief of the encyclopedia with Couch as her direct supervisor. From the beginning, Couch knew there were major problems with the encyclopedia and was aware that his new job would probably not be the beginning of a long career at Little & Ives. He wrote to Lambert Davis, director of the University of North Carolina Press, on October 11, 1959, describing the situation in which he found himself:

> I went with Little & Ives to help them straighten out an almost hopeless tangle they've gotten themselves into with the Oxford University Press. L&I has a contract with Oxford, one that could mean a lot to both parties financially. L&I is trying to avoid spending what is necessary to meet the contract and has been so misguided as to imagine that I, with my background of university experience, could help them to manage. I had told L&I they have no alternative but to perform as the contract provides, or give up the contract and lose their investment.[2]

Finances, though, were not his most pressing problem. The immediate issue for the company and for Couch was Sarah Martin's role as editor-in-chief of the encyclopedia revision.

Despite repeated demands, Sarah Martin had proven incapable of giving Harold Drimmer an adequate budget projection or a schedule for completing the project. When Couch arrived, Drimmer told him that he had to be firm with her and force her to develop a budget. Couch did this almost immediately and Sarah Martin indignantly told Couch that she would not be instructed by him, threatening to resign if Couch pushed her on the issue. Couch reported the incident to Drimmer who told him to sooth her and try to get whatever information on budgets and schedules from her that he could.

Couch took her to lunch a few days later, but when he broached the budget issue, she exploded. Couch reported to Drimmer, "Her conduct was such that, if the situation had been a normal one, I would have secured her resignation."

Couch laid blame for this impossible situation directly on Harold Drimmer and told him so. While Drimmer was forceful and direct with Couch in determining the needs of the encyclopedia, he was gentle with Sarah Martin and vacillating when meeting with her and Couch together over the issues. Couch accused Drimmer of having "not only permitted but encouraged the insubordination" of Sarah Martin.

In Couch's estimation, Sarah Martin was "not in a normal state." He told Drimmer that as long as she was in charge of the encyclopedia, it would be impossible to complete the work. She simply did not have the administrative ability to successfully handle the job of editor-in-chief. In the two and a half years she had occupied the position, she had been unable to secure a capable staff, she had "repeatedly falsified and misrepresented issues," and she suffered a fatal hubris that "will not allow her to accept help." Her greatest failure was her refusal to accept Couch's guidance.

Drimmer was in a quandary. He had hired Couch to solve a problem that Couch himself had created when he recommended Robert Murphy and then Sarah Martin to edit the work. Neither had worked out. Drimmer did promote Murphy out of that job, but Sarah Martin's position proved more problematic. The contract under which Little & Ives acquired the rights to the encyclopedia required that all revisions be approved by the OUP and Martin had established a strong relationship with Laura Salt, the in-house editor of the *Oxford Junior Encyclopedia*, who had been charged with overseeing the revision. Martin accomplished this by acquiescing to every suggestion and demand made by Oxford. Laura Salt had complete faith in Sarah Martin which, in Drimmer's view, was crucial for the successful completion of the project. While Sarah Martin was marginally competent and a temperamental problem for the company, her personal relationship with Oxford and Laura Salt was, to Harold Drimmer, essential to the progress of the work.

Laura Salt's role in the encyclopedia may not have been completely clear to Couch, and Drimmer had good reason for his view that Martin was essential because of her strong relationship with Salt. Laura Salt had been hired by the OUP in 1943 to work on the school textbooks published by the press. There was not a great deal to be done on these, though, and she was put in charge of developing a school-level encyclopedia. Laura Salt essentially had created The *Oxford Junior Encyclopedia*.

On October 26, 1959, Couch again explained the full situation as he knew it to Drimmer. The relationship between Laura Salt and Sarah Martin was detrimental to the encyclopedia. He recommended that Drimmer ask the OUP to have someone else in the United States appointed to take Laura Salt's place. Oxford University Press had made a fatal error in appointing Laura Salt to oversee the project. The person charged with final editorial approval of such an endeavor had to be an American, someone who knew the United States, and who was a capable editor. A British employee of the OUP working out of England could not accomplish such work no matter how extensive her experience had been in editing the British version. After Laura Salt had been removed, Couch recommended that Drimmer fire Sarah Martin and find someone else to take her place. Couch concluded his harangue of Drimmer by resigning from Little & Ives effective at the end of October 1959.[3]

Harold Drimmer convinced Couch to stay on at the job and Drimmer accepted Sarah Martin's resignation at the end of October 1959, when Couch took on the job of editor-in-chief for the *American Oxford Encyclopedia* himself. After the events, Couch wrote Laura Salt with details leading up to the separation of Sarah Martin from Little & Ives. It was a gracious letter in which Couch conceded that Sarah Martin had been charged with an impossible task.

Couch addressed two major issues in this letter to Laura Salt. The most important for him was the editorial agreement with the OUP under which she had the ultimate authority to reject articles for the revision. Sarah Martin had labored in slavish devotion to her interpretation of the standards of the OUP, but her task had been complicated by having no guidelines for authors of articles for the American revision. Couch's concern was that without explicit guidelines for style or at least good examples of the style demanded by the OUP for the revision, the effort would go forth in a vacuum. Authors of articles would not know what was expected or why an article could be seemingly arbitrarily rejected by Salt. Couch, as editor, could not adequately make assignments to authors under those circumstances.

Couch offered Salt an alternative to the existing contract under which he and Little & Ives would complete the revision. Drimmer wanted Couch to see the work through to the first printing, but he agreed with Couch that a better plan might be to pay the OUP the $400,000 budgeted for the revision and have Oxford take over full responsibility for the revision.

The second major issue he raised in this letter to Laura Salt was her relation to the revision if it was to be continued by Little & Ives. If the Americanization of the encyclopedia was to be successful, each volume should be edited by a scholar from a major American university and the general editorial responsibility should be held by an American. Couch suggested someone like journalist and historian Allen Nevins or liberal social historian Henry Steele Commager.

Couch was less cordial a few months later. He wrote Salt again on February 2, 1960, in frustration with her and the process at the OUP. He protested that she insisted on total editorial control, but refused to make the decisions needed to maintain a schedule that would ensure the timely production of the encyclopedia. Couch made an effort to soften his criticism by denying that he was "belligerent," assuring her, "I want peace and harmony and a good job done, just as much as you." But, he accused her of using the authority she claimed by the terms of the contract to create "paralysis of the function that both parties want to perform, endless talk about the paralysis, and endless lament over the time consumed by the talk." He entreated her to give her approval or disapproval of the volumes of the set that Sarah Martin had assured him were ready for publication. He told her that in giving her judgment, she should "ignore my opinion that no volume is yet in good condition." He simply wanted her to tell him where the revision stood with Oxford so he could proceed with his own schedule.[4]

By September 1960, the OUP had replaced Laura Salt on the project. Winifred Davin, a woman of some literary attainments who was married to Daniel Marcus Davin of Oxford's Clarendon Press, took over her duties. Davin proved to be as equally difficult for Couch as Laura Salt, but for different reasons.

On October 3, 1960, Couch wrote Davin with a complex list of complaints about the editorial policies and procedures imposed on him by the OUP. He objected that "Oxford has been and still is trying to set standards for us when we have demonstrated the inadequacy of Oxford's standards." He gave her a detailed critique of two articles, "Toleration" and "Anarchy," scheduled for the set in which she had both demanded cuts to adhere to the word count and insisted on additions that would inflate the length. He pointed out that the encyclopedia could be suitable for the home and meet the highest standards for educational institutions. If it reached that level of quality, though, it could stand on its own merits without the Oxford name. If it did not, it could only be sold through deception.

The contract Little & Ives had signed with the OUP was detailed and addressed, in addition to editorial policies, strictures on sales that prohibited the traditional door-to-door practices. Couch charged:

> What Oxford is doing is first, using the name Oxford to sell an inferior work; second, trying to force us to keep the work inferior, which will force us to use deceptive selling methods; and third, Oxford is expressing shock at the use of deception in selling, and threatening us with disaster if we use such methods.

The editorial policies enforced by the OUP guaranteed that the product would be defective and the strictures on selling that Oxford insisted upon guaranteed that it could not be sold. Oxford University Press had put Little & Ives in an impossible situation.

While Couch professed to Davin that having the Oxford University Press name on the encyclopedia was important to him and acknowledged, "our problem is to be reasonable to each other," he directly accused her of editorial malfeasance. If Oxford was holding him to the terms of the contract, he would hold Oxford and her to the terms of the contract. Since he had not heard from her within the thirty days specified by the contract with her approval or objections to articles he had sent, he would assume approval and would ignore any subsequent correspondence about the articles.[5]

Couch's letter to Davin had repercussions. She forwarded it to her superior, Colin Roberts, who immediately wrote Harold Drimmer in protest. He said he had hoped that a meeting he had had with Drimmer earlier in September 1960, had established a more cordial relationship between the OUP and Little & Ives than had obtained in the past. Couch's letter had destroyed that comity. Roberts took particular and pointed exception to Couch's assertion that Oxford was using its name to sell an inferior work. Roberts maintained that the *Oxford Junior Encyclopedia* had a high reputation and was a great commercial success while "Mr. Couch's encyclopedia" was an untested commodity. He cautioned Drimmer that he should do what he could to avoid more such letters from Couch and dangled the threat, "We hope to keep our lawyers out of these problems; but if statements such as those are made, I don't see how we are going to."[6]

Drimmer immediately showed this letter to Couch who retorted that Roberts's letter was simply another attempt to bury Oxford's errors. He told Drimmer, "I have made it perfectly clear that I am not willing to overlook the mistakes that Oxford has made and allow myself to be juggled into a position in which I can be held responsible for those mistakes."

Couch thought Roberts was "incapable of being reasonable," but was capable of resorting to legal action even without the possibility of winning. The essential point for Couch was, as he told Drimmer, Roberts "wants to muzzle me." Couch reminded Drimmer that his charge had been to get the work completed. He told Drimmer that the only possible way to do this and to retain the Oxford name on the encyclopedia would be to continue submitting the articles to Winifred Davin for approval, to follow her suggestions when they may improve the articles, and to cease giving her explanations of what he was doing in editing the work. Explaining what he was doing to the OUP only complicated the problem because, as he told Drimmer, "The treatment that Oxford gives to explanations that we have given them in the past shows a disposition to continue arguing when they have been proven wrong, or to ignore what we say." His preference, which he expressed to Drimmer, was to do exactly what Oxford said to do, but he refused to allow his name to be put on the encyclopedia if that policy was followed. He concluded, "If any way could be found in which I could withdraw completely from the project without embarrassment to you, I would be very glad to do so."

Couch knew Roberts had to be answered and drafted a letter for Drimmer to send in response, telling Drimmer, "If you do not say the following to Mr. Roberts, I think the firm will lose ground that it has won during this period." Couch reiterated the points he had made to Oxford in the past. Oxford University Press was responsible for the problems with Sarah Martin. Even though she was technically not an Oxford employee, she had been directed by Oxford employees. Since the OUP retained editorial control over the encyclopedia, the ultimate product was the responsibility of Oxford and the press either had to take over the full responsibility for the editing or allow Couch the freedom to do the job. Through Drimmer, Couch told Roberts, "You make my problems almost hopelessly difficult when you make it clear that you are willing to attribute to Mr. Couch responsibility so far you have not been willing for him to have." Couch concluded this letter by turning aside an aspersion Roberts had cast at him—that the *Oxford Junior Encyclopedia* was a commercial success and Couch's effort at revising it had no sales record. Roberts had complained, "I should have thought a little more modesty [on Couch's part] would be in place." Modesty was not among Bill Couch's virtues and he objected, through Drimmer, that the *Oxford Junior Encyclopedia* had only sold 100,000 copies in ten years while *Collier's Encyclopedia* sold that many sets in a year. This made Couch "ten times as good" as the Oxford editors, at least in the number of sets sold and over twenty-five times as good if Roberts considered the relative cost of each encyclopedia set rather than number of copies sold.[7]

Drimmer refused to use the letter and Couch was furious. By not taking the stand demanded by Couch, Drimmer relinquished complete editorial control over the encyclopedia to Oxford and Couch told Drimmer, "I wish to make it clear that I am unwilling to continue in a position in which I can be loaded either in private or public with responsibilities for decisions made by Oxford."[8]

By January 1961, Couch was disgusted with Oxford and was seriously considering complete break with the OUP. Little & Ives could make a success of a good youth encyclopedia without the Oxford name. Couch suspected that Oxford's obstinacy in editorial matters, particularly in the number of words allocated to individual articles, derived from the suspicion of the Oxford editors that Couch was attempting to create an adult encyclopedia from the *Oxford Junior Encyclopedia*. Couch protested that this notion was "fantastic" and it would take much more than an increase in size to make an adult encyclopedia from the mess of the *Oxford Junior Encyclopedia*. What Couch did want was a young people's encyclopedia that would be suitable for schools and home use. Creating that required the kind of careful editing and article space that he demanded.[9]

His battle with Oxford was over more essential issues than article length and word counts. On August 12, 1961, Couch wrote his good friend James J. Kilpatrick, who had asked his advice on writing a book on school segregation for Crowell-Collier. Couch advised him to do it, but not to lose sight of the fact that the central issue was not racial segregation or integration, but rather "the sovietization of the United States." He complained to Kilpatrick that his major challenge was attempting to edit "viciously misleading propaganda" from the *Oxford Junior Encyclopedia* to prepare it for an American market. The job was exacerbated by the constraints imposed on his editorial activity by Oxford and the person charged with overseeing revisions, Winifred Davin, had no reticence about her open and "strong pro–Communist sentiment." Couch told Kilpatrick that he was trying his best, "but I do not have the resources, the time, the unlimited energy to do anywhere nearly all that needs to be done."[10]

The problem of propaganda proved as perplexing a one for Couch at Little & Ives as it had been at *Collier's*. In May 1961, he wrote Ivan Bierly of the William Volker Fund with whom he had developed an extensive correspondence about the propaganda problem and told him that he had to personally write the article, "Democracy," for the encyclopedia after the person assigned to the piece sent "a version that evaded the issues." He confided to Bierly that Leo Strauss of the University of Chicago, a scholar who argued throughout his career that natural rights and natural laws were the substance of political existence, should have written the piece, but "both the volume editor and Oxford teeter on the verge, where they are not over the verge of extreme left-wingism." Couch sent copies of his article to Bierly telling him, "I send this stuff to you to show you the direction I would go if I had the power to do what I think ought to be done. In my opinion our public has not yet been completely corrupted."[11] Of course, the encyclopedia was being designed for school children between the ages of eleven and eighteen. The state of political corruption of this public was probably low.

The American Library Association (ALA), Couch's nemesis at *Collier's Encyclopedia*, raised its head in 1961 at a meeting Couch had in New York with Winifred Davin and others from the OUP interested in potential sales of the set. Couch and Drimmer had discussed the possibilities of ALA approval in the past, and Couch had conceded that the chances of a positive review by the ALA were no better than even. When Couch was asked pointedly at the meeting if he could assure the English visitors that the *American Oxford Encyclopedia* would be approved by the ALA's Subscription Books Committee, Couch hedged his answer telling them that "the set was very different from other sets on the market and that ALA might disapprove on account of these differences." Couch was startled that Winifred Davin had no interest in the issue and was totally unconcerned about the ALA and its potential impact on sales.[12] It confirmed to him, again, that the people who controlled the editorial policies of the encyclopedia had no idea of what they were doing in an American market.

The encyclopedia never got to the ALA's Subscription Books Committee. While several volumes were typeset and two actually produced, the complete set was never published. Marketing studies conducted by the OUP were discouraging and Oxford did not go through with the project. The investment Little & Ives had made in the editorial work was lost and the company eventually was forced to file for Chapter 11 bankruptcy.[13]

On January 25, 1963, Couch told Winifred Davin that he was leaving Little & Ives. Couch informed her that for several years he had been in extensive correspondence with a group of people at a small foundation about the issues of encyclopedias and education and they had invited him to join them. Couch's letter to her was gracious. He thanked her and Colin Roberts for their patience and cooperation in working with him on the *American Oxford Encyclopedia*.[14]

The small foundation Couch mentioned was the William Volker Fund, the major source of financial support for the Libertarian movement through the 1950s.[15] William Volker had enjoyed a long and successful career beginning in 1882 as a merchant of home furnishings headquartered in Kansas City, Missouri. He had built his business from a local store to a national concern over the years and had been active in philanthropy at both a personal and corporate level. Volker's generosity ranged from handing a few dollars to people walking into his office to major contributions to charitable institutions.

In 1932, Volker institutionalized his philanthropy by establishing the William Volker Charities Fund with himself, his wife Rose, and his nephew, Harold Luhnow, as trustees. Harold Luhnow had joined the William Volker Company in 1919, was promoted to regional sales manager in 1928, and later to general sales manager. When William Volker retired in 1945, Luhnow became head of the company and of the charitable foundation.[16]

Luhnow immediately made significant changes in the direction of the fund. In 1947, he used the fund to support the first meeting of economists and scholars that became the Mont Pelerin Society. The society was a loosely organized group of scholars opposed to socialism and statism and committed to the study of free-market economies. This first meeting was organized and directed by Fredrich Hayek whose book, *The Road to Serfdom*, had strongly influenced Luhnow and others in the emerging Libertarian movement in America. Hayek served as the president of the Mont Pelerin Society from its first meeting in 1947 to 1960. During these years, the society held ten international meetings.[17]

One of the major beneficiaries of the William Volker Fund under Luhnow was the Foundation for Economic Education (FEE). Indeed, the FEE functioned almost as a front for the Volker Fund. The FEE was established in 1946 to produce, publish, and distribute literature in support of Libertarianism and various conservative causes and was committed to informing businessmen, elected officials, and the general public about the threat of government intervention in business and economic development.[18] The Volker Fund was only one of many corporate contributors to the FEE, but it was by far the most generous. Harold Luhnow, through the fund, financed the start-up expenses of the FEE, guaranteeing the FEE's president, Leonard Read, enough support to ensure the success of the enterprise. The FEE reported that by 1950, the William Volker Fund had contributed $170,000. The next largest supporter for the period was General Motors for $50,000. To keep its name from public association with the first conference of the Mont Pelerin Society, Luhnow and the Volker Fund moved money through the FEE to pay the expenses. It was, according to the minutes kept by the FEE Board of Trustees, "a service performed for the William Volker Fund, which merely gave the Foundation the money for the handling of details and disbursements."[19] William Volker had always insisted on anonymity in his own charitable work, but Harold Luhnow took this further in keeping the name of the William Volker Fund from any direct association with Libertarian causes and programs. Luhnow actively promoted the appearance that there were numerous small independent groups all working toward the same purpose, to influence the American government to support a free market economy and suppress government intervention in American business activities.

The relationships among the FEE, the Volker Fund, and the Mont Pelerin Society were much closer than mere financial support. Leonard Read was a founding member and regular participant at meetings of the Mont Pelerin Society. Floyd Arthur "Baldy" Harper, one of the founders of the FEE and a co-director and chief recruiter for the William Volker Fund from 1958 to 1961, was also a founding member of the Mont Pelerin Society as was Herbert C. Cornuelle, author of an adulatory biography of William Volker, an officer with the Volker Fund, and Leonard Read's assistant at the FEE. Libertarian polymath Henry Hazlitt was a society founding member and vice-president of the FEE. Harold Luhnow became a member and regularly attended meetings. Loren Miller of the Volker Fund, the man responsible for encouraging William Volker to establish the fund in 1936, was at the first meeting. The two major figures in the Mont Pelerin Society from the beginning, Austrian economists Friedrich Hayek and Ludwig von Mises, had their salaries paid at the University of Chicago and New York University by Harold Luhnow, who had brought them from Europe and secured their appointments at those universities through the Volker Fund.[20]

There was some friction between the FEE and members of the Mont

Pelerin Society, who considered the FEE people to be a simple-minded bunch more interested in propaganda than the higher purpose of economic research.[21] The Mont Pelerin Society founders included such luminaries as Milton Friedman, who became an economic advisor to Barry Goldwater and later, President Ronald Reagan; French intellectual Bertrand de Jouvenel; Fritz Machlup, the economist who first recognized the economics of information; the president of Haverford College, Felix Morley; and philosopher Karl Popper. These were not men who readily engaged in political propaganda. They were serious scholars actively in search of the truth. Scholarly integrity, though, was insufficient reason to refuse the financial assistance offered by the FEE and the Volker Fund.

The FEE was so successful that it drew the attention of Drew Pearson, the most widely-read political columnist of the day, in his column, *Washington Merry-go-Round*. Pearson's column for March 24, 1949, took aim at the FEE calling it a "powerful lobby" that "has been flooding the country with propaganda aimed at undermining the Marshall Plan, rent control, aid to education and social security." He asserted, the "chief aim of this high-powered lobby is to oppose any act of Congress that raises living standards, if—it also lowers business profits." Pearson's central objection was that the FEE was recognized by the Internal Revenue Service as a tax-exempt organization. Its supporters, primarily big businesses, received significant tax benefits for contributions and members of Congress used their franking privileges to send out multitudes of FEE tracts across the country.

Pearson reported that the contributors to the FEE were clothed in secrecy, but he had obtained a list. His column included the names of several major corporations, but the William Volker Fund was absent.[22] Pearson had not actually gotten the complete list, but had sent his assistant, Jack Anderson, to the FEE offices in Irvington-on-Hudson, New York, and Anderson asked the president of the FEE, Leonard Read, for the list of donors. Read told him that the list was not given out, but he could look at it. Even though Read knew Anderson was a reporter, he innocently expected him to keep the names of the donors confidential.

Anderson's memory was incomplete, but the short list of twenty major corporations that were evading taxes while promoting their own right-wing agenda through FEE propaganda was sufficient to make the House of Representatives Select Committee on Lobbying Activities call the FEE to testify at a hearing held in Washington on July 18, 1950. The FEE was only one of several groups testifying in this series of hearings including the National Economic Council, the Committee for Constitutional Government, the Conference of American Small Business Organizations, Americans for Democratic Action, the Public Affairs Institute, and the Civil Rights Congress. These were organizations that spanned the American political spectrum from right to left. At this hearing, the FEE was represented by its president, Leonard Read, and Ivan Bierly in his capacity as executive secretary.

Frank Buchanan, chairman of the committee, opened the session by stating, "We are interested in learning more about the operations of these groups which have little personal contact with Members of Congress and yet have a tremendous influence in shaping national legislative policy." Read responded by saying that the FEE was a purely educational endeavor: "We are trying to find out how man can preserve his independence in a society where interdependence plays a major role."

The testimony focused on the publications and the funding of the FEE. When challenged by the committee that the publications were all on one side of legislative and economic issues, Read responded, "We are engaged in a highly specialized subject, attempting to further understanding, ourselves, the principles of the free market and the voluntary society, and the principles of a government of strictly limited powers."[23] In short, there was only one side.

The committee was especially interested in the relationship of the FEE to DeWitt Wallace's *Reader's Digest* since it was one that vastly expanded the impact of the FEE on American opinion. Wallace, kept his circulation figures a closely guarded secret. He feared the magazines from which he reprinted articles might raise their rates for reprinting if the owners knew of the immense circulation of the magazine. The best estimate would put its circulation at over ten million copies an issue in 1950 making it the most widely distributed magazine in America at the time.[24] Wallace had reprinted several FEE publications and was interested in publishing more. Leonard Read was also interested in that possibility and engaged in an on-going correspondence with the editors of *Reader's Digest* for several years. Interest was strong enough that in 1948, the *Reader's Digest* had asked for advanced copies of FEE publications so the magazine could have first chance to reprint them.

Leonard Read was coy when asked about the financing of the FEE. The committee had requested a full list of contributors and Read complied, but insisted on going on record that he was not legally required to make the list public and was giving it to the committee with the expectation that it would be kept confidential. Evidently, Read did not know that the proceedings and accompanying exhibits would be published as a government document. In his testimony before the committee, he elaborated on his objections to making the list public because the information, though true, did not tell the whole story— why people and corporations contributed. The list only told part of the story, and "half-truths submitted to the public, bearing the names of contributors, cast suspicion on the contributors." Further, Read insisted, it is a basic "right of a person or corporation to do with the fruits of his or its labor as he or it pleases so long as the actions are devoid of fraud, coercion, conspiracy, or pre-dation." Read was more circumspect when the committee counsel, Benedict FitzGerald, asked pointedly if he knew anything about the Volker Fund. Read responded simply, "I don't know a great deal about the fund itself. I know very little about the disbursals of its income."[25]

The publication program of the FEE was only one aspect of the Volker Fund's efforts to influence American opinion and politics. The FEE programs did not reach a major audience that Luhnow was eager to influence, the students of America's colleges and universities who were being indoctrinated into Com-munism by leftist faculty members. Influencing faculty members and admin-istrators was one goal of the FEE, but Luhnow wanted a deeper penetration of Libertarian ideas into American higher education. Ensuring that appropriate books were placed in college libraries became a major strategy to accomplish this.

In 1953, the Volker Fund commissioned a survey of academic librarians to determine how best to meet this objective. The survey was conducted by the Opinion Research Corporation which had been founded in 1938 by Claude Robinson and George Gallup to conduct public opinion surveys. Gallup left shortly after the company was established, leaving Robinson in control of the corporation. Claude Robinson was a founding trustee of the FEE, as was Harold Luhnow, and Robinson also served as FEE treasurer. The survey commissioned by the Volker Fund used a stratified sample of 218 accredited four-year colleges and universities and two-year colleges around the country. The Opinion Research Corporation developed two lists of fifty titles each—one list of right-wing books and another of left-wing publications. The survey generally found that the librarians did not favor one perspective over the other, but it also found that most libraries had few books on economics or politics.

Librarians welcomed donations of books if the books were suitable for the collections. In response to a pointed question in the survey inquiring about various organizations as sources of gifts, it was clear that librarians were deeply concerned about the objectivity of the sources and were suspicious of adding propaganda to their collections. Generally, they would accept gifts, but wanted to know the source and the biases the donor wanted to promote. One librarian pointedly complained in the survey that publisher Henry Regnery was a blatant propagandist who "sends us free books to try to influence the opinion of young students."[26] Of course, this was exactly what Luhnow was attempting to do.

Luhnow insisted that the William Volker Fund not be associated with the survey and the Opinion Research Corporation was careful to conceal the rela-tionship. He had no need to worry since very few of the librarians surveyed had heard of the Volker Fund. Encouraged by this survey, Luhnow established the National Book Foundation to send out short reviews to librarians from which they could select free copies of the books offered.[27]

In June 1955, the National Book Foundation began sending flyers to college librarians. These were elegant efforts—single folded sheets of laid paper with deckle edges with one to three book reviews set in letter-press covering the four pages. The heading, "The National Book Foundation Established to Serve American Libraries," was followed with an assertion that the foundation "was established to promote, in a modest way, the unhampered flow of information and ideas." There was no indication that the National Book Foundation was associated with the William Volker Fund. The flyers were sent to college libraries with a postage-paid card that the librarians could return to order free copies of the books reviewed.

Luhnow did not overwhelm the libraries. A new list was sent out only three or four times a year and in the nine years the foundation was active, only eighty-one books were offered. The presses of Yale, Harvard, and Chicago were represented and Henry Regnery had several books on the lists. Books published with subsidies from the Volker Fund were evident and Austrian economists Ludwig von Mises and Fredrich Hayek were well represented with four books each. The reviewers were drawn for the most part from the Advisory Committee of the National Book Foundation, all of whom had close ties to the Volker Fund. While the popularity of specific titles varied, the foundation usually sent out from 300 to 400 copies of each title in response to requests from college and university libraries.[28] There was, of course, no way to determine if any of these were actually read by the students Luhnow hoped to influence.

Luhnow's aspirations for what the Volker Fund could do extended beyond the academic world. Citizenship and economic education in schools and for educational foundations and any venue that could promote "finding and aiding thoughtful students and scholars to become more effective fountainheads for the promotion of freedom" were targets for the Volker Fund. To achieve this end, Luhnow insisted that the people employed and supported by the Volker Fund have total freedom to follow their ideas wherever they led. His avowed view was, "To promote freedom successfully, the promoter must himself be free."[29] However, the degree of freedom allowed was limited by the employee's commitment to the ideals Luhnow sought to promote.

Couch's involvement with the Volker Fund began in 1957 while he was still with *Collier's Encyclopedia* and had written to Kenneth Templeton, a fund official, proposing that the Volker Fund finance a "conference on the subject of Propaganda, Facts, and Objectivity." In pressing the need for such a conference, Couch recounted for Templeton the difficulties he had in convincing Everett

Fontaine, his nemesis at *Collier's Encyclopedia*, that Communist propaganda was not fact. He told Templeton that Fontaine

> is very much distressed when I tell him and keep on telling him that the Communists are skilled in the making of facts for propaganda purposes, that they do not label their facts as Communist facts, and that we are serving their purposes when we report the facts they want us to report and fail to report others that they do not want us to report.

The problem, Couch explained to Templeton, was that Fontaine was brought from the American Library Association to P. F. Collier as director of publications "to guarantee the quality, the objectivity, fairness and impartiality of the editorial work of the firm." His view of the issues involved would be supported by the ALA and by most of its members even though most librarians had no idea of what the term, *objectivity*, really meant. If *objectivity* was to be more than a mere "conjure term" as used by the social sciences, its usage must be defined clearly and the Volker Fund had the resources to construct a definition.[30]

Couch's proposal did not produce immediate results, but it did open a correspondence with Ivan Bierly, another officer with the Volker Fund. Kenneth Templeton's primary job with the Volker Fund was to find talent that fit the Libertarian model the fund was promoting under its director, Harold Luhnow. This recruitment effort included scholars needing support in their research and teaching as well as potential employees of the Volker Fund. Ivan Bierly's job at the time was essentially the same. Both Templeton and Bierly were active recruiters for the Libertarian cause.[31] Couch and Bierly carried on a cordial correspondence in which ideas of liberty, society, and morality were explored and Bierly soon came to consult Couch about possible projects for the Volker Fund.[32]

Couch wrote Bierly on December 7, 1958, to propose that the Volker Fund establish an "Institute for Propaganda Analysis at a university where there would be a chance to get honest and intelligent administration of such an organization." The occasion for this appeal was the firing of Eugene Davidson, director of the Yale University Press and a member of the advisory council of the National Book Foundation, by the president of Yale, Alfred Whitney Griswold. According to Couch, Davidson's offense was championing a "free society" by publishing books, particularly those of Ludwig von Mises, condemning government interference in a free-market economy. Bierly wrote back to tell Couch that financial support from the Volker Fund for his institute was improbable, but he wanted to meet with Couch personally.[33] Bierly had already identified Couch as a possible recruit for the Volker organization and the Libertarian cause.

By 1962, the conditions that prompted Luhnow to turn the fund toward promoting right-wing organizations had changed. The organizations the fund had supported and assisted through the 1950s had either run their course or were well enough established to need little financial support. Luhnow looked to make a more significant contribution to promote conservatism. He was becoming more convinced that merging economic and social conservatism with Christianity was a necessary step. In a press release dated March 15, 1962, Luhnow announced the dissolution of the Volker Fund, saying that the fund's assets would be distributed to other charitable agencies.[34] While he did continue some few of the charitable commitments the fund had already made, the major portion of the assets were redirected by Luhnow to the newly formed Center for American Studies.

On January 7, 1963, Harold Luhnow and Ivan Bierly attended a meeting in Chicago and asked Couch to fly there to talk with them about the future of a newly revitalized Volker Fund. There, Couch was offered a job in publishing with the new center. Couch, having been assured that the funding for the center would be available for the next twenty years and that more than minimal resources would be available for his own publishing projects, accepted the offer.[35]

Couch had no apprehension of falling into a nest of liberal vipers at the Volker Fund. The fund had defined conservatism in America for over a decade. At the age of sixty-two, Couch was not ready for retirement, but knew that this job would probably be his last. The center promised to outlast him and offered the financial and philosophical support necessary to enable him to do the work that was needed. The job had all of the necessary elements to provide a meaningful culmination to his career. He would be working on editorial projects with a group of colleagues who fully understood and were fully committed to the same conservative values that he had been championing since taking the job at *Collier's Encyclopedia*, if not before at the University of Chicago. One of Couch's major challenges at *Collier's* had been identifying conservative scholars who could write for the encyclopedia. He had begun to rely on a network of people, but it was never more than a lattice with more holes than nexus points. He continually asked his trusted advisors and contributors to recommend conservative scholars. At the Center for American Studies, he had a resident coterie of conservative scholars each of whom knew many more conservatives than Couch himself. His network would be virtually whole.

He knew that most Americans, even those in colleges and universities, would support his vision of America if they could and if they knew what that vision was. But, liberals owned the means of communication, of publishing, to the extent that even at the universities, a "powerful minority of pinkos" had taken control of the classrooms and the presses. True conservatives had been banned from academe. His problem had been finding conservatives who could and would speak out. For *Collier's*, he relied on people with whom he had engaged in the past, Richard Weaver, Russell Kirk, Donald Davidson, and Kenneth Colgrove. When Kenneth Colgrove asked Couch in March 1959, to send him a list of names of some genuine conservatives, Couch was at a loss. Since there was no agreement on a definition of the term, such a list was impossible. He told Colgrove, "I'm fairly sure a lot of people who think of themselves and are thought of as conservatives hold a position ... that is indistinguishable from that of the communists." Colgrove's task was complicated by the fact that people who looked and talked like conservatives could not be trusted: "just getting the names of people that you could be fairly sure wouldn't join the leftwing camp if they were offered enough money—would take months of study."[36]

Couch's primary contact with the Volker Fund had been Ivan Bierly. Couch had not, apparently, fully understood the degree to which Harold Luhnow had been influenced and motivated by evangelical Christianity in restructuring the Volker Fund. Luhnow explained his basic underlying assumption,

> It seems to me fantastic to assume that it is simply an historical accident that Western civilization, and particularly the United States of America, evolved in a situation that owes so much of its traditional view of man to Christian concepts and principles. Is there no reason why freedom as we have known it in this country in the last two centuries has not evolved under Islam, Buddhism, or other religious philosophies?

Luhnow's answer was that the kind of economic freedom the William Volker Fund promoted could only be possible in a Christian society. Luhnow committed the fund to the record with this in a public forum, a publication of the monograph series, the *William Volker Fund Series in the Humane Studies*.[37] Here, his proclamation of the centrality of Christianity to the conservative movement was constrained by his audience, people who might not accept his argument that Christianity was an essential basis for conservative economic and social policies.

He was much more open to the members of the staff of the Volker Fund. Shortly after he announced the dissolution of the Volker Fund, he addressed the staff elaborating on this theme. Luhnow maintained that the central reason for "the moral deterioration which has been in progress in America" for the past twenty years was the "deliberate *ignor*-ance" of "God's law, from which all other laws should be derived." The great failure of American democracy and of American society was the failure of Americans to accept "Christ as our divine leader."[38] Luhnow insisted that staff members of the newly formed Center for American Studies be people with a commitment to God and to Christ. He realized, though, the potential difficulties of this as a public position and mandated that this Christian purpose be presented to the public through the activities and publications of the center as a vague sense of a spiritual foundation for the center rather than as promoting evangelical Christianity.[39]

Bill Couch was not a perfect fit for Luhnow's Center for American Studies. While he had strong conservative credentials, he was not a Christian fundamentalist. His father had been a part-time Baptist minister and Couch had joined the Baptist Church at the age of nine, but he readily confessed that he had not been a church member since he was a teenager.[40] He was nominally a Christian, but his view of Christianity differed significantly from the evangelical crusade mandated by Luhnow. To Couch, the promotion of social, cultural, and political conservatism did not require the Kingdom of God or the blessing of Jesus Christ for legitimacy. He may not have been able to pass Luhnow's test of faith, but he could pass Ivan Bierly's and by the time Couch joined the group in California, Luhnow trusted Bierly completely to the exclusion of any other member of the Center for American Studies.[41]

Luhnow's trust in Bierly was not misplaced. Long before joining the group, Couch had professed his own basic belief in the importance of Christianity, even though he did have reservations about the difficulties that might be encountered in promoting it in the United States. Early in 1961, Bierly had asked Couch for his thoughts on the Volker Fund sponsoring a series of books timed for the American Bicentennial in 1976. Couch enthusiastically supported the idea, telling Bierly that he agreed that the principles on which the United States had been founded and followed represent the highest that have "been developed in western civilization and that this in turn rests on Christianity."

Couch sent Bierly a detailed plan for such a project with lengthy digressions on the nature of freedom and objectivity and the caution that such a project had to have the active participation of people at major universities to secure the necessary level of authority to keep it from being "ignored or treated as the utterance of a crackpot." The people who could legitimatize the project were at Harvard, Yale, Chicago, Columbia, Oxford, and Cambridge. Couch told Bierly he did not know exactly who they were, but he knew where they were to be found. Couch adumbrated to Bierly a plan for the center to publish books and articles and, eventually, an encyclopedia.

Bierly took Couch's sketchy outline and drafted a proposal to Luhnow following the elements identified by Couch. An encyclopedia of American studies was the major piece of the plan and became Couch's principle assignment when he joined the Center for American Studies. He enthusiastically set to work. By early July 1963, Couch had given Luhnow a detailed program for producing an encyclopedia with guidelines on the relative length of articles, the scope of the topics, the treatment of natural sciences and biographies, and the scholarly level desired. Couch drew on his experience at *Collier's* and at Little & Ives to develop a proposal that addressed the needs of an encyclopedia for the general reader without becoming embroiled in the controversies over objectivity and truth had that plagued him earlier.[42]

Couch lost no time in beginning the next phase of the plan he had outlined to Bierly; identifying potential contributors. Through the summer of 1963, he and Ivan Bierly began writing to virtually every prominent conservative in the country. Couch contacted literary critic Cleanth Brooks, *National Review* editor William F. Buckley, Jr., linguist Mario Pei, Leonard Carmichael, secretary of the Smithsonian, and even his former boss at *Collier's Encyclopedia,* John Ryan, among a multitude of others. Bierly wrote to Arthur Conrad of the Heritage Foundation, Milton Friedman, Felix Morley, Ludwig von Mises, and others, requesting meetings with them. Neither Couch nor Bierly told their correspondents what the proposed meetings were to address. Apparently, they divided the people they contacted based on their own personal friends and former colleagues and between the two of them, knew virtually everyone on the right in America.

If anyone asked about the topic of the meetings, Bierly and Couch sent them the same form letter they sent to everyone. With slight variations, they asked for advice on the encyclopedia. They did not ask for active participation, but merely for recommendations of people who could act as advisors and who would share their vision for the Center for American Studies. They specified that they wanted to identify scholars of American history who were "aware and deeply concerned with" the dynamic relationship between a free society and a free market and the ethical issues involved in both. They wanted to identify scholars who were concerned about the concentration of power in a central government and its potential to result in totalitarianism. They wanted scholars who were concerned that the *United States Constitution* was being mangled by the courts, and they asked for scholars who recognized that the role of religion as a personal commitment to Christianity is embodied in the *Constitution*.[43]

Couch, encouraged by his colleagues at the Center for American Studies, the promise of abundant funding, and his own certainty in the rightness of the project, persisted in his effort to secure reputable advisors and potential contributors and to refine the plan for the work. By November 1963, he could announce that the proposed encyclopedia had two purposes: first, "to present American experience as far as possible as it actually occurred, and in the light in which the actors understood this experience," and second, "to examine the quality of this light." The first purpose was purely descriptive and had already been accomplished by many scholars in many disciplines. The second, however, was something new that required the application of standards and scales of values that, like St. Augustine, laid emphasis on "belief as the foundation of knowledge." From these purposes, Couch formulated a creed to guide the development of the encyclopedia:

> While we regard beliefs as necessary to knowledge, we reject the view that one set is as good as another. We believe there is a true set and that to approach knowledge of this set is the most important thing that men can do on earth. We believe that the Judaeo-Greek tradition, the Western tradition, makes a closer approach to a true set of beliefs than any other. We believe that the continual examination of beliefs is necessary if they are to be kept alive and meaningful.

With this, Couch rejected the idea of an objectivity based on the absence of commitment to and even the denial of cultural values. Rather, he acknowledged that the search for truth is a commitment to the values, traditions, and the beliefs that form the Western tradition. Couch was attempting to make a complete break with orthodox American scholarship which demanded a perspective of cultural relativism in which the standards and values of "a band of thieves and murderers" would be valued equally with the standards and values of an Augustinian friary.[44]

Couch's aspirations for the encyclopedia were tempered by the staff members of the Center for American Studies who formed the editorial board of the encyclopedia. In addition to Ivan Bierly, these included Rosas John Rushdoony and David Hoggan. Both Rushdoony and Hoggan had been employed by the William Volker Fund before Couch joined the cause.

Couch realized as soon as he arrived in California that Rushdoony was a Christian fundamentalist. Having been raised as a Southern Baptist, Couch knew fundamentalism, but not at the depth that Rushdoony promoted. Rushdoony embraced the *Bible* as the received word of God and, for him, everything followed from that, including that the United States, as a Christian nation, should be governed by the laws of God and not man.[45] As a conservative, Couch was strongly opposed to collectivism and statism. Rushdoony also opposed collectivism and statism, but on grounds that differed significantly from those of Couch. In 1963, Rushdoony published *The Messianic Character of American Education: Studies in the History of the Philosophy of Education.* The book was a critique of public schools for which Ivan Bierly provided an introduction that concluded, "What the educationists have forgotten is that the sense of meaning and purpose in life which they take for granted was bought with the blood of saints from the time of the prophets and Jesus until this day." Bierly and Luhnow had brought Rushdoony into the center precisely to promote this vision of private Christian education in opposition to the secularized statism of the public schools.[46]

Rushdoony castigated public education as the ultimate evil of statism in which "the group, democracy, would inevitably be exalted above the individual and his freedom." This was a view that Harold Luhnow had long shared when he equated public education with socialism. To Rushdoony, democracy was the evil and public schools, by promoting democracy, denied the natural law of God. He laid direct blame for this on the rise of Unitarianism in the United States in the nineteenth century which made the Christian church "progressively irrelevant to the American experience as the schools became the working embodiment of the Unitarian faith in salvation by statist education." Indeed, the state and democracy had not only usurped the place of God and Jesus Christ in American society, it had replicated the rites and rituals of the church in those of statist education. Baptism and confirmation, natural rites of passage into a personal relation with God, had been replaced with the meaningless rituals of the first day at school and graduation.

The United States was founded as a Christian nation and the intrusion of modern liberalism, of democratic ideals, and of the government into American society had destroyed the special relationship of the nation as the New Israel with God. As one commentator has noted, Rushdoony's foundational belief was " the federal government invaded private life and began a campaign to replace the true fear and guilt that every sinner in the hands of an angry God ought to feel with a new narrative of guilt meant to emasculate its noblest citizens: Christian white men."

Couch did agree with Rushdoony about the invasive role of the federal government, but he was not prepared to accept Rushdoony's view of the causes. Couch condemned the targets of Rushdoony's outrage as "silly and not a national or world danger as are National Socialism and Communism." While Rushdoony's fundamentalism was inconsequential, Couch was dismayed by his viciousness in attacking anyone opposing him. He observed, "Rushdoony is anti–Catholic, anti–Semitic, anti–Negro, anti-just about everybody and everything except Rushdoony and his predestinate view."[47]

Rushdoony, however, was a minor irritant for Couch compared with the difficulties posed by David Hoggan. Couch dismissed Rushdoony as "a congenital liar, so much so that I am fairly certain that he believes his own lies."[48] He suspected both Rushdoony and Hoggan of being "Nazi sympathizers" from the beginning, but Rushdoony was more probably simply a liar with a turn toward a bizarre form of religious fundamentalism. David Hoggan posed a more serious concern.

In 1963, Hoggan published a book, *Der Erzwunge Krieg*, in Germany. It was a major revision of his Harvard doctoral dissertation that absolved the Nazi Party, Adolph Hitler, and Germany of culpability for World War II, laying the blame totally on the British. Hoggan's book was pilloried by Joseph Bauke in a review in the *New Leader* entitled, "Whitewashing the Third Reich."[49] Couch thought the review only marginally competent, but Bauke did see Hoggan's pro–Nazi sentiments and condemned him as an apologist for Adolph Hitler.

This was bad enough, but Rushdoony compounded the problem by rushing to Hoggan's defense with a letter to the editor that raised some minor quibbles about Bauke's criticisms. The editor allowed Bauke to reply to Rushdoony in the same issue in which his letter was published. Bauke parried each of Rushdoony's points, concluding that, "the kind of revisionism practiced by Hoggan and applauded by Mr. Rushdoony will eventually present us with a scholarly volume on Adolf Eichmann as a traffic manager."[50] Oberstrumbannführer Eichmann had only recently been captured by Mossad in Argentina and hung in Israel for his role in organizing and managing the deportation of European Jews to extermination camps during World War II.

What infuriated Couch most was Rushdoony's rhetorical question raised in defense of Hoggan, "Are we not under obligation to do justice historically to those with whom we may seriously differ?" Couch knew Rushdoony himself felt no such obligation.[51] Rushdoony's answer to those with whom he disagreed was simple and Biblical: he was on the side of God and God was right.

The May 18, 1964, issue of *Newsweek* published a short article on Hoggan that derided his claim that Hitler and the Nazis wanted peace and that the British had started the war. It noted that Hoggan's book had been published in Germany and that Hoggan had been lionized by the German right-wing and neo–Nazis. It observed that an English version of the book was to be published in fall, 1963, by Devin-Adair under the title, *When Peaceful Revision Fails*. The *Newsweek* piece also identified Hoggan as a lecturer at the Center for American Studies.[52]

Ivan Bierly responded weakly to this with a letter to the editor saying that Hoggan was not a lecturer since the center had no lecturers and, besides, Hoggan's employment had been terminated.[53] Officially, both Hoggan and Rushdoony had been fired from their jobs at the center on September 10, 1963, by Bierly "as a consequence of convincing evidence that we had a dangerous situation on our hands." While Rushdoony left, Hoggan stayed on at the center in a much reduced role until the *Newsweek* piece appeared. Couch did regret the decision after the *Newsweek* article was published, but he agreed with Luhnow and Bierly that since Hoggan's wife was about to give birth to their child and Hoggan had no means of support other than the center, he would be kept on the payroll to photocopy articles and do research at local libraries for the center. Couch said that he would have given the opportunity to someone "suspected of being a Communist" and was pleased that the people at the center agreed with him that "we have to put human beings first."

In Couch's mind, the damage had already been done. Hoggan's and Rushdoony's public association of the center with the Nazis had discredited it and the real fault was neither Rushdoony's nor Hoggan's but belonged to Harold Luhnow who had "allowed these men completely to deceive him." Even though Couch had repeatedly complained to Luhnow that Rushdoony and Hoggan were dangerous to the center, Luhnow refused to listen. Couch knew that Luhnow was a man who, like Everett Fontaine, "could not be brought to reason no matter how badly he had been deceived."[54]

From the start of his career at the University of North Carolina, Couch had always been anxious that he be taken seriously by the intellectual community. He thrived on controversy and was perfectly willing to create his own when none existed, but he insisted on creating his own and not having someone else do it for him. Luhnow, through his support of Rushdoony and Hoggan, had led the Center for American Studies into a situation that was impossible and had enmeshed Couch in an organization that was subjected to public ridicule through no fault of his, and even, in fact, over his repeated objections to the continued employment of those who had brought the public denunciation down on the organization.

Bill Couch was careful to document the chronology for his own record of the bizarre situation in which he found himself and kept detailed accounts of events. He was particularly meticulous in recording every detail of David Hoggan's relationship with the center. On May 27, 1964, he wrote Julian Falk, the president of Little & Ives, about his difficulties in California and appended a detailed chronology of Hoggan's employment at the center from the first approval of a grant from the Volker Fund in December 1957, to revise his dissertation for publication to a summary of a telephone call made by a *Newsweek* reporter to Ivan Bierly on May 25, 1964, inquiring about Hoggan's employment status with the Center for American Studies.[55]

Couch reported that Hoggan, after talking with Bierly, had visited him in the office on May 28, 1964, to say goodbye after having been permanently fired after the *Newsweek* article appeared. Couch told Hoggan, "It is impossible for us to be friends and you know very well that I have not been your friend at any time." When Hoggan wished Couch the best, Couch reported that he said, "I hoped very much he would see the terrible error he has been making and that when he sees it, it would not completely destroy him."[56]

The Hoggan affair had repercussions beyond those of public ridicule that Couch feared. On May 22, 1964, he wrote to Fred Wieck about a confrontation he had with two advisors to the Center for American Studies from the Hoover

Institution at Stanford University when they threatened to resign from the center over the Hoggan incident. Couch was incensed that the advisors would flee at the first sign of trouble. One of the advisors had joined Couch and Bierly for dinner after the meeting and spoke to Couch privately in praise of Rushdoony. When Couch told him that Rushdoony was a partisan of Hoggan, the advisor accused Couch of a purely personal animosity. When Couch told him that what he was saying in private should be said in public, the advisor became belligerent. The main fear of both advisors was that their names might be linked to the center and to Hoggan and they would be publically associated with a right-wing cause. This, of course, was a major concern for Couch, too, but he was more than willing to accept the advisors' resignations from the center. Couch wanted people who "help to bring clarification rather than to bring confusion." He told Fred Wieck, "If we face the facts and tell the truth, we can come through all this with an improved understanding of what needs to be done and determination to do it."[57] Couch desperately wished the mistake Luhnow had made in bringing Hoggan and Rushdoony to the center had not happened, but since it had and since it had become public, the only honorable course was to acknowledge it and learn from it.

When Harold Luhnow fell ill in 1963, Morris Cox became president of the William Volker Company. Cox controlled the Volker Fund but was officially second to Harold Luhnow in the administration of the Center for American Studies. On May 26, 1964, shortly after the *Newsweek* article had been published, Couch wrote Cox with a threat to resign from the center. He recounted that he had repeatedly warned Harold Luhnow that Rushdoony and Hoggan's Nazi sympathies threatened to undermine the legitimacy of the center to no avail and accused Cox of treating the issue as trivial. He wrote, "Your attitude says in effect that an offense of the gravest kind becomes an offense only when it becomes public. This is, in my view as thoroughly immoral a position as it is possible to take, and I have to protest with all that I have in me against your taking it." And, Couch did protest.

He made it clear to Cox that he would demand a financial settlement should he find it necessary to end his employment with the center and that this settlement would have to include Ivan Bierly. Bierly was a man of integrity who had been completely compromised by his service to Luhnow. Bierly was faithful to Luhnow and Luhnow had forced him "to do things that would make it extremely difficult, if at all possible, for Mr. Bierly to get another job."[58] Hiring and retaining David Hoggan and Rosas John Rushdoony were only part of Bierly's service to Luhnow.

Bierly did not know that Couch had written to Cox, but Couch, of course, had talked with Bierly about the gravity of the situation. They had agreed that

Harold Luhnow had to go and that the Center for American Studies had to be moved to another location that would make it possible "to exclude [people with] opinions and influences that have prevailed in the past and that might continue to feel they had the right to dominate." Couch and Bierly both dismissed the prospect of closing the center as "simply fantastic." Closing would do nothing to resolve the situation created by Hoggan and Rushdoony and, if the center closed at that point without a chance to redeem itself, "the name 'William Volker' and the name 'Harold Luhnow' will go on record for all future time as those of pro–Nazis."[59]

On June 4, 1964, Ivan Bierly presented a proposal to the Board of Directors of the Center for American Studies that elaborated on the discussions he and Couch had. Bierly outlined the problems arising from the Hoggan affair with particular emphasis on the flight of advisors from the center following the publication of the *Newsweek* article. He pointed out that the center had been established in 1963 with ten million dollars in assets from the Volker Fund, but the real wealth of the center "was the good will and the confidence of a great many scholars." That had been squandered by Rushdoony and Hoggan with Luhnow's support. The solution, Bierly told the directors, was to "make a sharp break with this past history" by removing Luhnow from all authority and moving the center to a new location. This and the development of a public statement of the mission of the center's program with the hiring of "the best PR counsel we can find" could reestablish the center's legitimacy in the public mind. The crucial issue for the center was that the success of its programs rested on people "with direct and continuing relationships to the center." These people, the advisors, the authors, and the publishers on whom the center relied, must be protected in their association with the center. The public perception that the center was involved with Nazis had failed to protect them.[60]

Morris Cox agreed, at least in part, with Bierly's and Couch's recommendations. Within a month, Cox drafted a proposal to move the center to the Hoover Institution at Stanford University. Cox's proposal amounted to simply transferring the programs, the purposes and commitments, the financial resources, and the existing personnel to the Hoover Institution completely. The center would retain control over its activities through its own directors and staff. Harold Luhnow was to remain titular president with Morris Cox as vice-president. Ivan Bierly would remain executive secretary and William Terry Couch would be retained as editorial director.[61]

The negotiations with the Hoover Institution were a final effort by Bierly, Cox, and Couch to save the center. Harold Luhnow had already decided to terminate the effort by July 1964, and had rejected Couch's assertion that this action would cloud all that the center had accomplished.[62]

On July 23, 1964, the Center for American Studies sent the Hoover Institution a formal proposal by which the center could be transferred to the Hoover Institution. Among other provisions, it specified that Harold Luhnow and Morris Cox were to be two of the three trustees of the center that were to be appointed by the William Volker Fund and that they had the authority to designate their own successors. The third trustee was to be David Packard, one of the founders of Hewlett-Packard, who was already a trustee of the Hoover Institution.[63]

David Packard had been a participant in the negotiations on the side of the Hoover Institution and Cox thought him sympathetic to the aims of the center and favorably disposed to the merger of the two interests. The point at which they clashed was over authority and control. Cox wanted the center to become an autonomous unit under the broad umbrella of the Hoover Institution and Stanford University. Packard insisted that the governing board of the center be under the control of the Hoover Institution and Stanford. This was unacceptable to Cox, who reminded Packard that the avowed purpose of the Hoover Institution, as expressed by its founder, Herbert Hoover, was "to demonstrate the evils of the doctrines of Karl Marx ... thus to protect the American way of life from such ideologies, their conspiracies, and reaffirm the validity of the American system." This was an aspiration with which Cox was in complete accord.[64]

Packard conceded that the objectives of the center and those of the Hoover Institution were close, but balked at the notion that any real research could derive from the purposes Cox articulated, telling him, "If the results of research are predetermined it no longer qualifies as research, but rather as studies for propaganda purposes." Packard insisted that any significant research must be conducted by people who "are free to pursue the truth in whatever direction their work would indicate." While Packard thought there was common ground, he insisted that the direction of the center had to be determined by the Hoover Institution and Stanford University and not by the advisors and directors of the Center for American Studies.[65]

David Packard was in a difficult situation. He had a personal relationship with Herbert Hoover who had, in the late 1950s, become deeply disturbed about the left-leaning faculty members and administrators of Stanford University. Further, the Hoover Institution was an autonomous unit at Stanford and members of the Stanford faculty and Stanford students had become increasingly concerned over the degree of autonomy the institution held and, more importantly, the purposes of the institution as articulated by Herbert Hoover and quoted to Packard by Morris Cox. To the Stanford community, this purpose was a direct violation of any definition of scholarly objectivity. In 1960, the issue had spilled out of the Stanford community into the national media. While Packard himself supported Hoover and subscribed to his vision of the Hoover Institution, he recognized that those principles did not fit well with the intellectual commitments of a major research university.[66] Adding another autonomous unit to the Hoover Institution with the philosophical commitments of the Center for American Studies would be politically impossible at Stanford University.

Cox answered that he had been clear from the beginning of the negotiations with the Hoover Institution about the purposes of the center. And, he had been especially clear that he would never turn the management of the center over to Stanford University. For Cox, this was the end of the negotiations and he wrote Packard, "We might as well recognize we have reached an impasse and terminate the conversation."

Couch had been an active participant in the negotiations. He had met with William Nichols, a trustee of the Hoover Institution, at least twice in July 1964, to discuss the merger. For Nichols, a major problem was Ivan Bierly, who Nichols and other Hoover trustees thought was a power-hungry incompetent who had driven the center to ruin. Couch argued in Bierly's defense that Bierly was only following Harold Luhnow's orders, but this argument failed to convince.[67]

Couch did not pass this personal reflection on to Bierly, but he did send Bierly a response to Packard's letter of September 8, 1964, in which he picked apart Packard's aspersions on the agenda of the Center for American Studies. The real issue for the center, he told Bierly, was the continuing public misperception of the center because of its early mistakes in hiring Rushdoony and Hoggan. It was a situation that had been corrected, but was still a part of Packard's and the other Hoover Institution trustees' thinking. Despite Cox's conviction that the negotiations were ended, Couch still had hopes that the center could find a home at Stanford even with the major obstacles that had to be overcome.[68] Within two weeks, though, Couch's hopes were dashed.

On September 23, 1964, the third of a series of meetings was held with E. Howard Brooks, the executive assistant to the vice-president and provost of Stanford, about the merger. It raised some serious issues for Couch. The first was the demand from the university that twenty-five percent of the center's budget be paid directly to Stanford University as overhead costs. Couch objected immediately. If the center was a good fit for the university, it could more properly use the money for its own activities and if it was not a good fit, the center should not be there.

The second issue was more fatal to the negotiations. When directly asked, Brooks could only find the names of a few faculty members at Stanford who might be sympathetic to the commitments of the center. Brooks pointedly mentioned that the Stanford administration was concerned about the balance of viewpoints among the faculty and singled out the problem of the Stanford economics department being dominated by Keynesians. Brooks told Couch that he hoped to bring Milton Friedman there "to establish a balance." Brooks, however, expected the center to attain a balance in its own work if it were to become a part of the Hoover Institution at Stanford, pointing to the books the William Volker Fund had supported as completely biased. The books were expressions of a commitment to Libertarianism and Austrian economics, failing to reflect more liberal research and opinion. Brooks said, "Stanford could not approve the development and expression of only one point of view." For Couch, the issue was simple: "The Center, with a fraction of the resources of the university, would be expected to achieve in all of its operations a 'balance' the university has been able, by Mr. Brooks own statement, to achieve in none." Couch wondered why, since the faculty at Stanford was overwhelmingly leftist, Stanford "did not welcome us with open arms" if a balance in perspective was the desired end.[69] The right-wing Center for American Studies would be an excellent counter to the left-wing Stanford faculty.

Morris Cox had closed the door on the Hoover Institution when he terminated his discussions with David Packard on September 10, 1964. Couch closed his own door with Stanford's provost less than two weeks later when he concluded that the Center for American Studies and the Volker Fund had made some major errors in the past, "But so far as I can see it has made none comparable in magnitude and importance to those it would make if it followed either Stanford's preachment or its practice."[70]

With this, Couch concurred with Cox that the negotiations were over. The failure, however, was neither a disappointment nor a surprise to Couch. Unless the mission of the center complemented that of the Hoover Institution, the center would need a degree of autonomy in the organization that, Couch knew, Stanford University would never allow. More seriously, he had no confidence that anyone at the Hoover Institution or Stanford University "could safely be entrusted with selection of advisors to the Center," an essential demand of Stanford's administrators.

Couch attributed the collapse of negotiations to the "malicious gossip" circulating about the Center for American Studies and the center's inability to counteract rumors and innuendo. By abandoning the center, Couch maintained, "we go far to add substance to the truth of the gossip around us." It would be a confession that he, Cox, and Bierly, "were incapable of consistency of purpose" and that their rhetoric of "commitment was mere talk." At the end, Couch absolved Luhnow from blame, even though he had had harsh criticism for him throughout. He told Bierly that he criticized Harold Luhnow "because the worst form of disloyalty is to fail to be honest with your boss on the matters of the greatest importance." Closing the center, however, would be a repudiation of everything Luhnow had accomplished through the Volker Fund and, Couch maintained, "do more serious damage to all concerned but most of all to Mr. Luhnow."[71]

Stanford University and the Hoover Institution were not interested in absorbing the center on the terms demanded by Morris Cox, and Cox, Ivan Bierly, and Bill Couch were unwilling to accept the terms offered by Stanford. The taint of Nazism, the propaganda agenda of the center, and what was perceived as the general mismanagement of the effort by Bierly and Couch, led the Hoover Institution officials to conclude that the Center for American Studies needed the legitimacy of association with Stanford University far more than the Hoover Institution needed the remaining assets of the William Volker Fund.

In September 1964, Harold Luhnow officially terminated the Center for American Studies. Ivan Bierly turned to more honest work selling California real estate. Harold Luhnow was placed in a retirement home a few years later and turned the remaining assets of the Volker Fund over to Morris Cox. Cox finally terminated the Volker Fund officially in 1978 in what has been described as a "murky deal" that established the Morris Arnold Cox Senior Fellowship at the Hoover Institution with the remaining assets of the Volker Fund. Rushdoony became an influential figure as a founder of the Christian Reconstructionist Movement, in the movement for home schooling, and in the establishment of Christian academies as alternatives to public education. In the 1980s, Rushdoony was frequently called on to testify in court cases in which the legitimacy of home schooling was questioned. David Hoggan continued a publishing career seeking to vindicate the Nazis, to prove the Holocaust was a Zionist hoax, and became a dim New Light in the Institute for Historical Review.[72] William Terry Couch retired to North Carolina.

8

The Human Potential
for Modernism

Retirement was not a comfortable situation for Bill Couch. He did maintain a vegetable garden most years, but was not constitutionally disposed to hobbies and after an active intellectual life, he was not about to take up oil painting or knitting to pass the time until his eventual end. Couch had, however, been involved in politics, the dispersal of power and decision-making in society, in one way or another, throughout his entire career. The events of the 1960s and early 1970s captured his attention, even though he no longer had a forum to comment publicly on them. The student unrest in the 1960s particularly dismayed him. The student reaction across the country to the shootings at Kent State University on May 4, 1970, in the wake of Richard Nixon's announcement that U.S. troops had entered Cambodia to destroy the bases of operation of the Viet Cong and North Vietnamese forces, distressed him. Couch rose up in defense of Nixon and his secret plan to end the war in Vietnam.

Couch knew that the student protests were led by a small group of "string pullers" who had duped naive students into following a course that was doomed to failure. He knew that these leaders were fully aware that their program of harassing the government would lead to violence when Americans of common sense finally had enough to "give the harassers the beatings they so richly deserved." To Couch, the tragedy at Kent State University was inevitable. Of course, he acknowledged that Americans had the Constitutional right to peacefully and respectfully petition their elected officials, but the Constitution allowed no right to demand change through threats of violence and intimidation. These were techniques of Communism as he had learned at the Southern Conference for Human Welfare. Couch referred to the student protestors as *mobs* "because there is no other [word] that correctly describes a group of disorderly people that uses numbers, continual harassment, and the threat of violence in the effort to intimidate and get compliance with its demands." For Couch, the question was not whether Richard Nixon was right or wrong in his policy in Vietnam or Cambodia, but rather whether mob rule should be accepted or rejected. In the case of Kent State, he concluded, "You have to respect the office of the President. You have to support police and soldiers when they are called out to stop mob violence. You have to remember that there would be no damage, no maiming, no deaths in the absence of mobs."

Bill Couch knew who to blame. The fault lay with liberal members of the faculties of America's universities who failed to teach their students to distinguish sense from nonsense. These faculty members were abetted by university administrators too cowardly to take a firm stand against the student mobs. These leftist academics were encouraged in their acts by members of Congress, particularly Senator J. William Fulbright, who chaired the Senate Foreign Relations Committee and publicly opposed the Vietnam War. Couch observed that since the war had no congressional approval, "aid and comfort by members of congress and the public to the enemy is not a treasonable offense, though it is a despicable one."

That the flames of revolution were fanned by the mass media, particularly the powerful one of television, was even more despicable. The "highly skilled and determined group" of radicals in control of the student mobs knew how to create occasions to make national news and used that knowledge to manipulate the media "in tying the hands of government." He named Walter Cronkite, of course, as one nationally prominent news commentator who was most easily manipulated.

Couch professed that he was completely baffled by the question of what the students wanted. He had listened to the newscasts and had heard many demands, but none that made sense to him. The only possible result he could see from the mob was totalitarianism. He certainly did not think this was a conscious objective for American students, but warned that while "the patience of the public, and particularly of the police, in the face of the violence in which the students have been involved has been admirable," that patience was quickly dissipating.[1]

Couch defended Nixon, but he did not consider him a true conservative in any meaningful sense any more than Donald Davidson could consider Couch a true Confederate in the 1930s, but when many in the country demanded Nixon's resignation over the Watergate scandal, Couch came to his defense. While Couch was deeply concerned about the "failure of nerve, and perhaps failure of understanding" that had led to Nixon's troubles, he knew that violence and criminal activity that characterized the United States in the 1960s and into the 1970s "called for extraordinary action." A Democratically controlled Congress was incapable of doing anything to subdue the lawlessness in the land and, indeed, did nothing but place obstacles in the way of those who would.

To Couch, criminals had more protection under the laws a Democratic Congress passed than the victims of their crimes. American universities, teaching that crime and violence were the fault of society rather than the criminal, had only sunk America into a slough of despond in which the natural state of American citizens was to be the prey of whomever would take advantage of them. The Democratic Party, in collusion with a small gang of student activists, had seized that opportunity.

To Couch, Richard Nixon was as much a victim as any other American. The Democratic Party had accepted Communism as a valid form of social and political order in World War II during the Roosevelt administration and the Republican Party could not have objected in wartime without the charge of treason being raised against them. Appeasement of Communists had become established as American policy and the Democratic Party was at fault. Couch fell short of directly blaming the Democrats for Watergate to Russell Kirk, but if the Democrats had not supported the Communists in World War II and the Republicans had not, from a misguided sense of patriotism, followed, Richard Nixon would not have felt the compelling necessity for maintaining secret surveillance of the Democratic Party. It was unfortunate, but Couch concluded, Richard Nixon was right. Couch's exoneration of Nixon for Watergate was simple: "There are times when the law has to be broken in order to maintain the law."[2] He only extended this concession to Nixon, not to the students protesting the war in Vietnam.

Couch had not left the Center for American Studies and the Volker Fund empty-handed. As part of his severance settlement from the fund, Morris Cox gave him $75,000 to work on a book, with his usual stipulation that the Volker Fund would not be publicly acknowledged. While Couch had been a prolific author of journal and magazine articles throughout his career, his only solely-authored book, *The Human Potential: An Essay on Its Cultivation*, published by Duke University Press in 1974, was a direct result of the Volker Fund grant.

By 1969, he had completed a first draft of a manuscript with the title, "Education: Illustrations and Necessities," and had begun the search for a publisher. He sent out a prospectus including sample chapters to several trade houses including Knopf, Morrow, and Farrar, Straus and Giroux. These publishers politely rejected the book for publication. Couch continued writing and revising the manuscript and, in December 1971, sent a complete manuscript, under the title, "The Human Potential," to the trade division of Oxford University Press, which also declined the opportunity.[3]

Duke University accepted the manuscript for publication in September

1972. Ashbel Brice, head of the Duke University Press, had sent the manuscript to two readers, both of whom recommended publishing. Both readers knew that Couch was the author and both, apparently, knew Couch if not personally at least by reputation and thought highly of him. Their major objection was that the book was too long. Brice told Couch that he was going to recommend that the press publish the book to its editorial board, but cautioned him that the financial prospects for sales would be an obstacle to approval.[4]

Couch's book certainly did not fit into the publishing program at Duke any better than it had into the programs of the other publishers to whom he had offered it. Brice, however, did send it out to be evaluated, perhaps because he felt a personal link with Bill Couch. Ashbel Brice was known to his staff as a man willing to publish a book based on his personal regard for the author. When Brice wrote Couch to tell him that he was recommending the book to the press's advisory board, he reminded him that Couch had hosted the first Association of American University Presses meeting he had attended in the mid–1940s."[5] Further, Couch offered an unusually large subsidy to Duke to publish the book. One thousand dollars was provided by the Volker Fund and two thousand dollars from Couch's own resources. At the October 4, 1972, meeting of the advisory board of the press when the book was accepted, board member Marcus Hobbs, professor of philosophy and provost of Duke University, voted to accept the manuscript, but suggested that Couch be encouraged to raise the subsidy by one or two thousand dollars.[6] Couch dug deeper and contributed another $1,000 to raise the total to $4,000 with $1,000 from the Volker Fund and $3,000 from his own money, though part or all of this may have come from his settlement with the Volker Fund.[7]

Couch knew enough about university presses to realize from the start that he had little chance to profit from the book. Royalties would not be paid to him until the first one thousand copies had been sold. At a retail price of $9.75, over 4,000 copies would have to be sold before his own $3,000 would be realized. But, he had hopes.

From his experience at the presses of the University of North Carolina and the University of Chicago, Couch knew that it would take aggressive promotion to sell the book. University presses usually send out review copies to a modest list of academic journals in a particular field. Because of the specialized nature of the books they publish, it is also customary for a press to ask authors to suggest possible reviewing journals for their books. The "Author's Questionnaire" sent to Couch by the Duke University Press asked for specific journals to which it could distribute review copies. Couch's only immediate idea was the *Journal of General Education*, then published by the Pennsylvania State University Press. Couch had worked with the journal's editor, Henry Sams, and his wife, Carol, at the University of Chicago. Couch ended a detailed account of his history with them in the questionnaire, to conclude, "My guess is that Henry and Carol will be puzzled by *The Human Potential* and won't be jarred by it out of their dogmatic slumber." The press had simply asked for the titles of journals and Couch gave the question a lengthy personal essay.

Couch recommended to the press, "The shotgun approach has to be made to the promotion of *The Human Potential*." He knew that without strong interest from people who had read the book, there would be no chance of reaching a broader audience. No reviewer could truly understand his book without preparation and the only way to adequately prepare readers would be to find people who would "give it their enthusiastic endorsement." If this could be done, Couch predicated, the review journals would have to pay attention to the book.[8]

On February 6, 1973, Couch sent Rachel Davies, the advertising and promotion manager at the Duke press, a list of names of people to whom he suggested galleys of the book might be sent in an attempt to elicit positive comments that could be used to promote it. Even if readers did not offer words that could be used in advertising, this approach might at least generate interest by encouraging influential people to read the book in hopes they would discuss it with other influential people. He told her:

> The enclosed list runs to between 50 and 100 or more names. Word of mouth promotion of a book is extremely important, and you may find it worthwhile to try to get more quotations. Free copies to a carefully selected list, with requests for opinions can be far the least expensive way and far the most effective way of getting a book started.

On the list he appended, there were sixty-eight names including many conservative writers he had worked with as contributors at *Collier's Encyclopedia*, such as Cleanth Brooks, Brand Blanchard, chairman of the philosophy department at Yale, and Russell Kirk. Also listed were friends from other parts of his career such as James J. Kilpatrick, Virginius Dabney, and Howard Mumford Jones as well as others, Robert Maynard Hutchins, John Hope Franklin, and Sidney Hook, with whom he had clashed in the past. He followed this a week later with another list of ninety-four newspapers, journals, and magazines that included every possibility, and some very vague possibilities, for reviewing the book such as *Kirkus*, *Time*, and the *Manchester Guardian*.[9] Couch was encouraging Duke University Press to adapt the techniques he had used earlier, particularly in the promotion of A. Frank Reel's *The Case of General Yamashita* at the University of Chicago Press.

Rachel Davies had a far more realistic idea of the potential sales of the book. She ignored Couch's requests for mass mailing of the book to the world at large, though she did send out review copies and the book slowly received some notice. Davies wrote to Couch on August 13, 1974, attempting to calm his growing anxieties. She agreed with him that it would be good for the book to be reviewed by the *New York Times*, but acknowledged, "I have to confess that it's been a long time since I've seen a Duke book mentioned therein." She assured him that the delay he had experienced in seeing reviews of the book was normal and "frequently an author waits over a year for any such mention."[10]

Any reviewer would have had a difficult time dealing with *The Human Potential*. Had an author submitted it to the University of North Carolina Press or the University of Chicago Press while Couch was in charge, he would probably have rejected it as a gallimaufry, one of Couch's favorite words of condemnation. The book, as the readers for Duke University Press noted, was too long and it was also too convoluted to serve as a coherent expression of Couch's central idea: the world was in a terrible state, ignorance was the root cause of that state, and salvation lay in the comprehensive collection of knowledge through a universal encyclopedia. The point of the book was the need to provide some essential element for general education that had not been offered in the past and, to demonstrate that need, Couch assessed the general state of learning. The first three hundred pages offered Couch's jeremiad on the deplorable state of education, knowledge, and learning in the western world.

To his credit, Couch warned the reader at the beginning when he admitted that providing the evidence of intellectual decay of western civilization that grounded his proposal was "the most difficult problem in the writing of this book." He advised that anyone who could accept that western intellectuals were already in Hell and the hand-basket had just left to pick up the next cohort of intellectually confused sinners "can safely skip this evidence and pass on to the last two chapters."[11]

Readers could skip. Reviewers could not. Louis Schneider of the sociology department of the University of Texas reviewed the book for *Annals of the American Academy of Political and Social Science*. It was a strongly positive review that concluded, Couch "is worth accompanying in his controlled rambles," but noted his writing was "often somewhat in the manner of free association."[12] Schneider was right. While Couch did produce more than an occasional well-turned sentence, he was too prolix for most readers, obscuring his meaning in a barrage of words and a flow of disjointed ideas. Further, his rambles were not particularly well-controlled. He jumped from idea to idea in a frequently random display of rhetoric.

Much of the book reads more as a commonplace book than it does an exposition with a central idea and purpose. While the book did have a plan and while Couch, at the end of his opening chapter, did explain the structure and how each chapter topic related to his conception of the whole, his argument is lost in the wealth of detailed digression he used to convolute his exposition. There is an opening chapter on Edmund Burke that worked its way to Communism, Robespierre, Adam Smith, and Margaret Mead only to lurch to an abrupt end with a comparison of Sophocles's and Jean Anouilh's treatment of Antigone. It is a *tour de force* that follows a logic, but not a logic that the average reader would be likely to ride to its conclusion. Two chapters on Marshall McLuhan, two chapters critiquing current American encyclopedias, particularly *Britannica*, and a chapter on the educational thought of Robert Maynard Hutchins followed by one on the failure of Hutchins's ideas on general education at the University of Chicago, suffer from similar difficulties. Couch used his book and its central idea to carry too much freight to the reader.

The final two chapters in which Couch outlined his proposal for a new encyclopedia are, after the morass of the first eleven, remarkable for their relative clarity. For the penultimate chapter, he had promised a cure for the plague afflicting western civilization, but only managed to hint at it by proposing that "an institute for general education in a free society" be established that would design and produce an encyclopedia specifically for general education. While such an endeavor would need financial backing at the beginning, it would eventually be self-sustaining through sales of the encyclopedia. The encyclopedia itself would be published by a commercial press, but the physical books would only represent a part of the program of his institute. A physical encyclopedia was too passive an instrument to effect the kind of cultural transformation Couch envisioned. He called for a sustained series "of public forums on topics of contemporary interest involving principles of perennial interest." He insisted that the effort be centered in a university community, but it could only have an informal connection to a university and should be governed by "public-spirited citizens, university faculty members, and university students" without the interference of university administrators.[13] A university was too corrupt an institution to be entrusted with a project of this importance. These were not new ideas for Couch. He had urged similar proposals to his superiors at *Collier's Encyclopedia* almost twenty years earlier with no results.

With *The Human Potential*, Couch made a statement he considered the culmination of his life's work. His major concern was that his book and his ideas be noticed and taken seriously. The book was reviewed, perhaps, as widely as any other university press book in the 1970s. *Library Journal* published a short positive review, and Couch was pleasantly surprised by the praise that appeared in *Choice*, the book review journal published by the Association of College and Research Libraries, a division of the American Library Association, even though it said the book's appeal may be limited to academics "or tavern discussions between self-educated longshoremen over a cold beer in July," a slighting reference to Eric Hoffer. Couch was gratified.[14]

These reviews encouraged Couch, but they were not in the publications he wanted and needed to bring the book to the attention of the audience he had tried to reach. He had failed with the *New York Times*, but he had hopes for the *Saturday Review* and on September 7, 1974, wrote the editor, Norman Cousins, directly. It was an unctuously polite letter asking if Cousins had received the review copy of *The Human Potential* sent by Duke University Press a few months earlier and telling him that he was having the press send another copy if the first had not been brought to his attention "since I believe you would be especially interested in it."[15] *Saturday Review* failed to review the book.

Couch persisted and turned to his friend, James Osler Bailey, professor of literature at the University of North Carolina, for help. Couch had sent Bailey a copy of the book in hopes of enhancing the word-of-mouth campaign he personally had mounted. Bailey had responded favorably to the book and, when Couch despaired of obtaining a review through Cousins, Couch asked him to review the book and attempt to get Cousins to publish it in the *Saturday Review*. Bailey wrote a review and submitted it to the *Saturday Review*. It was rejected. Couch responded by lambasting Bailey, not for the rejection, but for the incompetency of the review. The incident threatened their close friendship to the point that Bailey gently told Couch, "You might benefit from a vacation, for you seem unusually tense."[16]

Couch was unusually tense. He desperately wanted the book to be taken seriously by the same liberal intellectuals he was attacking, the ones who were not paying attention to the destruction of western civilization by the forces of ignorance, statism, and collectivism. He wanted reviews in the *Saturday Review*, in the *New York Times*, and in the *Wall Street Journal*, but these were not forthcoming. The only way Couch could possibly reach the general, literate, and engaged audience he wanted for his ideas would have to be through advertisement in the media. However, Duke University Press had no funds for the kind of advertising he wanted. As Mary Louise Back, Rachel Davies's replacement in promotions at Duke University Press, told Couch, "Alas, the really juicy places like the *New York Times* and *New York Review of Books*, and other such are out of reach for us."[17]

Even though the book did not receive attention from the major media, it did, as far as might reasonably be expected, receive notice in the scholarly community. In addition to the review in the *Annals of the American Academy of Political and Social Science*, it was reviewed by Alan G. Hill of Columbia University in *Sociology: Reviews of New Books*. Hill's review was generally positive. He was not, however, overly kind to Couch and concluded, "Despite the not inconsiderable defects of his book, Couch is to be commended for moving from a critique of the intellectual world, where many would have stopped, to a concrete proposal. We wish his encyclopedia project well."[18] This review brought a sharp rejoinder from Couch to the editor of the journal in which he picked it apart for three pages, focusing on Hill's characterization of Couch as a conservative. Since the term has "no internally consistent body of doctrine—or one that its adherents think is so," the charge was nonsense or, at best, irrelevant to the book. It was a lengthy rebuttal and Couch insisted at the end that if his letter was published, it must be printed in its entirety. The editor politely responded that responses to reviews in the journal were limited to twenty-five to fifty words.[19]

Two reviews in major academic journals and two solid reviews in major library book selection tools within a year after publication is a good record for most books from university presses. Mary Louise Back wrote to tell him so in April 1975, when she assured him that "you're overly pessimistic in thinking that the book is dead: it's generally the second and third year after publication that university press books receive most of their reviews, and I do expect more will come in on *The Human Potential*."[20]

She was right and Couch should have known this, but he persisted in his efforts to have his book read and reviewed as widely as possible by people who would be sympathetic to his cause. In August 1974, he wrote to Eliseo Vivas, associate editor of the conservative journal the *Modern Age*, asking him to review the book. Couch had published Vivas's first book, *The Moral Life and the Ethical Life*, at the University of Chicago in 1950. Like many of Couch's friends, Vivas declined, telling Couch, "Some time ago I promised myself never—but never—to review the book of a friend: after several experiences that turned out into disagreeable catastrophes." Vivas did, however, promise to contact Joseph Michael Lalley, the book review editor of *Modern Age*, who had in the past reviewed books on Vivas's recommendation.[21] Couch contacted Lalley directly, saying that he had already obtained a commitment to write a review from his friend E. Maynard Adams, professor of philosophy and chairman of the faculty at the University of North Carolina, which could be sent for consideration. Lalley asked Couch to send the Adams review to him if it would fit into the 1,000 to 1,500 words that the journal could accommodate.

Adams had earlier agreed to review Couch's book for the local newspaper in Chapel Hill since Couch strongly felt that the book's sales would be enhanced if North Carolina newspapers published reviews or at least notices of the book. Surprisingly, Couch was not familiar with the Chapel Hill newspaper. When he looked at it, he concluded that it was not an appropriate place for a review, even if the editor would publish it.[22] By the time Couch wrote Lalley, Adams had abandoned the task and never completed the review.

In the end, Lalley reviewed the book himself, publishing it in the summer, 1975, issue of *Modern Age*. It was a lengthy review that focused on a few of the particulars of Couch's central argument that condemned the "intellectual nihilism" of logical positivism, but failed to address Couch's encyclopedia proposal as an antidote to the philosophies that had poisoned the western intellectual tradition.[23] It was unsatisfactory to Couch.

If he could not get reviews in the *New York Times* and the *Wall Street Journal*, he knew he could rely another source, his good friend Russell Kirk and his periodical, the *University Bookman*. Kirk had read chapters of the book in manuscript as Couch was writing it and had told Couch, "Your book is lucid, but complex." Kirk suggested that Couch needed a restatement of his idea and should "consider prefixing to the book a sort of Argument or systematic table of contents common enough in the eighteenth and nineteenth centuries—a brief summary of the arguments of each chapter." Kirk was concerned about the accessibility of the book to the "common reader."[24]

Kirk's suggestions came too late. The book was already in press by the time he made them. Couch replied to Kirk asking him if he would give a whole issue of the *University Bookman* over to the book. Kirk agreed, telling Couch when the book was available, he would not only have two reviews for the journal, but he would also review it in his syndicated newspaper column, "To the Point," and promised a longer review of it for William F. Buckley's *National Review*.[25]

Kirk did a review for his newspaper column, but it was little more than a note. Buckley apparently declined to give over a page in the book review section of the *National Review* to Couch's book. Kirk did, however, use his column in the *National Review*, "From the Academy," in the June 7, 1974, issue for a review.[26] It was a purely descriptive account, but Kirk gave it more than he could in his newspaper column and ended by referring his readers to the reviews that were forthcoming in the *University Bookman*.

These reviews were more detailed and substantial. Kirk did not have enough copy with the two pieces to completely fill out the issue devoted to the book and had Couch himself contribute a review of the recently published *New Encyclopaedia Britannica* to the issue.[27] Couch, as could have been expected, found *Britannica* lacking, even though he did admit, "it is probably the best encyclopaedia now existing in the English language." His review picked *Britannica* apart with frequent side references to *The Human Potential*.[28]

The two reviews of *The Human Potential* that Russell Kirk published in the *University Bookman* disappointed Couch. One of the reviewers, Victor M. Cassidy, had served as an associate editor in technology for the *New Encyclopaedia Britannica*. Cassidy focused tightly on Couch's criticisms of *Britannica* in *The Human Potential*, rising to *Britannica*'s defense. Most of his review ignored

Couch's book completely and was devoted to explaining the difficulties of editing and producing the encyclopedia. Cassidy did acknowledge that Couch was correct in many of his criticisms, but concluded, "Mr. Couch overstates his case and makes impractical proposals" without recognizing that the *New Encyclopaedia Britannica* was a major positive development in encyclopedia design. Cassidy castigated Couch's book as "abominably written and organized—any editor could have shortened it by a hundred pages."[29]

Russell Kirk had specifically asked Frederick D. Wilhelmsen, professor of philosophy and politics at the University of Dallas, to address what Couch had written about Marshall McLuhan in the second review of Couch's book for the journal. Wilhelmsen did praise Couch "for having written one of the few significant books on general education that has been published in recent years," but took him to task in a closely reasoned essay for completely misunderstanding and misrepresenting Marshall McLuhan in *The Human Potential*.[30]

Couch was incensed when he read the reviews. He fired off a series of letters to Russell Kirk about the reviewers, complaining, "Their comments present me as an ignoramus, softened a little but still an ignoramus." He picked apart both Cassidy's and Wilhelmsen's critiques bit by bit in these letters saying that Wilhelmsen "simply hadn't read the book with care and thought seriously about what he was reading" and both reviewers were "utterly lacking in the background and skill necessary for fruitful discussion—but then so is a large part of the intellectual world.." Kirk replied that he had hoped for more positive reviews from the two and tried to reassure Couch telling him that "a sharply critical review, however, often does more to interest people in a book than does an ordinary humdrum review." Kirk told Couch that he would fit a response from him to the reviews into an upcoming issue of the *University Bookman*.[31]

The summer, 1975, issue carried Couch's response. It was a restrained reaction. While he privately condemned the reviewers as absurd and maintained that their reviews proved his contention in the book that "most of those of us who write haven't yet learned to read," he refrained from personal attacks on Cassidy and Wilhelmsen. Rather, he defended his own position and eloquently refuted the criticisms of the reviewers. He concluded by thanking them for their "stimulating comments" and expressing his gratitude to them for offering him the "occasion for this response." To promote his book, Couch had hoped to send out several hundred copies of the issue of the *University Bookman* containing the reviews, but the poor quality of the reviews and the incompetency of the reviewers dissuaded him from this.[32]

By 1979, Couch had given up on the book. He wrote a friend about the general nature of criticism and, specifically, about *The Human Potential*:

> I doubt whether any book has ever come into the world and been so completely ignored. In fact, the particular targets I took for attack have disappeared and were disappearing even before the book I wrote could be published. Who, it might be asked, could reasonably expect discussion of things gone and forgotten? Well, I did and I was mistaken. I assumed that our critics would still know that the old is constantly reappearing in new forms and perhaps under new names in the new. My argument in the book is that we have lost the basis for even the tentative knowing, for more than a moment of anything, so I cannot say I was greatly surprised at the it's come and it's gone treatment that my book got.[33]

It was not quite gone then, but in May 1983, Couch received a letter from Mary Louise Back telling him that the book was being remaindered. She offered him any or all of the final 112 copies at a twenty-five percent discount from the retail price. His royalty statement from the press at the end of 1983 stated that a total of 973 copies had been sold since its publication in 1974.[34]

The book itself was dead, but Couch's idea was not quite. Gregory William Sand, a visiting lecturer in history at the University of Missouri at Kansas City at the time, read the book and became interested in the possibilities outlined by Couch. Couch was delighted. His central hope for the book was that it might inspire someone to act on his proposal, but the reviewing media had failed to notice the book and he had given up on that prospect. While Couch was pleased that someone was interested in pursuing his ideas, he was not able to give the financial assistance that Sand sought, and directed him to Russell Kirk.[35]

Sand did write to Kirk who suggested that he might try the Marguerite Eyer Wilbur Foundation for possible funding for the project. Sand approached the Wilbur Foundation and also *Vera Lex* and the Natural Law Society, but to no avail.[36]

In June 1984, Sand wrote Couch asking him if he would become a member of an advisory board he was gathering for the project. Couch declined.[37] Couch knew that it would take an endowment of at least twenty-five to fifty million dollars to properly undertake the encyclopedia he had proposed.[38] Sand had no hopes of raising that amount and Couch had no desire to involve himself in an inadequately funded effort.

While Couch was writing *The Human Potential*, he received some encouragement that his career had not been forgotten or ignored. On August 3, 1970, Daniel Singal, a doctoral student in American history at Columbia University, asked Couch if he would be willing to be interviewed for the Columbia Oral History Office. The interview would be used for a chapter on Couch in Singal's dissertation.[39]

Couch agreed and on October 22, 1970, Singal met Couch at his home in Carrboro, North Carolina. It was a long session and Singal returned for additional sessions on November 11, 12, 13 and, finally, on November 21, to complete the series of interviews. During these meetings, Singal and Couch developed a close personal relationship that deepened as Couch commented on chapters of Singal's dissertation and its revision for publication and Singal read and offered constructive criticism of Couch's *The Human Potential*.[40]

As was the custom of the Oral History Office, the transcript of the interview was submitted to Couch for his corrections and emendations. The transcriber was dismayed to find that Couch had extensively edited it, treating the interview transcript as he would any manuscript submitted to him at a university press or at *Collier's*. The typist admitted that Couch's additions "do result in a substantial improvement of the transcript," but were so extensive "that virtually the entire manuscript will have to be retyped."[41]

Through Singal's dissertation and the revision of the work, Couch provided detailed corrections to Singal's text and elaborations on his own motivation as well as providing philosophical digressions in many directions. In one three page single-spaced letter about Singal's chapter on Howard Odum, in which Couch addressed the problems of heredity (both biological and cultural) and environment (both physical and social), in a general condemnation of Odum's cultural relativism, he concluded, "I still see no need for any revisions in the Chapter. I'm sorry to be so unhelpful."[42]

When it came to his own chapter, Couch was even more detailed. By 1975, Couch had deposited his own papers in the Southern Historical Collection at the University of North Carolina. What Singal wrote sent Couch to the Louis Round Wilson Special Collections Library in an attempt to validate his own memory. As Couch wrote to Singal at the end of 1975, "This has been a most interesting experience in that it tells me something of my own memory—how badly it can be misled." Couch had numerous corrections and objections to the chapter, some of which he concluded, after examining the record, that Singal was correct, but others that Singal was wrong. The two most substantial ones were Singal's account of Rayford Logan's book, *What the Negro Wants*, which Couch asserted was intended from the beginning to be part of a two volume set with Logan's volume representing the African American view and a second volume to represent the white view. Couch was approximately right. The two books were not proposed concurrently, but shortly after Logan's book was approved by the governors of the press, Couch announced that a companion volume to be written by prominent white southerners was under consideration.[43]

Couch's second problem was Singal's charge that in the 1930s, Couch held sympathy for the Communist cause. Couch objected strenuously to this imagined calumny, but admitted to Singal, "I have no difficulty in understanding how you came to your interpretation." Couch had sided with causes such as the

Sacco and Vanzetti case in which he aligned himself with Communists and had been actively involved in the early meetings of the Southern Conference for Human Welfare. He also readily confessed to being a New Dealer in the 1930s. These activities and associations, he maintained, were aberrations taken out of the context of his life and work.

Throughout these exchanges, Couch remained a cordial supporter of Singal's work. He assured Singal, "If you didn't slip on a few points, I'd begin thinking you were more than human" and concluded with a reassurance: "You will remember, I'm sure, you are the author and will do with all my notes what *you* see fit."[44] Couch would never have allowed this license to anyone submitting a book or article to him for publication. But, Couch's editorial judgment was moderated by Singal's interest in his life and his close attention to Couch's narrative.

Any man entering his eighth decade would naturally be concerned about the record he leaves as well as about his declining physical capacity. Knowing that his life's work would be documented in Daniel Singal's oral history and in Singal's dissertation reassured Couch on the first concern. His health, however, was suffering from the natural progression of his years.

Beginning in 1982, Couch was afflicted with arthritis to such an extent that he was only able to walk with difficulty. On the recommendation of his doctor, he began forcing himself to walk and within a year could manage to cover a mile and a half daily on the streets around his new home in Chapel Hill. It was not without a great deal of pain, but he persisted.

He approved of Daniel Singal's positive treatment of him, but found other public notices objectionable, especially those that came from what he thought should have been sympathetic sources. In 1979, the *National Review* published a letter to the editor in which Couch took Charles Kesler to task for an article published in the July 6, 1979, issue of the magazine. Kesler, a graduate student at Harvard, had written the piece as a tribute to Harry V. Jaffa, a historian then considered a senior figure in the conservative movement. Couch's letter, printed by the editor under the heading, "Muddled Messages," took both Kesler and Jaffa to task for their misinterpretation of the words *equality* and *liberty* in the *Declaration of Independence*. Couch particularly objected to what he had read into Kesler's essay when he accused Kesler and Jaffa of equating conservatism with *traditionalism*, a word that Couch proclaimed was meaningless because it did not signify anything more than continuity without recognizing that some continuities or traditions were better than others. They both had, Couch persisted, fallen into the trap of accepting the notion of cultural relativism without being aware that it was one in which all American scholars were ensnared.

Harry V. Jaffa responded to Couch's letter with an article in the July 11, 1980, issue of the magazine in which he demolished Couch's argument in terms that brought Couch's intellectual ability into question. Jaffa wrote a piece that was incisive and conclusively compelling and left Couch with little with which to shield himself from the charge of intellectual incompetence. At its kindest, Jaffe accused Couch of having "misunderstood and misrepresented—however unintentionally" the issues involved.[45]

Bill Couch left the discussion at that for the time. Two years later while in the glow of what he still considered his excellent treatment by Daniel Singal and amidst the distress of his increasingly bad health, he received a form letter from the *National Review* over William F. Buckley, Jr.'s signature asking why he had not renewed his subscription to the magazine. Couch was furious. He immediately began a letter to Buckley that opened, "Surely ... you do not expect a person to continue subscribing to a medium that has published virtual libels about him." He accused Buckley of arrogance and of not recognizing Couch's own importance to the conservative cause in America. Bill Couch's reply to Bill Buckley was long and convoluted, but in essence he condemned Buckley for not realizing that had the American Library Association not had him fired from *Collier's Encyclopedia*, Bill Couch and *Collier's* would have had the national conservative pulpit rather than Bill Buckley and the *National Review*. Buckley had the financial backing and the support to do what he wanted to define conservatism in American with no one above him to stop him as Couch had had at Chicago and Collier-Crowell. Couch scolded Buckley, "It takes an enormous ego, Mr. Buckley, to imagine as you appear to do, that you are the only person in the country to do work just as important as yours." Couch went on to enumerate Buckley's many failures with the *National Review*. Bill Couch was particularly upset since he considered himself at least partially responsible for Buckley's success. When Buckley began the magazine, he approached Couch and others to send out letters to friends asking them to subscribe. Couch sent him names and Buckley had letters typed in his office for Couch's signature.[46]

Buckley had sorely disappointed Couch in not realizing the potential of his magazine, but his major disappointment was Buckley's failure to suppress Jaffa's attack on him and his refusal to recognize that William Terry Couch's contribution to American conservatism was as significant as that of Buckley himself. Couch's dudgeon was real, but he knew that he was overextending it after three double-spaced pages of heaping abuse on Buckley without finding a conclusion. He never completed the letter and sent, instead, a more temperate response. He simply declined to renew his subscription to the *National Review* without elaborating on his reasons.

Couch's disappointment over Buckley's perfidy was assuaged to some extent by the publication of Singal's dissertation. The revision of Singal's dissertation was published in October 1982, by the University of North Carolina

Press under the title, *The War Within: From Victorian to Modernist Thought in the South, 1919–1945*. Couch received his advanced copy on August 12th and spent a week reading it before writing Singal to congratulate him on his achievement. When he did write to Singal he pronounced the book "excellent, possibly because it is so flattering of me—though you do rank me as a 'racist' but not perhaps as a thoroughly vicious one." Even with this, Couch's reaction to Singal's book was enthusiastically positive.[47]

After a month, Couch had more time to give the book the close careful reading he habitually gave to any book and wrote to Singal reaffirming his positive view of the book and of Singal as an historian. Singal responded, reporting that he had heard about a review that was coming out in the *New York Times Book Review* that "appears to be filled with fireworks, all very much favorable to our cause."[48]

The *New York Times Book Review* published David Herbert Donald's review of *The War Within* on October 31, 1982. It was a laudatory review that praised the book as "a first-rate piece of work." Unfortunately, Donald, chairman of the graduate program in American civilization at Harvard, singled out the chapter on Couch as an odd choice for inclusion, saying, "It is hard to see why Mr. Couch is considered a Modernist at all, and certainly he was not a major intellectual figure comparable to Odum, Faulkner or Tate."[49] Howard Odum, William Faulkner, and Allen Tate had all received their own separate chapters in the book.

Couch was furious. He wrote to the editor of the *New York Times Book Review* defending his right to be included in the book. Planting his tongue firmly in his cheek, he proclaimed he was as irrational as any Modernist and deserved his place in Singal's book, even though he admitted to lapses: "I cultivate my irrationality as strenuously as I can, but despite all my efforts, a little sanity now and then breaks through."[50]

Couch followed this a few days later with a more serious critique of Donald's review in which he assessed Singal's monumental achievement: "He brings together within a few hundred pages records of the shifts in commitments of persons of the highest honesty and intelligence from one body of doctrine to a contradictory body on questions of the greatest importance, e.g., whether there is any truth discoverable by human beings—or only a shifting body of opinion, not merely adjustments—the most important of all questions." The thrust of Couch's argument was that neither Singal nor Donald could, as Modernists, claim omniscience. That was reserved for theology. When Donald criticized Singal for including Couch among the Modernists, he was saying that Singal did not know enough about his own work "to choose the right subject, and did not know enough to choose the right parts." Donald did not realize that "he is asserting that he knows rightness when he sees it, whereas his Modernism denies that there is any rightness to see, and holds that even an opinion about rightness is nonsense."[51]

Donald's review caused a major rift between Couch and Daniel Singal. Singal himself dated the change in their relationship to December 1982, when Couch engaged him in a quarrel about the concept of Modernism in response to the review. Couch was upset over the review, but he was more upset over Singal's dismissal of what Donald said about Couch himself. Couch's own book had not made the review section of the *New York Times* and when he was finally noticed for his chapter in Singal's book, it was not flattering. Singal's advice to him, "Just remember the advice you use to give authors when unfavorable notices appeared and ignore the ones you don't like," rankled and he found little balm in Singal's words.[52] Couch's only effective course was to appeal to the editor of the *New York Times Book Review*.

Couch's series of letters to Harvey Shapiro, the *New York Times Book Review* editor, about the Donald review were remarkable in their focus. He habitually approached such confrontations with a barrage of ideas, information, and opinion, picking apart the points of contention from an array of perspectives that were usually notable for their range, their vitriol, and their incisive critiques of the myriad inconsistencies in the reviewer's words. Here, he focused on one major point, the omniscience of the reviewer, and stuck to that.

Couch finally abandoned any hope of getting satisfaction from Harry Shapiro when he submitted a detailed alternate review of Singal's book under the title "What Is Daniel Singal's Book The War Within About?" to him in December. In a dozen pages, he took both Donald and Singal to task for their failures: Singal, for placing him in the world of the Modernists without realizing the inconsistency in positing a dichotomy between Victorianism and Modernism that was based more on rhetoric than reality, and Donald for not seeing that Couch himself was a major player in the transformation. Couch cited Brand Blanchard of the philosophy department at Yale, W. J. Cash, author of *The Mind of the South*, Gertrude Himmelfarb, author of *Darwin and the Darwinian Revolution*, David Hume, John Milton, Gilbert Murray, author of *Five Stages of Greek Religion*, Karl Pearson on social Darwinism, Beardsley Ruml, chairman of the board of Macy's, Bertrand Russell, and John L. Stewart, author of *The Burden of Time*, among others, in support of his position. Here, Couch refuted his earlier facetious argument that he belonged because he was irrational by triumphantly asserting his rationality over the irrationality of both Singal and Donald when he concluded:

The book, *The War Within*, is among the most interesting, provocative and revealing books I have ever read about any particular society. In my opinion, the notions of both culture and modernism that dominate the book are the most dangerous errors of our time. But this is what makes the book of extraordinary value. I recommend it as a compendium of the most serious intellectual errors of our time, but it has to be read closely and with extreme care, otherwise it spreads the errors that if read with sufficient care it exposes.[53]

Couch, clearly, had major objections at this point to Singal's work. Shapiro declined to publish Couch's alternative review.[54]

Couch's review was part of a much longer *Apologia pro Vita Mea* that eventually ran to one hundred and sixty-nine pages under the working title, "The Critical Temperament at the Mourner's Bench." This title came from the bench at the front of a church where penitent sinners knelt to pray for forgiveness. Couch cited an incident recounted by his friend, Charles Wood, a lawyer in Roxboro, North Carolina, in which Wood, as an adolescent, was at the bench and raised his head from prayer to ask a question of the minister. The preacher's response was to slam Wood's head back to the railing, commanding him to shut up.[55] To Couch, the incident was an objective correlative to the treatment that his own objections to Singal's work had received.

In his expanded piece, Couch blamed Singal's academic preparation for the failures of the book. As an academic, Singal existed in "an almost hopelessly warped environment." It was an environment that accepted, as a basic postulate, the doctrine of cultural relativism, a notion that was abhorrent to Couch.[56] Couch was a firm believer in natural law, that there were standards of conduct in human relations that transcended cultures and societies. Indeed, Couch had long maintained that the search for natural laws, "an assertion of a regularity, a process of any kind that has been observed always and everywhere in human affairs," was the most important human activity and should be the fundamental quest of the social sciences.[57]

For Couch, the tragedy of western civilization was the abandonment of natural law for the notion that all cultures merit equal consideration and value. There is no better or worse. There are only differences. Singal's defect was to be so totally immersed in the academic faith of cultural relativism that he was unable to comprehend other philosophical perspectives.

Couch was correct. Daniel Singal's analysis of the phenomenon of southern Modernism was explicitly based on a paradigm of Modernism that incorporated cultural relativism and, specifically, the idea that research in cultural anthropology had destroyed the Victorian notion that civilization was "some vague spiritual quality cultured people possessed, but rather it was a set of traits and practices people invented to adapt to the particular environment they found themselves in." The issues of morality and values—of good and evil—had no place in a Modernist academic discussion of culture and civilization. To this,

Couch countered, "If the anthropologist has no ethical standards of his own, he lacks the basic qualification necessary to the effort to discover the truth about social ethics."[58]

In his introductory paragraph to the section of *The War Within*, "The Modernist Generation Arrives," in which the chapter on Couch appears, Singal articulated his thesis:

> By the late 1920s the process of intellectual change in the South entered what might be called its third stage. An increasing number of writers appeared whose sensibilities and style of thought could be identified beyond doubt as Modernist. For them, the debate that had started in the late nineteenth century was largely over. They began with the assumption that man was the human animal, that the universe was inherently irrational, that morality was embedded in history and not in immutable natural laws, and that personality was primarily determined by one's culture."[59]

Couch had argued with David Herbert Donald and the *New York Times* that he belonged in Singal's book, but his argument was based on Donald's assertion that "he was not a major intellectual figure comparable to Odum, Faulkner, or Tate." As Couch reread Singal's book and fully came to understand what Singal meant by *Modernism*, he came to agree with Donald that he was not a Modernist, at least in the sense constructed by Singal. Of course, he continued to consider himself as equal in importance to Odum, Faulkner, and Tate.

Couch had worked closely with Singal as he revised his dissertation for publication by the University of North Carolina Press. From the basic oral history Singal had done for Columbia University and subsequent interviews with Couch, Singal constructed an interpretation of Couch as a southern Modernist. In the preface to his book, Singal described his approach to the topic. As a basic assumption, Singal stated, "Ideas are not created by eras, or generations, or even schools of thought; they are generated by individuals through a complex interaction between the mind, intellectual influences, and the personal encounters with the world."[60] This is good history. Data is gathered. The information subjected to rigorous analysis. Conclusions are reached.

It was not, however, an approach that satisfied Couch. He objected to being dumped into the same pen as novelist Robert Penn Warren and the Odum crowd of Rupert Vance, Guy Benton Johnson, and Arthur Franklin Raper. The essence of his objection, though, derived from Singal's methods. He complained that at no time in the original interviews or in subsequent meetings and correspondence did Singal "ask me any questions intended to discover what I considered my most important beliefs." He had asked nothing about the things crucial to Couch: nothing about religion, nor metaphysics, nor philosophy, nor

212   William Terry Couch and the Politics of Academic Publishing

"about any basic commitments I might have." Couch concluded. "Perhaps he thought he could psychoanalyze me from what he got in the question and answer process beyond that which he recorded, as well as from my life history." He berated Singal for implying that he was a Communist or at least a "fellow traveler." Singal denied that he had done this, but Couch could read the accusation between the lines that Singal wrote and took objected to it. The charge, to Couch, supported his conclusion that "Singal didn't need either flimsy or solid evidence. His imagination, bias for Utopia, and absolute faith in sufficiently startling Freudian 'revelations' were all he needed."

Throughout the piece, Couch affirmed his general conclusion that "Mr. Singal's book is an invaluable compendium of the worst errors that are possible in human thought."[61] Further, he complained that Singal had provided no "grounds but his imagination for the Modernism he attributes to me."[62] Though Couch rejected being placed under the banner of Modernism, Daniel Singal was essentially correct. While Couch himself held strongly to the convictions he had developed at the University of North Carolina, at the University of Chicago, and at Crowell-Collier, convictions that provided him with a firm foundation in knowing right from wrong and sense from nonsense, he increasingly found himself trapped by the quicksand of Modernism. The consistent ethical and moral basis on which he constructed his sense of reality was eroding and his only recourse was to hold more firmly to the foundation of conservatism he had carefully constructed. Even though he had characterized himself using those terms, he bristled equally when Allen Tate condemned him as a *liberal* in the 1930s and Eli Oboler called him a *conservative* in the 1950s. For Couch, truth was truth and knew no place in a political spectrum. However, for Bill Couch, truth was becoming more and more elusive.

The protest movement against the Vietnam War and Nixon's troubled last term in office worried Couch as violations of the natural order of society. He found other developments even more distressing to his sense of natural law and moral absolutes. Events in South Africa in the 1970s over the governmental policy of apartheid and the demands for black majority rule in the country posed severe problems for his sense of the permanence of truth and eternal values. While he could, by then, acknowledge that white supremacy as the official policy of the American South was wrong, the idea of black supremacy in South Africa meant that "we are still almost as badly lost in the wilderness of absurdity as we have ever been."

Rule by political majorities was an evil no matter who might compose the majority and the problem lay in the nature of majority rule, not in the race of the majority. He objected to the use of the term, *black majority rule*, as it was being bandied about in the news and was concerned about the parallel with white supremacy saying, "I know only too well what would happen to any southerner of any prominence who was so ill-advised as even to suggest, without using the expression 'white supremacy' that the principle intended by this expression should be accepted generally throughout the United States." Essentially, it was the words, not their substance to which Couch objected and, as an editor and author, he was awed by the power of words: "Words, I repeat, when widely transmitted in public, can have tremendous influence."[63] Couch knew full well that words could hang you. They had at Chicago and at *Collier's*, and finally, at the Center for American Studies. Couch was firmly trapped in the morass that Daniel Singal saw as the fate of southern Modernists and "was lost in a world of paradox and moral relativism." Singal did see some hope in the emergence of "a new sense of guidance" to replace the loss of certainty by the Modernists, a "liberation from liberation itself," but Couch missed this in his wandering through the maze of cultural relativism and logical positivism.[64]

Couch blustered and threatened to sue Singal, the University of North Carolina, and its press for publishing the book." He might have done so had he had the money, but he settled for a hearing before the press's Board of Governors. Couch prepared a statement that he read to the board at a meeting on February 23, 1984, titled, "The Critical Temperament Leashed." It was a restrained presentation in which Couch admitted to his ultimate dissatisfaction: "I do not like the idea of being embalmed forever like an insect in amber in a book." Couch demanded that the press publish his rebuttal to Singal's interpretation, "The Critical Temperament at the Mourner's Bench," as a separate to be sent to all reviewers of the book, to all the booksellers who had handled the book, to anyone who had bought the book, and that the text of his rebuttal be added to all new printings of Singal's book. Couch's demand was rejected by the press.[65]

With that, the issue was officially concluded, though Couch did continue revising the statement until almost his death on December 10, 1988, in Charlottesville, Virginia. Ultimately, he blamed the University of North Carolina Press for the book and for what he had come to view as his disgrace. He wrote to a close friend in 1983, "I have had, and still have deep pride in my work with the Press and I can't help believing that the present management used Singal to bring me down a few notches." He feared that Singal's book would remain available in libraries forever while his rebuttal would never be heard. The fear was real to him. He had been proud of his work at the University of North Carolina Press, but the press had turned on him.[66] Throughout his life, he had wanted, above all else, to be taken seriously. His early spectacular success at the University of North Carolina had been followed by a series of equally spectacular failures. His head had been slammed into the railing of the mourner's bench by Robert Maynard Hutchins, then by Everett Fontaine and the American Library Association, and again by Oxford University Press. The debacle with the William Volker Fund and the failure of his book to gain the attention he desperately wanted did further damage and the University of North Carolina Press administered the final blow.

9

The Word
and the Rope

Most people who achieve positions of consequence in the world progress through careers that follow an upward path. Unless they are born to wealth and position, they generally begin at the bottom, increasing their influence and success until they cease being active in their fields. William Terry Couch's career differed from this typical pattern. His acme came at the beginning at the University of North Carolina and, while the University of Chicago might seem to have been a step upward, the events that led to his dismissal did not amount to success in any appreciable way. *Collier's Encyclopedia* offered him a greater popular audience for his work, but the job did not carry the prestige the university presses gave him. His subsequent jobs at Little & Ives and, finally, with the Center for American Studies were progressively lower points. It has been observed that rather than an Algerian progression of rags to riches, Bill Couch's career was a downward spiral from acclaim and national recognition to relative obscurity.

In 1958, Bill Couch published an article in *Modern Age* in which he cited the story, recounted by John Stuart Mill in *On Liberty*, about the Locrians, an ancient Greek tribal society that followed the custom in public meetings of allowing anyone objecting to the laws or customs under which their society operated to propose changes. A rope was placed around the speaker's neck and, if the assemblage approved of what was said, it was removed. If the people disapproved, the rope was used to hang the offender.[1] It is a correlative that aptly describes Couch's life and career. From his start at the University of North Carolina Press in the 1920s until his retirement from the service of the William Volker Fund's Center for American Studies in the 1960s, Couch's neck was always firmly in the noose. Even if the gate under him failed to drop as his opponents wished, the awareness of the noose constantly chaffed and forced him to consider his words carefully. But, it did not mean that he would refuse to say them when he thought it necessary.

Bill Couch received few accolades in his career. Editors and publishers do not generally hold positions of public prominence and his contributions to intellectual life were secondary to those of the writers he supported, encouraged, and brought to the attention of the public. When the University of North Carolina (UNC) honored him as one of five graduates who received its Distinguished Alumnus Awards at its 1972 University Day ceremony, he was gratified.

The announcement of the award pointedly stated that it was for his service as head of the university press 1925 to 1945. It specifically referred to his work publishing the books from Howard Odum's Institute for Research in Social Science as "perhaps his most signal achievement" at the university.[2] The credit given to Odum undoubtedly galled him, but he was pleased by the award and the recognition.

Arie Nicolaas Jan den Hollander wrote a letter to the university to be read at the awards ceremony. He and Couch had been friends since 1930 when Hollander spent time in Chapel Hill working on a book on southern rural life.[3] Even though Hollander was a sociologist, he and Bill Couch formed a close friendship that had lasted over forty years. In this letter, Hollander focused on Couch's notorious inability to refrain from any argument, but hastened to add "that he is one of the most rewarding men to disagree with," even while wondering "how excellent reasoning [and] irrefutable logic may carry Bill Couch to some highly debatable conclusions." For Couch, argument was the essence of human interaction. For him, winning an argument was as bad as losing one. The value of argument was in the interchange of ideas and to win or lose would put an end to the search for truth. He valued the argument itself more than its resolution and relished the joy of the challenge. Hollander characterized Couch as "a lover of truth, a champion of the causes he considers right, he is perhaps not a diplomat. He does not believe in compromise as an easy and safe way out."[4] This assessment is accurate but probably too kind. While Hollander found Bill Couch an agreeable companion in the intellectual clashes both men cherished, many others with whom William Terry Couch clashed found him irascible, bigoted, doctrinaire, and rigidly dogmatic.

Couch's enduring public reputation as a liberal had been firmly established by the end of his first decade at the University of North Carolina Press. By southern standards, the label was probably accurate, but Couch was more a follower of the New South creed than a proponent of the brand of liberalism that had motivated the Progressive Era in the North. Being a liberal at the University of North Carolina in the 1920s and 1930s was different from being a liberal in the North. He published books that dealt seriously with issues of race, of economics, and of southern mores, but he also personally supported the southern structure of racial segregation. He had been an active participant in the New Deal and a participant in the Southern Conference for Human Welfare, but abandoned both when confronted by government bureaucracy and by dogmatic Communists. His experiences at North Carolina began an intellectual, social, and political conservatism that deepened and intensified throughout his career.

Couch's early liberalism rested on a solid awareness of the problems of the South. The South, still suffering from the devastation of the Civil War, was afflicted with poverty, disease, ignorance, and a level of racial strife that distinguished it from other regions of the United States. It was a region that at a later period could almost be characterized as a third world country. Bill Couch effectively used his podium at the University of North Carolina Press to attack the flaws of the South through the books he published, even the books he published grudgingly for Howard Odum's Institute for Research in Social Science.

With the publication of *I'll Take My Stand* in 1930, a new intellectual force rose in the South in defense of the southern traditions that Couch and the sociologists at the University of North Carolina condemned. The Agrarians, associated with Vanderbilt University in Nashville, Tennessee, defended the traditions and institutions of the Old South against the encroachment of Modernism into the orderly agrarian society they felt represented the civilization of the South.

Couch crossed swords repeatedly with the Agrarians over the romantic yearnings of Allen Tate, John Crowe Ransom, and others who exalted the yeoman farmer and the land without recognizing that agriculture could not raise the South from its economic torpor. The South could only achieve its rightful place in American life through a manufacturing economy that could provide the kinds of jobs that enabled southern workers to earn a decent living and escape the chains of someone else's land.

Couch's argument against the Agrarians derived from his own belief in the New South creed. The fantastic notions that there was something noble in the Confederacy, that the Civil War destroyed a grand culture and society in the antebellum South, and that the Lost Cause could be resurrected were anathema to Couch. The mythopoeic posturing of the Agrarians and their misty reverence for a civilization that Couch knew had never existed infuriated him. He lost no opportunity to publicly challenge them even while recognizing their ability by publishing the books written by members of the Agrarian movement.

Bill Couch attributed the problems of the South to economics. If the economic situation of the South was such that African American and white workers had parity in wages and the dignity of labor was recognized, there would be no racial problems in the South. The southern system of labor, resting on the ignorance of the white and black laboring class, could not sustain an economy that would allow the amelioration of the desperate poverty, disease, and immorality common among both races in the South. In a South still paralyzed by the Civil War with ownership of the means of production held by the North and much of the population, both black and white, held by the mirror of chattel slavery known as sharecropping, the necessity for industrialization was obvious to him if the South was to achieve its rightful place with the rest of the country.

Virtually all New South proponents recognized that racial segregation was a viable and even beneficial means of organizing southern society. A major tenet of the New South creed held that the South should be left alone to solve its own racial problems. Couch, as a southerner, approved of this. Segregation was not a problem for him. He knew that separation of the races was necessary to preserve what was good and admirable in the culture of the South. He insisted, however, that equality be emphasized in the doctrine of *separate-but-equal*. When the lot of the laboring classes of whatever color was improved, when opportunities for economic betterment were available, and when the dignity of all labor was recognized and rewarded equally, there would be no racial problem in the South. This was central to Couch's conception of the New South.[5]

William Terry Couch transformed the University of North Carolina Press during his first decade. When he took over from Louis Round Wilson, the press was a bucolic operation content with printing the operational documents of the university, the occasional book written by a faculty member, and the few periodicals and journals the university sponsored. As a man committed to the New South, Couch was an intellectual entrepreneur who used the press and the university to transform the South through publishing books that, by revealing the truth, would stir the South from its stupor of customs and traditions.

As a publisher, Couch's contribution to the development of a New South lay in his enthusiastic attacks on the errors of the past. He was committed to publishing books that were controversial to the point that he occasionally brought condemnation on the university. Many members of the publishing board of the press and of the faculty attributed this to his own impulse for controversy. It was ultimately, though, from his commitment to creating a New South in which the cozy, misty reverence for the antebellum South would be destroyed by the truth.

Couch's clashes with Howard Odum over the books coming out of his Institute for Research in Social Science had little to do with what the research found, but rather with its presentation. The authors' essential meaning and the significance of their work was hidden under the murky jargon of the academic sociologist. Couch wanted to reach the southern public, not other scholars, and insisted that the texts be accessible to intelligent readers in the South. He wanted to change the mind of the South, not to make academic reputations for Odum's band of sociologists. If Couch ever thought that academic scholars and researchers could write the kinds of books needed to shake the South, he was early disabused of that notion by the offerings of Howard Odum and the members of the Institute for Research in Social Science. Their topics were the right ones and the data presented by the authors was sound, but the academic jargon was impenetrable to the common reader, and it was the common reader Couch desperately wanted to reach. The academics who could understand those books were irrelevant to social and economic change in the South. The legislators and community leaders who needed to understand the issues that confronted the South were essential to change and it was change that Couch wanted to effect through the press.

Couch had a strong, well-defined idea about the kinds of books that could promote change in the South. He did not wait for good manuscripts to be submitted, but actively sought out authors to write the books that should be written. He developed publishing projects and found people to produce them. He referred to this as *experimental publishing* and it was a new venture for an American university press. Under Couch's direction, the shape of academic publishing at the University of North Carolina changed dramatically and the press became a general southern publishing house modeled not on other American university presses, but on the trade houses, the commercial presses that published and sold books to an American reading public that could be influenced by ideas.

Couch was intensely aware of the power of words, but words, after all, are merely the means to convey ideas. He was more aware of the power of ideas. As an editor, Couch was passionately engaged in ideas and in their effective expression. He early rebelled against the arid conventions of academic social sciences at the University of North Carolina by insisting that authors bring the narrative to a personal level rather than the dispassionate statistics that characterized academic discourse. Data is abstract. Narrative is concrete. Couch's intent as an editor and publisher was to change society through the books he published and a concrete narrative affected people more than an abstract accumulation of data. The test was the author's ability to write. The content was a consideration, of course, but the literary excellence of the manuscript was always his primary consideration in evaluating a manuscript.[6]

The definition of *liberal* and *conservative* as either points on some political spectrum or as distinct categories of human behavior or belief defy precision. Throughout his life, Couch rebelled against any attempt by others to pen him in a category, even though he did, at times, describe himself as a liberal or a conservative and even as a right-winger. Couch may have accepted the labels in self-appraisal at various times, but they were merely tags of convenience since Couch rarely attempted to define his terms. He did offer Virginius Dabney a definition of liberalism for his book, *Liberalism in the South*, in 1932, but this only asserted "the notion of the dignity and worth of the individual." It was a definition that could equally be applied to conservatives or even his later involvement with Libertarianism. When Kenneth Colgrove asked him for a list of the names of true conservatives in 1959, he was stymied. The term, he told Colgrove, was meaningless and even those who appeared to be conservative were likely to become radical leftists if offered enough money to do so.[7]

George H. Nash in his *The Conservative Intellectual Movement in America since 1945*, a book that, since its first publication in 1976, has become part of the canonical literature of Libertarianism, refused to enter the "terminological thicket" in which a definition would have entangled him. He did, however, identify several areas that the term *conservative* would have to encompass that had characterized the movement since World War II. Libertarianism—resistance to the expanded roles of the state, particularly the national government that threatened private enterprise, individual rights, and the personal liberties of American citizens—has been a major focus of conservatism.

Rejection of cultural relativism, labeled *traditionalism* by Nash. is a second element. The decline of traditional religion and the loss of an ethos based in Christianity had created a society without roots in a set of shared beliefs and values had "produced an intolerable vacuum that was filled with demonic ideologies." One of the major ideologies that had found a foothold in cultural relativism was Communism. Anti-Communism is the third element Nash found that characterized American conservatism. Communism is an ideology that is foreign to the Anglo-American system of values. It had crept insidiously into American political and economic life, abetted by the liberal press and promoted by American educational institutions.

Alfred Regnery, son and heir of conservative publisher Henry Regnery, identified the same three areas that defined conservatism. He added a fourth group to these; conservatives characterized more by their methods than their intellectual underpinnings—the "young conservative journalists, publishers, and activists who shared many of the beliefs of the other three intellectual schools, but as popularizers were willing to challenge liberals and liberalism in a more public setting."[8] Bill Couch tried to use *Collier's Encyclopedia* and, particularly, its yearbooks as a journal of conservative opinion, but was thwarted by the liberals controlling the publishing company. When Couch attacked William F. Buckley, Jr., in 1982, he was attempting to place himself in the company of the journalists, but even he must have realized that he could never have attained the level of Buckley's influential *National Review* in the conservative community through *Collier's Encyclopedia*.

Bill Couch had joined in causes that were supported by Communists in the South while he was at the University of North Carolina. The point of confluence of Couch with the Communists, though, lay in his firm belief that source of the South's problems were economic, not political. In his writings and public activities at North Carolina, he frequently appeared to support some objectives of the Communist Party, but he was never a follower and had accepted the presence of Communists in the southern scene primarily because University of North Carolina President Frank Porter Graham accepted them.

Couch had also been a supporter of Franklin Roosevelt and the liberal programs of the New Deal in the 1930s. Bill Couch came into direct conflict with the Federal Writers Project as regional director in 1940 over its bureaucratic meddling in his publications. He quit the project in disgust over federal intrusion into affairs that he considered his own area of authority.

By the end of the 1930s, he had become completely disaffected with the Roosevelt administration and the New Deal. The federal government under Roosevelt had simply accumulated too much power to be compatible with Couch's ideals of democracy. The general public acceptance of Roosevelt's New Deal programs disheartened him. He eventually realized that the real threat to American democracy did not come from Communists or fascists, but from people who were unaware of the threat of power centralized in the federal government. These were the people, common citizens and municipal, county, and state level officials, who simply ignored the threat of federal control over the agencies, functions, and powers that should be exercised at local levels rather than by the federal government.[9] They were abetted in this by academic sociologists who embraced the notion that Communism was merely an alternative to the traditions, values, and beliefs that had shaped the United States.

When Couch went to the University of Chicago in 1945, his anti–Communism was firmly entrenched. Couch found the university rife with liberalism—a liberalism that to him bordered on Communism. He credited three books he published there for his eventual firing by University of Chicago Chancellor Robert Maynard Hutchins. These were Richard Weaver's *Ideas Have Consequences*, A. Frank Reel's *The Case of General Yamashita*, and Morton Grodzins's *Americans Betrayed*. Weaver's book assailed the western culture of nominalism—the rejection of universal truths in favor of a relativism that was independent of values in a culture. Reel's and Grodzins's books differed, attacking the military and the government of Franklin Roosevelt.

By this time, Bill Couch was an enthusiastic supporter of anything that would embarrass Franklin Delano Roosevelt or the federal government, or, preferably, both. He knew that Roosevelt's pact with the Soviet Union during World War II was the juncture that could destroy the United States. Any accommodation with the Soviet Union could only end badly. For him, the Communist Soviet Union was a worse threat to the Anglo-American tradition than Nazi Germany had been. Collusion with the Communists was a major turning point in the downward course of western civilization and the Roosevelt administration had enabled that.

As Couch became increasingly concerned over the intrusion of Communism and Communist propaganda into what he was publishing, his close reading of manuscripts became increasing nuanced. As an editor and publisher, Couch knew that America was being undermined by Communist propaganda so subtle that even the people writing were not aware of its danger and the evil they were innocently spreading. The tacit assumptions that economic regulations and controls were a natural function of a federal government, that federal power and authority should displace the rights of the individual states, and that federal power should triumph in disputes were rife in the writings of American scholars of all political persuasions.

When he published Weaver, Reel, and Grodzins at Chicago, he was, in part, reaching toward those issues, but at *Collier's Encyclopedia* his own Libertarian tendencies began to flower. Under the tutelage of Lucille Cardin Crain, editor and publisher of the *Educational Reviewer*, he learned to read the texts even more closely to find the underlying assumptions of statism and collectivism that informed the authors. Lucille Crain opened the first issue of the *Educational Reviewer* with her statement of purpose. She claimed that the publication was not "an attack on the academic world." Rather, it was to assist "those numerous teachers who honestly wish to confront with objectivity and honesty the concealed theories of collectivism."[10] Her own close reading of the textbooks revealed the assumptions underlying the words of the authors to expose their unacknowledged and, perhaps, unconsciously pernicious commitment to collectivism and statism as beneficial aspects of American political and economic life. With Crain's help, Couch learned how Communist propaganda subtly pervaded school and college textbooks. With this deepened critical perspective, he saw that the articles written for *Collier's* were equally infected. Couch learned not only to closely read the author's words, but also to read what the author did not say to unearth the pernicious propaganda underlying the writing.

His aversion to the liberal tendencies in American society and politics was rooted in his own conception of objectivity. Liberals defined *objectivity* as a dispassionate presentation of the facts. At least this is what Couch's nemesis at *Collier's*, Everett Fontaine, had demanded. Couch knew that facts simply served the arguments of the authors who could and did harvest those facts most suited to support their arguments. He also knew that the best people to write about almost any topic were not and could not be dispassionate. He actively pursued authors who held committed beliefs on the topics as the best equipped to adequately present the truth. The naked facts told the encyclopedia reader nothing. The interpretation of the facts gave the reader the significance needed to understand the truth.

His use of multiple authors, each writing to opposing sides on controversial topics, for articles in the encyclopedia was a practice that infuriated Fontaine and librarians. It was a technique, though, that Couch found useful to handle controversial subjects and represented his attempt to achieve some balance in the presentation. Authors would be biased in their presentation if only because of their acceptance of the liberal dogma of cultural relativism. Couch's conception of debate, however, clashed with the views of his immediate superior, Everett Fontaine, who insisted that a competent scholar could and should dispassionately explain the various sides of a controversial issue. For Couch, only those who held decided views on any issue, who were committed to a viewpoint, could speak with authority on a subject. Nobody could adequately represent the opposing sides of any topic for which there could be radically divergent points of view. Objectivity, at least the way liberals defined it, was an impossibility. The only rational approach was to engage the opposing views in a debate among their committed proponents.

Staged debates among opposing proponents of controversial issues, though, were used only sparingly by Couch in the encyclopedia's yearbooks. Fontaine raised strong objection to the technique, but the use of conservative writers for other articles outraged him even more. When Bill Couch proclaimed the purpose of the yearbook was to combat collectivism and statism and proceeded to encourage conservative authors to follow him into battle on the pages of the yearbooks, he violated every notion of objectivity and balance that Fontaine held. Fontaine's insistence on his own editorial policies, though, violated Couch's own conception of his role as editor-in-chief of the encyclopedia. He alone had the right to determine what should be published in the encyclopedia and its yearbooks.

Couch began his war on the foundations at Chapel Hill. The Rockefeller Foundation that funded the operations of Odum's Institute for Research in Social Science was the first object of his scorn. Foundation grants to Odum's institute and to individual authors to finance publication enabled them to control what was published by a university press. At North Carolina, the Rockefeller Foundation essentially controlled the direction of research in the social sciences through by-passing the editorial process that should be under the control of the university presses. The presses had established policies and procedures to ensure the quality of the research with a system of evaluation by qualified reviewers and an editorial procedure that was designed to ensure the quality of the writing. The demands of the foundations guaranteed neither quality research nor competent writing.

At Chicago, Hutchins's defection to the Ford Foundation and to the Fund for the Republic intensified Couch's hatred for foundations. At *Collier's*, the influence exerted by the American Library Association (ALA) in reference book publishing added it to the objects of Couch's scorn. The collusion between the ALA and Hutchins's Fund for the Republic demonstrated to him an overarching conspiracy with the Communists to control America. The cozy relationship between the major foundations and the ALA only confirmed this to Couch.[11] Indeed, Bill Couch's opposition to the ALA became almost obsessive. Its control over the success of reference books, its insistence on a standard of objectivity that Couch knew was impossible to attain, its commitment to complete freedom of information, and its constant crusade against censorship were enough to convince him that the ALA, like the foundations, was nothing more than a coalition of liberals united to destroy America. When the ALA refused to rise to his defense after Robert Maynard Hutchins fired him at Chicago and then became an active force in removing him from his job at Crowell-Collier, he knew that the foundations and American librarians were united in a concerted effort to suppress the truth and to spread a gospel of social and cultural relativism that could only lead to the dissolution of America as a civilization. The foundations and the ALA, under the direction of liberals, controlled not only the funds for research, but also the funds for publication of research. Ultimately, they controlled all that shaped the values of Americans by defining what constituted acceptable truth.

For Couch, the issue came down to power. When Robert Maynard Hutchins refused to allow him to publish Morton Grodzins's book on the Japanese internment during World War II, Couch accused him of intellectual dishonesty. It was a simple matter of Hutchins abusing the power of his position over the press. Couch argued Grodzins's case on the merits of his research and its value to the public. He was, he told Hutchins, appalled that the chancellor of the University of Chicago would take the position that the issue was not an ethical one, but a simple one of which party in the dispute had the most power. Couch and Grodzins had to bow to the demands of the University of California. Hutchins used his power in the attempt to suppress Morton Grodzins's book and ultimately to rid the University of Chicago of Bill Couch just as Everett Fontaine used the power of the ALA to suppress Couch's conservatism and, eventually, to rid Crowell-Collier of Couch.

The large philanthropic foundations had the power to control research and publication and the power to impose their will on the American people. The support of the Rockefeller Foundation, the Ford Foundation, and the Carnegie Corporation for a social science that promoted collectivism and statism under the guise of objective scholarship was an assault on all that was right and good. The pernicious belief that cultures and societies were all equal, that there was no better or worse, but simply different solutions to the problems of any society affronted Couch. He knew that the proper object of social science was to uncover the natural law of humankind. The focus had to be on the commonalities of human existence, not on the differences among cultures, and the elements that were common and good would reveal the path to perfecting human society. To modern American social scientists, Couch charged, appeasing the gods who caused the crops to fail with human sacrifices was a solution equally as valid as scientific agriculture. The major foundations had mounted "a determined, continuous, and powerful assault on the standards of civilized life" through their support of social scientists who were assiduously promoting cultural relativism and, ultimately, Communism in their work.[12]

Some smaller and less well-financed foundations were aware of the problem and were, as best they could, prepared to do battle. The William Volker Fund's Center for American Studies was among those. The Volker Fund's Center for American Studies promised Bill Couch an alternative to the university presses and the commercial realm through which he could fully realize his vision as an editor and publisher. Couch, though, was always concerned that his crusade against Communist propaganda and the intrusion of statism and collectivism, the precursors to Communism and totalitarianism, into American thought be taken as legitimate. The actions of Rosas John Rushdoony and David Hoggan that publicly associated the Volker Fund's Center for American Studies and Couch himself with the disreputable fringes of the right-wing proved too radical for him.

He tried to avoid the trap of radical rhetoric that would repulse the liberal readers he sought to influence, but the demands of his superiors in the publishing concerns in which he worked demanded more than he was willing to accept. The issues of a balanced and objective publishing program, the kind of approach demanded of *Collier's* by the ALA, were not ones Bill Couch had faced at either Chicago or North Carolina. There, he had published individual books that did express disparate philosophies. As an academic publisher, he produced books that explored all ranges of opinion. The authors balanced themselves. Conservative authors countered the liberal scholars and his list was balanced even though the individual books were not. The responsibility for objectivity was that of the authors. For each conservative book he published, there were many more by liberal scholars who were committed to spreading liberal propaganda. At *Collier's*, though, Couch himself was responsible as editor-in-chief in the same way as journal editors were responsible for what was published in their periodicals. At *Collier's* and at Little & Ives, he attempted to offer a conservative vision as a corrective to the liberal imbalance of competing reference sets. When he encountered the demand from Stanford University that the Center for American Studies present a balanced publication program when the university itself could not, he was nonplussed.

Couch's conservatism was firmly rooted in the traditionalism that both Nash and Regnery agreed was one of the defining characteristics of American conservatism. His belief in an order to human society was almost religious in nature. There was an order to the universe with a hierarchy from the amoeba to man and, from there, directly to God in a great chain of being.[13] It was, essentially, a Victorian rather than a Modernist faith. He categorically rejected cultural relativism and believed that the proper research arena of the social sciences was the pursuit of the ultimate values of natural law.

Of all human societies, Couch found those of Europe and, particularly, in the Anglo-American tradition, were the best. As a white, Anglo-Saxon, protestant, southern male, he could come to no other conclusion. Couch's insistence on maintaining racial segregation, even after the Civil Rights movement of the 1950s and 1960s, had its roots not in a virulent racism, but a firm belief that Americans of African descent represented a separate people. Even those African Americans who were thoroughly enculturated into white American society had to be excluded from full participation. No amount of enculturation could erase the basic difference of being black.

Bill Couch's traditionalism, his firm belief in natural law and his ardent faith in an ordered universe, should have precluded his consideration by Daniel Singal as a Modernist. Singal, though, only considered Couch's career at the University of North Carolina in a period before his conservatism had ossified. It was a period when Couch's reputation as a southern liberal and his eagerness to challenge the conventions of the South were sufficient for Singal to place him legitimately in the company of the Modernists.

At the end of the 1930s, Couch radically changed. His battles with Howard Odum and the Rockefeller Foundation that funded Odum and his institute's research and publication forced him to reject the fundamental notion of cultural relativism that had formed the basis for the social sciences in America. He knew that the purpose of a university press was to provoke change—

change in customs and mores, in politics, in economics, in education, and in all other aspects of human society. The idea of a social science that only described a society but did not aspire to remedy societal faults was a fraud. The dispassionate accumulation of facts and data without an explicit commitment to bettering the human condition could not accomplish change. It could only perpetuate the flaws of society. Cultural relativism, one of Daniel Singal's hallmarks of Modernism, was rejected by Couch almost from the beginning of his career.[14]

In a disorderly universe that could only be apperceived through irrationality, the ability to live in uncertainty, was a necessary virtue of a Modernist. Bill Couch did live most of his life in uncertainty, but he was steadfastly unhappy with the situation. Assailed from all sides by liberal Modernists who persistently failed to accept that there were essential underlying values to human existence and who rejected the necessity to examine those values, he was buffeted by uncertainty. As a publisher, Couch lived in hierarchies. He had subordinates in the organizations he served and had superiors above him. He lived in uncertainty, but it was within a structure that should have provided order. Couch's hierarchies failed to provide order because the liberals who controlled the positions above him were themselves Modernists who accepted a disorderly universe and human irrationality even while William Terry Couch demanded rationality.

As his career progressed and he was attacked by liberals in the publishing industry, the academic world, and by librarians, he held faster to his increasingly nuanced form of conservatism. He knew that the world was rational. It was the liberals who insisted on irrationality and who forced him into what were, to him, untenable publishing decisions. Bill Couch knew right from wrong and held tightly to his moral absolutes. When he finally broke his connection with the main-stream of publishing and went to the Volker Fund, he found that the extreme reaches of conservatism were as irrational as the liberal Modernists.

William Terry Couch was a Modernist, at least, in that he held conflict to be a positive value. Arie den Hollander recognized this when he cited Couch's ability to take an argument to conclusions that were logical, but wrong. Couch repeatedly followed his arguments to illogical conclusions more for the sake of the argument than for any desire for a conclusion. He railed against collectivism and statism as pathways toward totalitarianism. When faced, however, with committed right-wingers at the Center for American Studies, his certainty faltered. He refused to back down publicly, but privately admitted that there were collectivist programs and statist tendencies that were necessary to a functioning society. He could not accept Rushdoony's contention that public education was an evilly egregious example of both collectivism and statism in America or

David Hoggan's defense of Nazi Germany. Bill Couch could argue with anyone who had a glimmer of rationality, but Rushdoony and Hoggan had none.

There were obvious limits beyond which he would not go, even when his arguments might seem to lead there. He knew that an editor had to be a polymath and knew much of right-wing rhetoric was nonsense. But, further, he was always intensely aware that his audience had to be a wider one than the extreme right-wing could offer him and he had to control his rhetoric to appeal to that audience. Liberals would automatically dismiss the truth underlying radical bombast. He wrote, edited, and published to sway liberals toward the truth. There was a higher order than the chaos the liberals enjoyed, there was a hierarchy to the universe, and Bill Couch's world was, indeed, a rational place. He fought to make it rational.

Couch failed to meet Daniel Singal's criteria for Modernism at several crucial points after the period Singal wrote about. He could not accept cultural relativism. He refused to accept that irrationality was a natural human reaction to an unpredictable universe. He knew that there were moral standards and absolutes to which people should adhere. But, he certainly was contentious and he actively demonstrated the "critical temperament uninhibited by consideration of formal manners" that Singal maintained was a requisite for Modernism. While Bill Couch was almost always a gentleman in person, he refused to defer to manners when attacking error in his own writings or when publishing those of other authors. The books he published at the University of North Carolina and Chicago did not observe the niceties of civil discourse in assailing the South for its regional peculiarities or the federal government for its moral deficiencies. He refused to accede to inter-southern comity in his attacks on the Agrarians or to conventions of scholarly discourse in his battles with Howard Odum and the members of his band of sociologists.

Bill Couch used Singal's own terms when he wrote the two pieces attacking Singal's book *The War Within*. "The Critical Temperament Leashed" was the title of his presentation to the Board of Directors of the University of North Carolina Press in 1984. This was a concise abridgement of his much longer "The Critical Temperament at the Mourner's Bench" that he demanded the press publish as his rebuttal to Singal. This was rejected by the board, but the two pieces did demonstrate his own critical temperament. Singal cited the incendiary books Couch published for Odum's institute and other books dealing with the social, cultural and political situations of the South and Couch's insistence that writers dig into the mire southern reality rather than simply list the statistics as evidence of his critical temperament.[15] Couch repeatedly demonstrated the critical temperament that Singal found to be the *sine non qua* of Modernism during the period in his career that Singal covered. While Couch denied that he could possibly be a Modernist in the sense that Singal postulated, the two pieces he wrote in response to Singal's book show that his own critical temperament was intact late in life. He was not hindered by any sense of manners or moderation in his attack on what he considered Daniel Singal's scholarly excesses and flaws.

Daniel Singal was right that Bill Couch was a Modernist at the University of North Carolina and, if a man with deeply held conservative sympathies could be considered a Modernist, remained so for the rest of his life. Singal also successfully made the case that Couch deserved a place in the pantheon of southern Modernism through his work with the University of North Carolina Press and deserved the attention he received in *The War Within*. Couch did radically change scholarly publishing in the South. His subsequent career, though, was one of growing conservative convictions with a corresponding growing compulsion that those convictions had to be expressed in the books and articles he published. As a man who firmly believed in the power of the truth and the power of expressing that truth, he could do nothing other than use his editorial positions to further the truth as he saw it. This was not an obsession for William Terry Couch. It was his job.

Couch fit Daniel Singal's definition of Modernism about as well as he fit Nash's and Regnery's definition of a conservative. He expressed strong Libertarian tendencies as he developed his own sensibilities, but he rarely fit snugly into any specific group. On occasion, he attributed his conservatism to a reaction to the power of liberals in America, saying that had conservatives been in control, he would have opposed them as strongly as he opposed the liberals.[16] He certainly had a strong aversion to the use of power to resolve arguments, whether it was the power of the foundations to control publishing, the power of Chancellor Hutchins to suppress a book, the power of the American Library Association to control the sales of reference books, or the power of Stanford University to control the activities of the William Volker Fund. Power could be effective, but facts and logic—rationality—should be the means of resolution for any conflict. It is doubtful that he could have become a committed champion of liberalism had conservatives controlled positions of power in the government, the major foundations, the publishing industry, or the universities. His own conservatism was too well rooted in western traditions, too strongly based on an aversion to Communism, and too entrenched in his own commitment to oppose the state to allow him to espouse the virtues of liberalism.

Had conservatives held the power in America, though, he may well have opposed them simply from his own sense of Modernism. Rather than from any philosophical commitment, Bill Couch would have argued for the liberals out of sheer obstinacy. Throughout his career, he was always in search of an argument and always contentious with a well-developed critical temperament. He could and did take almost any side of an argument joyously and enthusiastically for the simple delight in the argument.

In 1948, he addressed a meeting of Phi Beta Kappa at the University of Chicago. He confessed to the audience,

> I am convinced that all men are in an important sense members of one another; but I am equally certain that the single individual, the lone person who takes his own way by himself, supported by his convictions and character, and who refuses to run with every trend that comes along, no matter how popular, is necessary to civilized life.[17]

He opposed collectivism and statism, but recognized they were a necessity in the modern world and, more fundamentally, that collective action was necessary to the functions of the state. However, he also affirmed that the individuated person was equally necessary. He refused to run with any trend and followed, as much as he could, his own convictions and character, especially when they countered the prevailing trends. Couch's personal tragedy was that he never held a position of power that was not ultimately controlled by men who blindly followed the trend of liberal orthodoxy. When he finally accepted a job with the William Volker Fund that promised him the freedom to follow his own convictions, it was with an organization that had followed his own arguments much further than he was willing to go.

Chapter Notes

Chapter 1

1. Daniel Joseph Singal, *The War Within: From Victorian to Modernist Thought in the South, 1919–1945* (Chapel Hill: University of North Carolina Press, 1982), 270–273; Wilson to Couch, May 31, 1926, Series 1, Folder 1, in the William T. Couch Papers #03825, Southern Historical Collection, Louis Round Wilson Special Collections Library, University of North Carolina at Chapel Hill; William Terry Couch, "Twenty Years of Southern Publishing," *Virginia Quarterly Review* 26 (Spring 1950): 171–185.

2. Reminiscences of William Terry Couch (1970), on page 114 in the Columbia Center for Oral History Collection.

3. Nell Battle Lewis, "The University of North Carolina Gets Its Orders," *Nation* 122 (February 3, 1926): 114–115; Couch to Lewis, January 16, 1927, Series 1, Folder 2, Couch Papers.

4. Couch, "Twenty Years of Southern Publishing," 174–176

5. Edward C. L. Adams, *Congaree Sketches: Scenes from Negro Life in the Swamps of the Congaree and Tales by Tad and Scip of Heaven and Hell with Other Miscellany* (Chapel Hill: University of North Carolina Press, 1927); Singal, *War Within*, 265–268; Couch, "Twenty Years of Southern Publishing," 172.

6. Elizabeth Villeponteaux, "William Terry Couch and the University of North Carolina Press" (Master's paper for the M.S. in L.S., University of North Carolina at Chapel Hill, 1989), 41.

7. Villeponteaux, "William Terry Couch," 21.

8. Reminiscences of William Terry Couch (1970), on page 135 in the Columbia Center

for Oral History Collection; Paul Green to Elizabeth Green, July 27, 1924, in Paul Green, *Letters of Paul Green, 1916–1981*, ed. Laurence G. Avery. (Chapel Hill: University of North Carolina Press, 1994), 103–104; John Herbert Roper, *Paul Green: Playwright of the Real South* (Athens: University of Georgia Press, 2003), 110–111.

9. Paul Green, "Introduction," in Edward C. L. Adams, *Congaree Sketches: Scenes from Negro Life in the Swamps of the Congaree and Tales by Tad and Scip of Heaven and Hell with Other Miscellany* (Chapel Hill: University of North Carolina Press, 1927), xi.

10. Singal, *War Within*, 266–267.

11. "We Are Called Down," [clipping from the *Durham (NC) Morning Herald* April 17, 1927]; Wilson to Couch, April 19, 1927; Couch to the Editor of *The Christian Century*, April 20, 1927; Oswald Garrison Williams to Couch, April 25, 1927, Series 1, Folder 2, Couch Papers.

12. Couch, "Twenty Years of Southern Publishing," 172; Villeponteaux, "William Terry Couch," 22.

13. Paul M. Gaston, *The New South Creed: A Study in Southern Mythmaking* (New York: Knopf, 1970), 72–79.

14. Luther Lee Bernard, "The Development of the Concept of Progress," *Journal of Social Forces* 3 (January 1925): 207–212; Harry Elmer Barnes, "Sociology and Ethics: A Genetic View of the Theory of Conduct," *Journal of Social Forces* 3 (January 1925): 212–231.

15. Wayne D. Brazil, *Howard W. Odum: The Building Years, 1884–1930* (New York: Garland Publishing Company, 1988), 426–35, 478–87; Willard B. Gatewood, Jr., *Preachers Pedagogues & Politicians* (Chapel Hill: University of North Carolina Press, 1966), 114–120.

16. William Terry Couch, "The University Press As an Aid to Scholarship," in The Association of American Universities, *Journal of Proceedings and Addresses of the Thirty-sixth Annual Conference Held at the University of Chicago October 25, 26, 27, 1934* (Chicago: University of Chicago Press, 1934), 138–139, 148; Couch to Graham, March 7, 1941, Series 1, Folder 11, Couch Papers.

17. Chester Kerr, *A Report on American University Presses* (n.p.: Association of American University Presses, 1949), 133–134.

18. Couch, "University Press as an Aid to Scholarship," 146.

19. Villeponteaux, "William Terry Couch," 32; *Books from Chapel Hill: A Complete Catalogue, 1923–1945* (Chapel Hill: University of North Carolina Press, 1946), xvii.

20. William Terry Couch, "That Learning Be Served," in *A Short History of the University of North Carolina Press: Essays by Former Directors, William T. Couch, Lambert Davis, & Matthew Hodgson Published on the Occasion of the Press's 75th Anniversary* (Chapel Hill: University of North Carolina Press, 1997), 5–8 ; Guy Benton Johnson and Guion Griffis Johnson, *Research in Service to Society: The First Fifty Years of the Institute for Research in Social Science at the University of North Carolina* (Chapel Hill: University of North Carolina Press, 1980), 17, 97, 110–118.

21. Singal, *War Within*, 280–281.

22. Couch to Dabney, June 8, 1932, Series 1, Folder 7, Couch Papers; Virginius Dabney, *Liberalism in the South* (Chapel Hill: University of North Carolina Press, 1932), 414–428.

23. Reminiscences of William Terry Couch (1970), on pages 204–205 in the Columbia Center for Oral History Collection; Couch to John B. Holt, November 7, 1935; John B. Holt to Couch, November 11, 1935, Series 8.1, Folder 453, Couch Papers.

24. [Couch, Comments on Vance's Human Geography in the South, Chapter 1], Subgroup 4, Series 1, "Vance, R. B. Human Geography in the South: A Study of Regional Resources and Human Adequacy" Folder, in the University of North Carolina Press Records #40073, University Archives, Louis Round Wilson Special Collections Library, University of North Carolina at Chapel Hill.

25. Kerr, *Report*, 93.

26. Couch to Jones, December 18, 1930; Jones to C. W. Ramsdell, April 28, 1930, Series 1, Subgroup 4, "Couch, W. T. Culture in the South" Folder 1 of 8, UNC Press Records.

27. Jones to Couch, December 27, 1930,

Series 1, Subgroup 4, "Couch, W. T. Culture in the South" Folder 1 of 8, UNC Press Records.

28. Jones to Couch, January 29, 1931; Couch to Jones, February 2, 1931, Series 1, Subgroup 4, "Couch, W.T. Culture in the South" folder 1 of 8, UNC Press Records.

29. Singal, *War Within*, 281–282.

30. Couch to Davidson, April 26, 1932; Couch to Lytle, April 30, 1932, Series 1, Subgroup 4, "Couch, W. T. Culture in the South" Folder 3 of 8, UNC Press Records.

31. Lytle to Couch, May 10, 1932, Series 1, Subgroup 4, "Couch, W. T. Culture in the South" Folder 4 of 8, UNC Press Records; Couch to Lytle, September 13, 1932, Series 1, Subgroup 4, "Couch, W. T. Culture in the South" Folder 5 of 8, UNC Press Records.

32. Lytle to Couch, October 26, 1932, Series 1, Subgroup 4, "W. T. Couch Culture in the South" Folder 5 of 8, UNC Press Records; Lytle to Tate, October 23, 1932, in Andrew Lytle and Allen Tate, *The Lytle-Tate Letters: The Correspondence of Andrew Lytle and Allen Tate*, ed. Thomas Daniel Young and Elizabeth Sarcone. (Jackson: University Press of Mississippi, 1987), 68; Couch to Davidson, October 21, 1932, Series 1, Subgroup 4, "Couch, W. T. Culture in the South" Folder 5 of 8, UNC Press Records.

33. Couch, "Memorandum to President Graham," July 13, 1938, Subgroup 2, Series 2, "Federal Writers Project 1936, 1938" Folder, UNC Press Records.

34. William Terry Couch, *Culture in the South* (Chapel Hill: University of North Carolina Press, 1934), 448–467.

35. Couch, *Culture in the South*, 455, 461–462, 469–471.

36. Frank Lawrence Owsley, "The Irrepressible Conflict," in *I'll Take My Stand: The South and the Agrarian Tradition* (New York: Harper, 1930), 61–91; Herman Clarence Nixon, "Wither Southern Economy?" in *I'll Take My Stand*, 176; Andrew Nelson Lytle, "The Hind Tit," in *I'll Take My Stand*, 234; Donald Davidson, "A Mirror for Artists," in *I'll Take My Stand*, 29.

37. "Introduction: A Statement of Principles," in *I'll Take My Stand*, ix-xx.

38. Couch, *Culture in the South*, vii-viii; Allen Tate, "A View of the Whole South," *American Review* 2 (January 1934): 411-432.

39. Couch, *Culture in the South*, x.

40. Donald Davidson, *Southern Writers in the Modern World*, Eugenia Dorothy Blount Lamar Memorial Lectures, 1957 (Athens: University of Georgia Press, 1958), 61.

41. William Terry Couch, "An Agrarian Programme for the South," *American Review* 3 (Summer 1934): 313–326; Ralph Barsodi, "Subsistence Homesteads: President Roosevelt's New Land and Population Policy," *Survey Graphic* 23 (January 1934): 11–14, 48; Maurine H. Beasley, *Eleanor Roosevelt: Transformative First Lady* (Lawrence: University Press of Kansas, 2010): 131–138; Marcia G. Synnott, "Hugh MacRae, Penderlea, and the Model Farm Communities Movement," *Proceedings of the South Carolina Historical Association* 57 (1987), 53–65; Paul K. Conkin, *Tomorrow a New World: The New Deal Community Program* (Ithaca, NY: Published for the American Historical Association [by the] Cornell University Press, 1959), 277–285: Reminiscences of William Terry Couch (1970), on pages 298–301, in the Columbia Center for Oral History Collection; Couch to Frank W. Prescott, November 10, 1937, Series 8.1, Folder 456, Couch Papers.

42. Couch, "An Agrarian Programme for the South," 326.

43. Michael O'Brien, *The Idea of the American South, 1920–1941* (Baltimore, MD: Johns Hopkins University Press, 1979), 178.

44. Virginia Jean Rock, "The Making and Meaning of *I'll Take My Stand*: A Study in Utopian-Conservatism, 1925–1939" (PhD diss., University of Minnesota, 1961), 233.

45. Thomas A. Underwood, *Allen Tate: Orphan of the South* (Princeton, NJ: Princeton University Press, 2000), 165–168; Lytle to Tate, June 1930; Lytle to Tate, spring 1930, in Andrew Lytle, *Lytle-Tate Letters*, 38–42; Couch to Frank W. Prescott, November 10, 1937, Series 8.1, Folder 456, Couch Papers.

46. William Terry Couch, "Economic Planning in the South," *Westminster Magazine* 23 (January–March 1935): 298–305.

47. Owsley to Couch, March 11, 1935; Couch to Owsley, March 14, 1935, Series 1, Folder 8, Couch Papers; Glenda Elizabeth Gilmore, *Defying Dixie: The Radical Roots of Civil Rights, 1919–1950* (New York: Norton, 2008), 67–105.

48. Davidson to Tate, January 12, 1934, in Donald Davidson and Allen Tate, *The Literary Correspondence of Donald Davidson and Allen Tate*, ed. John Tyree Fain and Thomas Daniel Young (Athens: University of Georgia Press, 1974), 288.

49. William Terry Couch, "The Agrarian Romance," *South Atlantic Quarterly* 36 (1937): 419, 430; Thomas W. Cutrer, *Parnassus on the Mississippi: The "Southern Review" and the*

Baton Rouge Literary Community, 1935–1942 (Baton Rouge: Louisiana State University Press, 1984), 130–131.

50. Davidson to Tate, March 31, 1937, in Donald Davidson, *Literary Correspondence of Donald Davidson and Allen Tate*, 302.

51. Tate to Brooks, November 15, 1938, in Cleanth Brooks, *Cleanth Brooks and Allen Tate: Collected Letters, 1933–1976*, ed. Alphonse Vihn (Columbia: University of Missouri Press, 1998), 56.

52. Donald Davidson, *The Attack on Leviathan: Regionalism and Nationalism in the United States* (Chapel Hill: University of North Carolina Press, 1938); Couch to Fred Wieck, May 18, 1953, Series 2, Folder 78, Couch Papers.

53. William Terry Couch, "American Peasants," *Virginia Quarterly Review* 10 (October 1934): 637–640.

54. Couch to Henry, January 2, 1932 [i.e., 1933], Series 1, Folder 7, Couch Papers.

55. Couch to Frank W. Prescott, November 10, 1937, Series 8.1, Folder 456, Couch Papers.

56. Federal Writers' Project, *These Are Our Lives, as Told by the People and Written by Members of the Federal Writers' Project of the Works Progress Administration in North Carolina, Tennessee and Georgia* (Chapel Hill: University of North Carolina Press, 1934), xv, 30–37, 418.

57. Couch to R. B. House, May 26, 1936; Couch to Henry O. Alsberg, April 22, 1938; Couch, "Memorandum to President Graham," July 13, 1938; Couch to J. W. Bailey, April 17, 1938; "Correspondence Relating to Difficulties Encountered under Agreements to Publish Books Produced by the WPA Writers' Program"; Couch to Comptroller General, Department of the Treasury, May 21, 1940; Couch to William R. McDaniel, June 6, 1940, Subgroup 2, Series 2, "Federal Writers Project, 1936, 1938" Folder, UNC Press Records; Singal, *War Within*, 285–286.

58. UNC Press. Board of Governors. [Minutes] May 14, 1940, Subgroup 1, Series 1, Box 1.1, "1922–1941" Folder, UNC Press Records.

59. Villeponteaux, "William Terry Couch," 39.

60. Wilson to Odum, January 5, 1929, Series 4, Box 34, Folder 603, in the Louis Round Wilson Papers #3274, Southern Historical Collection, Louis Round Wilson Special Collections Library, University of North Carolina at Chapel Hill.

61. William Terry Couch, "A University Press in the South," *Southwest Review* 19 (January 1934): 198–199.

62. Wilson to Odum, February 16, 1929, Series 4, Box 36, Folder 603, Louis Round Wilson Papers.

63. Odum to Wilson, [ca. February 20, 1929], Series 4, Box 36, Folder 603, Louis Round Wilson Papers.

64. Chase to Couch, February 1, 1930, Series 1, Box 1, Folder 5, Couch Papers.

65. Johnson, *Research in Service to Society*, 98; Villeponteaux, "William Terry Couch," 35.

66. *Books from Chapel Hill: A Complete Catalogue, 1923–1945*, xiv; Odum to Wilson, May 8, 1943, Series 4, Folder 604, Louis Round Wilson Papers; Couch to Odum, March 11, 1933, Series 1, Folder 7, Couch Papers.

67. C. Vann Woodward, *Thinking Back: The Perils of Writing History* (Baton Rouge: Louisiana State University Press, 1986), 17–18: John Herbert Roper, *C. Vann Woodward: A Southern Historian and His Critics* (Athens: University of Georgia Press, 1997), 3–4.

68. Singal, *War Within*, 128–129; Reminiscences of William Terry Couch (1970), on pages 204, 319 in the Columbia Center for Oral History Collection; Couch, "University Press in the South," 204.

69. Couch, *Culture in the South*, 433–434.

70. UNC Press [Annual Report November 1, 1938-October 31, 1939]; UNC Press Board of Governors [Minutes May 14, 1940], Subgroup 1, Series 1, "1922–1941" Folder, UNC Press Records.

71. William Terry Couch, "Books that Ought to be Written," *Library Quarterly* 12 (October 1942): 432.

72. William Terry Couch, "Regional Publishing," in *The Place of the University Press in American Education and Publishing: A Symposium Conducted by Earl Schenck Miers* (s.n., n.d.), 29.

73. Couch, "University Press as an Aid to Scholarship," 140–143; Reminiscences of William Terry Couch (1970), on pages 260–261, in the Columbia Center for Oral History Collection.

74. William Terry Couch, "Can Language Teaching Be Improved?" *Modern Language Journal* 14 (October 1929): 29.

75. UNC Press Board of Governors [minutes] January 13, 1937, Subgroup 1, Series 1, "1922–1941" Folder, UNC Press Records; *Books from Chapel Hill*, 175; Howard Russell Huse, *The Psychology of Foreign Language*

Study (Chapel Hill: University of North Carolina Press, 1931), 188–189; Howard Russell Huse, *Reading and Speaking Foreign Languages*. (Chapel Hill: University of North Carolina Press, 1945), 97.

76. Couch, "University Press as an Aid to Scholarship," 143–144.

Chapter 2

1. William D. Snider, *The Light on the Hill: A History of the University of North Carolina at Chapel Hill* (Chapel Hill: University of North Carolina Press, 1992), 208–209.

2. Ira Katznelson, *Fear Itself: The New Deal and the Origins of Our Time* (New York: Liveright, 2013), 149–151.

3. Katznelson, *Fear Itself*, 158–168.

4. "10 Points Drafted: Attempt Made to Unite All Conservatives and Moderates on Plan," *New York Times* (Late City Edition) 87 (December 16, 1937), 1, 4; John F. Manley, "The Conservative Coalition in Congress," *American Behavioral Scientist* 17 (November/December 1973): 223–247.

5. Susan Dunn, *Roosevelt's Purge: How FDR Fought to Change the Democratic Party* (Cambridge, MA: The Belknap Press of Harvard University Press, 2010): 70–72, 236–239.

6. Clark Foreman, "The Decade of Hope," *Phylon* 12, no. 2 (1951): 139–140.

7. National Emergency Council (U.S.), *Report on Economic Conditions of the South* (Washington, D.C.: United States Government Printing Office, 1938).

8. George Brown Tindall, *The Emergence of the New South, 1913–1945* (Baton Rouge: Louisiana State University Press, 1967), 636; Glenda Elizabeth Gilmore, *Defying Dixie: The Radical Roots of Civil Rights, 1919–1950* (New York: Norton, 2008), 269–270.

9. Harvey Klehr, *The Heyday of American Communism: The Depression Decade* (New York: Basic Books, 1984), 277; Clark Foreman, "The Decade of Hope," 138–139.

10. Warren Ashby, *Frank Porter Graham: A Southern Liberal* (Winston-Salem, NC: John F. Blair, 1980), 154–156; Linda Reed, *Simple Decency and Common Sense: The Southern Conference Movement, 1938–1963* (Bloomington: Indiana University Press, 1991), 32; Thomas A. Krueger, *And Promises to Keep: The Southern Conference for Human Welfare, 1938–1948* (Nashville, TN: Vanderbilt University Press, 1967), 29; William E. Leuchtenburg, *The White House Looks South:*

Franklin D. Roosevelt, Harry S. Truman, Lyndon B. Johnson (Baton Rouge: Louisiana State University Press, 2005), 114.

11. Ashby, *Frank Porter Graham*, 155; Foreman, "Decade of Hope," 141; Tindall, *Emergence of the New South*, 636.

12. Ashby, *Frank Porter Graham*, 155–156.

13. Linda Reed, *Simple Decency and Common Sense*, 53; Leuchtenburg, *White House Looks South*, 114.

14. William Terry Couch, "Southerners Inspect the South," *New Republic* 97 (December 14, 1938): 114, 168–169; Tindall, *Emergence of the New South*, 637; Ashby, *Frank Porter Graham*, 157; *Report of the Proceedings of the Southern Conference for Human Welfare, Birmingham, Alabama, November 20–23, 1938* (n.p., n.d.), 13; Krueger, *And Promises to Keep*, 58.

15. Couch, "Southerners Inspect the South," 169.

16. Maurine Hoffman Beasley, *Eleanor Roosevelt: Transformational First Lady* (Lawrence: University of Press of Kansas, 2010), 108–109.

17. Krueger, *And Promises to Keep*, 32.

18. Mark Solomon, *The Cry Was Unity: Communists and African Americans, 1917–36* (Jackson: University Press of Mississippi, 1998), 11–128; Robin D. G. Kelley, *Hammer and Hoe: Alabama Communists during the Great Depression* (Chapel Hill: University of North Carolina Press, 1990), 138–175.

19. Ashby, *Frank Porter Graham*, 160–161.

20. John Egerton, *Speak Now Against the Day: The Generation before the Civil Rights Movement in the South* (New York: Knopf, 1994), 296.

21. Walter Gellhorn, "Report on a Report of the House Committee on Un-American Activities," *Harvard Law Review* 60 (October 1947): 1193–1234; Couch to Graham, April 15, 1940, Series 1.1, Folder 1097, in the Frank Porter Graham Papers #1819, Southern Historical Collection, Louis Round Wilson Special Collections Library, University of North Carolina at Chapel Hill; Couch to Ralph McCallister, May 14, 1971, "Douty, Kenneth—Report 1956–1974" Folder in the Kenneth Douty Report and Letters, 1956: 1971 #3976-z, Southern Historical Collection, Louis Round Wilson Special Collections Library, University of North Carolina at Chapel Hill.

22. Couch, "Memorandum on Assistance to Democratic Peoples," April 12, 1940, Series 1.1, Folder 1097, Frank Porter Graham Papers.

23. Couch to Graham, April 15, 1940, Series 1.1, File 79, Frank Porter Graham Papers; Lee to Couch, May 13, 1940, Series 8.1, Folder 370, in the William T. Couch Papers #03825, Southern Historical Collection, Louis Round Wilson Special Collections Library, University of North Carolina at Chapel Hill.

24. Ashby, *Frank Porter Graham*, 164–166; Egerton, *Speak Now against the Day*, 298–299; Kenneth Douty, "Report on the Southern Conference on Human Welfare"; Couch to Ralph McCallister, May 14, 1971, "Douty, Kenneth—Report 1956,-1974" Folder in the Kenneth Douty Report and Letters.

25. Kenneth Robert Janken, *Rayford W. Logan and the Dilemma of the African-American Intellectual* (Amherst: University of Massachusetts Press, 1993), 145–166.

26. William Terry Couch "Publisher's Introduction," in Rayford W. Logan, ed. *What the Negro Wants* (Chapel Hill: University of North Carolina Press, 1944), xii–xiii.

27. William Terry Couch, *Culture in the South* (Chapel Hill: University of North Carolina Press, 1934), 433–434, 455, 467.

28. Gunnar Myrdal, *An American Dilemma: The Negro Problem and Modern Democracy* (New York: Harper, 1944).

29. Couch, "Publisher's Introduction," in *What the Negro Wants*, xiii, xiv, xvii; William Terry Couch, "Objectivity and Social Sciences," in *Scientism and Values*, ed. Helmut Schoeck and James W. Wiggins (Princeton, NJ: Van Nostrand, 1960), 48–49.

30. David W. Southern, *Gunnar Myrdal and Black-White Relations: The Use and Abuse of "An American Dilemma," 1944–1969* (Baton Rouge: Louisiana State University Press, 1987), 84; Walter A. Jackson, *Gunnar Myrdal and America's Conscience: Social Engineering and Racial Liberalism, 1938–1987* (Chapel Hill: University of North Carolina Press, 1990), 241–252.

31. William Terry Couch, "Are All Men Created Equal," *Negro Digest* 3, no. 3 (1945): 35–36.

32. University of North Carolina Press. Board of Governors, [Minutes, June 26, 1943], Series 1, Subgroup 1, Folder "1942–1944," in the University of North Carolina Press Records #40073, University Archives, Louis Round Wilson Special Collections Library, University of North Carolina at Chapel Hill.

33. W. E. B. Du Bois, *Against Racism: Unpublished Essays, Papers, Addresses, 1887–1961*, ed. Herbert Aptheker (Amherst: University of Massachusetts Press, 1985), 256.

34. Janken, *Rayford W. Logan*, 162–165.

35. "UNC Press Annual Report, 1940–1941," Subgroup 1, Series 1, Folder "1922–1941," University of North Carolina Press Records; Couch to David H. Stevens, October 6, 1941, Series 8.1, Folder 462, Couch Papers.

36. Ashby, *Frank Porter Graham*, 174–191.

37. UNC Press Board of Governors [Minutes] December 19, 1941, pp. 1–2, 11, 13, Subgroup 1, Series 1, Folder "1922–1941," UNC Press Records; Snider, *Light on the Hill*, 228.

38. Donald P. Bean, "The Pitfalls of Cooperation: Origins of the AAUP," *Publishers Weekly* 161 (June 28, 1953): 2610.

39. Couch to Members of the AAUP, November 22, 1941, Series 2, Directors Records, Subject Files: Association of American University Presses, Box 2.2, University of North Carolina Press Records.

40. Elizabeth Villeponteaux, "William Terry Couch and the University of North Carolina Press, 1925–1945," Master's paper for the M.S. in L.S., University of North Carolina at Chapel Hill, 1989, 58–64, 70; "UNC Press Annual Report, 1940–1941," University of North Carolina Press Records.

41. Milam to Couch, February 9, 1942; "Exhibit A" of "Survey," ALA. Department of Publishing and Cooperative Services *Circular Letters* (1942) volume 1, 145–147, Record Series 13/1/3, Box 2, American Library Association Archives, University of Illinois Library; Couch to Carl Milam, June 18, 1942, ALA. Department of Publishing and Cooperative Services *Circular Letters* (1942) volume 1, 125, Record Series 13/1/3, Box 2, American Library Association Archives, University of Illinois Library.

42. Couch to Carl June 18, 1942, ALA. Department of Publishing and Cooperative Services. *Circular Letters* (1942) volume 1, 125, Record Series 13/1/3, Box 2, American Library Association Archives, University of Illinois Library.

43. William Terry Couch, *Publishing at the University of Texas: Survey and Recommendations Made at the Request of the University Press Advisory Board*. Austin, [1945?].

44. Edward G. Holley, *The Library, Philanthropy, Publications, and UNC's Emergence as a Major American University* (Chapel Hill: Hanes Foundation, University of North Carolina at Chapel Hill, 1998), 16; Chester Kerr, *A Report on American University Presses* (n.p.: The Association of American University Presses, 1949), 25, 42, 115–116.

45. Couch to Graham, August 10, 1945, Series 1, Folder 19, Couch Papers.

46. Russell Kirk, *Academic Freedom: An Essay in Definition*, (Chicago: Henry Regnery, 1955), 90; Villeponteaux, "William Terry Couch," 77–79; Graham to Strube, March 7, 1955; Couch to Graham, March 9, 1955, Series 8.2, Folder 493, Couch Papers.

Chapter 3

1. Howard Mumford Jones, *Primer of Intellectual Freedom* (Cambridge, MA: Harvard University Press, 1949), 6–10.

2. Robert Maynard Hutchins, *The Higher Learning in America* (New Haven, CT: Yale University Press, 1936), 36.

3. Couch, "Hutchins and Full, Frank, Free Discussion," [ca. February 1954], 4, Series 7.1, Folder 222, in the William T. Couch Papers #03825, Southern Historical Collection, Louis Round Wilson Special Collections Library, University of North Carolina at Chapel Hill.

4. Correspondence from Brandt to Hutchins dated January 11, 1945 and June 5, 1944, quoted in "in re: statute creating University of Chicago Press," Series 2, Folder 42, Couch Papers.

5. Couch to Hutchins, July 24, 1945, Series 1, Folder 19, Couch Papers; "The University of Chicago, Exhibit B: Correspondence between Chancellor Hutchins and Mr. William Terry Couch," "Summary Report on the Couch Dismissal," Series IV, Folder 175, in the Louis Round Wilson Papers #3274, Southern Historical Collection, Louis Round Wilson Special Collections Library, University of North Carolina at Chapel Hill.

6. Wilson to White, October 6, 1954, Series IV, Folder 830, Wilson Papers; Wilson to Couch, January 25, 1951, Series 2, Folder 55, Couch Papers.

7. Hutchins to Couch, July 18, 1945, Series 1, Folder 19, Couch Papers.

8. Graham to Couch, August 6, 1945, Series 1, Folder 19, Couch Papers.

9. Couch, "Summary of Events, November 6 to November 20, incl.," 5, Series 2, Folder 73, Couch Papers; William Terry Couch, review of *Of Making Many Books: A Hundred Years of Reading, Writing and Publishing* by Roger Burlingame, *Library Quarterly* 17 (October 1947): 310.

10. Ben Mark Cherrington. *Methods of Education in International Attitudes* (New York: Bureau of Publications, Teachers College, Columbia University, 1934), 3–5; Roger Shugg,

"Publishing at Chicago: A Brief History of the University of Chicago Press," in *The University of Chicago Press: Catalog of Books and Journals, 1891–1965* (Chicago: University of Chicago Press, 1967), xxv; George Milburn, *The Hobo's Hornbook: A Repertory for a Gutter Jongleur* (New York: Washburn, 1930); Brandt to Bookfolder, July 25, 1944, Box 22, Folder 2, University of Chicago Press Records, Special Collections Research Center, University of Chicago Library; Reminiscences of William Terry Couch (1970), on pages 457–466 in the Columbia Center for Oral History Collection; Couch, "The Social Science Foundation Affair," Series 7.1, Folder 270, Couch Papers.

11. William Terry Couch, "Do Intellectuals Have Minds?" *Georgia Review* 1 (Fall, 1947): 309.

12. Fred Douglas Young, *Richard M. Weaver, 1910–1963: A Life of the Mind* (Columbia: University of Missouri Press, 1995), 31–60, 67–68, 156; Ted J. Smith, III, "How *Ideas Have Consequences* Came To Be Written," in *Steps Toward Restoration: The Consequences of Richard Weaver's Ideas*, ed. by Ted J. Smith, III (Wilmington, DE: Intercollegiate Studies Institute, 1998), 19–20.

13. Richard Weaver, *Ideas Have Consequences* (Chicago: University of Chicago Press, 1948), 36–37, 42, 44, 83–85, 131.

14. Young, *Richard M. Weaver*, 161–162; Henry Regnery, "A Southern Agrarian at the University of Chicago," in *The Vision of Richard Weaver*, ed. Joseph Scotchie (New Brunswick, NJ: Transaction Books, 1995), 160.

15. Smith, "How *Ideas Have Consequences* Came To Be Written," 2–4.

16. Joseph Scotchie, "Introduction: From Weaverville to Posterity," in *The Vision of Richard Weaver*, ed. Joseph Scotchie (New Brunswick, NJ: Transaction Books, 1995), 9.

17. "Foreign Markets for United States Books," *Publishers Weekly* 148 (September 1, 1945): 850; John B. Hench, *Books as Weapons: Propaganda, Publishing, and the Battle for Global Markets in the Era of World War II* (Ithaca, NY: Cornell University Press, 2010), 185–194.

18. Couch to Harry F. West, [n.d.], Series 7.1, Folder 224, Couch Papers.

19. "Money Needed by Europe to Implement Marshall Plan," *Publishers Weekly* 152 (October 4, 1947): 1786.

20. William Terry Couch, *It Costs Us Nothing* (Hinsdale, IL: Henry Regnery Company, 1948), 4, 9, 15.

21. Hench, *Books as Weapons*, 206–208; "Intellectual Imperialism" [Clipping from the *Washington Post*, March 16, 1948], Series 7.1, Folder 224, Couch Papers; Joseph V. Machugh to Couch, March 11, 1948, Series 7.1, Folder 224, Couch Papers.

22. Couch, *It Costs Us Nothing*, 8–9.

23. Couch to William Warren Smith, Jr., March 5, 1948, Series 7.1, Folder 224, Couch Papers; Couch to David Stevens, November 4, 1949, Series 7, Folder 45, Couch Papers.

24. American Textbook Publishers Institute, *Books in World Rehabilitation: A Memorandum for Members of the Congress of the United States, Department of State, Department of the Army, Department of Commerce* ([New York], 1948), 9.

25. Couch, "Grodzins AMERICANS BETRAYED," October 25, 1948, Series 2, Folder 64, Couch Papers.

26. Thomas to Fred Wieck, August 28, 1948, Series 2, Folder 64, Couch Papers.

27. tenBroek to Couch, September 24, 1948, Series 2, Folder 64, Couch Papers.

28. Couch to tenBroek, September 29, 1948, Series 2, Folder 64, Couch Papers.

29. Couch to Farquhar, September 30, 1948, Series 2, Folder 64, Couch Papers.

30. tenBroek to Couch, October 1, 1948, Series 2, Folder 64, Couch Papers.

31. Couch, "Grodzins AMERICANS BETRAYED," October 25, 1948, Series 2, Folder 64, Couch Papers.

32. Ernest Cadman Colwell, "The Publishing Needs of Scholarship," *Publisher's Weekly* 151 (February 1, 1947): 516–517.

33. Couch to Colwell, October 28, 1948, Series 2, Folder 64, Couch Papers.

34. Thomas to Leonard D. White, January 9, 1945; Grodzins to Thomas, August 9, 1945; Thomas to Grodzins, August 18, 1945, Box 216, Folder 5, University of Chicago Press Records.

35. G. Edward White, *Earl Warren: A Public Life* (New York: Oxford University Press, 1982), 65–67; Leo Katcher, *Earl Warren: A Political Biography* (New York: McGraw-Hill, 1967), 223–228; Peter T. Suzuki, "For the Sake of Inter-University Comity: The Attempted Suppression by the University of California of Morton Grodzins' *Americans Betrayed*," in *Views from Within: The Japanese Evacuation and Resettlement Study*, ed. Yuji Ichioka (Los Angeles: Asian American Studies Center, University of California at Los Angeles, 1989), 95–123.

36. Hankey to Grodzins, September 8,

1948; Grodzins to Couch and Tyler, October 7, 1948, Box 216, Folder 5, University of Chicago Press Records.

37. Wieck to Couch, December 30, 1948; Hutchins to Couch, December 30, 1948, Box 216, Folder 6, University of Chicago Press Records; Suzuki, "For the Sake of Inter-University Comity," 106.

38. Grodzins to Couch and Tyler, October 7, 1948, Box 216, Folder 5, University of Chicago Press Records; William Terry Couch, *It Costs Us Nothing*, 14–15.

39. Dorothy Swaine Thomas and Richard S. Nishimoto, *The Spoilage* (Berkeley: University of California Press, 1946); Dorothy Swaine Thomas, *The Salvage* (Berkeley: University of California Press, 1952); Jacobus tenBroek, Edward N. Barnhart, and Floyd W. Matson, *Prejudice, War and the Constitution* (Berkeley: University of California Press, 1954).

40. Thomas to Grodzins, July 24, 1946; Grodzins to Thomas, July 27, 1946, Box 216, Folder 5, University of Chicago Press Records; Suzuki, "For the Sake of Inter-University Comity," 11–12.

41. Suzuki, "For the Sake of Inter-University Comity," 107–108; tenBroek, *Prejudice, War and the Constitution*, viii, 190–202.

42. Suzuki, "For the Sake of Inter-University Comity," 108–109.

43. William Terry Couch, "A Case History in Book Publishing," *American Quarterly* 1 (Winter 1948): 303–305, 309–310; [Various correspondence]; Scherman to Couch, October 28, 1949, Series 2, Folder 50, Couch Papers.

44. Courtney Whitney to V. A. Rodriguez, January 7, 1950, Series 2, Folder 51, Couch Papers; Couch, "Whose Iron Curtain Is This," Series 2, Folder 50, Couch Papers; Couch to A. Frank Reel, January 31, 1950, Series 2, Folder 50, Couch Papers; A. Frank Reel, *The Case of General Yamashita* (Chicago: University of Chicago Press, 1949), 233–237; Larue Brown, "War Trial," *Nation* 169 (September 10, 1949): 257.

45. Couch to Regnery, May 2, 1951, Series 3, Folder 73, Couch Papers.

46. Whitney to V. A. Rodriguez, January 7, 1950, Series 2, Folder 51, Couch Papers.

47. "U.S. Advises Jap Press to Ignore Yamashita Book," [Clipping from the *Chicago Tribune*, October 7, 1949]; [Various telegrams October 7, 1949], Series 2, Folder 50, Couch Papers.

48. Couch to Elmer Thomas, October 14,

1949; Whitney to Roger Baldwin, October 15, 1949, Series 2, Folder 50, Couch Papers.

49. Whitney, "The Case of General Yamashita: A Memorandum," Series 2, Folder 51, Couch Papers.

Chapter 4

1. Couch to Crain, November 4, 1951, Series 2, Folder 77; Couch to Miss Perlman, January 5, 1951, Series 2, Folder 62, in the William T. Couch Papers, #03825, Southern Historical Collection, Louis Round Wilson Special Collections Library, University of North Carolina at Chapel Hill.

2. "Summary of Events, November 6 to November 20, incl.," Series 2, Folder 73, Couch Papers; Stephen O. Murray, "The Rights of Research Assistants and the Rhetoric of Political Suppression; Morton Grodzins and the University of California Japanese-American Evacuation and Resettlement Study," *Journal of the History of Behavioral Sciences* 27 (April 1991): 154.

3. Couch to Colwell, November 2, 1948, Series 2, Folder 65, Couch Papers.

4. Colwell to Couch, November 4, 1948, Series 2, Folder 65, Couch Papers.

5. Grant to Colwell, November 1, 1948; Cunningham to Couch, November 5, 1948, Series 2, Folder 65, Couch Papers.

6. Couch to Cunningham, November 9, 1948, Series 2, Folder 65, Couch Papers.

7. Couch to Joe Rotskoft, January 9, 1950, Series 2, Folder 32, Couch Papers.

8. "University of Chicago. Board of University Publications [Minutes], Friday, April 8, 1949," Series 2, Folder 67, Couch Papers.

9. Couch, "Interview with J. C. Cunningham," April 18, 1949, Series 2, Folder 67, Couch Papers.

10. "Report of Special Committee of the Board of University Publications," May 18, 1949, Series 2, Folder 75, Couch Papers.

11. Couch to Louis Round Wilson, November 12, 1945, Series 4, Box 31, Folder 175, in the Louis Round Wilson Papers, #03274, Southern Historical Collection, Louis Round Wilson Special Collections Library, University of North Carolina at Chapel Hill.

12. Couch to Matthews, November 30, 1949, Series 2, Folder 65, Couch Papers.

13. Couch to Hutchins, February 8, 1950, Series 2, Folder 65, Couch Papers.

14. "Minutes of a Conference with Messrs. Cunningham, Colwell and Matthews on Fri-

day, May 26, 1950," Series 2, Folder 67, Couch Papers; University of Chicago. Faculty Council. Committee on the Couch Dismissal. "The University of Chicago, Exhibit A: Summary Report of the Subcommittee on the Couch Dismissal," Series 4, box 31, Folder 175, Louis Round Wilson Papers.

15. Couch to Matthews, May 26, 1950, Series 2, Folder 67, Couch Papers.

16. Couch to Hutchins, May 26, 1950, Series 2, Folder 65, Couch Papers.

17. Couch to Wood, July 7, 1950, Series 2, Folder 43, Couch Papers.

18. University of Chicago. Board of University Publications. [Minutes], April 28, 1950, Series 2, Folder 67, Couch Papers.

19. "Minutes of a Conference with Messrs. Cunningham, Colwell and Matthews on Friday, May 26, 1950," Series 2, Folder 67, Couch Papers.

20. Couch to Colwell, June 8, 1950, Series 2, Folder 65, Couch Papers.

21. Krogman to Couch, August 22, 1950; Couch to Cunningham, August 24, 1950, Series 2, Folder 65, Couch Papers.

22. Couch to Krogman, August 1, 1950; Krogman to Couch, August 2, 1950, Series 2, Folder 65, Couch Papers.

23. Couch, "Summary of Events, November 6 to November 20, incl.," Series 2, Folder 73, Couch Papers.

24. Couch to Krogman, [three memos], November 13, 1950, Series 2, Folder 69, Couch Papers.

25. Trout to Couch, November 15, 1950, Series 2, Folder 68, Couch Papers.

26. "Summary of Events, November 6 to November 20, incl.," Series 2, Folder 73, Couch Papers.

27. Couch to The Office. Publishing and Printing Departments, November 13, 1950, Series 2, Folder 65, Couch Papers.

28. "The University of Chicago: Exhibit A: Summary Report of the Subcommittee on the Couch Dismissal," Series 4, Box 31, Folder 175, Louis Round Wilson Papers.

29. Cunningham to Couch, November 20, 1950, Series 2, Folder 52, Couch Papers.

30. Couch to Cunningham, December 9, 1950, Series 2, Folder 52, Couch Papers.

31. Hemens to Bean, November 13, 1950; Hemens to Bean, December 1, 1950, Box 216, Folder 7 University of Chicago Press Records, Special Collections Research Center, University of Chicago Library; Couch to Paul C. Hodges, November 20, 1950, Series 2, Folder 52, Couch Papers.

32. "The University of Chicago: Exhibit C: Summary Report of the Subcommittee on the Couch Dismissal"; Arnold Bergstraesser *et al.* to Colwell, November 23, 1950, Series 4, Box 31, Folder 175, Louis Round Wilson Papers.

33. Couch to Paul C. Hodges, December 8, 1950, Series 2, Folder 52, Couch Papers.

34. Couch to A. N. J. Den Hollander, October 4, 1951, Series 2, Folder 74, Couch Papers.

35. Couch, [Memorandum], April 21, 1948, Series 2, Folder 49, Couch Papers; Couch to Hutchins, October 28, 1949, Series 2, Folder 50, Couch Papers.

36. "News of the Week: The University of Chicago Council Reviews Dismissal of Couch," *Publishers Weekly* 158 (December 9, 1950): 2437–2438; Couch to Shep, December 28, 1950, Series 3, Folder 74, Couch Papers.

37. Daniel Joseph Singal, *The War Within: From Victorianism to Modernist Thought in the South, 1919–1945* (Chapel Hill: University of North Carolina Press, 1982), 280–281; Frank Hughes, "How to Fire a Professor: A Case History in Academic Freedom," *Freeman* 2 (December 3, 1951): 145–148; Alex L. Hillman, "The Case of Mr. Couch," *Freeman* 2 (January 28, 1952): 279–280; Kimpton to Hillman, December 13, 1951, Box 10, Folder 11, "Presidents. Papers. Addenda. Appointments and Budgets. 1946–1954," Special Collections Research Center, University of Chicago Library.

38. University of Chicago, Faculty Council, Subcommittee on the Couch Dismissal, "Summary Report of the Committee on the Couch Dismissal," Series IV, Folder 11, Louis Round Wilson Papers.

39. Couch to Laird Bell, January 31, 1951, Series IV, Folder 175, Louis Round Wilson Papers.

40. Mary Ann Dzuback, *Robert M. Hutchins: Portrait of an Educator* (Chicago: University of Chicago Press, 1991), 160–228; William H. McNeill, *Hutchins' University: A Memoir of the University of Chicago, 1929–1950* (Chicago: University of Chicago Press, 1991), 163; Frank Hughes, *Prejudice and the Press: A Restatement of the Principle of Freedom of the Press with Specific Reference to the Hutchins-Luce Commission* (New York: Devin-Adair, 1950), 46–48; Alex Beam, *A Great Idea at the Time: The Rise, Fall, and Curious Afterlife of the Great Books* (New York: Public Affairs, 2008), 40–41.

41. Harry S. Ashmore, *Unseasonable Truths: The Life of Robert Maynard Hutchins* (Boston: Little, Brown, 1989), 310.

42. Wilson to Hutchins, November 24, 1950, Series 2, Box 36, Folder 442, Louis Round Wilson Papers; Hutchins to Wilson, November 30, 1950, Box 10, Folder 11, "Presidents. Papers. Addenda. Appointments and Budgets. 1946–1954," Special Collections Research Center, University of Chicago Library.

43. Hutchins to Jones, November 27, 1950, Box 10, Folder 11, "Presidents. Papers. Addenda. Appointments and Budgets. 1946–1954," Special Collections Research Center, University of Chicago Library.

44. Couch to John Anderson, April 5, 1952, Series 2, Folder 75, Couch Papers; Couch to Grodzins, November 26, 1951, Series 2, Folder 74, Couch Papers.

45. Russell Kirk, *Academic Freedom: An Essay in Definition* (Chicago: Henry Regnery, 1955), 87; Couch to Wieck, November 18, 1952, Series 3, Folder 80, Couch Papers; Roger W. Shugg, "Publishing at Chicago: A Brief History of the University of Chicago Press," in *The University of Chicago Press: Catalogue of Books and Journals, 1891–1965* (Chicago: University of Chicago Press, 1967), xxvi–xxvii.

46. Couch to Dabney, January 3, 1951, Series 2, Folder 73, Couch Papers.

47. Roger Dakin to John Carroll, May 19, 1954, Series 7.1, Folder 222, Couch Papers.

48. Couch, "Hutchins and Full, Frank, Free Discussion" [ca. February 1954], Series 7.1, Folder 222; Couch to Buckley, March 7, 1954, Series 3, Folder 81, Couch Papers.

49. Buckley to Couch, May 19, 1954, Series 3, Folder 81, Couch Papers.

50. Milton Mayer, *Robert Maynard Hutchins: A Memoir* (Berkeley: University of California Press. 1993), 326–327, 330–336: "Editor's Corner: The Big Brainwash," *American Legion Magazine* 59 (October 1955): 6–7.

51. Couch to Wieck, November 18, 1952, Series 3, Folder 80, Couch Papers.

52. Couch to Kennelly, November 10, 1952, Series 3, Folder 80, Couch Papers.

53. U.S. Congress. House. Select Committee to Investigate Foundations, *Final Report of the Select Committee to Investigate Foundations and Comparable Organizations*, Eighty-second Congress, Second Session, H. Report 2514 (Washington, D.C.: United States Government Printing Office, 1952), 7; Couch to George de Huszar, February 26, 1953, Series 3, Folder 80, Couch Papers.

54. Kirk, *Academic Freedom*, 93.

55. Couch to Wieck, January 24, 1955, Series 3, Folder 80, Couch Papers.

56. Couch to Regnery, [Various Letters], Series 8.2, Folder 481, Couch Papers.

57. Reminiscences of William Terry Couch (1970), on page 301 in the Oral History Collection of Columbia University; Couch to Root, December 23, 1953, Series 8.1, Folder 328; Couch to Root, July 25, 1953, Series 2, Folder 72; Couch to Wieck, January 25, 1954, Series 3, Folder 81; Couch to Root, February 12, 1954, Series 8.1, Folder 328, Couch Papers; E. Merrill Root, *Collectivism on the Campus: The Battle for the Mind in American Colleges* (New York: Devin-Adair, 1961), 301.

58. Couch to John, January 29, 1951, Series 2, Folder 55, Couch Papers.

59. Leora Lewis to Couch, November 29, 1951; Couch to Lewis, December 17, 1951, Series 2, Folder 74, Couch Papers; Couch to Carter Harrison, June 16, 1951; Richard Ettinger to Couch, July 2, 1951, Series 2, Folder 75, Couch Papers; Francis M. Rogers to Couch, January 31, 1951, Series 2, Folder 78, Couch Papers; Couch to Wreden, April 23, 1951, Series 2, Folder 78, Couch Papers; Couch to Wolff, April 23, 1951, Series 2, Folder 78, Couch Papers; Couch to Melcher, April 23, 1951, Series 2, Folder 78, Couch Papers; Couch to Carl Harrison, April 23, 1951, Series 2, Folder 78, Couch Papers.

60. Couch to Wieck, June 11, 1952, Series 2, Folder 75, Couch Papers.

61. Couch to Wieck, May 18, 1953, Series 2, Folder 78, Couch Papers.

62. Couch to Carter Harrison, June 16, 1951, Series 2, Folder 75, Couch Papers.

63. June Melby Benowitz, *Days of Discontent: American Women and Right-Wing Politics, 1933–1945* (DeKalb: Northern Illinois University Press, 2002), 168–173; Jonathan Zimmerman, *Whose America?: Culture Wars in the Public Schools* (Cambridge, MA: Harvard University Press, 2002), 91.

64. Abbott Joseph Liebling, *The Wayward Pressman* (Garden City, NY: Doubleday, 1948), 159–163.

65. U.S. Congress. House. Select Committee on Lobbying Activities. *Conference of American Small Business Organizations: A Report of the House Select Committee on Lobbying Activities*, Eighty-first Congress, Second Session, House Report 3232 (Washington, D.C.: United States Government Printing Office, 1950), 10–11, 15–16, 23.

66. Lucille Cardin Crain, "A Declaration," *Educational Reviewer* 1 (July 15, 1949): 1.

67. *Educational Reviewer* 1 (October 15, 1949): 2.

68. Milo McDonald, review of *Secondary Education: Guidance—Curriculum—Method* by Charles Birkenshaw Mendenhall and K. J. Arisman, Educational *Reviewer* 4 (January 15, 1953): 3–4.

69. Felix Wittmer, review of *People in Literature* by Louella B. Cook, Walter Loban, and Ruth M. Stauffer, *Educational Reviewer* 5 (October 1953): 2–4.

70. Couch to Crain, June 30, 1951, Lucille Cardin Crain Papers, Coll. 095, Special Collections and University Archives, University of Oregon Libraries, Eugene, Oregon.

71. Zimmerman, *Whose America?*, p. 98–99.

72. Couch to Crain, September 3, 1951, Lucille Cardin Crain Papers.

73. Arthur D. Morse, "Who's Trying to Ruin Our Schools," *McCall's* 78 (September 1951): 26–7, 94, 108–9.

74. Couch to Crain, August 31, 1951, Lucille Cardin Crain Papers.

75. Crain to Couch, October 20, 1951, Lucille Cardin Crain Papers.

76. Lucille Crain, "Goodbye," *Educational Reviewer* 5 (October 1953): 1.

77. "Guide to the Lucille Cardin Crain Papers," (Col. 095) Special Collections and Archives, University of Oregon Libraries, Eugene, Oregon.

78. Couch to Crain, June 16, 1952, Lucille Cardin Crain Papers.

Chapter 5

1. Lee Shiflett, *Louis Shores: Defining Educational Librarianship* (Lanham, MD: Scarecrow, 1996), 101–105.

2. Peggy Sullivan, *Carl H. Milam and the American Library Association* (New York: H. W. Wilson, 1976), 124.

3. Shiflett, *Louis Shores*, 127–8.

4. Fontaine to Couch, June 6, 1952, Series 3, Folder 95, in the William T. Couch Papers #03825, Southern Historical Collection, Louis Round Wilson Special Collections Library, University of North Carolina at Chapel Hill.

5. William Terry Couch interview with Lee Shiflett, December 17, 1986, Chapel Hill, North Carolina.

6. Couch to Wieck, July 28, 1952, Series 2, Folder 75, Couch Papers.

7. Shiflett, *Louis Shores*, 128.

8. William Terry Couch, "Regionalism in Literature," *Southeastern Librarian* 3 (Spring 1953): 10; Couch to Frank W. Prescott, November 10, 1937, Series 8.1, Folder 456, Couch Papers.

9. Downs to Members of the Publications Board, February 11, 1953, "Library School, Miscellaneous, Library Trends (1) 1951–56" Folder, Record Series 35/1/3, Box 75, University of Illinois. Library. Deans Office. General Correspondence 1897–1979, University of Illinois Archives.

10. Downs to Kellam, July 27, 1953; Downs to Kellam, April 8, 1953, "Library School, Miscellaneous, Library Trends (1), 1951–56" Folder, Record Series 35/1/3, Box 75, University of Illinois. Library. Deans Office. General Correspondence 1897–1979, University of Illinois Archives; Robert B. Downs, *Perspectives on the Past: An Autobiography* (Metuchen, NJ: Scarecrow, 1984): 21.

11. Couch, "The Scholar and Gyges," Series 7.1, Folder 267, Couch Papers; Couch to Downs, February 19, 1954, "Library School, Miscellaneous, Library Trends (1), 1951–56" Folder, Record Series 35/1/3, Box 75, University of Illinois. Library. Deans Office. General Correspondence 1897–1979, University of Illinois Archives.

12. Downs to Couch, February 22, 1954, "Library School, Miscellaneous, Library Trends (1), 1951–56" Folder, Record Series 35/1/3, Box 75, University of Illinois. Library. Deans Office. General Correspondence 1897–1979, University of Illinois Archives.

13. Couch to Porter Kellam, February 26, 1954, Series 2, Folder 79, Couch Papers.

14. Helen Fuller to Paul Bixler, June 24, 1953, "CA-CZ Correspondence 1952–56" Folder, ALA Intellectual Freedom Committee, Record Series 69/1/5, Box 2, American Library Association Archives, University of Illinois Library; "A Special New Republic Report on Book Burning," *New Republic* 128 (June 29, 1953):7–17; Louise S. Robbins, "Toward Ideology and Autonomy: The American Library Association's Response to Threats of Intellectual Freedom, 1939–1969." (PhD diss., Texas Woman's' University, 1991), 185–199.

15. William Terry Couch, "The Sainted Book Burners," *Freeman* 5 (April 1955): 426.

16. Paul Bixler, "Libraries and Intellectual Freedom," in *Collier's 1954 Year Book Covering National and International Events of the Year 1953* (New York: P. F. Collier & Son, 1954), 333–336: Couch to Bixler, March 29, 1955, "CA-CZ Correspondence 1952–56" Folder, ALA Intellectual Freedom Committee, Record Series 69/1/5, Box 2, American Li-

brary Association Archives, University of Illinois Library.

17. Harold Lancour to L. Quincy Mumford, April 14, 1955, "Library School, Miscellaneous, Library Trends (1), 1951–56" Folder, University of Illinois. Library. Deans Office. General Correspondence 1897–1979, Record Series 35/1/2, Box 75, University of Illinois Archives; Couch to Wilson, April 30, 1955, Series 3, Folder 80, Couch Papers.

18. "They Have a Little List," *Newsletter on Intellectual Freedom* 3 (December 1954): 3- 4; "NODL List," *Newsletter on Intellectual Freedom* 3 (December 1954): 7; "Concerted Attack Charged in New Jersey," *Newsletter on Intellectual Freedom* 3 (March 1955): 1; Mary Anne Raywid, *The Ax-Grinders: Critics of Our Public Schools* (New York: Macmillan, 1962), 142.

19. Thelma King to Mrs. Alexander Long, April 29, 1955, "CA-CZ Correspondence 1952–56" Folder, ALA Intellectual Freedom Committee, Record Series 69/1/5, Box 2, American Library Association Archives, University of Illinois Library.

20. William Dix to Paul Bixler, May 5, 1955; Bixler to Dix, May 9, 1955; L. Quincy Mumford to Bixler, May 25, 1955, "CA-CZ Correspondence 1955–56" Folder, ALA Intellectual Freedom Committee, Record Series 69/1/5, Box 2, American Library Association Archives, University of Illinois Library.

21. Couch to Norsworthy, June 1, 1955, Series 3, Folder 95, Couch Papers.

22. Fontaine to Downs, June 9, 1955, Robert Downs Papers, "1955" Folder, Record Series 35/1/22, Box 4, University of Illinois Archives.

23. Couch to Fontaine, September 9, 1955, Series 3, Folder 109, Couch Papers.

24. William Terry Couch, "Preface," in *1953 Collier's Year Book Covering Events of the Year 1952* (New York: P. F. Collier & Son, 1953), v; Leland Rex Robinson, "Statism," in *1953 Collier's Year Book Covering Events of the Year 1952* (New York: P. F. Collier & Son, 1953), 659–663.

25. William Terry Couch, "Preface," in *Collier's 1954 Year Book Covering National and International Events of the Year 1953* (New York: P. F. Collier & Son), v; Russell Kirk, "Conservatism," in *Collier's 1954 Year Book Covering National and International Events of the Year 1953* (New York: P. F. Collier & Son), 156.

26. Russell Kirk, "Censorship," in *Collier's 1954 Year Book Covering National and Inter-*national Events of the Year 1953* (New York: P. F. Collier & Son), 85–89; Russell Kirk, "Great Britain: Report and Reflections," in *Collier's 1954 Year Book Covering National and International Events of the Year 1953* (New York: P. F. Collier & Son), 248–252; Russell Kirk, "Academic Freedom and Educational Standards," in *Collier's 1954 Year Book Covering National and International Events of the Year 1953* (New York: P. F. Collier & Son, 1954), 1.

27. Shores to Couch, July 29, 1954, Folder AB, in the Louis Shores Papers, Florida State University, School of Information.

28. Couch to Shores, March 19, 1958; Couch to Fontaine, May 30, 1953, Series 3, Folder 107, Couch Papers.

29. Couch to Wieck, July 8, 1953, Series 2, Folder 78, Couch Papers.

30. Karl Hess, Jack Anderson, Victor Lasky, and James A. Wechsler, "McCarthyism: A Debate," in *Collier's 1954 Year Book Covering National and International Events of the Year 1953* (New York: P. F. Collier & Son, 1954), 345–356.

31. Waite to Crain, July 13, 1953, Series 3, Folder 80, Couch Papers.

32. Couch to Crain, August 9, 1953, Lucille Cardin Crain Papers, Coll. 095, Special Collections and University Archives, University of Oregon Libraries, Eugene, Oregon.

33. Couch to Stockham, December 10, 1953, Series 3, Folder 85, Couch Papers.

34. Couch to Blanchard, September 1, 1954; Blanchard to Couch, September 13, 1954; Couch to Werkmeister, November 23, 1955; Couch to Fontaine, May 23, 1956, Series 3, Folder 108, Couch Papers.

35. Shores to Couch, August 7, 1954, Series 3, Folder 111, Couch Papers; Couch to Shores, August 7, 1954, AB13, Shores Papers; Kenneth Colgrove and Franklin L. Burdette, "Republic and the Language of War," in *Collier's 1955 Year Book: Covering National and International Events of the Year 1954* (NY: P. F. Collier & Sons, 1955), 536–538.

36. Colgrove to Couch, August 20, 1954, Series 3, Folder 98, Couch Papers; Couch to Fontaine, December 13, 1954, Series 3, Folder 98, Couch Papers; Couch to Shores, July 23, 1954, Folder AB13, Shores Papers; Shores to Couch, August 7, 1954, Folder AB13, Shores Papers; Couch to Shores, September 15, 1954, Folder AB13, Shores Papers.

37. Couch to Fontaine, December 19, 1954; Fontaine to Couch, December 20, 1954, Series 3, Folder 113, Couch Papers.

38. Couch, "What Kind of Man is Robert M. Hutchins," Series 7, Folder 297, Couch Papers.

39. Kenneth Colgrove and Willmoore Kendall, "Academic Freedom Hutchins Style: How a Distinguished Member of the University of Chicago Faculty, the Head of the University Press, Was Fired for Refusing to Suppress a Book," *American Legion Magazine* 61 (July 1956): 16–17, 54–56; Colgrove to Couch, June 28, 1956, Series 8.2, Folder 487, Couch Papers.

40. Robbins, "Toward Ideology and Autonomy," 223–225; *ALA Bulletin* 51 (December 1957): 833; *ALA Bulletin* 52 (July-August 1958): 503; United States. Congress. Senate. Committee on the Judiciary, *Proceedings against Mary Knowles for Contempt of the Senate*, Eighty-forth Congress, Second Session, Senate Report 1765, *Serial Set* Vol. 11887 (Washington, D.C.: United States Government Printing Office, 1956); Thomas C. Reeves, *Freedom and the Foundations: The Fund for the Republic in the Era of McCarthyism* (New York: Knopf, 1969), 117–125.

41. Couch to Aaron M. Sargent, April 8, 1952, Series 2, Folder 75, Couch Papers; Couch, "Foundations and Freedom," Series 7.1, Folder 204, Couch Papers; "1958 Liberty and Justice Book Awards," *ALA Bulletin* 52 (July-August 1958): 503.

42. Couch to Fontaine, December 2, 1953, Series 3, Folder 95, Couch Papers.

43. Couch to Fontaine, December 9, 1953, Series 3, Folder 95, Couch Papers.

44. Couch to The Editors, *The Saturday Review*, April 16, 1953, Lucille Cardin Crain Papers.

45. Couch to Hook, July 1, 1954, Series 3, Folder 92, Couch Papers.

46. Couch to Hook, July 13, 1954, Series 3, Folder 92, Couch Papers.

47. Hook to Couch, July 15, 1954; Couch to Hook, July 17, 1954; Hook to Couch, July 20, 1954, Series 3, Folder 92, Couch Papers.

48. Couch to Kirk, July 7, 1954, Series 3, Folder 92, Couch Papers.

49. Couch to Fontaine, July 20, 1954; Fontaine to Couch, July 20, 1954; Couch to Fontaine, July 21, 1954; Fontaine to Couch, July 21, 1954, Series 3, Folder 92, Couch Papers.

50. Couch to McPherson, March 31, 1956, Series 3, Folder 81, Couch Papers.

51. Couch to Kilpatrick, March 26, 1956; Couch to Kilpatrick, April 7, 1956, Series 8.2, Folder 498, Couch Papers.

52. "Georgian Details Integration Bars," *New York Times* (December 9, 1955): 24.

53. Couch to Cook, December 11, 1955; Cook to Couch, December 20, 1955, Series 3, Folder 80, Couch Papers.

54. Albert Hoyt Hobbs, "Social Science and Science," in *Collier's 1954 Year Book Covering National and International Events of the Year 1953* (New York: P. F. Collier & Son, 1954), 521–523.

55. William Terry Couch, "Objectivity and Social Sciences," in *Scientism and Values*, ed. Helmut Schoeck and James W. Wiggins (Princeton, NJ: Van Nostrand, 1960), 22–49; William Terry Couch, "Regionalism in Literature," *Southeastern Librarian* 3 (Spring 1953): 10.

56. Philip Selznick, "Natural Law and Sociology," in Center for the Study of Democratic Institutions, *Natural Law and Modern Society* (Cleveland, OH: World, 1963), 154–193.

57. Couch to Beale, February 20, 1954, Series 3, Folder 81, Couch Papers.

58. Couch to Norsworthy, November 17, 1955, Series 3, Folder 101, Couch Papers.

59. Russell Kirk and Glen Negley, "Academic Freedom: A Report," in *Collier's 1956 Year Book: An Encyclopedic Supplement and Review of National and International Events of 1955* (New York: P. F. Collier & Son, 1956), 1–6; Russell Kirk, "Colleges and Universities," in *Collier's 1956 Year Book: An Encyclopedic Supplement and Review of National and International Events of 1955* (New York: P. F. Collier & Son, 1956), 178–182; Lyle Blair, "Colleges and Universities: Comments," in *Collier's 1956 Year Book: An Encyclopedic Supplement and Review of National and International Events of 1955* (New York: P. F. Collier & Son, 1956), 182–183; Oboler to Carroll, April 11, 1956, Series 3, Folder 93, Couch Papers.

60. Couch to Hodges, June 29, 1956, Series 3, Folder 81, Couch Papers.

61. Shores to Couch, April 25, 1956, Folder AB, Shores Papers.

62. Howard Whitman and Howard G. Spalding, "Education: A Debate," in *Collier's 1955 Year Book Covering National and International Events of the Year 1954* (New York: P. F. Collier & Son, 1955), 190–203.

63. Fontaine to Couch, September 27, 1955, Series 3, Folder 111, Couch Papers.

Chapter 6

1. Couch to William H. Werkmeister, September 20, 1955, Series 3, Folder 108;

Fontaine to Couch, May 11, 1956, Series 8.2, Folder 491; Couch to Shores, June 3, 1957, Series 3, Folder 93, in the William T. Couch Papers #03825, Southern Historical Collection, Louis Round Wilson Special Collections Library, University of North Carolina at Chapel Hill.

2. "Article to Change Offensive Article on Christ," *Catholic Universe Bulletin* 83 (May 18, 1956): 1; Couch to Piper, June 6, 1956; Piper to Couch, August 2, 1956; Piper to Couch, February 20, 1957; McCool to Couch, [n.d.]; Couch to Piper, March 8, 1957, Folder AB-9, Louis Shores Papers, Florida State University, School of Information.

3. William Terry Couch interview with Lee Shiflett, December 17, 1986, Chapel Hill, North Carolina; *Aristotle's Metaphysics: Book Gamma.*

4. William Terry Couch, *The Human Potential: An Essay on Its Cultivation* (Durham, NC: Duke University Press, 1974), 344.

5. Couch to Kilpatrick, February 25, 1956, Series 8.2, Folder 498, Couch Papers.

6. Couch, "Tentative form #1: CE Policy on Controversial Issues," March 11, 1957, Series 8.1, Folder 368, Couch Papers.

7. Couch to Louis Shores, June 3, 1957, Series 3, Folder 99, Couch Papers; Lee Shiflett, *Louis Shores: Defining Educational Librarianship* (Lanham, MD: Scarecrow, 1996), 156.

8. Couch, "Policies, Procedures, and Objectives of Encyclopedia Publishing," Series 7.1, Folder 368, Couch Papers.

9. William Terry Couch, "Policies, Procedures and Objectives of Encyclopedia Editing," in Catholic Library Association, *Proceedings of the 33rd Annual Conference Held in Louisville, Kentucky, April 22–26, 1957, Kentucky Hotel* (Villanova, PA: Catholic Library Association, 1957): 91–106.

10. Couch to Shores, June 3, 1957, Box 3, Folder 93, Couch Papers.

11. Couch to Robert Blackburn, September 19, 1958; Couch to Norris Clark, April 8, 1959, Series 3, Folder 113, Couch Papers.

12. Couch to Ryan, March 25, 1957, Series 3, Folder 95, Couch Papers; Oboler to John Carroll, June 15, 1956, Series 3, Folder 92, Couch Papers.

13. Louis Shores, "Design for an Encyclopedia," Folder AA, Shores Papers; Shores to Couch, May 27, 1957, Folder AB, Shores Papers.

14. Fontaine to Couch, August 7, 1957, Series 3, Folder 109, Couch Papers.

15. Couch to Davidson, March 31, 1959, Series 3, Folder 84, Couch Papers.

16. Couch to Welch, March 31, 1958, Series 3, Folder 83, Couch Papers; Welch to Couch, March 16, 1959, Series 3, Folder 84, Couch Papers.

17. "End of a Success Story," *Time* 68 (July 9, 1956): 57–58; "Smith's Score," *Newsweek* 48 (December 7, 1956): 68.

18. Couch to Fontaine, February 7, 1958, Series 3, Folder 95, Couch Papers; Couch to Shores, February 8, 1958, Folder AB/20, Shores Papers; Couch to Shores, February 15, 1958, Folder AB, Shores Papers.

19. Couch to Ryan, February 12, 1958, Series 3, Folder 95, Couch Papers; Ryan to Fontaine, February 19, 1958, Series 3, Folder 101. Couch Papers; Couch to Gleason, March 17, 1958, Series 3, Folder 93, Couch Papers; Fontaine to Couch, September 26, 1955, Series 3, Folder 109, Couch Papers.

20. Fontaine to Couch, February 20, 1958; Fontaine to Couch, February 21, 1958, Series 3, Folder 95, Couch Papers.

21. Raymond Kilgour, "Reference and Subscription Book Publishing," *Library Trends* 7 (July 1958): 145.

22. Couch to Shores, December 18, 1958; Couch to Ryan, December 5, 1958, COL5 Binder, Shores Papers.

23. William Terry Couch, "Other Studies of Collier's Encyclopedia," November 17, 1958, Series 3, Folder 105, Couch Papers.

24. R. W. Apple, Jr., "The Gold Rush on Publisher's Row," *Saturday Review* 43 (October 8, 1960): 47; Couch to Kirk, May 10, 1959, Series 3, Folder 107, Couch Papers; Couch to Shores, May 7, 1959; Couch to Shores, May 12, 1959, COL5 Binder, Shores Papers.

25. Couch to Kirk, May 10, 1959, Series 3, Folder 107, Couch Papers.

26. United States. Federal Trade Commission, "In the Matter of the Crowell-Collier Publishing Company et al.," *Federal Trade Commission Decisions: Findings, Opinions, and Orders July 1, 1966, to December 31, 1966* (Washington: United States Government Printing Office, 1970): 977–1033.

27. Couch to Kirk, May 8, 1959, Series 3, Folder 107, Couch Papers.

28. Couch to Shores, May 7, 1959; Couch to Shores, August 2, 1959, COL5 Binder, Shores Papers.

29. Couch to Shores, May 22, 1959, COL5 Binder, Shores Papers; Couch to Shores, May 12, 1959, Series 3, Folder 84, Couch Papers: Couch to Kirk, May 10, 1959, Series 3, Folder 107, Couch Papers; Couch to Shores, May 15, 1959, COL5 Binder, Shores Papers.

30. Couch to Cole, April 27, 1959, COL5 Binder, Shores Papers.
31. Couch to Shores, June 4, 1959; Shores to Couch, June 6, 1959, COL5 Binder, Shores Papers.
32. Couch to Wieck, July 24, 1959, Series 3, Folder 84, Couch Papers; Couch to Shores, July 21, 1959, COL5 Binder, Shores Papers; Couch to J. J. Kilpatrick, August 12, 1961, Series 8.2, Folder 498, Couch Papers.
33. Ralph E. Ellsworth, *Ellsworth on Ellsworth.* (Metuchen, NJ: Scarecrow, 1980), 74–80; Ralph E. Ellsworth and Sarah M. Harris, *The American Right Wing: A Report to the Fund for the Republic, Inc..* University of Illinois Library School Occasional Papers Number 59 ([Urbana]: University of Illinois Graduate School of Library Science, 1960); Howard Margolis, "Right Wingers Seem Almost Everywhere: Notes on a Report to the Fund for the Republic," *Science* 134 (December 22, 1961): 2025–2027; Ralph E. Ellsworth, "Right-Wing Bibliography," *Science* 135 (February 23, 1962): 674.
34. Shores to Couch, July 28, 1959; Couch to Shores, August 2, 1959, Couch to Shores, August 21, 1959, COL5 Binder, Shores Papers; Couch to R. S. Lyons, August 8, 1959; Couch to Wieck, August 26, 1959, Series 3, Folder 84, Couch Papers; Reminiscences of William Terry Couch, (1970), on page 538 in the Columbia Center for Oral History Collection.

Chapter 7

1. Reminiscences of William Terry Couch (1970) on pages 539–540 in the Columbia Center for Oral History Collection.
2. Couch to Davis, October 11, 1959, Series 4, Folder 118, in the William T. Couch Papers #03825, Southern Historical Collection, Louis Round Wilson Special Collections Library, University of North Carolina at Chapel Hill.
3. Couch to Drimmer, October 10, 1959; October 26, 1959, Series 4, Folder 126, Couch Papers; Peter Sutcliffe, *The Oxford University Press: An Informal History* Oxford: Clarendon Press, 1978), 256–257.
4. Couch to Salt, November 11, 1959; Couch to Salt, February 2, 1960, Series 4, Folder 126, Couch Papers.
5. Couch to Davin, October 30, 1960, Series 4, Folder 126, Couch Papers.
6. Roberts to Drimmer, October 11, 1960, Series 4, Folder 127, Couch Papers.

7. Couch to Drimmer, October 13, 1960, Series 4, Folder 127, Couch Papers.
8. Couch to Drimmer, October 28, 1960, Series 4, Folder 127, Couch Papers.
9. Couch to Arthur Wilson, January 6, 1961; Couch to Eugene Rostow, November 7, 1960, Series 4, Folder 126, Couch Papers.
10. James Jackson Kilpatrick, *The Southern Case for School Segregation* (New York: Crowell-Collier, 1960); Couch to Kilpatrick, August 12, 1961, Series 8.2, Folder 498, Couch Papers.
11. Couch to Bierly, May 12, 1961, Series 4, Folder 118, Couch Papers.
12. Couch to Drimmer, July 31, 1961, Series 4, Folder 127, Couch Papers.
13. Reminiscences of William Terry Couch (1970), on page 553 in the Columbia Center for Oral History Collection.
14. Couch to Davin, January 25, 1963, Series 4, Folder 126, Couch Papers.
15. Brian Doherty, *Radicals for Capitalism: A Freewheeling History of the Modern American Libertarian Movement* (New York: Public Affairs, 2007), 62; Mary Anne Raywid, *The Ax-Grinders: Critics of Our Public Schools* (New York: Macmillan, 1962), 109–122.
16. Herbert C. Cornuelle, "*Mr. Anonymous": The Story of William Volker.* (Chicago: Regnery, 1951): 116–119, 125–126, 154.
17. Nicole Hoplin and Ron Robinson, *Funding Fathers: The Unsung Heroes of the Conservative Movement* (Washington, D.C.: Regnery, 2008): 24–25; Dieter Plehwe, "Introduction" in *The Road from Mont Pelerin: The Making of the Neoliberal Thought Collective,* ed. Philip Mirowski and Dieter Plehwe (Cambridge, MA: Harvard University Press, 2009): 18–26.
18. Doherty, *Radicals for Capitalism,* 157.
19. United States. Congress. House. Select Committee on Lobbying Activities, *Lobbying: Direct and Indirect: Part 8 of Hearings: Foundation for Economic Education, July 18, 1950,* Eighty-First Congress, Second Session (Washington, D.C.: United States Government Printing Office, 1953), 12, 50; "Minutes of Annual Meeting of Board of Trustees of the Foundation for Economic Education, Inc., May 20, 1947," in *Lobbying: Direct and Indirect.* 35.
20. Alfred S. Regnery, *Upstream: The Ascendance of American Conservatism* (New York: Threshold Editions, 2008), 184.
21. Plehwe, "Introduction," 15, 19; Kim Phillips-Fein, "Business Conservatives and the Mont Pelerin Society," in *The Road from Mont Pelerin: The Making of the Neoliberal Thought*

Collective, ed. Philip Mirowski and Dieter Plehwe (Cambridge, MA: Harvard University Press, 2009): 293–295.

22. Drew Pearson, "Foundation Accused as Lobby," *Washington Post* (March 24, 1949): 15B.

23. United States. Congress. House. Select Committee on Lobbying Activities, *Lobbying: Direct and Indirect*, 1, 9, 103, 105, 116.

24. James Playsted Wood, *Of Lasting Interest: The Story of the Reader's Digest* (Garden City, New York: Doubleday, 1958), 245; Samuel A. Schreiner, Jr., *The Condensed World of the Reader's Digest* (New York: Stein and Day, 1977), 87–88.

25. United States. Congress. House. Select Committee on Lobbying Activities, *Lobbying: Direct and Indirect*, 21, 58, 114, 181–184.

26. *A Study of College Libraries: A Survey for William Volker Charities Fund* (Princeton, NJ: Opinion Research Corporation, 1953), "Study of College Libraries" Folder, Box 1, William Volker Fund Records, 1953–1961, David M. Rubinstein Rare Book and Manuscript Library. Duke University.

27. Michael J. McVicar, "Aggressive Philanthropy: Progressivism, Conservatism, and the William Volker Charities Fund," *Missouri Historical Review* 105 (July 2011): 209, note 50.

28. "Books Offered through the National Book Foundation"; "Books Offered through the National Book Foundation (listed alphabetically by title)"; "Books Offered through the National Book Foundation (listed alphabetically by author)"; "Book Publication and Distribution Survey," "National Book Foundation" Folder, Box 1, William Volker Fund Records, 1953–1961, David M. Rubinstein Rare Book and Manuscript Library. Duke University.

29. Harold W. Luhnow, "Problems in the Promotion of Freedom," in Conference on the Necessary Conditions for a Free Society (1961: Princeton, N. J.), *The Necessary Conditions for a Free Society*, ed. Felix Morley (Princeton, NJ: Van Nostrand, 1963), 173–174.

30. Couch to Templeton, April 6, 1957, Series 5, Folder 132, Couch Papers.

31. George H. Nash, *The Conservative Intellectual Movement in America Since 1945* (Wilmington, DE: Intercollegiate Studies Institute, 2008), 214; Doherty, *Radicals for Capitalism*, 180.

32. Couch to Bierly, January 22, 1962, Series 4, Folder 118, Couch Papers.

33. Couch to Bierly, December 7, 1958; Bierly to Couch, December 10, 1958, Series 5, Folder 132, Couch Papers.

34. [Press release, March 15, 1962], "Research & Writing and Book Publication & Distribution Projects" Folder, Box 2, William Volker Fund Records, 1953–1961, David M. Rubinstein Rare Book and Manuscript Library. Duke University.

35. Luhnow to Couch, January 15, 1963, Series 5, Folder 132, Couch Papers; Couch to "Members of the Board of Directors of the Center for American Studies," June 24, 1964; Couch to Fred Wieck, September 5, 1963, Series 5, Folder 139, Couch Papers.

36. Couch to Colgrove, February 14, 1956; Couch to Colgrove, March 31, 1959, Series 8.2, Folder 487, Couch Papers.

37. Luhnow, "Problems in the Promotion of Freedom," 163.

38. Luhnow, "Can the United States of America Be the First Democracy in All History to Survive?: Speech by H. W. Luhnow to Employees, April 10, 1962," Series 5, Folder 132, Couch Papers.

39. McVicar, "Aggressive Philanthropy," 202–203.

40. Couch, [Resume, April 19, 1963], Series 5, Folder 132, Couch Papers.

41. Doherty, *Radicals for Capitalism*, 293

42. Couch to Bierly, March 11, 1961, Series 4, Folder 118, Couch Papers; "*American Bicentennial Project*: Tentative Draft for Criticism and Discussion, July 25, 1961," Series 5, Folder 145, Couch Papers; Couch to Luhnow, July 5, 1963, Series 5, Folder 143, Couch Papers.

43. [Various letters], Series 5, Folder 137, Couch Papers.

44. "Purpose of Encyclopedia, 11/7/63," Series 5, Folder 143, Couch Papers.

45. Milton Gaither, *Homeschool: An American History* (New York: Palgrave Macmillan, 2008), 135.

46. Ivan Bierly, "Introduction" in Rousas John Rushdoony, *The Messianic Character of American Education: Studies in the History of the Philosophy of American Education* (Nutley, NJ: Craig Press, 1968), xiv; Association of Christian Schools, *Schools Weighed in the Balance* (n.p.: St. Thomas Press, 1961); "Survey of Education: Report Number 11 Spring 1960," William Volker Fund Records 1953–1961, Box 1, David M. Rubinstein Rare Book and Manuscript Library. Duke University.

47. Raywid, *The Ax-Grinders*, 110; Rushdoony, *Messianic Character*, 87, 133–134, 281–282; Molly Worthen, "The Chalcedon Problem: Rosas John Rushdoony and the Origins of Christian Reconstructionism," *Church History* 77 (June 2008): 418; Couch to A. N. J.

den Hollander, March 22, 1964, Series 5, Folder 138, Couch Papers.

48. Couch to Fred Wieck, September 5, 1963, Series 5, Folder 139, Couch Papers.

49. Joseph Bauke, "Whitewashing the Third Reich," *New Leader* 46 (June 24, 1963): 28–30

50. "Revolutionary History," *New Leader* 46 (August 19, 1963): 26

51. Couch to Fred Wieck, September 5, 1963, Series 5, Folder 139, Couch Papers.

52. This was not published then but in 1989 as David L. Hoggan, *The Forced War: When Peaceful Revision Failed* (Cosa Mesa, CA: Institute for Historical Review, 1989); "In Defense of Hitler," *Newsweek* 63 (May 18, 1964): 82–83.

53. "No Lecturer," *Newsweek* 63 (June 15, 1964): 12

54. Couch to Morris Cox, May 24, 1964; Couch to Julian Falk, May 22, 1964, Series 5, Folder 139, Couch Papers.

55. Couch to Fred Wieck, May 22, 1964, Series 5, Folder 139; Couch to Falk, May 27, 1964, Series 5, Folder 139, Couch Papers.

56. "Memorandum to W. T. Couch Personal File," May 28, 1964, Series 8.1, Folder 379, Couch Papers.

57. Couch to Wieck, May 22, 1964, Series 5, Folder 139, Couch Papers.

58. Couch to Cox, May 6, 1964, Series 5, Folder 139, Couch Papers.

59. Couch to Fred Wieck, June 2, 1964, Series 8.1, Folder 378, Couch Papers.

60. Bierly to Members of the Board of Directors, June 4, 1964, Series 5, Folder 139, Couch Papers.

61. "A Proposal for a Center for American Studies Program at the Hoover Institution, Stanford University," June 24, 1964, Series 5, Folder 142, Couch Papers.

62. Bierly to Cox, September 11, 1964, Series 5, Folder 138, Couch Papers.

63. "Memorandum of Understanding July 23, 1964," Series 5, Folder 142, Couch Papers.

64. Cox to Packard, September 1, 1964, Series 5, Folder 142, Couch Papers.

65. Packard to Cox, September 8, 1964, Series 5, Folder 142, Couch Papers.

66. George H. Nash, *Herbert Hoover and Stanford University*, Hoover Press Publication, 369 (Stanford, CA: Hoover Institution Press, 1988): 144–149, 155, 157, 162–163, 168.

67. Cox to Packard, September 10, 1964, Series 5, Folder 142, Couch Papers; "WTC notes," August 10, 1964, Series 5, Folder 142, Couch Papers.

68. Couch to Bierly, September 10, 1964, Series 5, Folder 142, Couch Papers.

69. "WTC notes," August 10, 1964, Series 5, Folder 142, Couch Papers.

70. Couch to Bierly, September 24, 1964, Series 5, Folder 142, Couch Papers.

71. Couch to Bierly, September 11, 1964, Series 5, Folder 142, Couch Papers.

72. McVicar, "Aggressive Philanthropy," 204–206, 212 note 92; Stephen E. Adkins, *Holocaust Denial as an International Movement* (Westport, CT: Praeger, 2009), 157–158; Worthen, "The Chalcedon Problem," 402, 412–413; Gaither, *Homeschool*, 139, 187, 94.

Chapter 8

1. Couch, "The Student Mobs," Series 7.1, Folder 279, in the William T. Couch Papers #03825, Southern Historical Collection, Louis Round Wilson Special Collections Library, University of North Carolina at Chapel Hill.

2. Couch to Russell Kirk, May 24, 1974, Series 8.1, Folder 398, Couch Papers.

3. Couch to Frances, December 2, 1969; H. D. Vursell to Couch, December 4, 1970; James N. Garrett to Couch, October 10, 1969; Couch to James Raimes, December 22, 1971; Oxford University Press to Couch, December 27, 1971, Series 8.1, Folder 349, Couch Papers.

4. Brice to Couch, September 8, 1972, Series 8.1, Folder 348, Couch Papers; [Reader's Reports on *The Human Potential*, n.d.], Series 8.1, Folder 358, Couch Papers.

5. Brice to Couch, September 8, 1972, Series 8.1, folder 348, Couch Papers; Telephone conversation with former Duke University Press staff member, July 15, 2012.

6. "Duke University Press—Meeting of the Board, October 4, 1972," in "Editorial Advisory Board May 1971-June 1974" File, Duke University Press Records 1926–, Box 3, David M. Rubinstein Rare Book and Manuscript Library. Duke University.

7. Couch to Harold Luhnow, September 21, 1972, Series 8.1, Folder 358, Couch Papers; Couch to Ashbel Brice, May 7, 1973, Series 8.1, Folder 348, Couch Papers.

8. Duke University Press, "Author's Questionnaire," September 11, 1972, Series 8.1, Folder 353, Couch Papers.

9. Couch to Davies, February 6, 1973, Series 8.1, Folder 353, Couch Papers; Couch to Davies, February 14, 1973, Series 8.1, Folder 347, Couch Papers.

10. Davies to Couch, August 28, 1975, Se-

ries 8.1, Folder 346; Davies to Couch, August 13, 1974, Series 8.1, Folder 345, Couch Papers.

11. William Terry Couch, *The Human Potential: An Essay on Its Cultivation* (Durham, N.C.: Duke University Press, 1974), 4.

12. Louis Schneider, review of, *The Human Potential*, by William Terry Couch, *Annals of the American Academy of Political and Social Science* 415 (September 1974): 272–273.

13. Couch, *Human Potential*, 338–339.

14. *Library Journal* 99 (October 15, 1974): 2600; *Choice* 12 (March 1975): 122; Couch to Peter M. Doiron, April 15, 1975, Series 8.1, Folder 347, Couch Papers.

15. Couch to Cousins, September 7, 1974, Series 8.1, Folder 345, Couch Papers.

16. Bailey to Couch, April 17, 1974; Bailey to Couch [n.d.], Series 8.1, Folder 353, Couch Papers.

17. Couch to Davies, August 12, 1974; Couch to Back, September 7, 1974; Back to Couch, April 11, 1975, Series 8.1, Folder 340, Couch Papers.

18. Alan G. Hill, review of *The Human Potential*, by William Terry Couch, *Sociology: Reviews of New Books* 1 (August 1974): 194–195.

19. Couch to The Editors, *Sociology*, October 12, 1974; Cornelius W. Vahle, Jr., to Couch, October 17, 1974, Series 8.1, Folder 347, Couch Papers.

20. Back to Couch, April 11, 1975, Series 8.1, Folder 340, Couch Papers.

21. Vivas to Couch, August 17, 1974, Series 8.1, Folder 346, Couch Papers.

22. Couch to Adams, August 30, 1974; Adams to Couch, August 28, 1974; Lalley to Couch, September 8, 1974, Series 8.1, Folder 345, Couch Papers.

23. Joseph Michael Lalley, "On Putting It All Together," review of *The Human Potential*, by William Terry Couch, *Modern Age* 19 (Summer 1975): 308–312.

24. Kirk to Couch, December 1, 1972, Series 8.1, Folder 398, Couch Papers.

25. Couch to Kirk, December 5, 1972; Kirk to Couch, May 3, 1974, Series 8.1, Folder 398, Couch Papers.

26. Russell Kirk, "Encyclopedias and Our Afflictions," *National Review* 26 (June 7, 1974): 650.

27. Kirk to Couch, June 4, 1974, Series 8.1, Folder 398, Couch Papers.

28. William Terry Couch, "What Can't Be Found in the New Britannica," *University Bookman* 15 (Winter 1975): 35.

29. Victor M. Cassidy, "Does Couch De-

mand Too Much of the *Britannica?*" *University Bookman* 15 (Winter 1975): 36–39.

30. Frederick D. Wilhelmsen, "Couch on McLuhan," *University Bookman* 15 (Winter 1975): 40–47.

31. Couch to Kirk, April 11, 1975; Kirk to Couch, May 6, 1975, Series 8.1, Folder 398, Couch Papers.

32. William Terry Couch, "More about *The Human Potential*," *University Bookman* 15 (Summer 1975): 88–94; Couch to Eliseo Vivas, July 4, 1975, Series 8.1, Folder 352, Couch Papers.

33. Couch to Jerry Hirsch, September 27, 1979, Series 8.1, Folder 406, Couch Papers.

34. Back to Couch, May 19, 1983; [Royalty Statement: Duke University Press], September 13, 1983, Series 8.1, Folder 348, Couch Papers.

35. Couch to Sand, April 30, 1983, Series 8.1, Folder 397, Couch Papers.

36. Kirk to Sand, June 22, 1983; Virginia Black to Sand, August 11, 1983, Series 8.1 Folder 442, Couch Papers.

37. Sand to Couch, June 18, 1984; Couch to Sand, July 16, 1984, Series 8.1, Folder 443, Couch Papers.

38. Couch to Daniel Singal, November 15, 1975, Series 8.1, Folder 447, Couch Papers.

39. Singal to Couch, August 3, 1970, Series 8.1, Folder 447, Couch Papers.

40. Reminiscences of William Terry Couch (1970) in the Columbia Center for Oral History Collection; Couch to Singal, November 15, 1974, Series 8.1, Folder 447, Couch Papers.

41. [Unknown Transcriber] to Elizabeth B. Mason, May 5, 1971, Series 8.1, Folder 357, Couch Papers.

42. Couch to Singal, July 8, 1975, Series 8.1, Folder 447, Couch Papers.

43. Couch to Singal, December 31, 1975, Series 8.1, Folder 447, Couch Papers; University of North Carolina Press. Board of Governors, [Minutes, June 26, 1942], Series 1, Subgroup 1, Folder "1942–1944," in the University of North Carolina Press Records #40073, University Archives, Louis Round Wilson Special Collections Library, University of North Carolina at Chapel Hill.

44. Couch to Singal, December 31, 1975, Series 8.1, Folder 447, Couch Papers.

45. Charles Kesler, "A Special Meaning of the Declaration of Independence," *National Review* 31 (July 6, 1979) 850–859; William T. Couch, "Muddled Meanings," *National Review* 31 (September 4, 1979): 1126; Harry V. Jaffa, "Another Look at the Declaration," *National Review* 32 (July 11, 1980): 836–840.

46. Couch to Buckley, June 4, 1982, Series 8.1, Folder 361, Couch Papers; Buckley to Couch, November 10, 1955; Couch to Buckley, November 13, 1955, Series 3, Folder 80, Couch Papers.

47. Couch to Singal, August 19, 1982, Series 8.1, Folder 445, Couch Papers; Daniel Joseph Singal, *The War Within: From Victorian to Modernist Thought in the South, 1919–1945* (Chapel Hill: University of North Carolina Press, 1982), 296–301; William Terry Couch, "Publisher's Introduction" in *What the Negro Wants*, ed. Rayford Logan, ix-xxii. (Chapel Hill: University of North Carolina Press, 1944).

48. Couch to Singal, September 14, 1982; Singal to Couch, October 5, 1982, Series 8.1, Folder 445, Couch Papers.

49. David Herbert Donald, "What Set the Mind of the South Thinking?" review of *The War Within*, by Daniel Joseph Singal, *New York Times Book Review* 132 (October 31, 1982): 13, 37.

50. Couch to the Editor, *The New York Times Book Review*, November 18, 1982, Series 8.1, Folder 446, Couch Papers.

51. Couch to the Editor, *The New York Times Book Review*, November 23, 1982, Series 8.1, Folder 464, Couch Papers.

52. Singal to Couch, September 26, 1983, Series 8.1, Folder 450, Couch Papers; Couch to Singal, December 5, 1982, Series 8.1, Folder 445, Couch Papers; Singal to Couch, Series 8.1, Folder 446, Couch Papers.

53. Couch, "What is Daniel Joseph Singal's Book The War Within About?" Series 7.1, Folder 295, Couch Papers.

54. Shapiro to Couch, January 11, 1982 [i.e., 1983], Series 7.1, Folder 295, Couch Papers.

55. Couch to Wood, March 4, 1982, Series 8.1, Folder 476, Couch Papers; Couch, "The Critical Temperament at the Mourner's Bench," 1, Series 7.1, Folder 191, Couch Papers.

56. Couch, "Critical Temperament at the Mourner's Bench," 2, 10.

57. Couch, *Human Potential*, 69–70.

58. Singal, *War Within*, 6; Couch, "Critical Temperament at the Mourner's Bench," 9A, 16–17, 74, 40, 136.

59. Singal, *War Within*, 261.

60. Singal, *War Within*, xiv.

61. Couch "Critical Temperament at the Mourner's Bench," 20.

62. Couch "Critical Temperament at the Mourner's Bench," 3, 8. 4A, 20, 123G, 128; Singal, *War Within*, 294.

63. Couch to Singal, October 24, 1976, Series 8.1, Folder 451, Couch Papers.

64. Singal, *War Within*, 376–377.

65. Couch, "Critical Temperament at the Mourner's Bench," 8, 124B, 132; Couch, "The Critical Temperament Leashed," 4, Series 8.1, Folder 462, Couch Papers.

66. Couch to Georgia Nash, December 8, 1983, Series 8.1, Folder 451, Couch Papers.

Chapter 9

1. William Terry Couch, "The Word and the Rope," Modern *Age* 2 (Winter 1957–58): 4.

2. "Five Named 'Distinguished Alumni,'" [University of North Carolina] *Alumni Review* 60 (November 1972): 6.

3. Arie Nicolaas Jan den Hollander, *De Landelijke Arme Blanken in het Zuiden der Vereenigde Staten: Een Sociaal-historische en Sociografische Studie* (Gronigen, Netherlands: J. B. Wolters, 1933).

4. Hollander, "Letter to the U. N. C. Press To Be Read on October 12," September 25, 1972, in the William T. Couch Papers #03825, Southern Historical Collection, Louis Round Wilson Special Collections Library, University of North Carolina at Chapel Hill. Series 6, Folder 155.

5. Paul M. Gaston, *The New South Creed: A Study in Southern Mythmaking* (New York: Knopf, 1970), 5, 11, 25, 32–33, 35, 40, 60–63.

6. William Terry Couch, "Do Intellectuals Have Minds?" *Georgia Review* 1 (Fall 1947): 309.

7. Couch to Colgrove, March 31, 1959, Series 8.2, Folder 487, Couch Papers.

8. George H. Nash, *The Conservative Intellectual Movement in America since 1945* (Wilmington, Delaware: Intercollegiate Studies Institute, 2008), pp. xviii-xxi; Alfred S. Regnery, *Upstream: The Ascendance of American Conservatism.* (New York: Threshold Editions, 2008), 24–26.

9. Couch, "Centralization: The End of Democracy," Series 7.1, Folder 187, Couch Papers.

10. Lucille Cardin Crain, "A Declaration," *Educational Reviewer* 1 (July 15, 1949): 1.

11. George S. Bobinski, *Carnegie Libraries: Their History and Impact on American Public Library Development* (Chicago: American Library Association, 1968); Gary E. Kraske, *Missionaries of the Book: The American Library Profession and the Origins of United States Cul-*

tural Diplomacy, Contributions in Librarianship and Information Science, Number 54 (Westport, CT: Greenwood Press, 1985); Deanna B. Marcum, "Reclaiming the Research Library: The Founding of the Council on Library Resources," in *Libraries and Philanthropy: Proceedings of the Library History Seminar IX 30 March–1 April 1995, University of Alabama, Tuscaloosa* ed. Donald G. Davis, Jr. (Austin: Graduate School of Library and Information Science, University of Texas at Austin, 1996), 113–124; Robert Sidney Martin and Orvin Lee Shiflett, "Hampton, Fisk, and Atlanta: The Foundations, the American Library Association, and Library Education for Blacks," in *Libraries and Philanthropy: Proceedings of the Library History Seminar IX 30 March–1 April 1995, University of Alabama, Tuscaloosa* ed. Donald G. Davis, Jr. (Austin: Graduate School of Library and Information Science, University of Texas at Austin, 1996), 299–325; Wayne Wiegand, "Wresting Money from the Canny Scotsman: Melvil Dewey's Designs on Carnegie's Millions, 1902–1906,"

in *Libraries and Philanthropy: Proceedings of the Library History Seminar IX 30 March–1 April 1995, University of Alabama, Tuscaloosa* ed. Donald G. Davis, Jr. (Austin: Graduate School of Library and Information Science, University of Texas at Austin, 1996), 380–393.

12. W. T. Couch, "Foundations and Freedom," 11, Series 7.1, Folder 207, Couch Papers.

13. Arthur O. Lovejoy, *The Great Chain of Bring: A Study of the History of an Idea,* William James Lectures, 1933 (Cambridge, MA: Harvard University Press, 1936).

14. Daniel Joseph Singal, *The War Within: From Victorian to Modernist Thought in the South, 1919–1945* (Chapel Hill: University of North Carolina Press, 1982), 6–8.

15. Singal, *War Within,* 8, 276–279.

16. Couch to Aaron M. Sargent, April 18, 1952, Series 2, Folder 75, Couch Papers.

17. William Terry Couch, "Scholarship and Publishing," *South Atlantic Quarterly* 51 (1952): 522–523.

Bibliography

Unpublished and Archival Sources

American Library Association Archives, University of Illinois Library.

Duke University Press Records, David M. Rubinstein Rare Book and Manuscript Library. Duke University.

Frank Porter Graham Papers, #1819, Southern Historical Collection, Louis Round Wilson Special Collections Library, University of North Carolina at Chapel Hill.

Kenneth Douty Report and Letters, 1956: 1971, #3976-z, Southern Historical Collections, Louis Round Wilson Special Collections Library, University of North Carolina at Chapel Hill.

Louis Round Wilson Papers, #3274, Southern Historical Collection, Louis Round Wilson Special Collections Library, University of North Carolina at Chapel Hill.

Louis Shores Papers, Florida State University, School of Information.

Lucille Cardin Crain Papers (Col. 095), Special Collections and Archives, University of Oregon Libraries, Eugene, Oregon.

Reminiscences of William Terry Couch in the Columbia Center for Oral History Collection, Columbia University.

University of Chicago Presidents Papers, Special Collections Research Center, University of Chicago Library.

University of Chicago Press Records, Special Collections Research Center, University of Chicago Library.

University of Illinois. Library. Deans Office. General Correspondence 1897–1979, University of Illinois Archives.

University of North Carolina Press Records, #40073, University Archives, Louis Round Wilson Special Collections Library, University of North Carolina at Chapel Hill.

William Terry Couch interview with Lee Shiflett, 17 December 1986, Chapel Hill, North Carolina.

William Terry Couch Papers, #03825, Southern Historical Collection, Louis Round Wilson Special Collections Library, University of North Carolina at Chapel Hill.

William Volker Fund Records, David M. Rubinstein Rare Book and Manuscript Library, Duke University.

Published Sources

Adams, Edward C. L. *Congaree Sketches: Scenes from Negro Life in the Swamps of the Congaree and Tales by Tad and Scip of Heaven and Hell with Other Miscellany.* Chapel Hill: University of North Carolina Press, 1927.

Adkins, Stephen E. *Holocaust Denial as an International Movement.* Westport, CT: Praeger, 2009.

American Textbook Publishers Institute. *Books in World Rehabilitation: A Memorandum for Members of the Congress of the United States, Department of State, Department of the Army, Department of Commerce.* [New York]:1948.

Apple, R. W., Jr. "The Gold Rush on Publisher's Row." *Saturday Review* 43 (October 8, 1960): 13–15, 47–49.

Ashby, Warren. *Frank Porter Graham: A Southern Liberal.* Winston-Salem, NC: John F. Blair, Publisher, 1980.

Ashmore, Harry S. *Unsea¬sonable Truths:*

The Life of Robert Maynard Hutchins. Boston: Little, Brown, 1989.

Association of Christian Schools. *Schools Weighed in the Balance.* N.p.: St. Thomas Press, 1961.

Atkins, Stephen E. *Holocaust Denial as an International Movement.* Westport, CT: Praeger, 2009.

Barnes, Harry Elmer. "Sociology and Ethics: A Genetic View of the Theory of Conduct." *Journal of Social Forces* 3 (January 1925): 212–231.

Barsodi, Ralph. "Subsistence Homesteads: President Roosevelt's New Land and Population Policy." *Survey Graphics* 23 (January 1934): 11–14, 48.

Bauke, Joseph. "Whitewashing the Third Reich." *New Leader* 46 (June 24, 1963): 28–30.

Beam, Alex. *A Great Idea at the Time: The Rise, Fall, and Curious Afterlife of the Great Books.* New York: Public Affairs, 2008.

Bean, Donald P. "The Pitfalls of Cooperation: Origins of the AAUP." *Publishers Weekly* 161 (June 28, 1953): 2607–2610.

Beasley, Maurine Hoffman. *Eleanor Roosevelt: Transformative First Lady.* Lawrence: University Press of Kansas, 2010.

Benowitz, June Melby. *Days of Discontent: American Women and Right-Wing Politics, 1933–1945.* DeKalb: Northern Illinois University Press, 2002.

Bernard, Luther Lee. "The Development of the Concept of Progress." *Journal of Social Forces* 3 (January 1925): 207–212.

Bierly, Ivan R. "Introduction." In Rousas John Rushdoony, *The Messianic Character of American Education: Studies in the History of the Philosophy of American Education,* xi-xiv. Nutley, NJ: Craig Press, 1968.

Bixler, Paul. "Libraries and Intellectual Freedom." In *Collier's 1954 Year Book Covering National and International Events of the Year 1953,* 333–336. New York: P. F. Collier & Son, 1954.

Blair, Lyle. "Colleges and Universities: Comments." In *Collier's 1956 Year Book: An Encyclopedic Supplement and Review of National and International Events of 1955,* 182–183. New York: P. F. Collier & Son, 1956.

Bobinski, George S. *Carnegie Libraries: Their History and Impact on American Public Library Development.* Chicago: American Library Association, 1968.

Books from Chapel Hill: A Complete Catalogue, 1923–1945. The University of North Carolina Sesquicentennial Publications. Chapel Hill: University of North Carolina Press, 1946.

Brazil, Wayne D. *Howard W. Odum: The Building Years, 1884–1930.* New York: Garland Publishing Company, 1988.

Brooks, Cleanth, and Allen Tate. *Cleanth Brooks and Allen Tate: Collected Letters, 1933–1976.* Edited by Alphonse Vinh. Columbia: University of Missouri Press, 1998.

Brown, Larue. "War Trial." *Nation* 169 (September 10, 1949): 256–257.

Cassidy, Victor M. "Does Couch Demand Too Much of the *Britannica?" University Bookman* 15 (Winter 1975): 36–39.

Cherrington, Ben Mark. *Methods of Education in International Attitudes.* Contributions to Education, no. 595. New York: Bureau of Publications, Teachers College, Columbia University, 1934.

Colgrove, Kenneth, and Franklin L. Burdette. "Republic and the Language of War." In *Collier's 1955 Year Book Covering National and International Events of the Year 1954.* 536–538. New York: P. F. Collier & Sons, 1955.

Colgrove, Kenneth, and Willmoore Kendall. "Academic Freedom Hutchins Style: How a Distinguished Member of the University of Chicago Faculty, the Head of the University Press, Was Fired for Refusing to Suppress a Book." *American Legion Magazine* 61 (July 1956):16–17, 54–56.

Colwell, Ernest Cadman. "The Publishing Needs of Scholarship." *Publisher's Weekly* 151 (February 1, 1947): 516–517.

Conkin, Paul K. *Tomorrow a New World: The New Deal Community Program.* Ithaca, NY: Published for the American Historical Association [by the] Cornell University Press, 1959.

Cornuelle, Herbert C. *"Mr. Anonymous": The Story of William Volker.* Chicago: Henry Regnery, 1951.

Couch, William Terry. "An Agrarian Programme for the South." *American Review* 3 (Summer 1934): 313–326.

_____. "The Agrarian Romance," *South Atlantic Quarterly* 36 (1937): 419–430.

_____. "American Peasants." *Virginia Quarterly Review* 10 (October 1934): 636–640.

_____. "Are All Men Created Equal?" *Negro Digest* 3, no. 3 (1945): 35–36.

_____. "Books That Ought to Be Written."

Library Quarterly 12 (October 1942): 429–437.

_____. "Can Language Teaching Be Improved?" *Modern Language Journal* 14 (October 1929): 20–32.

_____. "A Case History in Book Publishing." *American Quarterly* 1 (Winter 1948): 303–310

_____. *Culture in the South*. Chapel Hill: University of North Carolina Press, 1934.

_____. "Do Intellectuals Have Minds?" *Georgia Review* 1 (Fall 1947): 307–315.

_____. "Economic Planning in the South." *Westminster Magazine* 23 (January–March 1935): 295–305.

_____. *The Human Potential: An Essay on Its Cultivation*. Durham, NC: Duke University Press, 1974.

_____. *It Costs Us Nothing*. Hinsdale, IL: Henry Regnery Company, 1948.

_____. "More About *The Human Potential.*" *University Bookman* 15 (Summer 1975): 88–94.

_____. "Muddled Meanings." *National Review* 31 (September 4, 1979): 1126.

_____. "Objectivity and Social Sciences." In *Scientism and Values*. Edited by Helmut Schoeck and James W. Wiggins, 22–49. Princeton, NJ: Van Nostrand, 1960.

_____. "Policies, Procedures and Objectives of Encyclopedia Publishing." In Catholic Library Association. *Proceedings of the 33rd Annual Conference Held in Louisville Kentucky April 22–26, 1957 Kentucky Hotel*. 91–106. Villanova, PA: Catholic Library Association, 1957.

_____. "Preface." In *Collier's 1954 Year Book Covering National and International Events of the Year 1953*. v–vi. New York: P. F. Collier & Son, 1954.

_____. "Preface." In *1953 Collier's Year Book Covering Events of the Year 1952*. [2 unnumbered pages]. New York: P. F. Collier & Son, 1953.

_____. "Publisher's Introduction." In *What the Negro Wants*. Edited by Rayford W. Logan, ix–xxiii. Chapel Hill: University of North Carolina Press, 1944.

_____. *Publishing at the University of Texas: Survey and Recommendations Made at the Request of the University Press Advisory Board* [Austin: 1945?].

_____. "Regional Publishing." In *The Place of the University Press in American Education and Publishing: A Symposium Conducted by Earl Schenck Miers*, 23–30. [N.p., 1941].

_____. "Regionalism in Literature." *Southeastern Librarian* 3 (Spring 1953): 5–10, 27.

_____. Review of *Of Making Many Books: A Hundred Years of Reading, Writing and Publishing*, by Roger Burlingame. *Library Quarterly* 17 (October 1947): 309–310.

_____. "The Sainted Book Burners." *Freeman* 5 (April 1955): 423–426.

_____. "Scholarship and Publishing." *South Atlantic Quarterly* 51 (1952) 519–527.

_____. "Southern Publishing." *Sewanee Review* 53 (Winter 1945): 167–171.

_____. "Southerners Inspect the South." *New Republic* 97 (December 14, 1938): 168–169.

_____. "That Learning Be Served." In *A Short History of the University of North Carolina Press: Essays by Former Directors, William T. Couch, Lambert Davis, & Matthew Hodgson Published on the Occasion of the Press's 75th Anniversary*, 3–9. Chapel Hill: University of North Carolina Press, 1997.

_____. "Twenty Years of Southern Publishing." *Virginia Quarterly Review* 26 (Spring 1950): 171–185.

_____. "The University Press as an Aid to Scholarship." In *Journal of Proceedings and Addresses of the Thirty-Sixth Annual Conference Held at the University of Chicago October 25, 26, 27, 1934*, by The Association of American Universities, 136–149. Chicago: University of Chicago Press, 1934.

_____. "A University Press in the South." *Southwest Review* 19 (Autumn 1934): 195–204.

_____. "What Can't Be Found in the New Britannica." *University Bookman* 15 (Winter 1975): 28–35.

_____. "The Word and the Rope." *Modern Age* 2 (Winter 1957–58): 4–9.

Crain, Lucille Cardin. "A Declaration." *Educational Reviewer* 1 (July 15, 1949: 1.

_____. "Goodbye." *Educational Reviewer* 5 (October 1953): 1.

Cutrer, Thomas W. *Parnassus on the Mississippi: The "Southern Review" and the Baton Rouge Literary Community, 1935–1942*. Baton Rouge: Louisiana State University Press, 1984.

Dabney, Virginius. *Liberalism in the South*. Chapel Hill: University of North Carolina Press, 1932.

Davidson, Donald. *The Attack on Leviathan: Regionalism and Nationalism in the United States.* Chapel Hill: University of North Carolina Press, 1938.

_____. "A Mirror for Artists." In *I'll Take My Stand: The South and the Agrarian Tradition*, 28–60. New York: Harper, 1930.

_____. *Southern Writers in the Modern World.* Eugenia Dorothy Blount Lamar Memorial Lectures, 1957. Athens: University of Georgia Press, 1958.

Davidson, Donald, and Allen Tate. *The Literary Correspondence of Donald Davidson and Allen Tate.* Edited by John Tyree Fain and Thomas Daniel Young. Athens: University of Georgia Press, 1974.

Doherty, Brian. *Radicals for Capitalism: A Freewheeling History of the Modern American Libertarian Movement.* New York: Public Affairs, 2007.

Donald, David Herbert. "What Set the Mind of the South Thinking?" Review of *The War Within*, by Daniel Singal. *New York Times Book Review* 132 (October 31, 1982): 13, 37.

Downs, Robert B. *Perspectives on the Past; An Autobiography.* Metuchen, NJ: Scarecrow Press, 1984.

Du Bois, W. E. B. *Against Racism: Unpublished Essays, Papers, Addresses, 1887–1961.* Edited by Herbert Aptheker. Amherst: University of Massachusetts Press, 1985.

Dunn, Susan. *Roosevelt's Purge: How FDR Fought to Change the Democratic Party.* Cambridge, Massachusetts: Belknap Press of Harvard University Press, 2010.

Dzuback, Mary Ann. *Robert M. Hutchins: Portrait of an Educator.* Chicago: University of Chicago Press, 1991.

Egerton, John. *Speak Now Against the Day: The Generation before the Civil Rights Movement in the South.* New York: Knopf, 1994.

Ellsworth, Ralph E. *Ellsworth on Ellsworth.* Metuchen, NJ: Scarecrow, 1980.

_____. "Right-Wing Bibliography." *Science* 135 (February 23, 1962): 674.

Ellsworth, Ralph E., and Sarah M Harris. *The American Right Wing: A Report to the Fund for the Republic, Inc..* University of Illinois Library School Occasional Papers no. 59. [Urbana]: University of Illinois Graduate School of Library Science, 1960.

Federal Writers' Project. *These Are Our Lives, as Told by the People and Written by Members of the Federal Writers' Project of the Works Progress Administration in North Carolina, Tennessee and Georgia.* Chapel Hill: University of North Carolina Press, 1939.

"Foreign Markets for United States Books." *Publishers' Weekly* 148 (September 1, 1945): 850.

Foreman, Clark. "The Decade of Hope." *Pylon* 12, no. 2 (1951): 137–150.

Gaither, Milton. *Homeschool: An American History.* New York: Palgrave Macmillan, 2008.

Gaston, Paul M. *The New South Creed: A Study in Southern Mythmaking.* New York: Knopf, 1970.

Gatewood, Willard B., Jr. *Preachers Pedagogues & Politicians: The Evolution Controversy in North Carolina.* Chapel Hill: University of North Carolina Press, 1966.

Gellhorn, Walter. "Report on a Report of the House Committee on Un-American Activities." *Harvard Law Review* 60 (October 1947): 1193–1234.

"Georgian Details Integration Bars," *New York Times* (December 9, 1955): 24.

Gilmore, Glenda Elizabeth. *Defying Dixie: The Radical Roots of Civil Rights, 1919–1950.* New York: Norton, 2008.

Green, Paul. "Introduction." In *Congaree Sketches: Scenes from Negro Life in the Swamps of the Congaree and Tales by Tad and Scip of Heaven and Hell with Other Miscellany*, by Edward C. L. Adams, vii–xvii. Chapel Hill: University of North Carolina Press, 1927.

_____. *Letters of Paul Green, 1916–1981.* Edited by Laurence G. Avery. Chapel Hill: University of North Carolina Press, 1994.

Hench, John B. *Books as Weapons: Propaganda, Publishing, and the Battle for Global Markets in the Era of World War II.* Ithaca, NY: Cornell University Press, 2010.

Hess, Karl, Jack Anderson, Victor Lasky, and James A. Wechsler. "McCarthyism: A Debate." In *Collier's 1954 Year Book Covering National and International Events of the Year 1953*, 345–356. New York: P. F. Collier & Son, 1954.

Hill, Alan G. Review of *The Human Potential: An Essay on Its Cultivation* by William Terry Couch. *Sociology: Reviews of New Books* 1 (August 1974): 194–195.

Hillman, Alex L. "The Case of Mr. Couch." *Freeman* 2 (January 28, 1952): 279–280.

Hobbs, A. H. "Social Science and Science."

In *Collier's 1954 Year Book Covering National and International Events of the Year 1953*, 521–523. New York: P. F. Collier & Son, 1954.

Holley, Edward G. *The Library, Philanthropy. Publications, and UNC's Emergence as a Major American University.* The Twelfth Hanes Lecture. Chapel Hill: Hanes Foundation, University of North Carolina at Chapel Hill, 1998.

Hoplin, Nichole and Ron Robinson. *Funding Fathers: The Unsung Heroes of the Conservative Movement.* Washington, D.C.: Henry Regnery, 2008.

Hughes, Frank. "How to Fire a Professor: A Case History in Academic Freedom." *Freeman* 2 (December 3, 1951): 145–148.

_____. *Prejudice and the Press: A Restatement of the Principle of Freedom of the Press with Specific Reference to the Hutchins-Luce Commission.* New York: Devin-Adair, 1950.

Huse, Howard Russell. *The Psychology of Foreign Language Study.* Chapel Hill: University of North Carolina Press, 1931.

_____. *Reading and Speaking Foreign Languages.* Chapel Hill: University of North Carolina Press, 1945.

Hutchins, Robert Maynard. *The Higher Learning in America.* New Haven, CT: Yale University Press 1936.

I'll Take My Stand: The South and the Agrarian Tradition. New York: Harper, 1930.

"Introduction: A Statement of Principle." In *I'll Take My Stand: The South and the Agrarian Tradition*, ix–xx. New York: Harper, 1930.

Jackson, Walter A. *Gunnar Myrdal and America's Conscience: Social Engineering and Racial Liberalism, 1938–1987.* Chapel Hill: University of North Carolina Press, 1990.

Jaffa, Harry V. "Another Look at the Declaration." *National Review* 32 (July 11, 1980): 836–840.

Janken, Kenneth Robert. *Rayford W. Logan and the Dilemma of the African-American Intellectual.* Amherst: University of Massachusetts Press, 1993.

Johnson, Guy Benton, and Guion Griffis Johnson. *Research in Service to Society: The First Fifty Years of the Institute for Research in Social Science at the University of North Carolina.* Chapel Hill: University of North Carolina Press, 1980.

Jones, Howard Mumford. *Primer of Intellectual Freedom.* Cambridge, MA; Harvard University Press, 1949.

Katcher, Leo. *Earl Warren: A Political Biography.* New York: McGraw-Hill, 1967.

Katznelson, Ira. *Fear Itself: The New Deal and the Origins of Our Time.* New York: Liveright, 2013.

Kelley, Robin D. G. *Hammer and Hoe: Alabama Communists during the Great Depression.* Chapel Hill: University of North Carolina Press, 1990.

Kerr, Chester. *A Report on American University Presses.* Association of American University Presses, 1949.

Kesler, Charles. "A Special Meaning of the Declaration of Independence." *National Review* 31 (July 6, 1979): 850–859.

Kilgour, Raymond. "Reference and Subscription Book Publishing." *Library Trends* 7 (July 1958): 139–152.

Kilpatrick, James Jackson. *The Southern Case for School Segregation.* New York: Crowell-Collier, 1960.

Kirk, Russell. *Academic Freedom: An Essay in Definition.* Chicago: Henry Regnery, 1955.

_____. "Academic Freedom and Educational Standards." In *Collier's 1954 Year Book Covering National and International Events of the Year 1953.* 1–5. New York: P. F. Collier & Son, 1954.

_____. "Censorship." In *Collier's 1954 Year Book Covering National and International Events of the Year 1953*, 85–89. New York: P. F. Collier & Son, 1954.

_____. "Colleges and Universities." In *Collier's 1956 Year Book: An Encyclopedic Supplement and Review of National and International Events of 1955*, 178–182. New York: P. F. Collier & Son, 1956.

_____. "Conservatism." In *Collier's 1954 Year Book Covering National and International Events of the Year 1953*, 151–156. New York: P. F. Collier & Son, 1954.

_____. "Encyclopedias and Our Afflictions." *National Review* 26 (June 7, 1974): 650.

_____. "Great Britain: Report and Reflections." In *Collier's 1954 Year Book Covering National and International Events of the Year 1953*, 248–252. New York: P. F. Collier & Son, 1954.

_____. "Prospects for a Conservative Bent in the Human Sciences." *Social Research* 35 (Winter 1968): 580–592.

_____. *The Sword of Imagination: Memoirs of a Half-Century of Literary Conflict.* Grand Rapids, MI: Eerdmans, 1995.

Kirk, Russell, and Glen Negley. "Academic Freedom: A Report" [and] "Academic Freedom: Two Views." In *Collier's 1956 Year Book: An Encyclopedic Supplement and Review of National and International Events of 1955*, 1–6. New York: P. F. Collier & Son, 1956.

Klehr, Harvey. *The Heyday of American Communism: The Depression Decade*. New York: Basic Books, 1984.

Kraske, Gary E. *Missionaries of the Book: The American Library Profession and the Origins of United States Cultural Diplomacy*. Contributions in Librarianship and Information Science, Number 54. Westport, CT: Greenwood Press, 1985.

Krueger, Thomas A. *And Promises to Keep: The Southern Conference for Human Welfare, 1938–1948*. Nashville, TN: Vanderbilt University Press, 1967.

Lalley, Joseph Michael. "On Putting It All Together." Review of *The Human Potential*, by William Terry Couch. *Modern Age* 19 (Summer 1975): 308–312.

Leuchtenburg, William E. *The White House Looks South: Franklin D. Roosevelt, Harry S. Truman, Lyndon B. Johnson*. Baton Rouge: Louisiana State University Press, 2005.

Lewis, Nell Battle. "The University of North Carolina Gets Its Orders." *Nation* 122 (February 3, 1926): 114–115.

Liebling, Abbott Joseph. *The Wayward Pressman*. Garden City, NY: Doubleday, 1948.

Logan, Rayford W., ed. *What the Negro Wants*. Chapel Hill: University of North Carolina Press, 1944.

Lovejoy, Arthur O. *The Great Chain of Being: A Study of the History of an Idea*. William James Lectures, 1933. Cambridge, MA: Harvard University Press, 1936.

Luhnow, Harold. "Problems in the Promotion of Freedom." In Conference on the Necessary Conditions for a Free Society (1961: Princeton, N. J.). *The Necessary Conditions for a Free Society*. Edited by Felix Morley, 161–177. Princeton, NJ: Van Nostrand, 1963.

Lytle, Andrew Nelson. "The Hind Tit." In *I'll Take My Stand: The South and the Agrarian Tradition*, 201–245. New York: Harper, 1930.

Lytle, Andrew Nelson, and Allen Tate. *The Lytle-Tate Letters: The Correspondence of Andrew Lytle and Allen Tate*. Edited by Thomas Daniel Young and Elizabeth Sarcone. Jackson: University Press of Mississippi, 1987.

Manley, John F. "The Conservative Coalition in Congress." *American Behavioral Scientist* 17 (November/December 1973): 223–247.

Marcum, Deanna B. "Reclaiming the Research Library: The Founding of the Council on Library Resources." In *Libraries and Philanthropy: Proceedings of the Library History Seminar IX 30 March–1 April 1995, University of Alabama, Tuscaloosa*. Edited by Donald G. Davis, Jr. 113–124. Austin: Graduate School of Library and Information Science, University of Texas at Austin, 1996.

Margolis, Howard. "Right Wingers Seem Almost Everywhere: Notes on a Report to the Fund for the Republic." *Science* 134 (December 22, 1961): 2025–2027.

Martin, Robert Sidney and Orvin Lee Shiflett. "Hampton, Fisk, and Atlanta: The Foundations, the American Library Association, and Library Education for Blacks." In *Libraries and Philanthropy: Proceedings of the Library History Seminar IX 30 March–1 April 1995, University of Alabama, Tuscaloosa*. Edited by Donald G. Davis, Jr. 299–325. Austin: Graduate School of Library and Information Science, University of Texas at Austin, 1996.

Mayer, Milton. *Robert Maynard Hutchins: A Memoir*. Berkeley: University of California Press. 1993.

McDonald, Milo. Review of *Secondary Education: Guidance—Curriculum—Method*, by C. B. Mendenhall and K. J. Arisman. *Educational Reviewer* 4 (January 15, 1953): 3–4.

McNeill, William H. *Hutchins' University: A Memoir of the University of Chicago, 1929–1950*. Chicago: University of Chicago Press, 1991.

McVicar, Michael J. "Aggressive Philanthropy: Progressivism, Conservatism, and the William Volker Charities Fund." *Missouri Historical Review* 105 (July 2011): 191–212.

"Money Needed by Europe To Implement Marshall Plan." *Publishers' Weekly* 152 (October 4, 1947): 1786.

Morse, Arthur D. "Who's Trying to Ruin Our Schools." *McCall's* 78 (September 1951): 26 7, 94, 108 9.

Murray, Stephen O. "The Rights of Research Assistants and the Rhetoric of Political

Suppression: Morton Grodzins and the University of California Japanese-American Evacuation and Resettlement Study." *Journal of the History of the Behavioral Sciences* 27 (April 1991): 130–156.

Myrdal, Gunnar. *An American Dilemma: The Negro Problem and Modern Democracy.* New York: Harper, 1944.

Nash, George H. *The Conservative Intellectual Movement in America since 1945.* Thirtieth-Anniversary ed. Wilmington, DE: Intercollegiate Studies Institute, 2008.

_____. *Herbert Hoover and Stanford University.* Hoover Press Publication 369. Stanford, CA: Hoover Institution Press, 1988.

National Emergency Council (U.S.). *Report on Economic Conditions of the South.* Washington, D.C.: U.S. Government Printing Office, 1938.

Nixon, Herman Clarence. "Whither Southern Economy?" In *I'll Take My Stand: The South and the Agrarian Tradition,* 176–200. New York: Harper, 1930

O'Brien, Michael. *The Idea of the American South, 1920–1941.* Baltimore, MD: Johns Hopkins University Press, 1979.

Owsley, Frank Lawrence. "The Irrepressible Conflict." In *I'll Take My Stand: The South and the Agrarian Tradition,* 61–91. New York: Harper, 1930.

Pearson, Drew. "Foundation Accused as Lobby." *Washington Post* (March 24, 1949):15B.

Phillips-Fein, Kim. "Business Conservatives and the Mont Pelerin Society." In *The Road from Mont Pelerin: The Making of the Neoliberal Thought Collective.* Edited by Philip Mirowski and Dieter Plehwe, 280–301. Cambridge, MA: Harvard University Press.

Plehwe, Dieter. "Introduction." In *The Road from Mont Pelerin: The Making of the Neoliberal Thought Collective.* Edited by Philip Mirowski and Dieter Plehwe. 1–42. Cambridge, MA: Harvard University Press, 2009.

Raywid, Mary Anne. *The Ax-Grinders: Critics of Our Public Schools.* New York: Macmillan, 1962.

Reed, Linda. *Simple Decency and Common Sense: The Southern Conference Movement, 1938–1963.* Bloomington: Indiana University Press, 1991.

Reel, A. Frank. *The Case of General Yamashita.* Chicago: University of Chicago Press, 1949.

Reeves, Thomas C. *Freedom and the Foundations: The Fund for the Republic in the Era of McCarthyism.* New York: Knopf, 1969.

Regnery, Alfred S. *Upstream: The Ascendance of American Conservatism.* New York: Threshold Editions, 2008.

Regnery, Henry. "A Southern Agrarian at the University of Chicago." In *The Vision of Richard Weaver.* Edited by Joseph Scotchie, 145–161. New Brunswick, NJ: Transaction Books, 1995.

Report of the Proceedings of the Southern Conference for Human Welfare, Birmingham, Alabama, November 20–23, 1938. [N.p., n.d.].

"Revolutionary History." *New Leader* 46 (August 19, 1963): 26.

Robbins, Louise S. "Toward Ideology and Autonomy: The American Library Association's Response to Threats of Intellectual Freedom, 1939–1969." PhD diss., Texas Womans' University, 1991.

Robinson, Leland Rex. "Statism." In *1953 Collier's Year Book Covering Events of the Year 1952,* 659–663. New York: P. F. Collier & Son, 1953.

Rock, Virginia Jean. "The Making and Meaning of *I'll Take My Stand*: A Study in Utopian-Conservatism, 1925–1939." PhD diss., University of Minnesota, 1961.

Roper, John Herbert. *C. Vann Woodward: A Southern Historian and His Critics.* Athens: University of Georgia Press, 1997.

_____. *Paul Green: Playwright of the Real South.* Athens: University of Georgia Press, 2003.

Root, E. Merrill. *Collectivism on the Campus: The Battle for the Mind in American Colleges.* New York: Devin-Adair, 1961

Rushdoony, Rousas John. *The Messianic Character of American Education: Studies in the History of the Philosophy of American Education.* Nutley, NJ: Craig Press, 1968.

Schneider, Louis. Review of *The Human Potential,* by William Terry Couch. *Annals of the American Academy of Political and Social Science* 415 (September 1974): 272–273.

Schreiner, A. Samuel, Jr. *The Condensed World of the Reader's Digest.* New York: Stein and Day, 1977.

Scotchie, Joseph. "Introduction: From Weaverville to Posterity." In *The Vision of Richard Weaver.* Edited by Joseph

Scotchie, 1–17. New Brunswick, NJ: Transaction Books, 1995.

Selznick, Philip. "Natural Law and Sociology." In Center for the Study of Democratic Institutions. *Natural Law and Modern Society*, 154–193. Cleveland, OH: World, 1963.

Shiflett, Lee. *Louis Shores: Defining Educational Librarianship*. Lanham, MD: Scarecrow, 1996.

Shugg, Roger W. "Publishing at Chicago: A Brief History of the University of Chicago Press." In *The University of Chicago Press: Catalog of Books and Journals, 1891–1965*, xi–xxxiii. Chicago: University of Chicago Press, 1967.

Singal, Daniel Joseph. "The Development of Modernism: Intellectual Life in the South, 1919–1941." PhD diss., Columbia University, 1976.

_____. *The War Within: From Victorian to Modernist Thought in the South, 1919–1945*. Chapel Hill: University of North Carolina Press, 1982.

Smith, Ted J., III. "How *Ideas Have Consequences* Came to Be Written." In *Steps Toward Restoration: The Consequences of Richard Weaver's Ideas*. Edited by Ted J. Smith, III, 1–33. Wilmington, DE: Intercollegiate Studies Institute, 1998.

Snider, William D. *Light on the Hill: A History of the University of North Carolina at Chapel Hill*. Chapel Hill: University of North Carolina Press, 1992.

Solomon, Mark. *The Cry Was Unity: Communists and African Americans, 1917–36*. Jackson: University Press of Mississippi, 1998.

Southern, David W. *Gunnar Myrdal and Black-White Relations: The Use and Abuse of "An American Dilemma," 1944–1969*. Baton Rouge: Louisiana State University Press, 1987.

"A Special New Republic Report on Book Burning." *New Republic* 128 (June 29, 1953):7–17.

Sullivan, Peggy. *Carl H. Milam and the American Library Association*. New York: H. W. Wilson, 1976.

Sutcliffe, Peter. *The Oxford University Press: An Informal History*. Oxford: Clarendon Press, 1978.

Suzuki, Peter T. "For the Sake of Inter-University Comity: The Attempted Suppression by the University of California of Morton Grodzins' *Americans Betrayed*."

In *Views from Within: The Japanese Evacuation and Resettlement Study*. Edited by Yuji Ichioka, 95–123. Los Angeles: Asian American Studies Center, University of California at Los Angeles, 1989.

Synnott, Marcia G. "Hugh MacRae, Penderlea, and the Model Farm Communities Movement." *Proceedings of the South Carolina Historical Association* 57 (1987): 53–65.

Tate, Allen. "A View of the Whole South." *American Review* 2 (January 1934): 411–432.

TenBroek, Jacobus, Edward N. Barnhart, and Floyd W. Matson. *Prejudice, War, and the Constitution*. Japanese American Evacuation and Resettlement, vol. 3. Berkeley: University of California Press, 1954.

Thomas, Dorothy Swaine. *The Salvage*. Japanese American Evacuation and Resettlement, vol. 2. Berkeley: University of California Press, 1952.

Thomas, Dorothy Swaine, and Richard S. Nishimoto. *The Spoilage*, Japanese American Evacuation and Resettlement, vol. 1. Berkeley: University of California Press, 1946.

Tindall, George Brown. *The Emergence of the New South, 1913–1945*. History of the South, vol. 10. Baton Rouge: Louisiana State University Press, 1967.

Underwood, Thomas A. *Allen Tate: Orphan of the South*. Princeton, NJ: Princeton University Press, 2000.

United States. Congress. House. Select Committee on Lobbying Activities. *Conference of American Small Business Organizations: A Report of the House Select Committee on Lobbying Activities*. Eighty-first Congress, Second Session. House Report 3232, Serial Set Vol. 11385. Washington, D.C.: United States Government Printing Office, 1950.

United States. Congress. House. Select Committee on Lobbying Activities. *Lobbying: Direct and Indirect: Part 8 of Hearings: Foundation for Economic Education, July 18, 1950*. Eighty-First Congress, Second Session. Washington, D.C.: United States Government Printing Office, 1953.

United States. Congress. Senate. Committee on the Judiciary. *Proceedings against Mary Knowles for Contempt of the Senate*. Eighty-forth Congress, Second Session, Senate Report 1765, *Serial Set* Vol. 11887. Washington, D.C.: United States Government Printing Office, 1956.

United States. Congress. House. Select Committee to Investigate Foundations. *Final Report of the Select Committee to Investigate Foundations and Comparable Organizations*. Eighty-second Congress, Second Session, House Report 2514, *Serial Set* Vol. 11578. Washington, D.C.: United States Government Printing Office, 1953.

United States. Federal Trade Commission, "In the Matter of the Crowell-Collier Publishing Company, et al.," *Federal Trade Commission Decisions: Findings, Opinions, and Orders July 1, 1966 to December 31, 1966*. Washington, D.C.: United States Government Printing Office, 1970: 977–1033.

Villeponteaux, Elizabeth. "William Terry Couch and the University of North Carolina Press, 1925–1945." Master's paper for the M.S. in L.S., University of North Carolina at Chapel Hill, 1989.

Weaver, Richard. *Ideas Have Consequences*. Chicago: University of Chicago Press, 1948.

White, G. Edward. *Earl Warren: A Public Life*. New York: Oxford University Press, 1982.

Whitman, Howard, and Howard G. Spalding. "Education: A Debate." In *Collier's 1955 Year Book Covering National and International Events of the Year 1954*, 190–203. New York: P. F. Collier & Son, 1955.

Wiegand, Wayne. "Wresting Money from the Canny Scotsman: Melvil Dewey's Designs on Carnegie's Millions, 1902–1906." In *Libraries and Philanthropy: Proceedings of the Library History Seminar IX 30 March–1 April 1995, University of Alabama, Tuscaloosa*. Edited by Donald G. Davis, Jr. 380–393. Austin: Graduate School of Library and Information Science, University of Texas at Austin, 1996.

Wilhelmsen, Frederick D. "Couch on McLuhan." *University Bookman* 15 (Winter 1975): 40–47.

Wittmer, Felix. Review of *People in Literature*, by Louella B. Cook, Walter Loban, and Ruth M. Stauffer. *Educational Reviewer* 5 (October, 1953): 2–3.

Wood, James Playsted. *Of Lasting Interest: The Story of the Reader's Digest*. Garden City, NY: Doubleday, 1958.

Woodward, C. Vann. *Thinking Back: The Perils of Writing History*. Baton Rouge: Louisiana State University Press, 1986.

Worthen, Molly. "The Chalcedon Problem: Rosas John Rushdoony and the Origins of Christian Reconstructionism." *Church History* 77 (June 2008): 399–437.

Young, Fred Douglas. *Richard M. Weaver, 1910–1963: A Life of the Mind*. Columbia: University of Missouri Press, 1995.

Zimmerman, Jonathan. *Whose America?: Culture Wars in the Public Schools*. Cambridge, MA: Harvard University Press, 2002.

Index

www.ingramcontent.com/pod-product-compliance
Lightning Source LLC
LaVergne TN
LVHW090254171224
799303LV00007B/194